Psychiatry in the American Community

Psychiatry in the American Community

H. G. WHITTINGTON, M. D.

INTERNATIONAL UNIVERSITIES PRESS, INC.
New York   New York

This book is dedicated to my co-workers in community mental health in Kansas. Special recognition goes to G. C. Coniglio, ACSW, Stan Mahoney, Ph.D., Susan Ellermeier, and Mrs. Jessie Irwin.

Contents

Foreword

This book is designed to serve as a stimulus for individual thought and study, or for group discussion. An attempt is made, then, to be provocative and stimulating, and to avoid an air of finality or dogma. The suggested readings, likewise, are chosen to present, when possible, a diversity of views, and to serve as a further stimulus for thought and discussion.

Although the greater portion of the book has been written by a psychiatrist, it is hoped that the content will be sufficiently general to make the material usable for seminars in graduate departments of psychology and social work, as well as in psychiatric residency training programs.

It is interesting in looking through the suggested readings, to note how many of the publications have committee or organizational authorship. It will be some years before any one professional person can possibly have a full grasp, and understand in depth, the complex field of community mental health. However, it is hoped that this introductory textbook will present with candor and directness the thinking and attitudes of one practitioner in the rapidly changing and growing area of community mental health theory and practice, and that this may be of some benefit to readers and students.

I

Community Mental Health Services: Something New?

Psychiatry has long been a sporting ground for extremists of all persuasions. Theories of etiology, systems of nosology, rationales of treatment, estimates of prognosis, definition of practitioner roles—all have fallen prey to the propagandist; the developers and expounders of systems and schools; the dilettantes and the demagogues; the men of much knowledge and little wisdom; the proponents and the opponents; the builders-up and the tearers-down; the formalists and the existentialists; the analysts and the synthesizers; the reductionists and the holists; the meddlers, pryers, peekers, and probers; the spiritualists and the materialists; the facilitators and the intruders; the euphemists and the neologizers.

Today another "new" development threatens the orderly growth of psychiatric theory and practice and the steady expansion of knowledge in the behavioral sciences. Fadism is not unique to the mental health disciplines; it is a prominent feature of 20th century civilization. The new, the progressive, the novel, the modern, have all been exalted as high social values. In contrast, science emphasizes a process of discovery by which the immutable laws of nature are unfolded: truth's being "in style" and "out of style," while not foreign to science, is always unwelcome and suspect.

Community mental health has become the style of the moment in psychiatry. Probably before the ink is dry on this

1

book, disillusionment and reaction will already have been voiced. The pendulum swings, action yields, faith is sire to disbelief. Let us, then, approach this entire topic and the chapters that follow with a sense of historical perspective, of commitment without religiosity, and with—above all—the scientific attitude: to observe, to conceptualize, to generate hypotheses, to test these "hunches," to retain the valid and discard the spurious. Being human, we cannot claim or realistically pursue omniscience; we can, however, learn from experience.

Why all this furor about community mental health practice? There have always been mental health practitioners— of various names and diverse persuasions—in communities. So why glorify community psychiatry as a movement, and devote a book to it? The question may be examined from several vantage points.

HISTORICAL PERSPECTIVE

All too often, what is labeled as an historical view of events, is in fact only a kind of intellectualized "Monday morning quarterbacking." One faces, in interpreting social events, the same dilemma encountered in evaluating the import of various events in the associative anamnesis: which events that have preceded an occurrence have any genetic significance in relationship to the described occurrence? So it is with looking at antecedent events, and speculating upon their relationship to the increased emphasis in recent years upon community psychiatric practice. One can describe certain developments or trends, but speculation about causes must always be subjected to critical scrutiny by others.

There are a number of interrelated social and professional events that bear upon the present emphasis on social or community psychiatry. At the most generalized extreme, one can see the current either-or dichotomy existing between community psychiatric services as opposed to state hospital psychiatric services, as only a reflection of a 180-year-old conflict in our American society between the Jeffersonian and Hamiltonian view of social organization. The struggle between centralized and decentralized social organization in the fields of government, education, industry, and every other aspect of our national life is, in all likelihood, only reflected in the current ferment and change concerning the organization of mental health services in this country. We are, all of us, whether we like to think so or not, inextricably bound up in the matrix of our society, and in our professional affairs we cannot help but see reflected basic social and political conflicts and problems.

Now, the conflicts referred to above are essentially a disagreement as to whether strong centralized national services—the federalist system—offer the greatest prospect of preserving individual and national freedom, and promoting the public good; or whether decentralized services, administered by the states and communities of the republic, can best meet the public need and preserve individual and national freedom.

Perhaps another way of stating the same problem, and putting it in a still more general concept, is the basic conflict in all societies between pluralism versus monolithism. Arnold Toynbee, in his historical writings, postulates that monolithism characterizes a particular phase in the development of higher societies, usually preceding a decline and decay of the civilization. In his view, there are continually forces towards the centralization of power, authority, and wealth; and counterforces towards the decentralization, dispersion, and distribution of power, authority, and wealth in a society. In Toynbee's judgment, the gradual erosion of local and regional autonomy and the steady ascendency of the central state in matters of government, religion, art, and science, may be considered an antecedent and perhaps causal

event in the eventual decline of a civilization. Our American
society has been characterized by a more conscious awareness
of these antipodal trends, and a more active involvement in
self-conscious regulatory mechanisms, than has any preceding
civilization. One may see the anti-trust laws, the constant
testing and retesting of states rights, and the consistent opposition to federal participation in education as being evidences of strong self-corrective factors which temporarily
reverse or at least slow down the processes of centralization.
Of course, one cannot, in all truth, state that these forces
towards decentralization and maintenance of local social and
governmental autonomy have really been successful in re-
versing the trend towards monolithism in our society; there
is considerable evidence that increasingly larger portions of
national wealth, power, and authority have in effect become
more and more centrally held.

Probably more pertinent to community mental health
theory and practice has been the impact of the Second World
War upon the generation that now occupies positions of
leadership. The events of the 1940's impressed all thinking
citizens, whether they were participants or spectators, with
the tremendous impact of social forces upon individual
behavior. We relearned that below certain levels of caloric
intake organized society cannot exist, and if the caloric
intake is decreased further all the usual standards of decent
behavior between individuals tend to disappear. We watched
millions of Germans seemingly abandon lifelong habits of
social behavior and responsibility, and act in brutal and
destructive ways. We had before us the horrible spectacle
of genocide, and the walking skeletons that emerged from
the prison camps after the war. We observed a Christian nation, and a nation from the Asiatic heritage, behave in ways
so similar as to suggest that the apparent cultural dissimilarities were only a deceptive mask that could be thrown away
easily. How could any behavioral scientist, faced with the

horrible and shocking events of the Second World War, proceed calmly on his way concerned only about intrapsychic forces, and interrelationships between id, ego, and superego? For all the attempts to relate the outbursts of brutality and aggression to nationally shared patterns of psychosexual development, the evidence was at best unconvincing. Could we really be expected to believe that all those millions of Germans and millions of Japanese had such similar childhood familial constellations, and such similar childhood psychosexual development, that their sadistic behavior was explained entirely by traditional psychoanalytic theory? Most behavioral scientists, rather, were compelled to come to grips with the social determinants of behavior, and to begin to broaden their field of investigation and inquiry concerning the causes of human behavior.

The professional historical determinants that have led to the current emphasis in community psychiatry are equally diverse and difficult to assess. Confining ourselves to the United States, we can notice a series of actions and reactions involving the whole climate, attitude, and structure of psychiatric services over the past century.

Dorothea Dix has been so widely acclaimed, and perhaps rightly so, as a heroine and messiah for the mental health movement, that a different position is risky. However, if we look behind the religiosity, the moralism, the emotional appeal, and the sentimentalism involved in her crusade, we can view it as a rather sad chronicle. Here was a woman, well intentioned but essentially ignorant in the ways of the world, who was deeply impressed and moved to action by the frequently cruel and inhumane treatment afforded the mentally ill in local jails and alms houses in this country. In her desire to ameliorate their condition, she essentially indicted the society which allowed such conditions to persist, proclaimed local government incapable of providing more humane care, and urged the assumption of total responsibility for the mentally ill by state government. In fact, in her zeal she went beyond this and in 1848 urged the national government to cede public lands to the state, the sale of which was to be earmarked for the improvement of the care of the insane. Her plan was finally passed by both houses of Congress, and called for the setting aside of 12,225,000 acres. It was only because of President Pierce's veto on constitutional and states rights grounds that the bill failed to become law in 1850, thereby thwarting Miss Dix's campaign to have the insane become "wards of the nation." The basic assumption, which nowhere seemed to have been very seriously challenged, was that local communities were incapable of caring in a humane and adequate manner for the mentally ill, and that this function must be taken over by the state. Another increasingly popular concept was that these state facilities should be, as indeed they did become, large institutions where many patients could be brought together in the name of efficiency and economy.

The factors that led Miss Dix's religious and moralistic campaign to achieve such notable success, and to bring about a consensus among all responsible persons that local governmental units were unable to care for the insane, are beyond the scope of this book. It is likely, however, that mental illness was already a little bit "beyond the pale" as far as the mainstream of American medicine was concerned. The increasing emphasis on the careful description of syndromes, the elucidation of pathology, and the discovery of specific etiology for illness—all of which were becoming more prevalent in the world of scientific medicine—rendered psychiatry, in its ignorance and confusion, increasingly mysterious and unchallenging to the physician.

As so often happens with Messianic movements, the followers of the leader tend to make somewhat greater claims than did the founder himself. Miss Dix seemed to be primarily concerned with humane custody, and did not propose the reorganization and centralization of services for the mentally ill on the basis that it would afford a great improvement in curability. However, this was not true of all the physicians who came to supervise the institutional treatment of the mentally ill. For example, in 1826 Dr. Ely Todd of the Hartford Retreat reported that he cured 91.3 per cent of all cases during the year 1826. Dr. Samuel Woodward, Superintendent of the State Lunatic Hospital at Worcester, reported in 1833 that 82.25 per cent of the patients admitted during the first year were recovered. By 1842, Dr. William All, Superintendent of the Ohio Lunatic Asylum at Columbus, reported 100 per cent recoveries.

Again, we observe over a period of a few years, one of those curious swings and reversals of opinion which have so afflicted the psychiatric profession. In 1840, for example, Dr. Luther V. Bell of McLean Asylum reported "the records justify the declaration that all cases, certainly recent—recover under a fair trial." Only seventeen years later, however, he wrote, "I have come to the conclusion that when a man once becomes insane he is about used up for this world."

What are we to make of this strange vacillation between the cult of incurability and the cult of curability? We can follow it beyond 1857, for that matter, and observe a long period during which medical opinion concerning the curability of the insane languished at a low ebb. We can observe a slight recrudescence of the cult of curability following the First World War, and, following the Second World War, a more striking and still persisting cult of curability which received a transfusion insuring prolonged life from the advent of the tranquillizing drugs.

We might wonder, then, if the community mental health movement is an attempt of the profession to come to grips with the fact that it has once again overextended itself, overpromised what it can do, overestimated the efficacy of treatment of the mentally ill. We might wonder if we are once again being confronted with our profound ignorance about the causes of various types of mental illness, and are attempting to move out in some new direction to offer some new chimerical hope in order to bolster a flagging mid-twentieth century cult of curability.

Other professional historical trends, undoubtedly contributing to the current emphasis in community mental health, can be traced back to the turn of the century. Most of the early community mental health services were concerned with delinquency, such as the Chicago Juvenile Psychopathic Institute established in 1909 by William Healy. In 1921, Thomas W. Salmon organized a conference on Prevention of Juvenile Delinquency, which led to a five-year demonstration program of child guidance clinics under the auspices of the Commonwealth Fund and the National Committee for Mental Hygiene. Over the years between the two great wars, an increasing number of child guidance clinics were established, gradually expanding their conception of service beyond the original court-related or juvenile delinquency service, and developing a model of practice which involved the use of psychiatrists, clinical psychologists, and psychiatric social workers.

The most recent professional event related to the emphasis on community mental health service is the report of the Joint Commission on Mental Illness and Health, established by Congress in 1955. One of the themes running through the report of this Commission was an indictment of state mental hospitals as they currently exist, and an emphasis on the development of community programs and community resources of many kinds. In a way, such a deemphasis of the role of the traditional state hospital becomes a sort of self-fulfilling prophecy. One might wonder, in other words, what young psychiatrist of ability would choose to assume a long-term position on the psychiatric staff of a state hospital, when such institutions are clearly regarded as vestigial evidences of previous psychiatric failures.

In fact, an unplanned social-professional development has apparently been taking place which would tend over the long run to decrease the influence of the state psychiatric hospital in American psychiatry, and to impede the continued professional leadership of psychiatrists working in that setting. In terms of mental health manpower, the Joint Commission points up that nearly one-fourth of all physicians in state mental hospitals were residents and most of these were foreign trained. In other words, the vast majority of American medical graduates entering psychiatry chose to do so in training settings other than state hospitals.

These foreign physicians, even if they remain in this country following the completion of training, would require a longer time to assume positions of leadership and responsibility in American psychiatry than would American medical graduates. Most of the faculty in medical schools are recruited from psychiatrists trained in university medical settings, which means that a cycle of interrelated events is set up which causes serious long-range problems for the state mental hospital. That is, the majority of the faculty of the university psychiatric department would have been trained in a university setting, and not in a state hospital setting. They will tend to select out the most able medical students and interns, and encourage them to enter medical school residency training programs. They will, in effect, probably have biased medical students during their training *against* a residency in a state hospital setting, and towards a residency in a medical school setting. Other factors being equal, the less able and less desirable residents would tend, then, to gravitate towards the state psychiatric hospitals, in addition to the foreign medical graduates. We can see a process developing over the years which would suggest—no matter what is the "best solution" or what is scientifically most defensible—that the state psychiatric hospitals will become more and more isolated from the mainstream of American psychiatry, will become more and more difficult to staff, and will become more and more hard pressed to offer adequate services to their patients.

LOGISTICAL-ECONOMIC ASPECTS

In looking at the trend towards decentralized mental health services, we must not leave out the logistical and economic factors involved. One very real factor is that there are simply more professional people in all of the disciplines now than there were ten or even five years ago, and this number is steadily increasing. Psychiatry, for example, is the third most popular field of specialty training in American medicine today, exceeded only by medicine and surgery. Over 1,000 psychiatrists are expected to complete training each year, and to continue to swell the ranks of American psychiatry. Equivalent gains are being made by psychology and social work. As these numbers of highly specialized, intensively trained, reasonably mature individuals become available on the job market, the pressure to move out of the psychiatrically better supplied urban areas will become greater. In other words, no matter whether there were a "community mental health movement" or not, the likelihood is that we would find more and more of all the specialties practicing their professions in smaller communities over the years ahead. Certainly, similar developments have been noticed in other medical specialties, such as surgery and internal medicine.

The increased income available to many American citizens since the war is a relevant economic factor. With the steadily rising level of family income, despite the heavy inroads made by the current tax burden, the feasibility of affording private or part-pay psychiatric service—rather than having the state assume total responsibility—becomes increasingly great.

With this higher income of many individuals, there is an apparent, and probably real, increased spread between the upper-middle-class and upper-class segments of our population, and the lower socioeconomic classes whose relative income tends to remain fairly stable. Increasingly, then, we have to face the fact that our state hospitals have become treatment resources, and often depositories, for the lower middle-class and lower socioeconomic classes in our society. A double standard of treatment has increasingly developed, which has increasingly troubled our American social conscience and sense of professional responsibility. With the American genius for compromise, the community mental health center program—stressing, as it does in actuality, a compromise between the state medicine and the private practice models—can be seen as an understandable sociological development.

Personal or Leadership Aspects

As behavioral scientists, we should not get so wrapped up in looking at "the big picture" that we leave out the role that individuals play, and the significant impact that they have on the course of human events. While many leaders in American psychiatry could be singled out, the impact of Robert Felix, Director of the National Institute of Mental Health, must be recognized as being singular. He and his associates have, in the ferment and turbulence of the American psychiatric scene in the last decade, hammered out the blueprints and basic concepts of the community mental health center.

Mention has already been made of the significant impact of the Joint Commission on Mental Illness and Health, under the able leadership of Jack R. Ewalt, M.D.

Most recently, ex-president John F. Kennedy delivered the first message to the Congress of the United States on Mental

Illness and Mental Retardation. This can be regarded as a significant milestone in the social "coming of age" of psychiatry, and is affording considerable impetus to the progress of the reorganization of psychiatric services along community lines. To quote briefly from that speech:

> Yet mental illness and mental retardation are among our most critical health problems. They occur more frequently, affect more people, require more prolonged treatment, cause more suffering by the families of the afflicted, waste more of our human resources, and constitute more financial drain upon both the Public Treasury and the personal finances of the individual families than any other single condition.
>
> There are now about 800,000 such patients in this Nation's institutions—600,000 for mental illness and over 200,000 for mental retardation. Every year nearly 1,500,000 people receive treatment in institutions for the mentally ill and mentally retarded. Most of them are confined and compressed within an antiquated, vastly overcrowded, chain of custodial State institutions. The average amount expended on their care is only $4 a day—too little to do much good for the individual, but too much if measured in terms of efficient use of our mental health dollars. In some States the average is less than $2 a day.
>
> The total cost of the taxpayers is over $2.4 billion a year in direct public outlays for services—about $1.8 billion for mental illness and $600 million for mental retardation. Indirect public outlays, in welfare costs and in the waste of human resources, are even higher. But the anguish suffered both by those afflicted and by their families transcends financial statistics—particularly in view of the fact that both mental illness and mental retardation strike so often in childhood, leading in most cases to a lifetime of disablement for the patient and a lifetime of hardship for his family.
>
> This situation has been tolerated far too long. It has troubled our national conscience—but only as a problem unpleasant to mention, easy to postpone, and despairing of solution. The Federal Government, despite the nationwide impact of the problem, has largely left the solutions up to the States. The States have depended on custodial hospitals and homes. Many such hospitals and homes have been shamefully understaffed, overcrowded, unpleasant institutions from which death too often provided the only firm hope of release.
>
> The time has come for a bold new approach. New medical, scientific, and social tools and insights are now available. A series of comprehensive studies initiated by the Congress, the executive branch, and interested private groups have been completed and all point in the same direction. . .

I propose a national mental health program to assist in the inauguration of a wholly new emphasis and approach to care for the mentally ill. This approach relies primarily upon the new knowledge and new drugs acquired and developed in recent years which make it possible for most of the mentally ill to be successfully and quickly treated in their own communities and returned to a useful place in society.

These breakthroughs have rendered obsolete the traditional methods of treatment which imposed upon the mentally ill a social quarantine, a prolonged or permanent confinement in huge, unhappy mental hospitals where they were out of sight and forgotten. I am not unappreciative of the efforts undertaken by many States to improve conditions in these hospitals, or the dedicated work of many hospital staff members. But their task has been staggering and the results too often dismal, as the comprehensive study by the Joint Commission on Mental Illness and Health pointed out in 1961. Some States have at times been forced to crowd five, ten, or even fifteen thousand people into one large understaffed institution. Imposed largely for reasons of economy, such practices were costly in human terms, as well as in a real economic sense. . .

If we launch a broad new mental health program now, it will be possible within a decade or two to reduce the number of patients now under custodial care by 50 percent or more. Many more mentally ill can be helped to remain in their own homes without hardship to themselves or their families. Those who are hospitalized can be helped to return to their own communities. All but a small proportion can be restored to useful life. We can spare them and their families much of the misery which mental illness now entails. We can save public funds and we can conserve our manpower resources.

1. Comprehensive community mental health centers. Central to a new mental health program is comprehensive community care. Merely pouring Federal funds into a continuation of the outmoded type of institutional care which now prevails would make little difference. We need a new type of health facility, one which will return mental health care to the main stream of American medicine, and at the same time upgrade mental health services. I recommend, therefore, that the Congress (1) authorize grants to the States for the construction of comprehensive community mental health centers, beginning in fiscal year 1965, with the Federal Government providing 45 to 75 percent of the project cost; (2) authorize short-term project grants for the initial staffing costs of comprehensive community mental health centers, with the Federal Government providing up to 75 percent of the cost in the early months, on a gradually declining basis, terminating such support for a project within slightly over 4 years; and (3) to facilitate the preparation of community plans for these new facilities as a necessary preliminary to any construction or staffing assistance, appropriate $4.2 million for planning grants under the National

Institute of Mental Health. These planning funds, which would be in addition to a similar amount appropriated for fiscal year 1963, have been included in my proposed 1964 budget.

While the essential concept of the comprehensive community mental health center is new, the separate elements which would be combined in it are presently found in many communities: diagnostic and evaluation services, emergency psychiatric units, outpatient services, inpatient services, day and night care, foster home care, rehabilitation, consultative services to other community agencies, and mental health information and education.

These centers will focus community resources and provide better community facilities for all aspects of mental health care. Prevention as well as treatment will be a major activity. Located in the patient's own environment and community, the center would make possible a better understanding of his needs, a more cordial atmosphere for his recovery, and a continuum of treatment. As his needs change, the patient could move without delay or difficulty to different services—from diagnosis, to cure, to rehabilitation—without need to transfer to different institutions located in different communities.

SCIENTIFIC ASPECTS

Sociologists have made some of the most significant contributions to the entire field of mental health practice in the last 15 years. While their studies of the sociological aspects of mental illness and emotional disorder have not aroused as great an interest and understanding among psychiatrists as they might, their detailed studies of the social variables affecting the treatment process and the treatment milieu have attracted the attention and interest of many mental health practitioners. These sociological studies proved a very potent antidote for the overpreoccupation with behavioral determinants of the first five years of the individual's life, and have served to remind us again that the human being is an amazingly plastic and adaptable creature. It is ironic that the social scientists should have to remind us of something that biological scientists should have been aware of: that man is, in every aspect of his functioning, an extremely malleable and variable individual, and is continually influenced by all aspects of his environment.

The advent of the tranquillizing drugs, and later of the psychic energizing drugs, has of course been a significant milestone in the development of psychiatric practice. Shortened hospitalization stays—that can at least be partly attributed to the drugs—and the increased possibility of returning patients rapidly to the community from the hospital, led to a total reorientation of hospital practice. Many of the management problems that occupied so much of the staff's time and energy in the past became less frequent. Concerns with restraint, control, and discipline began to give way to a more permissive and "open door" policy. It is only a step from unlocking the doors of the hospital, to wondering about moving the hospital itself into the larger community. The availability of these potent new drugs, also, cannot help but reawaken in psychiatrists many of their atrophied feelings of kinship with the medical profession, and remind them of their scientific heritage.

Aspects of Public Opinion

Ever since the mental hygiene movement began in this country around the turn of the century, there have been unremitting and increasingly effective efforts to educate the public about mental illness. Since the Second World War, the voices—both professional and lay—have risen to a crescendo, as we have tried to bring home to the citizen the enormity of the mental health problem and also the feasibility of providing improved care. The Congress of the United States was aware of this problem even before the citizenry as a whole, largely because of the experience in the Second World War when one and three-quarter million men were rejected for military service and three-quarter million were discharged because of mental and emotional disorders. In 1946, Congress passed the National Mental Health Act to assist the States in improving community mental health services. Shortly after that, the National Institute of Mental Health was formed by the United States Public Health Service and was charged with administration of the national mental health program. Over two-thirds of all the psychiatric outpatient resources in this country have been developed since 1946, witnessing the very rapid growth of a community mental health program, which may be regarded as both a technological innovation and a social revolution.

During this period, the National Association for Mental Health has become an increasingly effective agent for public information and for lobbying.

In all this public education and information about mental illness, several facts bear noting:

1. First of all, there has been much less mental health education than there has been mental *illness* education. Much of the emphasis has been on impressing various individuals with how many people have mental illnesses, what a serious national problem it is, and how desperately it needs attention.

2. The sociologists speak of two processes involved in the development within society of any profession. The first process, that of legitimization, lies in the society's accepting that there is a need for a certain profession. In other words, the existence of illness would be seen as legitimizing the development of a healing profession. It would seem that much of the effort in mental health education has gotten "stuck" on this question, long after this fact has been generally accepted by informed and responsible citizens in our society.

3. The second sociological process, that of validation, is more complex and difficult. It involves the acceptance by society that the profession, which has a legitimate reason for existing, is in actuality effective in dealing with the problem. For example, there is legitimate need for healing persons in our society, so the profession of chiropractor may be seen as a legitimate profession. However, viewed from the stand-

point of science, it is not a valid profession, since there is no evidence that it materially benefits the course of disease. Some of the public information and education activities have been directed to this process of validation—of convincing the public that the mental health disciplines can indeed influence favorably the outcome of many patients of mental and emotional illnesses—but this has been relatively ineffectual. It is a difficult kind of matter to handle, since it borders so closely upon advertising and threatens, thus, to violate professional taboos.

On the other hand, there has also been a tendency to overstate some of the claims of what mental health professionals can do, with a kind of latter-day "cult of curability." In the view of many professionals, we have considerably "oversold" psychiatry to the public. The average individual remains simply unconvinced, however, that mental health practitioners can, in reality, offer curative services in the sense that the other healing practitioners, who have a valid role in our society, can.

Prominent in the mainstream of efforts geared to modifying public opinion, are the abundant "how to" articles appearing in various magazines, advising people how to raise their children, how to adjust in marriage, how to have a happy sexual life, how to live with their tensions, and on and on ad infinitum. In a way, this vulgarization, with its coincident inaccuracy and contradiction among "authorities," has been the most pernicious influence in the entire mental health public information campaign over the past decade.

Whatever role these various genetic determinants may play, the "community mental health movement" is upon us. Shifts and realignments in mental health practices [1] are occurring. It is the intention of this book to examine various aspects of

---

[1] The term "mental health practice" is an interesting euphemism itself. It is used, by and large, to describe activities that are largely treatment-oriented: mental *illness* practice. Part semantics, part word-magic, part declaration of intent—to develop preventive health services—it is a symptom of unrest, uncertainty, and the struggle within psychiatry itself.

the practices of psychiatry, psychology, social work and related disciplines in a community setting. The observations are unalterably bound up in our own personal and professional experiences in the provision, evaluation, and administration of community mental health services. We present to the reader, then, a body of experience, more or less systematically organized, from which we have attempted to derive generalizations which may serve as crude guidelines or bench marks for those who subsequently travel the routes we have explored.

No matter what we may think of "the community mental health movement," how we appraise its effects or discern its historical antecedents, one thing is certain: a period of growth and expansion, of testing the limits of applicability of these concepts, lies ahead of us, and in all probability the rate of growth will be governed by factors influencing all technological change (National Science Foundation, 1961).

1. As the number of firms in an industry adopting an innovation increases, the probability of its adoption by a non-user increases.

2. The expected profitability of an innovation influences the probability of its adoption.

3. For equally profitable innovations, the probability of adoption tends to be smaller for innovations requiring relatively large investments.

4. The probability of adoption of an innovation is dependent on the industry in which the innovation is introduced.

5. If an innovation displaces very durable equipment, the probability of its adoption is lessened.

6. The probability of adoption will be higher in firms that are expanding at a relatively rapid rate.

7. All other factors being equal, the probability of the adoption of an innovation increases with time.

As applied to the "mental health industry," items 1, 2, 3,

4, 6, and 7 predispose, in all likelihood, to a very rapid diffusion, while item 5, related to the investment in large state mental hospitals, would impede growth. However, the cards would seem to be stacked in favor of a rapid spread of community mental health concepts in the years ahead.

SUGGESTED READINGS

Bahn, A. (1963), Gains in outpatient psychiatric clinic services, 1961. *Ment. Hyg.*, 47:177-188.

Conservation of Human Resources: A Guide to the Kansas Program for Community Mental Health Services (1964). Topeka: Board of Social Welfare.

Jaco, E. (1960), *The Social Epidemiology of Mental Disorders.* New York: Russell Sage Foundation.

James, M. (1962), *Social Psychiatry.* Springfield, Ill.: Charles C Thomas.

Kennedy, J. (1964), Message from the President of the United States relative to mental illness and mental retardation. *Amer. J. Psychiat.*, 120: 729-737.

Kotinsky, R. & Witner, H. L., eds. (1955), *Community Programs for Mental Health. Theory, Practice, Evaluation.* Cambridge: Harvard University Press.

Ozarin, L. D. (1962), Recent community mental health legislation—a brief review. *Amer. J. Pub. Hlth.*, 52:436-442.

Proceedings of National Congress on Mental Illness and Health (1962). Chicago: A.M.A.

Ridenour, N. (1961), *Mental Health in the United States: A Fifty-Year History.* Cambridge: Harvard University Press.

II

Organization of Community
Mental Health Services

Community is as difficult to define as is mental health: the community of mankind, of nations, of our nation, state, region, county, town, neighborhood? We must avoid a counterextremist position: Dorothea Dix said that counties and towns could not care for the mentally ill, so that the state or the nation must do so; we must eschew the counter-proposal, that the county and town can necessarily provide better mental health services to all patients than can the state, the region, or the nation.

The Joint Commission on Mental Illness and Health reports:

> The local community, with all the help it can get, must mount the attack [against mental illness]. [But,] In several sections of the nation virtually nothing is being done. In others, highly complex constellations of resources exist for the advancement of mental health. The big cities are relatively rich in these resources, whereas the rural areas are likely to be entirely barren. Severe shortages of adequately trained personnel were found in every area the authors investigated. Hardly an agency or service could be found with sufficient financing [Robinson et al., 1960].

The most refreshing and promising trend in psychiatry lies in the adoption of a pluralistic approach toward the prevention, treatment, and rehabilitation of mental illness, emotional disorder, and behavioral disturbances. In the Joint Commission's study (Robinson et al.), for example, reference is made to many community agencies: public health, welfare, court services, the schools, recreation, churches, family agencies, planning bodies, and mental health clinics. The present volume is designed to look specifically at the community mental health clinic—or center, as it is coming to be called—in interrelationship with other caregiving agencies within the community. Subsequent chapters will be devoted to specific interrelationships.

In this chapter, an attempt will be made to present a conceptual frame of reference—based on the medical model —for viewing and organizing the function of community mental health centers. Other conceptual models, which are complementary rather than antagonistic, will be used elsewhere in this book; the authors will endeavor in each instance to explicate their ideational underpinning.

What Is a Comprehensive Community Mental Health Center?

The concept of the comprehensive community mental health center is essentially a series of proposals for the deployment of professional persons in different ways than they have been used previously. The pattern developing over the years has utilized mental health professionals in specialized facilities, working in relative isolation from other agencies within the community with fragmentation of services resulting. Clinical services for emotionally ill patients were often unavailable. Continuity and comprehensiveness of care were sacrificed in order to maintain agency and professional autonomy.

The comprehensive community mental health center is, in essence, a proposal to develop mechanisms within the community to provide, for all citizens, mental health services that are available, comprehensive, and continuous. In addition, the comprehensive community mental health center concept emphasizes that specialized psychiatric services are *embedded in a matrix of helping agencies in the com-*

munity, and an essential part of the responsibility of a comprehensive community mental health center involves provision of mental health consultation services to these other caregivers in the community.

These considerations are well summarized in a recent publication of the U.S. Department of Health, Education and Welfare entitled "Concept and Challenge: The Comprehensive Community Mental Health Center."

This chapter attempts to translate the proposals summarized in the federal publication into possible applications for Kansas, and to thus provide an example of how planning for mental health services proceeded in a specific state.

ADMINISTRATIVE ORGANIZATION

It is necessary to emphasize that comprehensive community mental health services need not be under one roof, nor under the administrative direction of one agency. Rather, joint planning, sharing of responsibility, and exercise of authority in the prevention and treatment of mental and emotional illness may best be implemented by an inter-agency coordinating body.

Table 1 outlines possible organization of a new comprehensive community mental health center where local mental health services are nonexistent. In this proposal, the elements of a comprehensive mental health center are combined into one administrative organization. Of the eleven comprehensive community mental health centers that may eventually develop in Kansas, it is estimated that eight may organize on this model.

In contrast, Table 2 outlines an organization that will probably prove more appropriate for the three urban areas of Kansas City, Topeka, and Wichita, where many existing

TABLE 1

Organization of Single Comprehensive Agency

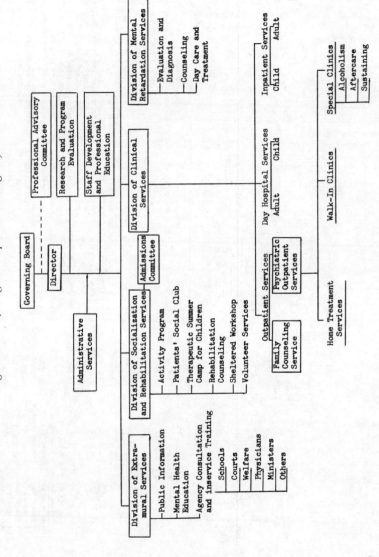

TABLE 2

Organization and Integration of Independent Agencies for Comprehensive Services

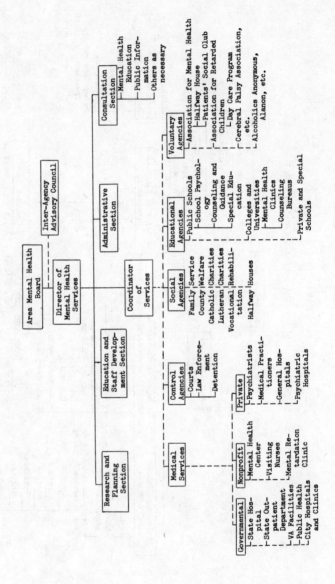

and independent agencies may be utilized so long as some mechanism is provided for overall coordination.[1]

The intent of the organizational schema in Table 1 is to provide for four operating divisions of a single comprehensive agency: a division of extramural services, a division of socialization and rehabilitation services, a division of clinical services, and a division of mental retardation services. In addition, there will be supportive services in the areas of administration, research and program evaluation, and staff development and professional education.

A well-trained, experienced, and able psychiatrist could best fulfill the function of overall director of the agency. However, in the absence of such a properly qualified person to serve as full-time director of the agency, the division of clinical services would, as a minimum, have to be directed by a board-qualified psychiatrist.

To discuss each of these divisions in turn:

The Division of Clinical Services

This division would provide the full spectrum of services now existing in outpatient clinics, child guidance centers, psychiatric units in general hospitals, and day hospital services. The number and types of personnel required to provide this spectrum of services would, of course, vary with local needs and the availability of personnel.

In this particular organization, there was no attempt to divide services into child and adult departments, since this arbitrary definition has seemed less and less functional in recent years, with increasing emphasis upon treatment for the entire family. It *may* be desirable to differentiate out-

---

[1] This is similar to the New York City Community Mental Health Board, described in Chapter 19 of *Handbook of Community Psychiatry and Community Mental Health*, edited by Leopold Bellak, Grune & Stratton, New York, 1964.

patient services along the dimensions that are indicated in Table 1. It seems evident that not all of the families consulting a community mental health center need, or properly should, receive a comprehensive psychiatric evaluation involving psychiatric interviewing, social work interviewing with relatives, and psychological testing of the patient. A significant number of persons seeking help from a comprehensive community mental health center are asking, in reality, for counseling or casework assistance with their emotional reactions to current situational dilemmas. Many of these individuals could be offered service directly by social work staff, as indeed already is offered in separate family counseling or service agencies. The crucial issue that arises, however, is the proper mechanism for sorting of patients, so that they enter either family counseling service or psychiatric outpatient services. In usual agency practice the psychiatric social worker performs the function of intake; not infrequently, the least experienced and qualified member of the social work staff performs the intake function. It is proposed that the function of intake, and the process of making crucial judgments concerning the future course of the patient's treatment program, should be *borne by that member of the clinical staff who holds the greatest seniority and is most qualified.* Ideally, this should be an experienced psychiatrist, well-founded in psychotherapeutic principles and practice, but with an essentially eclectic orientation towards the treatment of the mentally and emotionally ill.

An overriding issue deserving comment is professional personnel organization within the division of clinical services. One model of organization prevalent in state psychiatric hospitals is to have a chief of social work, a chief of clinical psychology, chief of nursing, and so forth. It is urged, however, that this mode of organization be abandoned, and that the staff of the comprehensive mental health center be organized into functional units. That is, there would be a number of teams, with varying proportions of psychiatric, psychological, and social work time, assigned to the outpatient service. They would each have specific commitments in terms of time and caseload to various aspects of the outpatient program. Each functional team would be differentiated, in terms of authority and responsibility, in only two dimensions: team leaders and team members. Since the psychiatrist bears the final medical, social, and legal responsibility for patient care, he should serve as the leader of each of the functional teams if possible. Similar organization should obtain with the other sections under the division of clinical services. The senior member of each professional discipline (psychiatry, clinical psychology, and psychiatric social work) should serve on the staff of the psychiatrist-director of the division of clinical services, and work with him in an advisory capacity, in setting policy and determining administrative procedures. However, there should be no line relationship to him from the chiefs of each of the professions Personnel at the operational level should be protected from double control and double accountability which might occur.

The psychiatric outpatient services, in addition to offering more or less conventional outpatient evaluation and treatment, may well develop modalities that utilize somewhat different models of treatment, and also additional personnel.

There is a considerable body of experience with the walk-in clinic, based on the concept that immediately available assistance will often prevent a more severe illness, and an unnecessarily extended treatment course. Consequently, provision should be made so that there is always one staff person at the clinic, without appointments, who may be seen immediately. In most settings, this should probably not be a permanently differentiated function, but one that may be handled by rotation among the senior qualified professional persons.

Home treatment services are nothing new in psychiatry, and have been utilized in this country, Russia, England, the Netherlands, and many other places for a long period of time. However, there has been a reawakened interest in this modality of treatment in the United States in recent years, and recent demonstrations have shown its usefulness in the management and treatment of a variety of patients. The capability of having the psychiatric team, in whole or in part, visit with the patient and his family, and prescribe and supervise the treatment program in the patient's home, has been demonstrated with considerable conviction in the case of the psychotic patient and the person with organic brain disease. The home treatment service, in addition to utilizing the basic professional team of the outpatient department, should also have on its staff, nurses with training and experience in public health principles and practice, and in psychiatric nursing. A staff of trained and qualified nurses would allow the provision of ongoing supportive care and supervision for many patients, seriously ill enough to need this kind of support, in the home milieu or in nursing homes.

In addition, it may be desirable to establish services to meet the needs of special patient groups. It would seem impossible, with our present professional resources, to provide standard psychiatric evaluation and psychotherapy for all the alcoholics who might need or be willing to accept treatment. It will often be desirable to develop special programs utilizing part-time services of community medical practitioners to provide suppressive medication, the services of specially trained subprofessional alcoholism counselors, and the services of mental health nurses. Particular emphasis in the community alcoholism control program should be based upon protective services for the children of alcoholics, and supportive services for spouses of alcoholics. In other words, attention should not be focused entirely upon the direct treatment and rehabilitation of the alcoholic, but should be given to many aspects of providing supportive services for individuals exposed to the results of alcoholism.

Aftercare services to patients returning from state hospitals might likewise need to be developed in a special program. Considerable experience has been gained in recent years with the use of brief contact psychotherapy, in conjunction with medication, in order to provide readily available aftercare services for patients returning to the community from state psychiatric hospitals.

In addition, similar sustaining clinics may prove useful for the support of other groups, not necessarily hospitalized, such as patients with chronic dependency problems.

The provision of day and night treatment services, sometimes referred to as day and night hospitals, has been proven both in this country and abroad to be useful for many patients, to be effective treatment modalities, and to be economical and feasible. At least 25 per cent of the adult patients now being hospitalized in state psychiatric hospitals, and probably well over 50 per cent, can be treated with equal effectiveness in community day hospital programs. In addition, many adults who cannot receive optimum help from outpatient psychotherapy, but who do not need hospitalization, can benefit greatly from the treatment program of a day hospital. Children, as well, can be treated effectively and economically in day hospital programs. Experience in such centers as the Des Moines Child Guidance Clinic indicates that it is feasible to organize and operate day treatment programs for children within a comprehensive community mental health center. In addition, many centers should experiment with other methods of treatment such as the week-end hospital, particularly useful for working men, and of great potential usefulness in western Kansas where the day hospital may be of limited usefulness due to sparse population distribution.

Inpatient services may be provided in the local general

hospital, or in a special inpatient unit in a community mental health center. Experience in Kansas has indicated that only about 10 per cent of the patients who are hospitalized up to 30 days in a psychiatric unit in a local general hospital are transferred to a state psychiatric hospital. The local psychiatric unit provides useful treatment for patients who can benefit from a milieu treatment experience. In other words, it would make available effective treatment for many patients who cannot now be treated effectively in the community.

Inpatient treatment services for children are characteristically expensive and difficult to administer. Their great scarcity in the state institutions makes the development of inpatient programs for children and adolescents in the comprehensive community mental health center a concern of high priority. Further study will be necessary to determine whether an inpatient facility for children and adolescents can properly be organized and administered within the context of the community general hospital.

The important consideration in developing an inpatient unit is *not*, as people often believe, the provision of beds and physical space alone. Rather, it is the development of a sound staffing plan, the employment of competent staff, and the provision of an administrative structure to guarantee continuing inservice training and proper supervision for all psychiatric personnel.

Division of Extramural Services

This division may be directed by a clinician from one of the three basic disciplines; by a trained mental health educator; by a person with a background in community organization or human relations; or by a person with training and experience in public education and information.

The duties of the section would include the development of an ongoing public information program designed to inform the citizens of the mental health area, and especially the agencies and caregivers of this area, about the services, potentialities, and problems of the comprehensive community mental health center. The intent should clearly not be that of "a public relations department," i.e., to sell the services of the center or to extoll its virtues. Rather, the presentation of a realistic picture of the capabilities and limitations of the center, and an attempt to encourage the management of patients by other community caregivers whenever possible, should be central to the operating philosophy and practice of the division of extramural services.

Mental health education will play an increasing role in the development of a network of preventive services within the community. The mental health educator should have special training and experience, making him able to use educational techniques in presenting scientifically valid and useful information concerning normal personality growth and development, family life, mental hygiene, and the recognition and management of emotional and mental problems. The mental health educator would serve as a consultant and program assistant to the associations for mental health and retarded children in the area; would be a resource person for working in public schools, to assist them in developing curriculum guides and materials for such areas as sex education, normal growth and development, emotional aspects of family life, recognition of mental and emotional problems, principles of mental hygiene, and problems of daily living, which would be integrated into the curriculum at all levels of the educational system.

The agency consultation and inservice training program would provide consultee-centered consultation to other community caregiving agencies such as schools, courts, welfare, physicians, ministers, and others. In addition, personnel in this section would be available to participate, upon request, in the inservice training operations of other community caregiving agencies.

Some persons believe that mental health consultation is a special skill or subspecialization within the professions of psychiatry, psychology, and psychiatric social work. Some states' programming calls for special persons who spend all of their professional efforts in providing mental health consultation. In our judgment, it is probably desirable (at our present stage of development and knowledge) to utilize, on a part-time basis, the augmented skills of clinicians working primarily in the clinical services, in order to provide mental health consultation to other community caregivers.

It will probably be desirable to have at least one person, trained and experienced in mental health consultation, to serve the overall purposes of coordination, planning, and supervision for agency consultation and inservice training.

Division of Socialization and Rehabilitation Services

It is becoming increasingly clear that many psychiatric patients can benefit greatly from socialization and group experiences which are not necessarily under medical supervision. For a sharply focused program with definitive goals, it will be necessary to structure a day hospital program which allows for the prescription and supervision of milieu therapy by a psychiatrist. However, many patients with chronic social and interpersonal disabilities, whose treatment will be prolonged and whose community adjustment will continue to be tenuous for perhaps many years, will benefit from a variety of socialization and rehabilitation services from a comprehensive community mental health center.

Trained adjunctive therapists, and in many instances properly trained and supervised volunteers, can provide an activity program which will have continuing therapeutic value for the mentally and emotionally ill. Some programs may be used preventively for high-risk groups in the community, such as the adult mentally retarded and the aging citizen.

An increasing body of experience about the usefulness of social clubs for patients has been accumulated in recent years. A social club may be the direct responsibility of the comprehensive mental health center, the association for mental health, or some other volunteer community group.

Many children can be helped significantly by outpatient psychotherapy in conjunction with family casework and could derive additional benefit from a therapeutic summer camp. Associations for retarded children have been sponsoring summer camps for the retarded with considerable success. It may be desirable for the comprehensive mental health center to participate in or actually operate a summer camp for the retarded and other groups of special disabilities, as well as for the emotionally ill child.

Volunteers have proved of great usefulness in the state hospital system, and in all likelihood can make a significant contribution to many activities in the comprehensive community mental health center.

Rehabilitation counselors, a special sheltered workshop and rehabilitation work setting would be of marked usefulness to many, particularly the chronic psychotic, the mentally retarded, and borderline patients. In our judgment, serious consideration should be given to developing a sheltered workshop for patients with many different kinds of disabilities, rather than differentiating workshops along strictly diagnostic lines such as the mentally retarded, the mentally ill, the physically handicapped, and so forth.

The director of the division of socialization and rehabilitation services may be a senior and experienced group social worker. However, a capable individual from any of the three basic disciplines could assume directorship of this division.

If the director of the division of socialization and rehabilitation services is not a psychiatrist, an admissions committee, composed of the director of the division of clinical services and several clinicians from his staff, would be necessary to approve the referral of each patient to any of the services within the division of socialization and rehabilitation, to approve the prescription for the type of services to be offered, and to periodically review the caseload and activities of the division.

Division of Mental Retardation Services

Psychiatry does not have total or even major responsibility for the provision of services for the mentally retarded, but rather shares this responsibility with education, rehabilitation, medical, and other agencies. The comprehensive mental health center definitely should include *part* of the services needed for continuous, comprehensive, and available care for the mentally retarded, however.

Comprehensive evaluation and diagnostic services, which would include medical, neurological, psychological, psychiatric, social, and vocational-educational evaluation, should be available.

Specialized counseling services may be developed in some comprehensive mental health centers in order to provide a fixed point of reference for the mentally retarded. That is, specially trained subprofessional mental retardation counselors might be employed, in order to afford continuing contact with and assistance to the families of the mentally retarded over the entire life span of the retarded individual. These persons would provide for needed care, and would make use of available resources both within and outside the comprehensive community mental health center to see that the multiple needs of the mentally retarded are met.

In addition, the comprehensive community mental health center may well operate a day care and treatment program for the mentally retarded who are too young to go to the public schools, too emotionally or behaviorally disturbed to participate in special classes for the educable and trainable, and/or too old to continue attending public schools.

SUPPORTIVE SERVICES

Sufficient and appropriate administrative services should be provided to support and maintain the clinical and consultative services of the four operating divisions of the comprehensive community mental health center. Administration is not a purpose unto itself, but exists *only* to make the function of the clinician and other professional people as effective, effortless, and available as possible.

Because many of these activities are new, and because scientific principles have not been firmly established for the practice of comprehensive community mental health services, it is especially necessary to have a research and program evaluation section. All centers should conduct systematic programmatic inquiry. Only in such a way can the program of the agency be tailored to best meet community needs, and a body of scientific knowledge about the application of behavioral sciences be accumulated. In some mental health centers, more basic research may be possible.

As in all industries where technological advances are rapid, at least 5 per cent or 10 per cent of staff time and agency budget will probably need to be budgeted for inservice training and staff development. Without this constant attempt to upgrade the knowledge and skills of the staff, obsolescence and demoralization may occur.

In addition, it is vital that community mental health centers assume a more central role in the supervised training experience of psychiatrists, clinical psychologists, psychiatric social workers, nurses, and adjunctive therapists.

SUMMARY

The comprehensive community mental health center is a concept for the deployment of professional resources in order to provide patient care that is comprehensive, continuous, and available; and to provide a spectrum of services aimed at primary, secondary, and tertiary prevention of mental and emotional disability. As such, it may be under one administration or it may not; it may be under one roof, or it may not. But it will definitely be a part of one community, and should be supported and directed primarily by the community it serves. The comprehensive community mental health center is embedded in the matrix of other helping agencies, with which it has collaborative and cooperative relationships.

Tables 3 to 9 suggest possible staffing plans and salary costs for a comprehensive community mental health center to serve a population of approximately 100,000.

LEVELS OF CARE
IN HEALTH SERVICES

In recent years, community-based mental health services have expanded rapidly. They have sprung up largely on the basis of local interest, and have been stimulated by local leadership, financed by local funds, and governed by local citizen boards. This development has come about because the lay person, the informed citizen leader, and the professional and semiprofessional caregiver in the community have not been satisfied with the availability of mental health services for local residents. Neither have they felt that the traditional caregivers in the community—general physicians, ministers, county welfare workers, volunteers, court and probation officials, law enforcement agencies, school personnel, etc.—have been entirely successful in meeting the mental health needs of the citizens of most communities. The community mental health movement does *not* imply dissatisfaction with the state hospital system. Rather, it suggests satisfaction with, and acceptance of, the usefulness of hospital treatment for seriously ill individuals; *and it is*

TABLE 3
Mental Health Services

Activity	Staff	No. Persons	Training	Salary From	To
Outpatient Evaluation & Treatment	Psychiatrist	3	3 yr. residency	$ 45,000	60,000
	Psychologist	3	1 Ph.D., 2 M.A.	24,000	30,000
	Social Worker	4	M.S.W.	30,000	36,000
Day-Hospital (29 spaces)	Psychiatrist	1	3 yr. residency	$ 16,000	20,000
	Psychologist	½	Ph.D.	4,500	6,000
	Social Worker	2	M.S.W.	15,000	18,000
	Nurse	2	1 RN, 1 LPN	9,000	11,000
	Adjunctive Therapist	2	Degree in OT, RT, MT	8,000	11,000
	Aides	2	IST	6,500	8,000
Psychiatric Unit in a General Hospital (20 beds)	Psychiatrist	1	3 yr. residency	$ 16,000	20,000
	Psychologist	½	Ph.D.	4,500	6,000
	Social Worker	2	M.S.W.	15,000	18,000
	Adjunctive Therapist	1	Degree in OT, RT, MT, etc.	4,000	5,500
Patient care personnel	Head Nurse	1	Psychiatric Nurse	5,000	6,500
	Assistant	1	Psychiatric Nurse	4,500	5,500
	Staff RN	8	RN+IST	36,000	36,000
	LPN	6	LPN+IST	20,000	20,000
	Aides	3		9,500	9,500
				$267,500	321,500

TABLE 4

Aftercare Services

Activity	Staff	No. of Personnel	Training	Salary	
				From	To
Nursing Services	1) Director of Aftercare Services	1	RN with public health psychiatric training or experience	$ 6,000	8,000
	2) Mental Health Nurses	3	RN or LPN with IST	12,000	18,000
Family Counseling	Casework Aides	2	B.A.+IST	8,000	11,000
Medical Services	Part-time Medical Consultant	½	M.D.+IST	6,000	10,000
			Medication	$32,000	47,000
				5,000	10,000
				$37,000	57,000

TABLE 5

Mental Retardation Services

Activity	Staff	No. of Staff	Training Required	Salary From	Salary To
Diagnostic & Appraisal Service	Pediatrician	1	M.D.+trn.+experience MR	$12,000	20,000
	Clinical Psychol.	1	Ph.D. with MR emphasis	9,500	12,000
	Social Worker	1	Medical or Psycho. M.S.W.	7,500	11,000
Family Counseling Service	Counsellor	3	B.A.+IST	10,800	18,000
Day Care & Treatment Center (40 spaces)	Director	1	Special Education	6,000	8,500
	Activity Aides	2	IST	6,000	9,000
	Training Assistants	8	IST	24,000	36,000
				$75,800	114,000
			Supplies	6,000	6,000
				$81,800	120,500

TABLE 6
Rehabilitation Services

Activity	Staff	No. of Positions	Training	Salary From	Salary To
Director of Service	Vocational Rehab. Supervisor	1	Voc. Rehab. training or counseling psychologist	$ 5,000	10,000
Rehabilitation Counseling	Voc. Rehab. Counselors (psychiatric)	4	B.A. + IST	$14,400	25,000
Sheltered Workshop (40-80 spaces)	Supervisor	1	Variable	4,800	7,000
	Voc. Teachers	4	Variable	16,000	20,000
	Rehab. Aides	4	Variable	14,400	18,000
	Industrial Representative	1	Variable	4,000	6,500
				$58,600	86,500
			Supplies	5,000	10,000
				$63,600	96,500

TABLE 7
Alcoholism Services

Activity	Staff	No. of Positions	Training	Salary From	Salary To
Family Counseling	Alcoholism Counsellors	4	B.A.+IST	$14,400	22,000
Medical Ser.	Part-time Medical Consultant	1 full-time equivalent	M.D.+IST	12,000	20,000
			Medication	2,000	5,000
				$28,400	47,000

TABLE 8
Court Consultation Services

Activity	Staff	Positions	Training	Salary
Diagnostic & Appraisal Services	Psychiatrist	½	M.D.+Special Trng.	$11,000
	Psychologist	½	Ph.D.+Special Trng.	6,000
	Psychiatric Social Worker	1	M.S.W.	8,500
Consultation Services for Probation & Parole Officers	Court Consultant	1	M.S.W. & Special Trng.	10,000
				$35,500

TABLE 9

Research, Training and Program Analysis Section

Activity	Staff	Positions	Training	Salary From	Salary To
Director	Behavioral Scientist	1	Ph.D.	$ 8,500	11,000
Program Analysis	Program Analyst	1	Variable	6,000	8,500
Biostatistics	Statistician	1	Variable	4,000	8,000
Research Activities	Research Assistant	3	Variable	12,000	15,000
				$30,500	42,500
			Statistical	500	2,000
			Operations Supplies	300	750
				$31,300	45,250

precisely because of the success of the hospital program that citizens have wanted services of equal quality readily available within their own communities for individuals whose illness or social disability does not warrant removal from the community for treatment in a psychiatric hospital.

However, the growth of these new services in the communities has resulted in considerable confusion and anxiety on the part of professionals working in more traditional mental health settings. There have been professional concerns that psychiatry was "spreading itself too thin," or that it was "prostituting" itself or "becoming too concerned with what the public wants rather than what science demands."

When this confusion, doubt, and anxiety are distilled, it seems that a conceptual frame of reference, a structure within which to view the continuum of different types of mental health services, is lacking.

This chapter proposes an adaptation of the military model of the *chain of* evacuation, which conceives of different echelons of medical care, as the model by which we can structure our thinking about the full spectrum of mental health services. In other words, different agencies offer services of varying scope and types, with interrelationships and interdependency between agencies. Four levels of service are differentiated.

First Level of Care: "Counseling"

Traditionally there have been many professions, individuals, and organizations within the structure of the total community which have provided care for individuals experiencing difficulties with living. These individuals may be defined by the community as having mental illness, as being emotionally ill, maladjusted, bad, criminal, normal but confronted with situational difficulties, etc. However, public health personnel, physicians, welfare workers, school psychologists, special education personnel, teachers, juvenile and district judges, mental health associations, ministers, voluntary social agencies, and many other individuals and groups are available, and characteristically attempt to help those who are experiencing difficulties that we might label mental or emotional illness. They play particularly crucial roles in (a) *casefinding* and referral for more definite diagnosis and (b) crisis intervention (with the "preventive" implications that Gerald Caplan and his co-workers have emphasized); (c) providing *psychiatric first-aid;* and (d) affording *mental health education* to various individuals and groups within the community.

None of the subsequent echelons of service supplants or displaces the workers in the first echelon. Rather, if we extend the military analogy, we would see the first level as being equivalent to the company aid-men, litter-bearers, battalion aid-station personnel, and battalion surgeon of a combat unit.

Second Level of Care: "Community Center"

The majority of the mental health centers that have been developed in Kansas over the past two decades fall essentially within this level. Generally, they can be described as mental health consultation centers. In addition to providing psychiatric evaluation and outpatient treatment, they also afford consultative services to first echelon caregivers. Such consultation may center about the patient or be directed towards increasing the caregiver's effectiveness. They have also played a role in providing emergency consultation regarding inpatient care while patients are treated in the local hospital or awaiting transfer to residential psychiatric treatment centers. They have become increasingly active in evaluating a patient and his environmental situation to assess the need for hospitalization in state and private hospitals ("precare"), and also in providing direct "aftercare" services to persons who return to the community from hospitals.

This echelon of service could be compared to the regimental clearing station where patients are treated and sent back restored to duty or else referred to more definitive treatment facilities.

Every community and every county has facilities that could be classed in the first echelon of mental health care. All community-based mental health consultation centers should provide second echelon care.

Third Level of Care: "Comprehensive Community Mental Health Center"

The third echelon of care, which might be likened in our military analogy to the field hospital, would offer additional services, including inpatient treatment in psychiatric units in the general hospital for adult patients; day hospital services for children or adults; and home treatment services which would allow for the treatment of some of the seriously ill within the community. In our judgment, probably one third of the needed second echelon community mental health centers should expand and add third echelon services, becoming, in effect, comprehensive community mental health centers. They would have one or more "sister mental health centers," which would offer only second echelon services and would refer patients for additional care to the third echelon comprehensive center which serves that area.

At this point, patients in effect skip from the second echelon type of service to the fourth echelon of service, the state psychiatric hospital, because none of our present community mental health facilities provide the range of services subsumed under the term "comprehensive community mental health center."

Fourth Level of Care: "State Hospitals"

Psychiatric hospitals, the fourth echelon of service, will continue functioning very much as they are at present. However, two changes that would materially affect the profile of hospital practice are suggested.

First, the clinical role would be *more intensive* and *less extensive*. The state hospital would be treating a smaller total number of patients. The average length of hospitalization, and the average severity of illness, might increase. The state hospitals should not continue to try to be "all things to all men." Traditionally, the role of the specialized medical facility, whether it is for medical illness or surgical conditions, has been to handle *the most difficult and complicated cases*— not to admit all comers with mild, moderate, and severe illnesses. *It would seem that the redefinition of the role of the state mental hospital as a referral and consultation center, to assist in the diagnosis and treatment of difficult and severe mental illness, would inevitably enhance its prestige and stature, rather than decrease it.*

The second proposed change would develop the mental hospital as a source for consultation services. We would propose that in addition to its traditional role as a treatment institution, it also assume the important responsibility in providing consultation services to second and third echelon facilities, and also expand its *responsibilities in the area of inservice training for personnel working in second and third echelon facilities.* In other words, the state hospital would redefine its role as a backup and resource agency for second and third echelon mental health services.

These interrelationships are indicated in Table 10 and Figure 1.

TABLE 10

	First Echelon	Second Echelon	Third Echelon	Fourth Echelon
Generic Class	Community Caregiver (Nonpsychiatric)	Community Center	Comprehensive Mental Health Center	Residential Treatment Community or State Hospital
Auspices	Local Governmental Local Private	Local Governmental Local Voluntary	Local Governmental Local Voluntary State Participation	State
Directing Agency	Varied	Local Mental Health Board	Area Mental Health Board	Superintendent
Advisory Group	Local, Varied	Local, Varied	Local, Varied	Regional Advisory Group
Activities	1. Casefinding & Referral 2. Crisis Intervention 3. "Psychiatric First Aid" 4. Mental Health Education	1. Consultation to 1st Echelon Agencies 2. Evaluation & Outpatient Treatment 3. Emergency Inpatient Care 4. Precare and Aftercare 5. Training and Research	1. Consultation to 2nd Echelon Agencies 2. Evaluation & Outpatient Treatment 3. Emergency Inpatient Care 4. Precare and Aftercare 5. Training and Research	1. Consultation to 2nd & 3rd Echelon Services 2. Brief and long-term hospitalization 3. Training and Research 4. Rehabilitation Services

TABLE 10—Continued

First Echelon	Second Echelon	Third Echelon	Fourth Echelon
		6. Rehabilitation Services 7. Inpatient Treatment for 30 days (Adult) 8. Day Hospital Service for Adults and Children 9. Home Treatment Services 10. Comprehensive Services for Retarded 11. Services for Alcoholics	

	First Echelon	Second Echelon	Third Echelon	Fourth Echelon
Personnel involved directly in service	1. Physicians, private 2. Public health personnel 3. County welfare 4. School personnel 5. Court juvenile officers 6. Child service league	1. Physicians, private 2. Public health personnel 3. County welfare 4. School personnel 5. Court juvenile officers 6. Child service league	1. Physicians, private 2. Public health personnel 3. County welfare 4. Psychiatrist 5. Clinical Psychologist 6. Psychiatric Social Worker	1. Physicians, private 2. Public health personnel 3. County welfare 4. Psychiatrist 5. Clinical Psychologist 6. Psychiatric Social Worker

7. Mental health associations 8.	7. Mental health associations 8. Ministers 9. Psychiatrist 10. Clinical Psychologist 11. Psychiatric Social Worker 12. Public Mental Health Nurse 13. Psychiatric Nurse 14. Mental Health Educator	7. Public Mental Health Nurse 8. Psychiatric Nurse 9. Mental Health Educator 10. Ancillary Therapists 11. Psychiatric Aides	7. Public Mental Health Nurse 8. Psychiatric Nurse 9. Mental Health Educator 10. Ancillary Therapists 11. Psychiatric Aides
Operational Orientation Medical or Non-medical	Medical or Non-medical	Medical	Medical
Population Served Variable	50,000+	100,000-300,000	700,000-1,000,000
Annual Expenditures of population at risk Unknown	$1.00 per capita per year	Additional $3.00 per capita per yr.	Additional $9.00 per capita per year
Facilities needed Variable	Outpatient Offices	1. Outpatient Offices 2. Day Hospital Facilities 3. Hospital Unit (general hosp.)	Extensive State Hospital Facilities

TABLE 10—Continued

First Echelon	Second Echelon	Third Echelon	Fourth Echelon
		4. Rehabilitation Unit	
		5. Day Care Center for Retarded	

FIGURE 1

Mental Health Services

A schematic diagram of interrelationships among the four
proposed echelons of service.

A tabular summary of functions
of the four proposed echelons of
service.

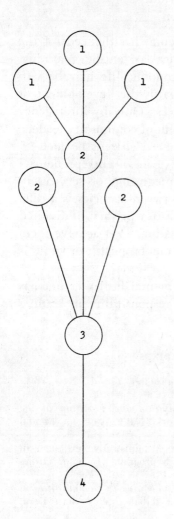

First Echelon
"Community Caregivers"

Casefinding and referral
Crisis intervention
"Psychiatric first aid"
Mental health education

Second Echelon
"Mental Health Center"

Consultation to first echelon
Evaluation and outpatient treatment
Emergency inpatient care
Precare and aftercare
Training and research

Third Echelon
"Comprehensive Community
Mental Health Center"

Consultation to second echelon
Evaluation and outpatient treatment
Inpatient treatment
Precare and aftercare
Training and research
Rehabilitation services
Day and night hospital
Home treatment services
Services for retarded and alcoholic

Fourth Echelon
"State Hospital"

Consultation to third echelon
Brief and long-term hospitalization
Training and research
Rehabilitation services

SUMMARY

The following key concepts have been underlined in this chapter:

1. Planning
2. Coordination
3. Integration

No community can meet the mental health needs of the citizens without careful, methodical, scientific planning. Many aspects of our social and economic life may be self-regulating. This is less true as regards the development of regional health and welfare resources. Only by interagency planning, involving a broad spectrum of community leaders, can the needs of emotionally disturbed citizens be met.

Coordination is difficult to achieve in an entrepreneurial and competitive society; just as integration of services to ensure free movement of clients between agencies is a difficult goal in a society which emphasizes privacy, individual initiative and the right of the individual. Yet achieve them we must, if an effective community mental health program is to be realized.

The comprehensive community mental health center has a crucial role and an inescapable responsibility in leading the way.

SUGGESTED READINGS

Albee, G. W. (1959), *Mental Health Manpower Trends*. New York: Basic Books.

Barhas, A. F. et al. (1952), *The Organization and Function of the Community Psychiatric Clinic*. New York: Nat'l Assoc. for Mental Health.

Bindman, A. J. & Klebanoff, L.B. (1960), Administrative problems in establishing a community mental health program. *Amer. J. Orthopsychiat.*, 30:696-711.

Binzley, R. F. & Forstenzer, H. M. (1959), *A Guide to Communities in the Establishment of Psychiatric Clinics*. Albany: N. Y. State Dept. of Mental Hygiene.

Characteristics and Professional Staff of Outpatient Psychiatric Clinics (1957), Public Health Monograph No. 49. Washington, D.C.: U.S. Dept. of Health, Education & Welfare.

Davies, S. P. (1960), *Toward Community Mental Health: A Review of the First Five Years of Operations under the Community Mental Health Services Act of the State of New York.* New York: New York Association for Mental Health.

The Elements of a Community Mental Health Program (1956). New York: Milbank Memorial Fund.

Freyhan, F. A. & Mayo, J. A. (1963), Concept of a model psychiatric clinic. *Amer. J. Psychiat.*, 120:222-227.

Leighton, A. M. (1959), *My Name is Legion: Foundations for a Theory of Man's Response to Culture.* New York: Basic Books.

Perkins, M. E. (1964), The organization and administration of the New York City Community Mental Health Board. In: *Handbook of Community Psychiatry and Community Mental Health,* ed. L. Bellak. New York: Grune & Stratton.

Programs for Community Mental Health (1957). New York: Milbank Memorial Fund.

Progress and Problems of Community Mental Health Services (1959). New York: Milbank Memorial Fund.

Rosen, I. M. (1964), A new social problems clinic—rationale and community response. *Amer. J. Psychiat.*, 120:779-781.

Westman, J. C., Vaughan, R. A., & Frull, J. P. (1964), Organization of a psychiatric clinic for children. *Arch. Gen. Psychiat.*, 10:332-336.

III

The Nurturant Society: An Introduction to Community Organization

The task set forth for this chapter is obviously impossible, just as a single chapter on "psychiatric theory and practice" would be doomed to incompleteness. The field of sociology, and applied aspects commonly referred to as community organization, is complex and extensive, and will obviously elude summarization in one chapter. However, the intent is to give a broad conceptual frame of reference, to introduce certain concepts, to stimulate the interest and curiosity of the reader, and to provide a basis upon which to accrue further knowledge.

CONCEPTS

Certain basic ideas are woven into the study of community life, and into the application of acquired knowledge towards the modification of social processes.

The first concept is that society is *organized*. That is, the parts and elements of the community are interrelated, and have structure and meaning.

Related to this is the concept that these relationships between elements and society may be *described* in a variety of ways. The participants may be enumerated and an answer be given to the question of *Who?* The purpose of the various elements in the social fabric may be elucidated, and com-

mentary made on the question of *Why?* The means by
which social groups and subgroups accomplish their purposes
may be described, and a commentary given on *How?* The
end product (resulting from the interaction of participants,
who are pursuing certain purposes, by specific means) may
be described in terms of outcome, and an answer given to
the question of *What?* The relationships involved in the life
of a community may be described in other ways as well. For
example, interactions between groups may be described, and
elements of mutuality, interdependency, competition, or
combat may be spelled out. Or, as one final example, the
focus of study may be on the medium of communication
used between and within the subgroups within the larger
society, and emphasis thus focused primarily upon the flow
of messages throughout the information network.

A study of community organization is also based on a belief
that society is *purposive.* That is, the relationships within
and between groups are designed to accomplish certain ends,
whether these goals are immediately evident or not.

A central concept in the study of society is that processes
within the social organization are *caused,* and are not random
events. This concept has led to a relatively new idea in man's
view of himself: the causes of social interactions and behavior are tied to inherent limitations in the behavior
repertoire of mankind, are susceptible to study, and *are predictable so long as the field of forces is relatively well-known.*
Prior attempts to explain social behavior, and to regulate it,
have been based upon the assumption that there were certain
God-determined rules governing human interactions, and
that human life was regulated by the observance of these
rules, with disaster occurring when divine scriptures, or other
taboos, were violated or broken.

With a causal and scientific frame of reference, it is reasonable to assume that social organization may be studied,
and the approach may be essentially a diagnostic one. The

exact approach to the study of society may vary along a number of dimensions. For example, the approach may be macroscopic—concentrating upon nations, regions, or multi-national communities—or may be microscopic, dealing with, for example, the organization of the extended family within a single community. The approach may be historical, relating antecedent events to current developments; or it may be essentially cross-sectional, describing social structures, processes, and relationships as they exist at the present moment. The description of the elements of society may be either static or dynamic, emphasizing either content or process; as with the study of psychotherapy, there is a deceptive lure to the descriptive approach since it ostensibly eliminates "observer bias." Yet, in the final analysis, the dynamic approach, which emphasizes cause and effect relationships between elements, is likely to be most productive. The study of social process likewise may emphasize formal elements of organization and interrelationship, or take a functional approach and look at informal or operational elements.

There are many other ways in which the study of society may be organized. Primary inquiry may deal with the demographic aspects of the population being studied, such as age distribution, sex, education, economic level, racial and ethnic background, marital status, and so forth.

Concepts of ecology may be borrowed more or less intact from biology, and an attempt made to broadly describe transactions involving man and his environment, both animate and inanimate. Such transfer of the ecological model is possible, but requires care because of the unique characteristics of the human animal: his reliance on language and symbolic processes.

The primary focus of inquiry may deal with governmental aspects of organization, associational aspects, or economic aspects. Or, the focus may be upon individual leadership figures, and their effect upon the community. On the other hand, the focus on individual leaders may be broadened and a general examination conducted of the power structure within the community.

A study of human organization indicates that all societies have developed certain normative standards for members in the society. Usually, there are more or less specific role definitions on the basis of age and sex. The range of "normalcy" is defined by each social group, and varies even from subgroup to subgroup, in the range and strictness of the normative sanctions. Likewise, there is wide variation among groups concerning the fate of the deviant who does not fall within normative standards, ranging from tolerance to the death penalty. Every society also has strict normative values concerning the full range of interpersonal behavior, although the extent to which these values are explicit, clearly defined, and generally adhered to varies considerably. All societies have standards and taboos concerning the management of aggressive drives, sexuality, competitive and exploitative strivings, and for the maintenance of property rights.

Inherent in the study of community organization is the belief that change occurs in societies. Such change is purposive even if it is not planned, and is goal-oriented even if it is not effective. One goal of the community mental health practitioner, then, is to understand the processes effecting changes in the community with sufficient depth so that goal-orientation and purposive aspect may be rendered more effective through the "management" of social forces.

COMMUNITY PROBLEMS

We do not need to go far to discover some of the problems that a study of communities would reveal to us in America of the 1960's. Many of these social ills have direct and major impact upon the whole field of mental health and mental illness. For example, prejudicial stereotyping, scapegoating and denial of civil liberties to certain ethnic and other mi-

nority groups in American society clearly have implications
not only for the mental health of those discriminated against,
but for the emotional functioning of the oppressor. The
scapegoating mechanism seems to be deeply engrained in
human personality organization, and probably appears in all
societies. Whether difficulty and adversity are ascribed to
a mystical force (possession by the devil), forces in the neighborhood (influx of various ethnic groups), or to an external
threat (the Communists), the human organism often needs
to reconstruct reality in order to protect wishes and delusions
of omnipotence from the imprint of the hard reality of mis-
fortune, by ascribing blame to some malevolent force. It is
doubtful if any amount of wishing, "do-gooding," or middle-
class morality will abolish prejudicial attitudes and behaviors.
The task of mental health workers is to focus on the mental
health implications of such prejudicial behaviors, and attempt to minimize the threat that such community patterns
hold for personality integrity and functioning.

Increasing centralization in government, industry, finance,
and idea-production has been a fact of social evolution for
the past century. It is important in looking at such processes
to sort out value judgments and moralistic attitudes. For
example, an immediate phrase that comes to mind is, "power
corrupts, and absolute power corrupts absolutely." This is
probably a misleading concept, and is a little like saying that
having a gun causes someone to be a murderer. Power only
allows a person to implement his own value system with
greater freedom, and does not in itself distort, pervert, or
overpower the individual.

Centralization does, however, raise serious problems in
our democratic society. We have been loath to vest excessive
power in one individual or institution within our pluralistic
society, and have set up an elaborate system of checks and
balances to prevent a monopoly on power and authority by
any individual or group. The effectiveness of this system is

based, in the final analysis, on the involvement of the voter
and the informed citizen. To the extent that social processes
are distant, inscrutable, and seen as being monolithic and
"too big to fight," the invaluable act of participation by
informed citizens will be difficult to maintain at a high level;
and it is precisely at the point that the involvement of the
informed citizen drops when centralization of power and
authority accelerate.

Improvements in communication render a system of centralized authority much more workable, from an administrative and logistical standpoint, than at any time in the past.
It is possible for one man or a group of men to effectively
make decisions governing the lives of millions of human
beings in all corners of the earth, because of vastly accelerated
communication processes. The delegation of decision-making
power to lower echelons, in the world of today, must be a
rational and purposive decision on the basis of management,
whereas in the world of the past, factors of time, distance, and
communication lag dictated such delegation as mandatory for
simple administrative efficiency.

Has the increased effectiveness of the communication system more than counteracted the centralization of decision-
making processes within our society? Is the informed citizen
even more knowledgeable about and involved in the affairs
of the day through television and other media? Certainly,
the immediacy of the television medium, and its effective use
in current-events reporting gives the observer a sense of
intimacy about world-shaking events. Whether this sense
of involvement may, in fact, be spurious and misleading, is
another question. Seeing the outcome of decisions that have
already been made, or at least the outcome that is presented
for public consumption, is a long way from active knowledge about and involvement in decision-making processes. A
passive spectator at a football game, for example, is a quite
different animal than an active participant in the game.

Some of these same processes of passive and vicarious participation may convert politics, war, and international rivalry
into "spectator sports."

Bureaucratization is another element of current social life
that has received wide commentary. It has been termed an
outgrowth of the increasing complexity of today's world, and
of the demands upon government made by rapidly changing
and complex events. There is nothing inherently bad or
wrong about bureaucracy, except when it results in governmental organizations becoming less accountable, less sensitive
to public opinion, and less manageable by duly elected or appointed officials.

The mobility of our society is frightening to behold, both
in terms of socioeconomic and actual physical change. It is
a rare man who lives in the same community, in the same
house, and pursues the same occupation as his father. We
move within towns, we move within states, we move from
one part of the country to another, and increasingly we move
to foreign lands. This mobility produces severe stresses and
strains in our social structure, which was established essentially on the basis of a stable agrarian and small manufac-
turing economy. As one concrete example, residency requirements for psychiatric hospitalization, welfare assistance, and
voting do not take into account the enormous interstate
mobility in the world of today.

Just as there has probably been an increasing centralization of authority, there has been paradoxical diffusion of
responsibility. The manipulation of bureaucratic organizations and processes is one way in which this may be accomplished. The diffusion of responsibility, at a more immediate
level, comes home whenever one sits down with a group of
agencies in the community to talk about cooperative planning
for meeting mental health or other needs of citizens. It becomes immediately clear that everybody wants as much

authority as he can get, as little responsibility as possible, and no accountability at all.

The rapid accumulation of scientific knowledge about things and about people has produced some serious stresses in our society. The model of democratic government was established at a time when the contribution that science had to make to the management of human events was negligible. The Industrial Revolution, the discoveries of Sigmund Freud, and the atomic bomb have changed all this. Should we now have, then, a democracy or a technocracy, where trained experts and scientists make decisions concerning the common welfare? The judgment of the scientist—or more appropriately, the wisdom of the scientist—has not been demonstrated with sufficient frequency or clarity to give us serious reason for abandoning our formula of "government for the people, of the people, and by the people."

PLAN FOR WHAT?

Community life is complex, and the functions that must be performed by subunits of even a very small American town are manifold. It is important for the mental health practitioner to view mental health services as only a piece in the total mosaic, and to maintain the proper humility and perspective in his attempts to improve the plight of the mentally ill. The community must plan for and provide the following activities:

1. Employment
2. Housing
3. Recreation
4. Transportation
5. Utilities
6. Food and Materials
7. Helping Services
   a. Welfare

   b. Medical
   c. Social Services
   d. Mental Health Services
   e. Courts and Court-related Services
   f. Rehabilitation Services
 8. Education and Training
 9. Centers for Community Life
   a. Churches
   b. Neighborhood Centers
   c. Auditoriums, etc.
10. Minimization of Noxious Influences
   a. Public Health Services
     (1) Air Pollution Control
     (2) Water Pollution Control
     (3) Rodent Control
     (4) Infectious Disease Control, etc.
   b. Sewage Disposal
   c. Garbage Disposal
   d. Law Enforcement and Courts

CHANGE

The community does change, in ways that are often imperceptible, for reasons that are often unclear, and to accomplish goals that are often poorly defined. How does this come about?

In general, for group behavior as for individual behavior, the status quo tends to persist. In all human events, individual or collective, the best predictor of future behavior is past behavior. Agencies of society, like individuals, resist change. Social morés, taboos, normative standards, the institutions of church and the law, all resist and slow down social change, whether it is needed or not needed, whether it promises to be successful or not successful, or whether desired by the majority or not desired by the majority.

Change *does* occur, sometimes with surprising rapidity, when certain requirements are met. When the discordance between widely held values, and current social reality, becomes very great and apparent, change will occur—either in the direction of modifying the value system, or reorganizing and changing social institutions. Discrepancies between public or verbalized morality, and private or operational morality, are often very great. The process may resemble what has been happening in divorce proceedings in our country over the past 50 years. Public morality holds that marriage is a sacred institution, should be protected and maintained by society, and should be terminated only when clear and grievous cause has been demonstrated by one party. The divorce laws in most states reflect this set of values and moralistic judgments. Private morality, on the other hand, has increasingly held that two people who do not care for each other, who find each other incompatible, and who are unable to maintain a harmonious and mutual relationship, should not be forced to live together. In the pursuit of happiness, promised to us as American citizens, the ancient institution of marriage should not be allowed to interfere. Consequently, divorce *practice* has come to conform with private morality, with a widespread disregard or operational modification of basic divorce laws. Only now are serious movements underway in some states for the amendment of divorce statutes, so that once again public morality and private morality, in the field of marriage and divorce, may be rendered more congruent.

Change may also take place when it is obviously necessary for survival. However, the behavior of many Jewish ghetto groups under occupation by the Nazis in World War II, provides clear evidence that behavioral changes and social reorganizations geared to survival will not *necessarily* occur, even under the most acute circumstances.

Social change will ensue when it is felt to be advantageous

or profitable to a considerable segment of the population to institute such changes. For example, our free enterprise philosophy holds that government should not engage in business activities. Yet, when a community becomes convinced that it is necessary to have industrial enterprises in order to maintain the economic and social health of the community, government may often be encouraged and indeed forced to engage in such enterprises as the development of industrial land areas, provision of utilities and roads at no expense to the occupants, and suspension or reduction of taxation upon such industries: a role in which government is directly subsidizing and supporting private entrepreneurs.

If few people actively oppose a social change, it is much more likely to come about. In reality, it is often more important in American community life to know the number of persons who actively and vocally oppose a change, rather than the numbers who actively and vocally support it. Most changes are viewed by the average citizen with relative indifference, and with little sense of personal or ego involvement. The management of social change, then, often requires the neutralization or reeducation of the vocal minority who oppose a change. Or, it may suffice to convince responsible governmental leaders that the amount of opposition is really quite small, so that they will feel sufficient support from the electorate to institute needed changes.

Community institutions may change in response to normative demands from the nurturant society. That is, the maintenance of a familial oligarchy in specific communities may be rendered more difficult by the fact that this deviates from the normative pattern of social and political life in the region, state, and nation. Likewise, changes in practices of segregation in communities are brought about not only by direct legal action, but also by covert pressure from national public opinion.

THE MANAGEMENT OF CHANGE

Management and manipulation are words that are closely linked. The community organizer, however, is theoretically devoted to assisting the community in recognizing and achieving community goals, not to imposing the goals of the organizer.

What does the person interested and involved in community organization attempt to accomplish? First of all, he would need to understand the communication network, and to insure insofar as possible that appropriate messages, with a minimum of static and distortion, flow along all relevant channels in the communication net. Second, he would be concerned, prior to the institution of any change, that a study of the effects of this change upon other aspects of community life should be done, and, to the extent that is feasible, an ecological approach be applied. He would be furthermore concerned that in the planning process, all vested interest groups be involved in defining goals, deciding upon means, and determining responsibility and accountability. He would be interested consistently about public opinion, or rather more specifically about the attitudes of a whole variety of publics: the vocal minority opposition, the man on the street, the political leader, the opinion setter, church leaders, newspaper editors, radio and television commentators, and so forth.

In summary, he would be trying to accomplish the following tasks: 1. To insure that there is a widespread recognition of the problem. 2. To insure that there is widespread conviction of a need for action to cope with the problem. (In other words, that there is a process of social legitimation whereby society define the problem as one that needs action.) 3. To insure the involvement of a broad cross section of community opinion-setters and power figures in discussing possible solutions to the problem. 4. To insure that a ra-

tional planning process is undertaken to involve consideration of alternative courses of action, their cost, available
scientific knowledge concerning effectiveness or lack of effectiveness, and feasibility or practicality of implementing specific courses of action. 5. To insure that a consensus is
reached concerning the most desirable course of action. 6.
To insure that responsibility is assumed, accountability is
defined, and commensurate authority is ascribed to the
agency or social unit which is to institute the needed change.
7. To insure, insofar as possible, that processes for evaluation
and appraisal of the effectiveness or lack of effectiveness of
the implemented change are planned for and carried forth.
8. If at all possible, to encourage a process of social validation
after the innovation is introduced, by which consensus is
reached that the innovation is a needed and effective one,
which at least partly meets the need and solves the problem
which led to its institution.

There are a number of mechanisms by which these processes may be implemented. Most urban areas have a health
and welfare planning council, usually supported by United
Fund or Community Chest, which operates with the explicit
or implicit sanction of health and welfare agencies within
the community, and is responsible for organizing community
planning activities. These councils were themselves a social
innovation, designed to provide some interagency planning
for regional development, without sacrificing the vigor and
spirit of innovation of a system of independent, essentially
entrepreneurial agencies. The health and welfare planning
councils have had mixed success, but even the worst of them
is usually an improvement over having no mechanism for
community-wide planning.

A wide variety of voluntary interagency associations, either
with or without full-time staff, have also been developed in
different areas. A council of social agencies is a mechanism
for rural and smaller urban areas, to provide some oppor-

tunity for interagency communication, sharing, and planning, which in larger urban areas would be served by the full-time staff of a health and welfare planning council. Councils of social agencies usually have an abundance of good intentions, but characteristically suffer from diffusion of purpose and overexpansion of membership. Chambers of commerce may, and quite properly should, develop special subcommittees for consideration of health and welfare-related matters. Certainly, studies of the factors involved in industrial relocation have clearly shown that the presence or absence of good services of various kinds for prospective employees—educational, medical, psychiatric, recreational—is important to the industrialist seeking a new plant site.

Or, change may quite simply come about through operation of the ongoing institutions of government. Legislative enactments at the state level, or at the county or community level, may institute changes. Administrative decisions, within limits set by law, may bring about significant social reorganizations. Even though governmental policy is largely determined by public opinion, there are considerable governmental resources designed to mold and develop specific public opinions necessary to bring about needed social changes.

The role of the community mental health center in community organization is not clearly defined at the present time. The center should certainly be embedded in the matrix of other helping agencies, and at least an active co-participant in interagency planning. Whether all or some community mental health centers can and should assume additional responsibility for leadership in planning for services affecting the mental health of the citizens, is open to question. Critics point out that clinical training is not adequate for, or even necessarily useful in, the mastery of community organization skills. The present author tends to disagree with this attitude and rather sees the task as primarily the translation of the knowledge of human behavior from the clinical context, into the frame of reference of the larger society. Although this transfer would require discarding certain models that are dear to the clinician, it would not involve abandonment of basic insights about human behavior, interpersonal process, and group behavior. It would require a significant modification in the clinician's role, changes in emphasis on various aspects of interpersonal behavior, and a careful rethinking of issues of responsibility and authority.

But it would seem, if the community mental health center is to take seriously its concern about the prevention of mental illness, that the staff must be involved in a variety of roles in community-wide planning for the amelioration of conditions contributing to mental ill health, and for the development of resources for promoting the development of healthy, adequate personalities.

Suggested Readings

Bennis, W. G., Beene, K. D., & Chin, R., eds. (1961), *The Planning of Change.* New York: Holt, Rinehart, and Winston.

Converging Social Trends—Emerging Social Problems (1964). Washington, D.C.: U.S. Dept. of Health, Education & Welfare.

Duhl, L. J., ed. (1963), *The Urban Condition.* New York: Basic Books.

Hallock, A. C. K. & Vaughan, W. T. (1956), Community organization—A dynamic component of community mental health practice. *Amer. J. Orthopsychiat.,* 26:691-706.

Hatt, P. K. & Reiss, A. J., Jr., eds. (1957), *Cities and Society: The Revised Reader in Urban Sociology.* Glencoe, Ill.: Free Press.

Howe, L. P. (1964), The concept of the community; some implications for the development of community psychiatry. In: *Community Psychiatry and Community Mental Health,* ed. L. Bellak. New York: Grune & Stratton.

Hughes, C. C. et al. (1960), *People of Cove and Woodlot: Communities from the Viewpoint of Social Psychiatry.* New York: Basic Books.

Lippitt, R., Watson, J., & Westlen, B. (1958), *The Dynamics of Planned Change: A Comparative Study of Principles and Techniques.* New York: Harcourt, Brace.

Merton, R. K., Broom, L., & Cottrell, L. S., eds. (1959), *Sociology Today, Problems and Prospects.* New York: Basic Books.

National Conference on Social Welfare (1958), *Community Organization*. New York: Columbia University Press.

Stevenson, G. S. (1956), *Mental Health Planning for Social Action*. New York: Blakiston.

Sussman, M. B., ed. (1959), *Community Structure and Analysis*. New York: Crowell.

IV

The Team: Role Definition
and Interrelationships

At present, most community mental health services utilize
small staffs. For example, in a study of outpatient services
for the year 1954-55, 76 per cent of the reporting outpatient
clinics employed nine or fewer staff persons (U.S. Department of Health, Education and Welfare, 1957). One-fifth of
all clinics provided fewer than ten professional manhours
of service per week, and the median was 74 professional
manhours per week. At the upper end of the scale there were
23 clinics (22 per cent) which provided 1,000 or more manhours weekly. The majority of the larger centers were those
operated by the Veterans Administration, Department of
Health, Education and Welfare, clinics affiliated with medical schools and other universities and colleges, and clinics
operated by city boards of education. In contrast, state
mental hospital clinics averaged only 7 manhours per week.
The median full-time clinic provided 176 professional manhours of service weekly, compared with 15 professional manhours for the median part-time clinic.

For the purposes of the report cited above, an outpatient
psychiatric clinic was defined as one where a psychiatrist was
in attendance at regularly scheduled hours and assumed the
medical responsibility for all the patients in the clinics. In
one-tenth of all the clinics, it was found that psychiatrist
manhours represented less than 10 per cent of the total manhours. The median number of psychiatrist manhours per

100 total professional manhours was 32. For all 9,522 total clinical professional staff reported operating in these centers, 43 per cent were psychiatrists, 22 per cent clinical psychologists, 26 per cent psychiatric social workers, and 9 per cent other disciplines. In contrast, of the 188,141 total clinic professional manhours per week, 30 per cent were provided by psychiatrists, 25 per cent by clinical psychologists, 38 per cent by psychiatric social workers, and 7 per cent by other disciplines. In other words, more of the psychiatrists had part-time positions than did the other disciplines, and in terms of total clinic professional manhours, psychiatric social workers provided the largest number of hours reported.

Five of every ten full-time clinics and one of every ten part-time clinics had professional trainees in addition to their regular full-time and part-time staff. There was about one trainee to every four regular full-time and part-time staff members for each of the three major professions, consisting of 1,912 trainees in clinics, of whom 88 per cent were doing graduate work and receiving supervised work-learning experience in a psychiatric clinic as an integral part of the training program for one of the three major professions of psychiatry, clinical psychology, or psychiatric social work.

Subsequent data (Bahn et al., 1963) while revealing steady quantitative growth, do not indicate any major shifts in patterns of organization, staffing, or service.

In other words, when we begin to look at professional and staff role definition and interrelationships between various disciplines in the usual community mental health setting at the present time, we are really talking about a small group relationship in which numbers are relatively small, hierarchical distinctions somewhat blunted, and a setting which permits of a high degree of intimacy and sharing among staff members.

However, such a milieu enhances certain psychological and social problems for the participants. An environment of this nature is not at all like the situation in which the bulk of professional training takes place, even at the present time. Major training institutions tend to be large, somewhat isolated from the general community, hierarchically organized, with marked status differentiations, and with firmly defined role definitions for various professions. The larger training institutions have a tendency to look "inward" psychologically, and to be relatively protected from external pressures and from influences that might have a disturbing effect on the established equilibrium.

In contrast, the usual community mental health center, is, by its very size, fluidly organized, subject to great pressures and stresses from external forces, and provides an environment in which certain aspects of interpersonal behavior may become heightened. For example, the problems of psychological closeness and emotional involvement in a small staff, working together in a confined physical situation and dealing with disturbed children and adults, on a day-in and day-out basis, are bound to grow. In many smaller communities, off-the-job relationships between staff members and their families are equally intense. Supervisor-supervisee distinctions, consultant-consultee differentiations, the organization of the decision-making process, involvement in planning, assignment of work loads, division of responsibilities—all begin, in a community mental health center, to take on some of the richness, complexity, and depth of interpersonal transactions within the family situation. In other words, the staff of the community mental health center may come to have some of the characteristics of a primary group, rather than a secondary reference group. Problems of ambivalence, intensity of involvement, inability to be "indifferent" to each other, struggle for leadership and followship positions, rivalry for gratification of dependency and prestige needs, struggle for recognition and reward—all may grow intense within the community mental health center.

Complicating all of these problems, have been fluctuating role definitions between and within the various mental health disciplines. At present, clearly defined and socially reinforced patterns of behavior for each of the disciplines are not well delineated. Some of the social controls of behavior are lacking in the community mental health setting, and the staff is thrown back upon its own resources to resolve difficulties and to strive for the achievement of democratic group interaction without having to surrender to mediocrity or abandoning initiative and leadership.

In order to clarify some of these issues, the following table outlining various specialization levels, representative specialties, treatment and diagnostic modalities available, typical cases, and prohibited areas of functioning is presented. There is also an attempt to differentiate between the various specialization levels on the basis of professional, personal, and social criteria. Undoubtedly this attempt will be distasteful to many readers, since the general trend nowadays is to "blur" professional discipline boundaries, and to move toward some generalized role description for "the mental health worker." However, while each discipline should, in the author's judgment, continue to extend its diversity and depth of functioning, so that areas of overlap and shared responsibility will undoubtedly continue to grow, each discipline has a unique identity, unique historical and professional background, and offers potentially unique contributions.

The author has no illusions that this chapter, or indeed a whole book on this subject, could resolve the problems that exist within, and between, all of the mental health disciplines at their present state of evolution. Indeed, it seems certain that these problems will be resolved through the give and take of social interaction over the years ahead, and cannot be dissolved by any authoritative and/or authoritarian statement.

Although the concept of "medical responsibility," often

Table 1

Role Definition of Mental Health Practitioners

Specialization Level	Representative Specialties	Treatment & Diagnostic Modalities Available	Typical Cases	Should Not Attempt to Treat:
1	Vocational Counselor; Pastoral Counselor; M.D. with counseling aptitude & training; Student Personnel Worker; School Guidance Worker; Personnel Counselor	Listening; abreactive experience; Reassurance & encouragement; Clarification of problem; "Rational Problem Solving"; Providing needed information	Reality, situational, adjustment problems	All below, *plus* those in which subjective discomfort is moderate-severe & persistent
2	Counseling Psychologist; Psychiatric Social Worker; M.D. with some psychotherapy training	As above, *plus*: Interpretation about interpersonal modes and defensive maneuvers; Judgment of severity of psychological illness and decision about referral for definitive treatment	As above, *plus*: Mild neurotic reactions; Mild personality problems	Cases in which there is deterioration in ego functioning (reality assessment, judgment, planning, delay of impulse, etc.)

#				
3	Clinical Psychologist	As above, *plus*: Complete diagnostic evaluation (testing & interview) plus establishment of rational treatment plan; Expressive psychotherapy with proper training	As above, *plus*: Moderately severe neuroses; Moderate personality problems; "Ambulatory" schizophrenics	
4	Psychiatrist	As above, *plus*: Medication for depression; "Psychotic" symptoms (delusions, thought disorders, etc.), or anxiety; Hospitalization; Neurological & medical evaluations	As above, *plus*: Severe neuroses; Severe personality problems; Psychotic reactions; Organic brain syndromes; Psychophysiological illnesses	Cases in which: 1. Patient is suicidal 2. Patient is assaultive 3. Medical-neurological complications are present 4. Medication is a necessary part of treatment (i.e., severe depressions, acute psychoses, etc.)

TABLE 1—Continued

Criteria	Specialization Level 1	Specialization Level 2	Specialization Level 3	Specialization Level 4
Professional Criteria				
1. Theoretical orientation	"Common-sense" orientation; reliance on conscious motivation as explanation; carry-over of lay attitudes	Varies widely: a. Psychiatric SW: either diagnostic or functional approach. Tend to emphasize social & situational determinants. b. Counseling: No concept of illness. c. MD: Variable. No theory regarding personality development.	Variable, but generally multifactorial, sophisticated, & broad. Concepts of personality development, sickness & therapy.	Variable. Generally integrates biological, social & psychological parameters. Complex & internally consistent theoretical framework.
2. Clinical training	No systematic exposure to seriously ill individuals	a. Psych. SW: Contact with but no direct respon. for seriously ill patients. b. Counseling Psychol.: No systematic exposure to seriously ill patients. c. MD: Variable	Variable, but usually affords contact with broad range of patients.	Broad as to age, types of illness, treatment modalities, etc.

3. Duration, breadth, & complexity of training	Brief, narrow un-complex training in relation to other spec. levels	Slights biological determinants of behavior. Still emphasis on conscious determinants & rational problem solving.	Broad but with considerable irrelevant content; often poorly integrated & inadequately coordinated.	Prolonged, broad, complex.
4. Intensity & closeness of supervisory contacts during training.	Inconsistent	a. Psych. SW: tends to be well-structured & close b. Counseling psych.: tends to be loosely structured, brief. c. MD: Variable	Extremely variable. Lack of strong philosophy for supervisory function. Generally far from ideal.	Usually well-structured & with theoretical basis for supervisory function. Attempts to make student aware of his neurotic distortions.
Personal Criteria 1. Maturity of Individual*	Variable	Variable	Variable	Variable

* Under the concept of "maturity" in a clinician, we might include such traits as:
Ability to tolerate dependency in others, and to *selectively* gratify or frustrate such wishes.
Relative freedom from voyeuristic impulses.
Mutuality dominant over exploitative and manipulative modes of interaction.
Ability to tolerate anger without retaliation.
Ability to set limits and to be lovingly firm.
Without need to "buy love" by "helping" people.

TABLE 1—Continued

Criteria	Specialization Level 1	Specialization Level 2	Specialization Level 3	Specialization Level 4
2. Freedom from neurotic illness	No systematic attention to this variable	a. Psych. SW: emphasizes need for personal psychotherapy. b. Counseling: minimizes need for personal psychotherapy. c. MD: Variable.	Personal psychotherapy or analysis not stressed. Some avoidance of recognizing neurotic symptoms in colleagues.	Personal psychoanalysis is encouraged in most centers. Diagnostic approach applied to colleagues' idiosyncrasies.
3. Practice experience	Variable	Difficult for counseling psychol. to obtain heterogeneous experience.	Can choose between wide range of opportunities.	Can choose between wide range of opportunities.
4. "Medical responsibility"	With exception of M.D., concept of "responsibility" is poorly developed & not institutionalized.	Poorly developed in counseling psychology training, where autonomy of client is stressed.	Concept is poorly developed, and is at odds with model of the "dispassionate scientist."	Highly developed; an extension of medical school training.
5. Professional Identity	Vague & shifting	1. Psych. SW: solid & consistent. 2. Counseling: hybrid & shaky. 3. MD: Solid & consistent.	Conflict between clinician-academician model.	Some strain with traditional medical identity; some identity diffusion.

Social Criteria				
1. Definition of role by society	Seen as closer to the common man; more like you & me; "Dutch Uncle"; common sense, practical approach	Seen as specialist who has technical info. not generally available. SW has some stigma of welfare & charity	Unable to differentiate from psychiatrist	Still seen as "alienists"; strange people; money-hungry; not really doctors, etc.
2. Fee paid for services	Fee is relatively small or nonexistent	Fee is usually small or nonexistent	Variable, but generally below Level 4 for same services.	Generally high. On private basis available only to upper 15-20% of income groups for extended treatment.

used in these discussions, is one of conventional respectability and sounds wise and good, it is difficult to define exactly what medical responsibility actually is, as contrasted with psychological or social work responsibility. In all truth, none of the three disciplines has placed a high enough value on administrative and/or leadership skills, to give the development of these attributes very great attention in the trainee and/or supervised experience portion of the curriculum. The medical profession tends to assume that this right of leadership is theirs, and that other disciplines are acting as usurpers when they attempt to assume such authority. By and large, the medical profession tends to see other clinical workers as "ancillary personnel" who should work under the supervision and direction of licensed physicians. Psychiatric social work has—but even here there are notable exceptions—tended to accept this role ascription. In contrast, clinical psychology sees itself as a distinct profession, performing many functions that are not inherently or even distantly medical in nature, and is attempting to develop a set of ethical principles and internal regulating devices to insure its continued functioning as a separate profession.

What all this adds up to, is that team practice is indeed a cumbersome, time-consuming, tiring, exasperating, and difficult undertaking at best. The success or lack of success that any particular group of clinicians experiences in practicing as a team depends upon a number of factors. First of all, it hinges upon the models for professional functioning and interprofessional behavior that were set during the training and early work experience of the professional persons involved. In some training settings the dominant discipline tends to hire submissive, and often untrained or partly trained professionals in the other two disciplines. For example, in one psychological training clinic the alleged psychiatrist is not recognized by his peers as being a specialist in psychiatry, and upon more than one occasion the only social worker has been without any formal training or degree in social work. It is understandable how a clinical psychologist trained in this setting could not help but be, from his early exposure to derrogated professionals in the other disciplines, extremely limited in his understanding of, and support for, team practice. Similarly, some clinical psychologists and psychiatric social workers are trained in state psychiatric settings where the majority of the physicians, while labeled psychiatrists, have no formal education entitling them to that appellation. In psychiatric training settings, psychologists may be hired who have less than ideal training, and are often assigned relatively routine and unimaginative testing tasks. Social workers may be used for a variety of functions such as scheduling appointments, collecting information about patients that could easily be obtained by clerical personnel, and performing essentially welfare-like tasks. Likewise, psychiatric nurses in some mental health centers serve as traffic managers, and replenish various office supplies and other stocks that are needed by the staff.

In addition to this very crucial formative experience in the lives of each of the professionals, the unique interpersonal relationships that develop within the small group will, of course, affect group functioning and intragroup tensions.

Similarly the kinds of pressures, encouragements, provocations, and harassments to which the mental health center is subjected by external forces—such as its governing board, community pressure groups, and so forth—will be reflected in tensions within the staff which may, or may not, lead to healthy conflict resolution and more mature group functioning.

The emotional health or ill-health of individual staff members must, inevitably, enter into how they function together as a group. No matter how much we stress social process and interpersonal transaction, each of the persons brings to the group experience a particular preparatory set which will, to a great extent, determine the ways in which he perceives and responds to situations, as will his manner of interaction with other people.

The primary responsibility of the director of the community mental health center, which transcends all of his other responsibilities, is to see that the groups of individuals who make up the staff of the center work together in such a way that they can make their optimum contributions as professional people to the community that they serve. The good leader will, inevitably, be more concerned with his responsibility to his staff, than with the privileges or prerogatives which his position affords him. Since his is a final responsibility for the operation of the clinic, he can expect reasonable respect and cooperation on the part of his staff members, and a higher financial reward for his efforts. He should also demand from his staff, to the extent that they are able to give it, active sharing of responsibility for the operation of the community mental health center. He can ask them to share this responsibility with him only if he allows them commensurate authority. He will be particularly plagued with problems of favoritism, and with the need to consider the overall program of the mental health center at all times.

It would be desirable if each of the directors of the 1,500 or so outpatient psychiatric clinics could be well suited by education, experience, personality, and personal maturity to assume this high leadership function and discharge it with integrity and honor. This will, of course, never entirely be the case. As has been true in all major conflicts—whether war, or fights against disease, or social disorder—young persons will be commissioned and promoted to positions of responsibility much earlier than they are ready for them. The leaders in all of our disciplines at the community level tend to be young, relatively inexperienced, insecure personally and professionally, and without the years of experience and maturation that would be desirable prior to the assumption of positions of major responsibility. In the judgment of the author, this means that the importance of the consultant from outside the agency will be very great in the transitional years ahead.

It would seem desirable that each community mental health center have a senior clinician from one of the disciplines, with a considerable background of experience in a variety of community mental health settings, who would be available on a regular basis as a consultant to assist with problems of the agency as a whole. This consultant could help the staff formulate policies, decide upon division of responsibilities, determine inservice training needs and priorities, lay out program guidelines, and resolve difficulties that arise in the interpersonal functioning of the staff.

Most importantly, the consultant would be available to work regularly with the director of the clinic, to help him develop his leadership and administrative skills, and to resolve problems that arise during the course of his apprenticeship as a director of a community mental health center. This consultant would be primarily the agent of "the agency" in the abstract sense, which is to say that his superordinate aim would be to assist in the provision of optimum mental health services to the community; secondarily, he would be the agent of the director of the center, with whom he would regularly work and assist in a confidential relationship. The role of the consultant would not be supervision, nor would it be psychotherapy, nor would it be a usurpation of the functions of the director of the mental health center. Rather, it would be client-centered consultation to assist the director, and the other staff persons at the center, in recognizing and resolving the emotional dilemmas which interfere with the utilization of their basic technical knowledge and skill towards the attainment of a mutually shared, consensually held goal.

The state mental health authority can, undoubtedly, play a significant role by setting a model in terms of the inter-professional relationships that are demonstrated in the central office staff and in terms of the models of interpersonal behavior that are demonstrated in the relationship of the state mental health authority to the community mental health centers. If the state mental health authority adopts a dogmatic, authoritarian, rigid and controlling approach toward the community mental health centers, it will be of little help to the centers in resolving internal staff problems and participating in desirable growth. On the other hand, no matter how effective the state mental health authority may be, there are built-in limitations in terms of its relationship, in a consultant role, with the community mental health center. A large part of this consultative relationship must, inevitably, be provided by senior clinicians who are not identified either with the local agency or with the state mental health authority.

SUGGESTED READINGS

Becker, H.S. et al. (1961), *Boys in White: Student Culture in Medical School*. Chicago: Chicago University Press.

Freud, S. (1926), *The Problem of Lay Analysis*. New York: Brentano, 1924.

Holt, R. R. & Luborsky, L. (1958), *Personality Patterns of Psychiatrists*. New York: Basic Books.

Kelly, E. L. & Fiske, D. W. (1951), *The Prediction of Performance in Clinical Psychology*. Ann Arbor: University of Michigan Press.

V

The Prevention of Mental Illness

The concept of prevention, like all idealistic endeavors, runs the risk of being too easily dismissed. The clinician cannot help thinking at times that attempts at prevention are only dishonest escapes from the realities of clinical practice: that he will no longer be concerned about the shortage of treatment facilities and the inadequacy of present treatment methods, but will instead look towards the grand hope of preventing mental disorder. The practicing clinician is entitled to a certain arrogance, perhaps, by virtue of the trials and frustrations that he must suffer at the hands of his patients.

However, it becomes increasingly clear that we must attempt to conceptualize some preventive activities in our total mental health programming. We could become hopelessly bogged down in a discussion and obsession about what constitutes mental health. However, the excellent book by Marie Jahoda (1958) explored this comprehensively, and the reader is referred to it for a more complete discussion.

For the purposes of this chapter, it seems desirable to adopt the focus of preventive psychiatry as "the prevention of recognizable mental disorder" (Gerald Caplan, 1959).

This circumscribed definition, however, does not reduce the dimension of the problem. Recent studies such as the Midtown Manhattan Survey, and the studies of Leighton and his group in Nova Scotia indicate that only 18 to 20 per cent of the total population are entirely free of psychiatric symptoms. It would seem, then, that emotional illnesses are almost as common as dental caries.

We need a scientific model with which to order our thinking. Physicians think first of the classical public health model in such terms as a specific pathogenic agent, transmitted by some vector, to a susceptible individual who becomes infected. The infection might be either latent (without symptoms), and the case would be a "carrier," or the individual might have overt symptoms, and the case would be called a "patient." This model is effective in thinking about certain mental illnesses. Nutritionally caused mental illness such as pellagra, infectious illness such as syphilitic brain disease, or virulent encephalitis provide examples of mental disorder in which this model is very functional.

In other kinds of mental and emotional illness the findings of human geneticists have become increasingly important. Porphyria, phenylketonuria, amaurotic familial idiocy, and Huntington's chorea are examples of hereditarily determined illnesses. There is also an increasing body of evidence to suggest that many illnesses classified as schizophrenic also have significant hereditary determinants.

In some cases of mental retardation, specific, organic brain traumata occur as a result of toxemia or other complications of pregnancy, the birth process, or the neonatal period. It is also possible, although not well-documented, that minimal organic brain damage may contribute to mental and emotional disturbance. A host of traumatic brain injuries—both the massive and obvious brain injuries of automobile accidents, and the minimal and covert injuries of athletic performers—contribute to mental and emotional impairment in a direct and obvious way. Organic brain changes during aging are also amenable to the usual medical frame of investigation, and can be fitted into the model of disease specificity and unitary causation.

However, for the vast majority of illnesses that we now

lump under the large heading of "mental and emotional illness," the medical model, with its emphasis on unitary and specific causation, is not particularly appropriate. It is the intent of this paper to propose an alternative model.

MODES OF PREVENTION

Initially, we need to introduce the concepts of primary, secondary, and tertiary prevention.

Primary prevention involves utilization of procedures to prevent or reduce the incidence and prevalence of recognizable mental or emotional disorder. It is important to emphasize that in this public health endeavor, as in all others, one must think in terms of population statistics, rather than in terms of individual cases. In evaluating results, then, we want to utilize statistical studies of the prevalence of certain disorders in populations that had been subjected to primary preventive activities, as opposed to those that had not.

By secondary prevention, on the other hand, we refer to the early diagnosis and prompt treatment of beginning mental and emotional disorders. In evaluating the results of this sort of program, prevalence and incidence rates would not be of primary concern; instead, we would be concerned with *disability rates* in the population at large following a long-term program of secondary prevention.

Tertiary prevention includes treatment and rehabilitation services for those with recognizable and fully developed mental and emotional disturbances. In evaluating results, we would again be interested in disability rates.

PREVENTIVE MODALITIES

Various approaches to mental health programming in different cultural settings have been reported. Such activities as mental health education, casefinding and secondary prevention, liaison-interpretive functions, and the various activities that can be summed up under the rubric of "promotion of a climate for mental health maintenance" might be included. To discuss each of these in turn:

1. Mental Health Education

The ineffectiveness of mental hygiene courses in preventing or curing mental illness is generally accepted. However, this does not vitiate the importance of education at all levels of our society concerning personality functioning and dysfunctioning, even though it is impossible to prove that such education makes the individual citizen a better human being, or a more compassionate friend to a troubled person. As a matter of fact, studies of all types of education have, in general, indicated a dearth of proven attitudinal changes resulting from education, per se. Yet we are not inclined to abandon general or liberal arts education, any more than we would forsake mental hygiene or mental health education. Over the years, researchers in this area have commented upon the deficiencies in knowledge concerning mental health, particularly in the case of significant caregivers in the community, such as teachers. There have been good surveys of mental health hygiene principles and practices, and increasingly there are soundly conceived attempts to study the effects of mental health education.

Until we have more definitive knowledge in this field, mental health education will probably have to be carried forward, as much education is, on the basis of faith. The Joint Commission on Mental Illness and Health has recommended that mental health education not be the responsibility of the clinical disciplines, but that ancillary personnel such as health educators, journalists, teachers, and so forth be involved in mental health education. Local mental health associations also play a crucial role in this endeavor, and should probably carry the major burden of responsibility

for mental health education both at the state and local
level.

2. Liaison-interpretive Functions

Despite the awkwardness of the title, this topic is separated
from the general rubric of mental health education because
it is, legitimately, more the concern of professional clinicians.
The opinion-setters in every community, many of whom are
also caregivers within the social structure of the community, must be informed and presented with accurate
appraisals of the functions of mental health facilities. Ongoing services of interpretation, correction of distortions,
and mutual collaboration toward superordinate goals must
be constantly woven into any community mental health
program. Studies in relatively "closed" subcultures, such as
the university community, emphasize clearly, the importance
of the attitudes of opinion-setters and caregivers in determining the readiness of the population to make use of mental
health services and its ability to benefit from them.

3. Casefinding and Secondary Prevention

In returning to essentially a medical model, we find ourselves thinking in terms of mobile X-ray units, blood examinations etc., as they are characteristically used in the detection and diagnosis of such pathologic conditions as tuberculosis and latent syphilis. However, the whole process of
casefinding and secondary prevention is considerably more
complicated when it involves mental and emotional illness.
For example, with physical illness we make the assumption
(before embarking on a program of casefinding) that effective
treatment is available, and that the patient will be better off
having his illness discovered. This is by no means certain,
at the present time, in all cases of mental and emotional
illness. Many recoveries from mental illness result from es-

sentially self-curative processes of the organism. We have
no definite evidence, for example, that the early detection of
"incipient schizophrenia" would necessarily result in a more
favorable lifelong adjustment.

Another problem that we immediately confront is the
question of prevalence. Prevalence studies in the general
population, as well as in special subcultural groupings such
as university populations, have substantiated the view that
many more individuals are experiencing emotional problems
in any given population than are actually seen as patients.
Surveys have also demonstrated convincingly, both the high
prevalence rates of emotional and mental illness and the
chronicity and seriousness of the illnesses. The logistical
problems are enormous. If the definition of adequate casefinding is to identify and attempt to treat all people who
are experiencing emotional illness, our resources in the
mental health field are immediately overtaxed beyond all
possibility of resolution. We must think, then, either in terms
of some system of priorities for providing services, and
identify those problems with the most social or "contagious"
urgency; we must enlist persons other than the mental health
disciplines for providing care for these individuals; and/or
we must wait until some "mass treatment" technique becomes available.

Even with these two serious problems temporarily ignored,
we come up against the question of whether there are sufficiently reliable and sensitive instruments for detecting
emotional illness. Even though group psychological tests do
not afford the accuracy that might be ideally hoped for,
they are useful for detecting individuals who are experiencing emotional difficulty. By and large, the better studies
suggest that measurement along several dimensions proves
to be more satisfactory for prediction. In addition to the
psychological test, we would also want to utilize such measures as peer ratings and judgments by persons in supervisory

or caregiving roles. For example, the studies by Bower concerning identification of emotionally ill children within the school setting, clearly demonstrate that it is practical to utilize school personnel in early casefinding. Another paper of Bower's entitled "School Characteristics of Male Adolescents Who Later Became Schizophrenic," offers convincing evidence as to the practicality of predicting a subsequent psychotic illness from behavioral judgments made by teachers while the individual is still in high school. Current trends along these lines would seem to indicate that we can anticipate an increasing wealth of predictive tools in the future.

Even if we accept the idea that it *is* possible to do casefinding and secondary prevention, we must ask whether it is necessary. We might reason that if patients experiencing a mental or emotional disorder do experience psychic pain, why could we not rely upon self-diagnosis and self-referral for treatment. Without the aid of any special studies, our experience as clinicians would convince us that a part of the illness that we call schizophrenia, involves a tendency to reject help and to withdraw from supportive contacts with other human beings. After all, help-seeking behavior is sophisticated and far along the evolutionary scale; animals at a lower stage of evolution do not characteristically seek out help when they are injured. Neither does a severely psychotic or regressed individual. Impressionistic findings from our clinical experiences can be supported by a study done in Texas, which showed that only 40 per cent of the individuals who were hospitalized in a state hospital for psychiatric reasons were known to any agency to be emotionally disturbed during the three years prior to their hospitalization. That is, patients experiencing a severe emotional illness by and large do not seek help until they become so disturbed that they are forced to do so by their families or other agents of the community. In essence, many of them "appear on the door step" of the hospital. Obviously, if we are to strive for early diagnosis and early treatment, this state of events is not desirable.

We next must ask whether there is any demonstrated benefit to be derived from a program of casefinding and early treatment. Although we do not have definite evidence based upon a total community, or an entirely representative sample, we do have early findings from some relatively "closed" subcultures. These beginning studies have been carried on mainly in the milieu of the college, which of course is a preselected population. The work of Spielberger at North Carolina is most noteworthy in this regard. His efforts at screening for high-anxiety students among entering freshmen, and offering prophylactic counseling, have resulted in a demonstrated decrease in academic dropout and increase in academic performance, as well as a general overall improvement in social adjustment. However, more extensive and refined studies remain for the future.

4. Climate for Community Mental Health

Social psychology, social psychiatry, and industrial psychiatry have made rapid strides in recent years in delineating some of the connections between the individual's social milieu and the state of his mental health. Unfortunately, much of this research has gone relatively unnoticed and unutilized by the practicing clinician. Much of the research has been focused upon industrial and college settings, but increasingly we have a body of data dealing with the general community. In looking at such a broad area as the "climate for optimum mental health functioning," we have to avoid the dangers of becoming overdiffuse and must strive to maintain a focus. Some of these particular foci may be summarized as follows:

a. The life situation crisis. This has been an area for preventive mental health efforts in several social institutions.

Individuals experiencing a crisis in their life situation may suffer a high risk of experiencing dysfunctional, maladaptive, or "sick" behavior. In addition, individuals at moments of life crisis are also more susceptible to external influences and are more amenable to change. An elaboration of this model would hold that other people in the interpersonal and social milieu of the individual experiencing a life crisis may be crucial in determining the severity of maladaptive behavior and the eventual outcome of the individual's response to crisis. Prototypical life crisis situations would include enrollment in kindergarten, movement from elementary to junior high school, movement into high school, disappointment in love, vocational choice, graduation from college, marriage, divorce, bereavement, economic setbacks, pregnancy, childbirth, weaning, etc.

b. *The high-risk trauma approach.* We would concede that there are certain kinds of traumata, certain kinds of afronts to the individual organism, which entail a high risk of some kind of sociopsychological decompensation or "sickness." We would like to think, then, of some prophylactic or preventive intervention following the trauma, with the belief that the risk of subsequent illness is sufficiently great so that the attempt to "nip it in the bud" is justified. In this group we might include those individuals with physical handicaps, sensory defects (such as blindness or deafness), the mentally retarded, the academically ungifted, including those with reading and speech difficulties, and so forth.

c. *Maladapted behavior as a focus for preventive psychiatry.* There are many types of behavior which are not usually labeled as illness, but which are maladaptive in the particular social milieu of the individual, and may be used as a focus for psychiatric intervention. Fitting into this category are the minor antisocial behaviors, academic underachievement, social awkwardness, self-defeating attitudes, etc. Viewed within the context of communication theory, most behavior is seen as a communication to other significant persons in the interpersonal milieu of inner distress. Consequently, the sooner the communication of internal distress can be perceived by significant caregivers in the environment, and some kind of return communication afforded as recognition of the distress, the less disturbed will the behavior be, the less severe and less regressive will the decompensation become, and the more quickly will the individual be able to reconstitute at a higher level of homeostatic functioning.

d. *The use of the institutional system as an agent for mental health*. A number of activities that are usually considered administrative are directly relevant to the climate for mental health. For example, personnel policies, plans for staffings, plans for staff development, policies for promotion, economic policies, and retirement planning directly and indirectly affect the climate for mental health within any social milieu.

MENTAL HEALTH CONSULTATION

As we look at the above enumerated models, we must immediately come to grips with the question as to how we, as mental health specialists, can exert any influence upon such a diversity of situations. Obviously, we cannot think in terms of "treating" all the individuals who experience a life situation crisis, who are exposed to some kind of high-risk trauma, or who evidence mild maladapted behavior. Neither can we expect to control all administrative decisions, nor run all the social institutions of our country.

We must, in other words, develop some models which we, as consultants, can use in our services to the other caregiving and caretaking individuals in our society. Hopefully, we will be able to use these models with some conviction that this will result in an eventual modification of institutional norms and processes, supportive services for individuals ex-

periencing high-risk trauma and life crisis situations, or showing maladapted behavior, as well as more efficient casefinding
and early treatment. In Chapter VI we will distinguish between the several types of consultation.

In thinking about prevention of mental illness within the
context of the community, then, we would conceive of the
mental health disciplines, usually situated in the community-
based mental health center, as influencing the overall mental
health of the population by providing consultative services
to the other caregiving persons in the community. The
main responsibility at levels of primary and secondary prevention, therefore, would rest with the community caregivers who have existed in our society for long periods of
time prior to the evolution of specialized mental health
services. We would think of assisting the teacher, minister,
family physician, welfare worker, public health department,
other caregiving agencies such as Red Cross, and various
citizen groups that are interested in problems related to
mental health. Only at the level of secondary prevention,
where one becomes concerned with definitive casefinding and
formal treatment, do the mental health disciplines begin to
assume a primary responsibility. In adopting this frame of
reference, then, we begin to see the mental health workers
as assuming only a fraction of the responsibility for a community's program in preventive mental health services.

EVOLUTION OF MENTAL HEALTH SERVICES

It is important, as we plan for prevention, to keep in mind
that social agencies undergo evolutionary processes. We must
remember that mental health centers, as all social institutions, experience a process of growth and change as they
develop within the context of the community. In their book,
Explorations in Social Psychiatry, Leighton and Longaker
describe the mental health center as a community innovation, and list a number of steps in the evolution of this

agency which they consider characteristic of this type of social innovation. The steps that they describe are as follows:

Aspect One: An institution is formed in a community to bring an innovation into practice.

Aspect Two: The new institution establishes a basic connection with some pre-existing social organization in the community.

Aspect Three: The existence of a new institution can be recognized by a majority of community members.

Aspect Four: From a wide range of specific sentiments regarding the new institution, three main types emerge: positive, indifferent, and negative.

Aspect Five: The full potential of the institution is limited for a time by sentiments and perceptions in the community. [It is very important to keep this fully in view: the role of the institution, as perceived by the mental health experts, can seldom be accepted and fully supported by the community for a long period of time.]

Aspect Six: By meeting the felt needs of the community, the institution facilitates changes in perceptions and sentiments. [In other words, as in psychotherapy with a very sick patient, the initial focus must be on meeting the perceived needs and perceived desires of the community, in terms of developing relationships so that a change in modes of functioning can be made by the mental health facility, and so that "demands" can be made upon the community at a later date. It must be stressed that this is not an initial step and occurs later in the evolution of any agency in the community.]

Aspect Seven: As a result of changes in perceptions and sentiments, bridges of communication develop between the institution and various parts of the community.

Aspect Eight: Demands from the community increase in frequency and in range of types. [The second half of this sentence is particularly important, since one would anticipate (and inevitably see) an increase in the variety of problems about which the mental health expert is consulted.]

Aspect Nine: The institution alters its function and approaches more nearly the fulfillment of its primary goals.

Aspect Ten: The institution draws individuals and organizations into participation in its functions. The community in turn draws the institution and its members into other community functions.

The tables following are presented to illustrate application of various ideas concerning prevention of mental illness to the university population, the prevention and control of psychiatric illness in the public school, and two schema for shared responsibility of state and local agencies in implementing a comprehensive mental health program.

TABLE 1

Prevention of Mental Illness in a University Population

Technique	Aim	Target Group or Problem	Agent	Method
A. Casefinding and Secondary Prevention	To discover and place in treatment emotionally ill individuals as soon as possible after the onset of symptoms.	1. The neurotic student. 2. The "pre-psychotic" student and early psychotic. 3. The psychosomatic student. 4. The dysfunctional character problem. 5. The symptomatic "adjustment problem" that does not improve with nonclinical support.	1. Student health service 2. Faculty	a. Screening all entering students' medical history. b. Referral of psychosomatic problem. c. Referral of the "sick call rider." a. Sensitization to problems of students. b. Clarification of criteria for referral. c. Clarification of technique of referral. d. Resolution of faculty ambivalence/resistance to psychiatric and/or student personnel program.

TABLE 1—Continued

Technique	Aim	Target Group or Problem	Agent	Method
				e. Ongoing feedback to and education of faculty, with concomitant decrease in social distance.
			3. Student body	a. Publicize availability.
				b. Educate as to criteria for seeking help.
				c. Combat stigmatization.
				d. Emphasize confidential nature of relationship.
				e. Student leadership training.
			4. Student personnel services	a. As for faculty.
				b. Leadership education and in-service training.

B. Life-situation Crisis	To support functional, individual adaptive reactions to physiological, psychological, and socio-cultural stress; to minimize regressive personality change and promote individual growth.	1. Sexually concerned. 2. Religious-ethical conflict. 3. Love disappointments. 4. Academic indecision. 5. Strife with parents. 6. Parental breakup. 7. The married undergraduate. 8. Loss of significant person.	1. Student leaders	a. Student leadership workshop b. Mental health workshop
			2. Student advisor in dormitory	a. Consultation with student personnel services Re: in-service training and supervision b. Direct contact in group process to clarify role modes, conflictual areas, etc.
			3. House "mothers"	a. As 2a. b. As 2b.
			4. Academic advisors	a. As 2a. b. Special group training series to discuss role of faculty in personality development of young adults, etc.

c. Screening test-questionnaire instruments for entering students.

d. Sensitization of student advisors.

TABLE 1—Continued

Technique	Aim	Target Group or Problem	Agent	Method
			5. Student Personnel Services	a. Ongoing consultation and collaboration Re: matters of student welfare b. Support for improving program c. In-service counseling training.
C. High-risk Trauma	To offer supportive, prophylactic assistance to groups in whom a relatively high incidence of psychosocial decompensation may be anticipated.	1. Reading and Study Skill groups	1. Reading and Study Skill groups	a. Supportive contact with R&SS groups. b. Support & Assistance to R&SS group leaders. c. Individual and/or group counseling.

		2. The socially rejected.
		  a. "Greek" rejects.
		  b. Minority groups.
		  c. Foreign students.		

		3. The physically handicapped.		

D. Maladaptive Behavior

To re-evaluate such behavior in terms of motivation and meaning, and to extend appropriate helping measures.

1. The underachiever.
2. The peer-group misfit.
3. The "college delinquent"—skipping classes, cheating, drinking, etc.
4. Antisocial behavior: voyeurism, stealing, etc.

1. Student Personnel Services
   a. Ongoing consultation to clarify issues.
   b. Encouraging & facilitating referral for evaluation where appropriate.
   c. Promoting "feedback" communication.
   d. Defining two roles of psychiatrist:
      1) As agent of university.
      2) As agent of patient.

2. Faculty
   a. As B4b.
   b. Communication with faculty where possible (i.e., approval of student) about special problems.

3. Students
   a. As A 3a-e.
   b. As B 1b.

TABLE 1—Continued

Technique	Aim	Target Group or Problem	Agent	Method
E. The Institutional System as Agent for Mental Health	To serve as catalyst-consultant-specialist-"impartial" agent in conceptualizing institutional problems and their effects on students; and to lend support to institutional strengths that promote a healthy milieu for personal growth and development.	President Academic Deans Personnel Deans Other key administrative personnel	1. Psychiatric Consultant	a. Administrative consultation and/or collaboration: 1) program-centered 2) problem-centered b. Consultation concerning special programs.

TABLE 2

School Mental Health: Prevention and Control of Psychiatric Illness

Levels of Prevention	Primary Prevention				Secondary Prevention	Tertiary Prevention
Focus of Prevention	Modification of Institutional Norms and Processes	High Risk Trauma	Life Crisis	Maladaptive Behavior		
Prototypical Problems	Poor promotion policies Poor personnel policies Poor staffing plans	Retardation Sensory deficit Crippling	Divorce of parents Death in family Absence or illness of parent	Learning and/or reading disability Speech impairment "Predelinquent" school dropout	Adjustment reaction Mild neurotic or personality reaction Delinquency	Psychosis Severe neurosis or personality disorder Antisocial behavior
School Resource Personnel	School psychologist Counseling and guidance personnel Classroom teacher Special education teacher School nurse					

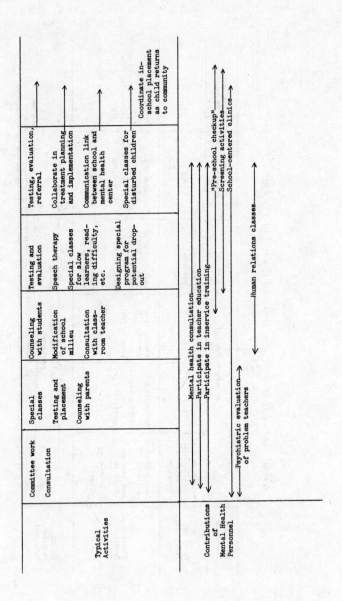

TABLE 2—Continued

TABLE 3

The Prevention of Mental Illness
Approach A

Epoch	Target Areas	Operational Aim	Responsible Agency	Feasibility
A. Heredito-Congenital Nucleus of Personality	1) Hereditary (PKU, Mongol. schiz., etc.)	Primary prevention by eugenics	State Board of Health	+ −
	2) Congenital	a) Prenatal factors	State Board of Health	+
		b) Complications of pregnancy and birth process	" "	+
B. Noxious Influences within the Nuclear Family	1) Preparation for parenthood	Parent education	" "	+
	2) Mothering of the infant	a) Parent education	State Board of Health & Comm. MH Services	+ −
		b) Supportive contacts for mother		
	3) Maintenance of stability of family in face of stress	a) Social Case Work Support	Comm. MH Services & Dept. Soc. Welfare	+
		b) Homemaker service	Dept. Social Welfare	+ + +
		c) Financial assistance	Dept. Social Welfare	+ + +
		d) Psychiatric treatment	Comm. MH Services	+ + +
		e) Marriage counseling	Comm. MH Services	+ + +

TABLE 3—Continued

Epoch	Target Areas	Operational Aim	Responsible Agency	Feasibility
C. Influences during Childhood	1) Within the school	a) Stimulate ego growth for increased coping ability	Dept. of Public Instruction	+
		b) Availability of Mental Health Consultation to School Personnel	Comm. MH Services	+
		c) School Psychology; counseling & guidance	Dept. of Public Instruction	+
		d) Psychiatric case consultation	Comm. MH Services	+
		e) Human Relations education; Sex education; Psychology	Dept. of Public Instruction	+
		f) Milieu for promoting positive Mental Health	Dept. Public Instruction & Comm. MH Services	+ −
	2) Other small group settings	a) Recreation opportunities	Local Agencies	+
		b) Youth groups	Local & Nongovernmental	+
		c) Religious groups	Nongovernmental	++
		d) Delinquent groups	Law enforcement & Comm. MH Services	
		e) Group living situations	Dept. Soc. Welfare & State Health Dept.	+

3) "Therapeutic" vs. rejecting attitude in community	Establish adequate community mental health centers and other helping services for children	Comm. MH Services & Dept. Social Welfare	+
4) Noxious agents	a) Brain damage secondary to infection	State Dept. of Health	+
	b) Brain damage secondary to trauma	" "	+
	c) Brain damage secondary to nonalcoholic toxic substances	" "	+
D. Influences during Adulthood	1) Within college		
	a) Stimulate ego growth	Board of Regents	+
	b) Avail. of Mental Health Consult. & clinical services in universities	Board of Regents & Comm. MH Services	+
	c) Counseling and guidance	Board of Regents	+
	d) Human Relations Education	" "	+
	e) Maintenance of milieu for positive mental health	" "	+

TABLE 3—Continued

Epoch	Target Areas	Operational Aim	Responsible Agency	Feasibility
	2) Other small group settings	a) Recreation opportunities	Local agencies	+
		b) Youth groups	Local Nongovernmental	+
		c) Religious groups	Nongovernmental	++
		d) Delinquent groups	Law enforcement & Comm. MH Services	+
		e) Industrial personnel practices	Comm. MH Services	+
	3) Community attitudes	Establish adequate community mental health centers & other helping services for adults	Comm. MH Services & Dept. of Social Welfare	+
	4) Neurotoxic agents	a) Infection	State Dept. of Health	+
		b) Traumatic	" "	+
		c) Nonalcoholic toxic	" "	+
		d) Alcoholic	Comm. MH Services	−
	5) Special services	a) Vocational counseling	Employment Security & Bd. of Voc. Edu.	+
		b) Vocational rehabilitation	Voc. Rehab.	+
		c) Premarital counseling	Churches CMH Services	+

E. Aging and Senescence	1) Social	a) Foster accepting community attitudes	Dept. Social Welfare	+
		b) Enlightened Retirement Planning	"	−
		c) Provisions for socialization and recreation	" " & Local Agencies	+ − +
		d) Adequate financial support	Dept. of Social Welfare	+
	2) Physical	a) Provision of adequate medical care	Dept. of Social Welfare	+
		b) Prevention of diseases of old age by dietary management, exercise, etc.	State Dept. of Health	+ −
		c) Adequate nursing home care when indicated	State Dept. of Health	+
	3) Psychological	a) Casework assistance	Dept. Social Welfare	+ +
		b) Psychiatric treatment	Comm. MH Services	

TABLE 4

Possible Modes of Prevention and Responsible Agencies
Approach B

Socio-Psycho-Biological Problem	Etiologic Possibilities	Est'd Prevalence in Kansas*	Primary	Agencies	Secondary	Agencies	Tertiary	Agencies
Mental Deficiency	A. "Psychological" or "Idiopathic" mental deficiency	44,000	Eugenic Control	Planned Parenthood Leagues; Dept. Health Dept. Social Welfare	Remedial Training	1. Dept. of Public Instruction	1. Residential Treatment and Training	Division of Institutional Management
						2. Assoc. for Mental Retardation		
					Rx of adjustment problems	3. Community MH Services	2. Vocational Rehabilitation	Vocational Rehabilitation
	B. "Pathological" Mental Deficiency	2,200						
	1. Genetic abnormality		Eugenic Control	Dept. of Health	Casefinding & early Rx	Dept. of Health	Institutional Treatment	Division of Institutional Management
			Heredity Counseling					
	2. Prenatal factors		Parent Education VD Prevention Prenatal care	"	Pediatric care	1. Family Physician	Institutional Treatment	Division of Institutional Management
						2. Dept. of Social Welfare		
Mental Deficiency (cont'd)	3. Perinatal and postnatal factors		Physician education Well-baby clinic Hospital procedures	Dept. of Health	Pediatric care	Family Physician Dept. of Social Welfare	Institutional Treatment	Division of Institutional Management

* Population 2,200,000

Category	Type	Number	Primary Prevention	Agency	Remedial	Agency	Tertiary	Agency
	4. For all types "Pathological" mental deficiency				Remedial Training	1. Assoc. for Mental Retardation 2. Dept. of Public Instr.	1. Residential care and Rx	Division of Institutional Management
Organic Brain Disease	Traumatic Toxic Senile	2,500	1. Industrial Health Programs 2. Accident Prevention 3. Control of toxic drugs	Dept. of Health	Rx of adjustment problems	Comm. MH Services	2. Vocational Rehabilitation	Vocational Rehabilitation
Psychoses & Neuroses	1. Minimal brain damage a. Traumatic	16,300 Psych. 94,000 Neurot. from all causes	a. Improved obstetrical care	Dept. of Health	Diagnosis & rehabilitation	1. Comm. MH Services 2. Voc. Rehab. 3. Private Physician	Hospital Rx Nursing Home	1. Division of Institutional Management 2. Dept. of Health
Psychoses & Neuroses (cont'd)	b. Infectious 1) Childhood exanthema 2) Virus encephalitis		Immunization Mosquito & epizootic control	Dept. of Health "	1. Diagnosis 2. Family casework 3. Medication 4. Psychotherapy	Comm. MH Services	Institutionalization	Division of Institutional Management

TABLE 4—Continued

Socio-Psycho-Biological Problem	Etiologic Possibilities	Est'd Prevalence	Primary	Agencies	Secondary	Agencies	Tertiary	Agencies
	2. Early maternal deprivation		Support for mothering	Dept. Soc. Welfare Dept. of Health	Casework or treatment for mother	Comm. MH Services	Institutional care for child	Dept. Social Welfare
	3. Disturbed family milieu		Family life education Premarital counseling	Dept. Health Comm. MH Services	Marriage counselling Individual Psychotherapy Social casework	Comm. MH Services Comm. MH Services Comm. MH Services Dept. Soc. Welfare	Family therapy Foster home care	Comm. MH Services Dept. Social Welfare
	4. "Social Climate"		Climate for mental health In: Industry Public Schools Colleges Communities	Community Mental Health Services	Casefinding, referral, and/or counselling Industry Public schools Colleges Communities	Community Mental Health Services	Psychiatric treatment availability for all ages and groups	Community Mental Health Services
			"Mental health education"	..	Special problems of aging population	Dept. of Health		
			Community recreation, youth groups, etc.	Local Agencies				

Condition		Prevalence	Church activities	Local Agencies		Psychiatric treatment	Comm. MH Services
Psycho-physiological Reactions	Same as for neuroses and psychoses	54,000	Same as for neuroses and psychoses	Same as for neuroses and psychoses Improved Gen'l Medical Dx & Rx	Comm. MH Services Dept. of Health	Same as for neuroses and psychoses, plus	Comm. MH Services
Behavior Disorders a) Antisocial	Same as for neuroses and psychoses	unknown	Same as for neuroses and psychoses	Same as for neuroses and psychoses, plus Juvenile Courts: 1) Diagnostic & consultative services 2) Consultative help to probation officers	Comm. MH Services	BIS, GIS Hutchinson Penitentiary Community Follow-up	Division of Inst. Mgmt. Bureau Prisons Local Courts Comm. MH Services
b) Alcoholic	Same as for neuroses and psychoses	24,000	Same as for neuroses and psychoses	Same as for neuroses and psychoses, plus Improved Rx by Local Physician Hospital facilities in community hospitals	Community Mental Health Services	Same as for neuroses and psychoses, plus Group support *Specialized* psychiatric treatment resources	AA Division of Inst. Mgmt. Comm. MH Services

Note: Prevalence figures are minimal.

114 PSYCHIATRY IN THE AMERICAN COMMUNITY

SUGGESTED READINGS

Beck, A. T. & Tuthill, R. W. (1963), Childhood bereavement and adult depression. *Arch. Gen. Psychiat.,* 9:295-302.

Coleman, J. V. (1951), Appraising the contribution of the mental hygiene clinic to the community: II. In the promotion of mental health. *Amer. J. Orthopsychiat.,* 21:83-93.

Gurin, G., Veroff, J., & Feld, S. (1960), *Americans View Their Mental Health.* New York: Basic Books.

Leighton, A. H., Clausen, J. A., & Wilson, R. N., eds. (1957), *Explorations in Social Psychiatry.* New York: Basic Books.

Mental Disorders: A Guide to Control Methods (1962). New York: Amer. Publ. Hlth. Assn.

Ojemann, R. H. (1957), *Four Basic Aspects of Preventive Psychiatry.* Iowa City: State University of Iowa.

The Prevention of Disability in Mental Disorders (1962), Mental Health Monograph 1. Washington, D. C.: U.S. Dept. of Health, Education & Welfare.

Rose, A. (1955), *Mental Health and Mental Disorder.* New York: Norton.

Symposium on Preventive and Social Psychiatry (1958). Washington, D.C.: Walter Reed Army Institute of Research.

VI

The Consultation Program

Mental health consultation has become, in recent years, a community psychiatric technique of primary importance. Briefly, mental health consultation entails the deployment of a professional mental health worker to assist community caregivers in such settings as schools, courts, public health departments, welfare departments, and so forth, so that these agencies may make a quantitatively larger and qualitatively better contribution to the mental health of the total community.

The current widespread interest in mental health consultation results from the impingement of several reality factors upon the developing field of community psychiatry. Some of these are as follows:

1. Prevalence and incidence studies have been revealing ever-larger percentages of the total population's experiencing symptoms of mental or emotional disorder.

2. Increasing recognition has been given to the fact that patients reach psychiatrists quite some months or years after the onset of emotional difficulties, and have characteristically already been in contact with a number of nonmental health professionals or subprofessional caregivers within the community.

3. There has been an increasing recognition—as for example through the study of the Joint Commission on Mental Illness and Health entitled *Americans View Their Mental Health*—that the average American still prefers, and does

habitually turn, first to minister, physician, or some other nonpsychiatric person in the community, for assistance with a wide spectrum of difficulties.

4. Increasing sophistication of clinical practitioners about the structure and functioning of our society, and the integration of sociological insights into clinical theory and practice, has clearly brought home the social relatedness and social rootedness of all behavior, and of all attempts to modify human behavior.

5. The existing manpower shortages in all mental health fields, and projections that indicate no great amelioration of this condition, have impressed upon mental health practitioners, the need to involve other manpower resources in the provision of services.

6. Attempts that have been made by the mental health profession to treat seriously disturbed citizens, and/or those whose deviancy is troubling to the larger community—such as the schizophrenic, the law offender, the alcoholic—in isolation from other community agencies, without their assistance or involvement, have not led to particularly striking results.

7. General developments in the field of psychoanalytic theory, focused upon the functions of the ego and the devices by which the individual copes with reality, have given rise to an increased interest in preventive mental health activities that can strengthen the coping ability and minimize regressive tendencies in personality functioning at moments of stress.

The most widely known proponent of mental health consultation is Gerald Caplan, who has defined mental health consultation as

> . . . the interaction between two professional persons—the consultant who is a specialist, and the consultee, who invokes his help in regard to a current work problem with which he is having some difficulty and which he has decided is within the consultant's area of competence. The work problem involves the management or treat-

ment of one or more clients of the consultee or the planning of a
program to cater to such clients.

An essential aspect of consultation, as defined here, is that the
professional responsibility for the client remains with the consultee.
The consultant may offer help for clarification, diagnostic interpretation, or advice on treatment, but the consultee is free to accept or
reject all or part of this help. Action for the benefit of the client
which emerges from the consultation is the responsibility of the
consultee.

Another essential aspect of this type of consultation is that the
consultant engages in the activity not only in order to help the
consultee with his current professional problem in relation to a
specific client or program, but to add to his knowledge and lessen
areas of misunderstanding, so that he may in the future be able
to deal more effectively with this category of problem. This definition applies not only to a single consultant dealing with one
consultee, but equally to one consultant and a group of consultees
or a group of consultants and a single consultee or group of consultees [Caplan, 1964a, pp. 212-213].

The practice and principles of consultation are not really
new, however, as the past two decades have seen an increasing
body of literature on the subject. Another definition of
mental health consultation is as follows:

Mental health consultation is a process of interaction between a
mental health professional and one or more consultees for the purpose of increasing the consultee's awareness of, and ability to manage, the mental health components of his work. This goal is
achieved by the consultant as he helps the consultee to clarify and
find solutions for current mental health problems either in relationship to specific clients, or to programs and practices of the consultee's
organization as these influence the mental health of groups of
clients. The process proceeds optimally where there is a positive
relationship between consultant and consultee, based on mutual respect and trust. The nature of this relationship has been described
as a 'co-ordinate' one. This emphasizes the fact that the consultant
has no administrative control over the consultee and that each has
his own area of competence [Haylett and Rapoport, 1964].

The discussion of consultation can focus upon purposes,
types, methods, and outcome.

Purposes

Most of the recent literature on mental health consultation has justified it as a method to reduce the overall incidence and prevalence of recognizable mental and emotional disorder and disability within the total population at risk. In other words, the major purpose which has been assigned has been a public health goal: the prevention of mental illness.

There are a number of other purposes for the consultation process, that, in our experience, make it a worthwhile parameter of community mental health practice, independent of the question as to whether it actually prevents mental and emotional illness or disability. Some of these goals are as follows:

1. *As a method of controlling input of patients.* If all community agencies and individual caregivers carry patients along until they feel incapable of proceeding, and then refer them—often precipitously—to the community mental health center, there is little control over the volume, type, or scheduling of these cases. The only way that the center can then reduce the steadily mounting demand, or limit a steadily increasing heterogeneity of demands, is by providing poor service and developing a bad reputation in the community. Ongoing consultation with community agencies and caregivers, a constant process of interpretation of the functions of the mental health center, assistance in caring for specific types of cases by other agencies, and a pattern of consultation about a referral prior to actual initiation of referral, allow the mental health center some control over the nature, number, and spacing of applications for direct clinical service. To rephrase this, with the high prevalence rates of mental illness existing in our communities and the scarcity of professional manpower, the choice may be whether to have patients on a waiting list at the community mental health center, or on the service rolls or waiting list of some

other agency; by and large, the second alternative is more desirable.

2. *Social credit is established.* Any agency, and all individuals, develop a certain "social credit rating" in dealing with other individuals and groups within the community. A willingness to do things for other caregivers, while seldom immediately repaid, builds up a backlog of debts and obligations which the agency may call upon at moments of crisis or special need.

3. *Effect on the staff of the mental health center.* Isolation, partly self-chosen and partly ascribed by the community, while protecting the individual mental health practitioner and the mental health agency in certain ways, leaves them vulnerable to progressive alienation from the nurturant culture, and fosters the development of group delusional thinking and ritualistic behaviors. The provision of consultative services to other community caregivers, so long as the mental health professional is willing and able to learn, himself, can keep the mental health center constantly attuned to the realities of community life, and the multiple needs of citizens and agencies.

4. *Public relations.* All mental health centers must cope with long-standing prejudices against the mentally and emotionally ill, rejection of them, and fear of mental health practitioners and agencies. By providing genuine assistance to a broad spectrum of community caregivers, the mental health center develops a group of "boosters" who form an important part of the opinion-setters of any community.

5. *Modification of consultee behavior.* Even if it cannot be demonstrated that the consultation process decreases the prevalence of mental illness and/or disability, the consultation process may be helpful to individual consultees, and allow them to perform their nonmental health-related activities in a freer and more effective fashion.

6. *Effect on consultee agency practice.* Likewise, the consultation process may be helpful to agencies in improving communication between staff members, conceptualizing and improving the decision-making process, and modifying a whole variety of agency practices. These modifications may or may not have any effect upon the general mental health of the community, but may be worthwhile modifications or improvements for their intrinsic value, or because of improvement in services offered in nonmental health-related areas.

Types of Mental Health Consultation

Considerable effort has been expended in classifying the different types of consultation. The efforts of Gerald Caplan are noteworthy in this regard, and will be summarized below:

> [In client-centered case consultations,] the problems encountered by the consultee in a professional case are the focus of interest; the immediate goal is to help the consultee find the most effective treatment for his client. Educating the consultee so that he may in the future be better able to deal unaided with this client or class of clients is a subsidiary goal. Since the primary goal is to improve the client, the consultant's fundamental responsibility is to make a specialized assessment of the client's condition and to recommend an effective disposition or method of treatment to be undertaken by the consultee. The consultant's attention is centered on the client, whom he will probably examine with whatever methods of investigation his specialized judgment indicates is necessary in order to arrive at an adequate appraisal of his difficulty.
>
> [In program-centered administrative consultation,] . . . the consultant is called in by consultee, or, more often, by a group of consultees to help with current problems and the administration of programs for the prevention, treatment, or rehabilitation of mental disorder. The problems may relate to any aspect of the program, including the planning and administration of services and policies governing the recruitment, training, and effective utilization of personnel. In response to the needs expressed by the consultees, the focus of the consultant is a specialized assessment of the current program or policy predicament, and recommendation of a plan of action to resolve the difficulty. As in the previous types of consultation, educating the consultees so that in the future they will be

better able to deal on their own with such a difficulty is a subordinate goal.

[In consultee-centered case consultation,] the focus of the consultant. . .is on the consultee, rather than on the particular client with whom the consultee is currently having difficulties. True, the problems of this client were the direct stimulus for the consultation request and will form the main content area of the consultation discussion, and a successful consultation will usually lead to an improvement of the consultee's handling of the current case, with consequent benefit for the client. But, in contrast to client-centered case consultation, in which the consultant's main interest is diagnosing the difficulties of the client, his primary endeavor in the present instance is to assess the nature of the consultee's work difficulty and to help him overcome it.

[For consultee-centered administrative consultation,] . . . the primary goal. . .is to help consultees master problems in the planning and maintenance of programs for the prevention and control of mental disorder and in the interpersonal aspects of agency operation. As with program-centered administrative consultation, this method is often applied in group situations and is directed toward helping a group of administrators, but it is not infrequently invoked by an administrator on an individual basis. Since a specialist assessment of the administrative problem is not demanded, it is quite feasible to operate with an individual administrator and restrict consultation help to his area of institutional life [Caplan, 1964a, pp. 214-230].

The work of Caplan and his associates has been of enormous value in helping all mental health practitioners develop a conceptual frame of reference for the consultation process. However, at least one author has suggested that there should be a differentiation in the classification between process and content (Mahoney). The *process* of consultation occurs between a consultant and a consultee, and *is always consultee-centered*. In contrast, the *content* will be determined by the presenting problem of the consultee, and can be divided (according to Dr. Mahoney) into the seven categories listed below:

[1. Client consultation (client seen).]
[2. Client consultation (client not seen).]
[3. Syndrome consultation.] Here the consultee seeks the help of the consultant in understanding and coping more effectively with actual or potential clients having certain characteristics in common.

The consultee does not see the consultant concerning a specific client, but concerning a group of clients with common characteristics. For example, a caseworker in a county welfare department may seek consultation from a mental health specialist in a community mental health center to increase his understanding and effectiveness in working with chronically passive, dependent clients.

[4. Situation consultation.] Here the consultee seeks the help of the consultant in understanding and coping more effectively with actual or potential clients in situations that are similar. The client characteristics may vary widely here, but the situation remains the same or similar. [For example, a pastor seeks consultation with a community mental health practitioner concerning the situation of death in a family, and the process of grief and mourning.]

[5. Program consultation.] Here the consultant's help is requested concerning various programs or services offered by an agency or contemplated by an agency in the future. These may include special workshops, conferences, research projects, the establishment of special classes for the handicapped, and so on. The consultant's help is requested for a particular program or service within the agency, and not with the entire agency structure.

[6. Administrative consultation.] The consultee, usually an individual with administrative responsibilities, requests consultation concerning administrative policy and practices.

[7. Community consultation.] The consultee seeks consultation concerning the agency's relationships with other groups, agencies, and individuals, outside its own organization.

Methods

Mental health consultation shares the characteristics of a number of related processes: education, inservice training, psychotherapy, collaboration, and supervision.

However, the more sharply the consultation process can be delineated from such related functions, in theory if not in practice, the more effective can understanding of the process and results become. In terms of the relationship between mental health consultation and education, to quote Dr. Mahoney again:

In general, mental health consultation proceeds from the immediate presenting problem (with transfer of learning as a secondary result), while formal education usually proceeds from general principles through specific applications. . . . mental health consultation does

not prepare the consultee to assume a different professional or vocational role. It is a process whereby he becomes better able to function
in his current role; it is a resource to be used by a person already
trained and educated in his profession.

Particular emphasis should be given to the concept that
consultation, for the most part, should only be afforded
persons with basic training in their profession. The relationship of consultation to inservice training deserves close
examination. If the mental health practitioner allows himself to offer mental health consultation to *all* members of
an agency, regardless of their level of training or competence,
he may passively condone, and be participating in, the per-
petuation of an undesirable situation. For example, if a
mental health practitioner offers consultation to all members
of a county welfare staff, he may be simultaneously offering
consultation to persons with a high school education, those
with partial or complete college education, those with a
master's degree in social work, and those with a master's
degree combined with considerable experience and additional education. By an indiscriminate offering of consultation to all of these persons, he participates in an insidious
attempt to blur distinctions between different training and
skill levels in the agency, and participates in a hoax, passing
off untrained persons as professional practitioners. It would
be wise, in other words, to see the consultation process as
being something only to be used "by a person already trained
and educated in his profession."

However, there may be inservice training needs in an
agency in which the mental health practitioner may be asked
to participate. They should be clearly labeled as such and
differentiated from ongoing consultation. The aim would be
to provide specific, new material and new content related to
the agency's expectations of the individual receiving training.

There are many similarities between the consultation

process and psychotherapy as well as many dissimilarities. Table 1 is an attempt to summarize some of the techniques commonly used in psychotherapeutic relationships, and to indicate the frequency with which they should be employed in mental health consultation. Mental health consultation is a process that is just as complex as psychotherapy, and requires the same careful training, including supervision and apprenticeship, as does psychotherapy. It is difficult to learn by reading or formal didactic study alone. Thorough training and experience in psychotherapy is, however, an excellent

TABLE 1

Utilization of Psychotherapeutic Behaviors in Mental Health Consultation

		Never	Rare	Occasional	Frequent
1.	Listening				X
2.	Accepting				X
3.	Empathizing				X
4.	Clarifying				X
5.	Questioning			X	
6.	Confronting		X		
7.	Interpreting current events in terms of genetic past	X			
8.	Pointing out similarities in apparently unrelated behaviors, feeling, perceptions of client			X	
9.	Explaining			X	
10.	Directing or Instructing			X	
11.	Reassuring				X
12.	Sharing responsibility for client behavior			X	
13.	Discussing dreams and fantasies	X			
14.	Discussing parapraxes			X	
15.	Discussing feelings toward other persons such as:				
	a. Clients				X
	b. Personnel of other agencies			X	
	c. Supervisors			X	

preparation for mental health consultation, since there is a large area of transfer of skills and experience from psychotherapy to consultation. Changes which are required in emphasis, in goals, and in methods can be acquired most effectively and surely through supervised practice.

In differentiating the collaborative process from the consultative process, the issue of responsibility is most important. The consultant does not assume a direct responsibility as he does in collaboration or in supervision. The supervisor, in addition to having responsibility for the supervisee, also has a responsibility to the agency and the client; the consultant does not have this sort of relationship, nor the power and the authority that the supervisor holds.

EVALUATION OF RESULTS

Little has been done to prove the usefulness of mental health consultation. In using this process, the mental health agency in effect is acting on enlightened faith, and is attempting to cope with reality factors using the best information and professional consensus available. In this light, no criticism can be levelled against an agency for using an essentially unproved method, so long as it is done with proper care and discretion, so long as adequate training and experience of the mental health consultant is guaranteed, and so long as the agency attempts to evaluate the process and its usefulness.

SUGGESTED READINGS

Caplan, G. (1964), *Principles of Preventive Psychiatry*. New York: Basic Books.

Halleck, S. L. & Miller, M. (1963), The psychiatric consultation: questionable social precedents of some current practices. *Amer. J. Psychiat.*, 120:164-169.

Lindemann, E. (1945), Symptomatology and management of acute grief. *Amer. J. Psychiat.*, 102:101-141.

McCann, R. V. (1962), *The Churches and Mental Health.* New York: Basic Books.

Parker, B. (1958), *Psychiatric Consultation for Non-Psychiatric Professional Workers.* Public Health Monograph #53, Public Health Service Publication #588. Washington, D.C.: U.S. Dept. of Health, Education & Welfare.

Rosenbaum, M. & Berger, M., eds. (1963), *Group Psychotherapy and Group Function.* New York: Basic Books.

Shoup, V. V. (1962), The relationship of the community mental health center with other community agencies. *Minnesota Welfare,* Summer Issue.

VII

Consultation with Health Agencies

Full-time local health units existed in 73 per cent of the counties in the United States in 1956 (Robinson et al., 1960, p. 18). The community mental health practitioner must define the nature of his relationship with this public health unit—which often holds seniority in terms of lifetime in the network of community agencies—as well as consider how mutually supportive roles may be evolved. Many thoughtful professionals have maintained, with good logic, that the community mental health program should be one division of the public health program—just as are communicable diseases, maternal and child health, etc. This position, and the counterarguments, are summarized neatly by Dr. Paul Lemkau:

> The arguments in favor of this rest mainly on the fact that the health department is involved in all other planning for the community health and it is logical that this large area should not be excluded. Furthermore, the local health department is the only health agency that is established in the community; it is unwise to duplicate this existing organization by other administrative structures to deal purely with mental health problems. The health department has access to a considerable portion of young children and their parents through the well child stations; these can easily offer mental health education, casefinding, and supportive treatment. Finally, the health department has developed public health nursing services which are available to carry out counseling and other services, both in a clinic setting and, particularly, in the home. . . .
>
> These cogent arguments are countered by others who point out that the technical procedures of mental health work are very different than traditional public health practice, and that health officers and public health nurses are not equipped for this task . . . [Arieti, 1959].

At the present time, the organization of health services in the United States is very complex at all levels of government and society. Before discussing in more detail, the relationship between the mental health program and the public health department, it is appropriate for us to review the purpose, organization, and functioning of the typical local health department in the United States. A variety of definitions is possible. One example is as follows:

> Public health is the Science and Art of (1) preventing disease, (2) prolonging life, (3) promoting health and efficiency through organized community effort for (a) the sanitation of environment, (b) the control of communicable infections, (c) the education of the individual in personal hygiene, (d) the organization of medical and nursing services for the early diagnosis and preventive treatment of disease, and (e) the development of a social machinery to insure everyone a standard of living adequate for the maintenance of health, so organizing these benefits as to enable every citizen to realize his birthright of health and longevity [Winslow, 1920].

Or, a more recent definition is that rendered by the House of Delegates of the American Medical Association in 1948, defining public health as:

> The Art and Science of maintaining, protecting and improving the health of the people through organized community efforts. It includes those arrangements whereby the community provides medical services for special groups of persons and is concerned with the prevention or control of disease, for persons requiring hospitalization to protect the community and with the medically indigent.

In practice, local health departments should have at least the following seven departments (American Public Health Association, 1951):

1. Vital statistics
2. Environmental sanitation
3. Communicable disease control
4. Laboratory services
5. Maternal and child health
6. Chronic disease control and promotion of adult health
7. Health education

Now, it is to be noted in the definitions quoted, and the description of the basic functions of a local health department, that mental health or psychiatric problems and services are not singled out for special attention. While it is quite appropriate to point out that such problems probably come under the heading of medical services, there are also sufficient elements of uniqueness and distinctness in mental health problems to make this specific omission noteworthy. It is also certainly true that public health education and practice, in a vast majority of settings, have stressed primarily the mechanistic, physical, infectious model of disease.

This is not to say that public health teachers and practitioners have been uninterested in mental health. There has been a considerable and increasing amount of verbalized concern about incorporating mental health problems into public health services. The amount of verbalized interest has varied inversely with the prevalence of infectious and epidemic illness, and directly with the popularity and financial support of mental health endeavors. The mental health professional has tended to feel, at times, that one of Parkinson's laws is operating: the amount of work expands to occupy the available personnel. Such a cynical observer might comment that with the decline of public concern about infectious illness, due largely to an actual real decline in infectious and epidemic illness, persons trained in more traditional public health practices have been looking for ways to fill up their available and no longer fully occupied time.

Likewise, the great popularity of mental health endeavors, during a period of relatively low interest in organized public health programs, might cause the distrustful observer to wonder about the motivation of public health practitioners in becoming involved in mental health endeavors. Some public health practitioners have, quite honestly, verbalized their desire to "latch onto the popularity of mental health," in order to expand and promote their own public health program.

Now, whatever the truth or lack of truth might be in these general kinds of suspicions and concerns—and probably upon close scrutiny, the observer might find them to be true in some instances, and totally untrue in others—there are certain basic issues that present themselves concerning the interrelationship between mental health and public health personnel. A committee of the American Public Health Association (1962), in a recent publication, has discussed the deficiencies that exist in the training of public health personnel and mental health personnel. They say, "the gaps in knowledge and skills which commonly exist among public health physicians, nurses, sanitarians, biostatisticians, and other public health professionals are different from—and to some extent complement—the gaps in the training background of psychiatrists, psychiatric social workers, clinical psychologists, and other mental health workers" (p. 62).

In this publication there is considerable discussion of the various gaps in the knowledge and skill of workers in the two fields. The committee felt that many public health workers have difficulty in recognizing psychiatric cases, and that additional training and inservice consultation would be desirable. The committee stated that health workers need to know more about epidemiology of mental disorders, and to have some acquaintance with, and understanding of, various methods of investigating such disorders. Likewise, experience on the part of public health personnel in making their specialized skills available to, and bringing them to bear upon, mental health programs is necessary in a community-wide endeavor. Health officers should be aware of administrative relations and programs of the full spectrum of psychiatric and other mental health services, as well as the nature and extent of mental disorders, of current psychiatric theories and practice, in addition to problems involving the administration of community psychiatric programs.

The Committee also concluded that mental health workers have gaps in their knowledge and skill. They stated:

> Probably the most important area in which psychiatric specialists will require additional knowledge and skill is that of public health practice. This includes the basic philosophy and point of view of the field of public health. Crucial here is emphasis on prevention and promotion, and on the community rather than the individual as a patient. There is an ideology, a set of values, a set of orientations, which characterizes the public health 'approach' to problems of health and illness. Part of this approach is a sense of 'responsibility' on the part of the public health administrator for the total health problems within his jurisdiction [p. 70].

It was also held by the committee that training in epidemiology and biostatistics for professional mental health workers is most usually insufficient to prepare them for community mental health practice. Community mental health administration requires skill in problem solving that leads to the setting of priorities for program development. The report also stated:

> The administrator who is a psychiatrist specialist must be conversant with both the theory and practices of community organization. This includes knowledge of the structure of communities— formal as well as informal and manifest as well as latent. He must be able to appraise communities in relation to mental health needs, but also in more general terms. There are special skills involved in the stimulation of community awareness. The administrator needs to know and understand the complicated social and power structure of communities and also the equally complicated network of community organizations, groups, and agencies [p. 72].

Particularly important, and often missing in the knowledge and skill of mental health workers, is ability in consultation and education activities with other professionals. A considerable portion of this chapter will be devoted to an explication of types of consultation and educational activities that may be appropriate in the relationships of a community mental health agency to a local health department.

Issues of control and authority are almost certain to arise in any relationship between two such agencies. The evidence would indicate that a community mental health program may function well as a division of a public health department, or it may function badly. Experience would also indicate that an independent mental health agency may conduct a high- as well as a low-quality community program. Among other things, this would suggest that administrative structure should be viewed as an instrument, rather than an end in itself. It furthermore suggests that there is a wide variation in both local and state situations as well as in the qualifications and characteristics of the personnel responsible for the program.

The National Opinion Research Center conducted, for the National Institute of Mental Health, a study of the relationship between mental health activities and local health departments. They confirmed that there exists a wide range of program emphases and priorities in mental health services under various auspices. Two of their general conclusions, quoted in the publication by the U. S. Department of Health, Education and Welfare, are relevant here:

> A large majority of public officials in mental health and a smaller majority of officials in public health, also believe that the hospital and community program should be integrated as part of the same total program. If the trend continues toward development of more local responsibility in mental health centers, on the one hand, and toward reduction of the patient load in state mental hospitals, on the other, the problems associated with this type of integration will lessen and the need for it will increase.
>
> Mental health programs cannot afford, at this stage of their development, to be absorbed by, or lost in, other programs. The degree of formal autonomy is a more open question. The NORC study summarized above, indicated considerably more agreement on integration (especially of hospital and community programs), and, at least, the implications of visibility, than on the issue of formal autonomy from departments of public health [Report of the Surgeon General's Ad Hoc Committee on Mental Health Activities, 1962, p. 39].

In considering the furor about jurisdiction and control, the authors of this same publication go on to state:

Two major problems heighten the issue of how mental health programs are best organized in relation to public health and other programs: (1) Where there is failure to have clearly defined goals, status considerations are highlighted, the importance of formal organizational structure is exaggerated, and interagency rivalries are generated; and (2) We lack adequate prevalence, incidence, and other kinds of epidemiological data which would clearly define need. Careful studies of interagency relations in terms of need should be made to assure that the person who is seeking help and is unfamiliar with the complexities of agency services, does not have to run a form of obstacle course to attain the particular assistance he needs. Such studies would, by clearly defining needs, prevent programs from becoming entrenched and oriented to programs as such, instead of securing services based on the needs of given populations. Clearly defined goals would also prevent interagency rivalries and keep status considerations and the importance of formal organizational structure at a minimum [p. 40].

Now, what most of these comments add up to is, that if people behaved with reason and scientific fidelity, interagency rivalries could be resolved. In truth, people do not always behave reasonably, and science is usually confined to the laboratory and seldom operant on the testing ground of interagency conflict. Among mammals, territorial behavior is perhaps most prevalent in the human, although handled symbolically and disguised by many rationalizations and social conventions. In our society, innate tendencies to such behavior—to stake off and defend a "territory" against intruders—are reinforced by reasonably consistent cultural conditioning for competitive, exploitative, and entrepreneurial behavior.

This book cannot attempt to spell out a method for the resolution of conflict between counterposed or vested interest groups. Indeed, such a solution should have wide currency in the fields of international and governmental relationships, as well as in the mental health area. We can only strive, to the best of our human ability, to seek constantly for superordinate goals, as the key to conflict resolution. If two opposing agencies can agree upon a common goal, which they want badly enough, the possibility of interagency collaboration increases markedly.

Likewise, while contact or togetherness do not necessarily resolve conflicts—and in some instances may make disagreements clearer, more sharp, and less resolvable—the resolution of conflict *without* open and mutual communication is unlikely. Communication between agencies will be enhanced to the extent that equivalent levels in the hierarchy of the two organizations maintain the dialogue, and that interagency relationships have the sanction of top-level governing boards and administrators.

Collaboration and genuine communication may often begin best by the initiation of a joint service project, which will allow professionals from different fields to work together around the focus of individual cases. Dealing with patients tends to bring forth the more humanitarian and responsible sides of our professional repertoire of behaviors, and talking about cases may often be more productive than talking about policies.

It would be an oversimplification in reality to state that *all* competition is bad, and that collaboration and mutual respect will always necessarily best advance the cause of the mentally ill or potentially ill individual. The system of free enterprise has worked so well precisely because it is geared to certain basic human impulses towards aggressive and competitive behavior. To the extent that such competition is not harmful, but results in a genuine improvement of program in one or both of the agencies involved in such a competition, it should nowise be branded as harmful. In fact, group morale and staff esprit may gain considerable stimulation by such a friendly, or even unfriendly, competition between two agencies. Competition becomes harmful, however, at the point that patients become pawns or tools in the conflict; or at the point where interagency rivalry results in a community reaction that leads to partial withdrawal of support from one or the other agency.

MENTAL HEALTH ACTIVITIES IN LOCAL HEALTH DEPARTMENTS

The mental health worker may be able to make a contribution in overall planning for the development and administration of public health services at the local level. An increasing body of knowledge concerning the impact of administrative practices, personnel policies, decision-making procedures, and group processes within an organization may be useful to the administrator of the public health program in developing an organization to implement overall and long-range community health goals.

In planning for specific local health activities, mental health concepts, knowledge, and experience may be useful to the public health administrator. The interrelationship between biological, social, and psychological determinants of health and illness has become increasingly understood in recent years. The mental health professional, to an increasing extent, occupies a crucial and important position between traditional medicine on the one hand, and the behavioral sciences on the other. He is, or attempts to be, at the same time a scientist, a practitioner, and a liberal humanist. The psychiatrist, particularly, because of his background in medicine may be able to serve a crucial role in assisting the public health administrator and his staff understand, incorporate, and integrate principles from psychology, sociology, and the other behavioral sciences.

The initial task of the mental health practitioner, when participating in a local public health department, may properly lie in assisting public health personnel improve upon traditional services. Increasing experience has been gained, in a variety of settings, with methods of human relations training, designed to increase sensitivity of the participants to nuances of interpersonal communication, and to familiarize them with salient features of group behavior. Under the leadership of the human relations training lab in Bethel, Maine, and their associates, the T-group technique has been utilized in sensitivity training for a wide range of individuals. This is one of the techniques that may be of use to local public health departments in upgrading the performance level and effectiveness of their personnel. The vast majority of employees of a local health department— whether they are involved in tuberculosis control, venereal disease, environmental sanitation, accident prevention, services to crippled children, services to well babies and their mothers, direct clinical services to indigent or deprived groups, or health education—in the final analysis are successful or unsuccessful to the extent to which they can form meaningful, collaborative, goal-oriented relationships with other persons. Often the other persons are socially and economically disadvantaged, relatively uneducated, ill, or emotionally disturbed, rendering the achievement of an effective relationship even more demanding.

Whether the mental health professional should himself provide human relations training depends upon his particular training and experience background. Clinical competence, or even competence in group psychotherapy, does not necessarily indicate a capacity for conducting successful T-group sessions.

Also, careful consideration must be given to whether the human relations training should be done within the context of the health department. Problems may arise when training groups are formed that cut across status and hierarchical levels of an organization, and involve people who work together on a day-by-day basis in an intensive group experience. It often may be the better part of valor for key personnel to receive sensitivity or human relations training in programs outside the work context of the agency.

In addition to such specialized training, the mental health professional may participate effectively in ongoing inservice training designed to heighten and reinforce the public health worker's awareness of interpersonal and group dynamics in his day-by-day work. Case discussions, individual consultation with staff members, and even formally or didactically oriented inservice training courses may prove useful.

In health departments where relatively untrained and inexperienced persons must be employed because of financial and other limitations, the mental health professional may participate in the inservice training program in a number of ways. He may provide basic information about human personality functioning and psychiatric disorder. He may bear partial or primary responsibility for training in interview techniques. In many public health endeavors, such as venereal disease control, a successful mastery of good interview techniques is really essential. If the mental health professional is willing and able to adapt his clinical psychiatric methods to the demands of various public health activities, he may make a genuine and important contribution to the overall functioning of the local health department.

The work of the public health nurse overlaps and intermingles with that of the mental health practitioner in many ways. In preventive activities, the public health nurse's involvement in maternal and child health activities gives her a focal and potentially crucial role in the prevention of mental illness, since she characteristically serves a segment of the population in which the prevalences of mental illness and mental retardation are high. In her work with the chronically ill, the school population, with aging citizens, and with a variety of high-risk groups such as crippled children, the blind, etc., the public health nurse does make a significant contribution to the overall mental health of the community, and may make an even larger contribution with effective collaboration with mental health specialists.

The first requirement of such a relationship is the establishment of open and mutual communication. Because the dialogue between public health nurse and mental health practitioner is in the final analysis case-related, it is probably best to structure and perpetuate the relationship between mental health staff and public health nursing staff around the focus of clinical problems, rather than around didactic or theoretical discussions. Since in public health nursing the nurse carries a responsibility that is different, both qualitatively and quantitatively, from that of the general duty nurse in the hospital, attention must be given on the part of mental health staff, particularly psychiatrists, to restructuring the doctor-nurse relationship in the direction of mutuality and complementarity, rather than following the characteristic authoritarian model. Within this mutual and complementary relationship, an ongoing dialogue should continue between mental health and public health nursing personnel. Whether these consultative relationships are structured as group activities, or as individual consultations, will vary with the particular context, needs, and personnel of the agency.

However, one basic rule which must not be violated is that consultation between mental health personnel and nursing personnel should be done only with the full knowledge and approval of the director of the agency, followed up by cooperative planning with the director of the public health nursing section, who will be kept informed about, and involved in, the program at all times.

Increasingly, public health nurses have been playing an important role in the aftercare of mentally ill patients returning to the community. If continuity of care is to be maximized, the contact of the public health nurse with the family of the patient should actually begin prior to, or immediately following, the patient's admission to the hospital. The task of the public health nurse should be to work, in full communication and cooperation with the staff of the mental hospital, towards developing a discharge plan and preparing the family for the return of the patient. With their knowledge of community resources, public health nurses can make a valuable contribution, working with the hospital, toward developing a realistic plan for post-discharge care for the individual patient. Since many patients are discharged from the hospital on medication, it is essential that the nurse be familiar with current psychiatric medication, so that she may participate in its supervision. Likewise, it is important for her to have a wide range of knowledge about, and experience with, social and health agencies within the community, as well as special educational and recreational resources.

Characteristic types of problems tend to arise in establishing such a program. Foremost is the fact that public health nurses are, by and large, heavily committed in current work assignments, and planning should realistically ask whether the addition of another responsibility, without a commensurate increase in number of personnel and appropriate in-service training, is realistic. Relationships with state mental hospitals in such a cooperative program are not always happy. The mental hospital, often at a distance from the community, may exhibit one type of verbal behavior and another type of action-oriented behavior: it may talk about the need for aftercare services, but seldom refer patients to appropriate community resources. Attitudes of possessiveness, jealousy, and fearful withdrawal on the part of state hospital personnel must be accepted with understanding and patience by the personnel of the community agencies in their attempts to deal with these overworked, undersupported, much maligned public servants who have been doing the dirty work of our society for many generations, and have been helping to sweep under the rug the faulty products of our human assembly line. It cannot be denied that the secretive attitudes characteristic of state hospital personnel, and the unwillingness to release appropriate information to public health nurses and other community agencies, do present an obstacle to the ongoing community mental health effort. However, these tendencies must be viewed against the background of a long-established medical tradition which has held as a sacred value, the privacy of the individual patient.

On the other hand, research indicates that the usual readmission occurs at a point of social crisis in the readjustment of the patient to the community. At this point of crisis, significant "gatekeepers" within the community are often called into play—such as the probate judge, police, county welfare department, public health department. To the extent that they are knowledgeable about, and involved in, the aftercare treatment of the patient, they will be able to discharge their heavy responsibility to both the community and to the patient with wisdom and compassion. To the extent that they are ignorant and uninvolved, they may well reflect community attitudes of intolerance, punitiveness, and rejection. It is to the best interests of the vast majority of seriously ill psychiatric patients, returning to communities from our state hospitals, to have significant caregivers or gatekeepers within the community informed about the major aspects of their illness and aftercare needs.

Relationships between public health nurses and social workers are characteristically fraught with distrust and ambivalence. Strong feelings of rivalry, often centered around the person of the psychiatrist, may develop. In assisting nursing and social work personnel to resolve their differences, the physician—whether he be public health administrator or psychiatrist—carries a particular and peculiar burden of responsibility and authority. To the extent that he is impartial and fair, and demonstrates in action as well as words that the needs of the patient must remain tantamount and that all professional people may make important contributions to patient welfare, he can assist in resolving the differences between public health nurses and social workers. To the extent that he is inconsistent, seducible, or partial, he will perpetuate and widen the breach between the two disciplines.

Health education has played a vital role in developing an informed citizenry able to participate effectively in health care. The basic model of health education lies very close to the usual educational model, in which a body of objective information is made available to a motivated and willing learner, who can incorporate the knowledge and use it in his day-to-day life.

In mental health education, whether the audience is a "well and normal" group, or a group that may be significantly disturbed (such as the parents of mentally ill children or the relatives of hospitalized mental patients), the rational educational model is only partly appropriate. To the extent that mental health education is successful, it must take on some of the process elements of psychotherapy, and allow for individual and group catharsis, sharing of experience, the element of group consensus, and the resolution of ambivalent feelings and attitudes. Current educational programs for mental health educators are strongly rooted in traditional public health, and consequently offer little preparation for effective mental health education. Whether mental health education, in the years ahead, will evolve out of health education as a specialty; or whether mental health education is more properly and intimately related to the behavioral sciences, such as psychology and counseling, will remain to be seen. It is to be hoped that new and experimental programs for the development of mental health educators will emerge in academic settings, and that the mental health educator will have an ever larger role to play, not only in the public health department but within mental health agencies of all sorts.

SUMMARY

In summary, there can be no question that the social role of the public health department and the mental health agency is closely interrelated and to some extent interwoven and overlapping. There is considerable agreement, as well, that mental health personnel and public health personnel have significant contributions to make to each other's understanding and practice. There is very little consensus, however, as to whether the mental health agency should be a subdivision of the local health department. One need look only as far as San Mateo County to see an example of an excellent, thriving, and vigorously experimental mental health department flourishing under the auspices of a local health department; on the other hand, there is Kansas, a state in which attempts to integrate mental health services and local health departments between 1948 and 1961, to a large extent failed.

Competition between agencies and between groups is not necessarily bad. It is a practice in which Americans are quite competent, and for a long time now competition has been one of the mainsprings of our social life. Competition may be harmful, or it may be helpful. One of the tasks of the practitioner and administrator, in public health and mental health alike, should be to cope with and minimize *harmful* competition—and "harmful" should be defined in terms of the effect upon the patient or recipient of services, not upon the constituent agency—but not to be compelled by any neurotic need for "togetherness," to merge programs that are in part basically incompatible, and often in such different stages of development as to make them uncomfortable bed fellows at best.

SUGGESTED READINGS

Arden House Conference (1961), *Mental Health Teachings in Schools of Public Health*. New York: Columbia University School of Public Health and Administrative Medicine.

Dorsey, J. R., Matsunga, G., & Bauman, G. (1964), Training public welfare nurses in mental health. *Arch. Gen. Psychiat.*, 11:214-222.

Hanlon, J. J. (1964), *Principles of Public Health Administration*. St. Louis: C. V. Mosby Co.

Holtzgrew, M. M. (1961), *The Role of the Public Health Nurse in Mental Retardation*. St. Louis: Child Development Clinic.

Mental Health Activities and the Development of Comprehensive Health Programs in the Community (1963). Washington, D.C.: U. S. Dept. of Health, Education & Welfare.

Program Area Committee on Mental Health (1962), *Mental Disorders: A Guide to Control Methods*. New York: Amer. Public Health Association.

Reman, D. W. (1962), *Mental Health in the Community Public Health Program*. Austin, Texas: The Hogg Foundation for Mental Health.

Robinson, R., DeMarche, D. F., & Wagle, M. K. (1960), *Community Resources in Mental Health*. New York: Basic Books.

Services for Children with Emotional Disturbances: A Guide for Public Health Personnel (1961). New York: Amer. Public Health Association.

Surgeon General's Ad Hoc Committee on Mental Health Activities (1962): *Mental Health Activities in the Development of Comprehensive Health Programs in the Community*. Washington, D. C.: Public Health Service.

Williams, R. H., ed. (1962), *The Prevention of Disability in Mental Disorders*. Mental Health Monograph Number 1, Washington, D. C.

VIII

Consultation with Welfare and Social Agencies

The welfare system, in the United States, is surrounded by emotional and doctrinaire attitudes. It is a frequent target of politicians of all persuasions, of every caliber, at every level of government, and in every section of our country. The term "welfare," has many of the characteristics of a projective test, into which people may read all of their concerns about shifting social values and a changing society.

Why should consultation be offered by the community mental health center to the staff of the county welfare department? Simply because the welfare personnel, whether they choose to or not, whether they are trained or not, whether they are competent or not, come in contact with people that are caught up in a wide variety of life crisis situations, deal with those who have experienced high-risk trauma, and see daily all forms of maladaptive behavior. In other words, they provide services to a population with a heightened risk of mental illness, and may serve to either decrease or increase the likelihood of deteriorating mental health for their clients.

What are some of the groups served? The state welfare departments, and their county departments—whether they be semi-independent units, or offices of the state welfare department—administer financial assistance to aged persons in the community, disbursing funds from both federal and state resources. In April of 1964, in Kansas, approximately one per cent of the state population was receiving old age assistance, which averaged $80.72 per person per month. The welfare department may serve merely as a disbursing agent; or, the personnel having proper training and motivation, may provide a wide variety of assistance to these older citizens at times of stress in their lives.

Mothers attempting to maintain families without the presence and support of a husband may be assisted through another category of public assistance—aid to dependent children. In April of 1964, one and one-half per cent of the population of Kansas was receiving aid to dependent children, with an average monthly amount per individual of $36.23. Again, the welfare workers with proper training and motivation may provide a wide variety of supportive, counseling, and preventive mental health services for the mothers and the children. Or, they may deal with clients in a mechanical, routinized, bureaucratic fashion, and be insensitive to the special needs, problems and potentialities of their clients.

About one person in every four thousand in the state of Kansas, in April of 1964, was receiving aid to the blind, averaging $78.06 per month per person. Again the role of the welfare worker in assisting a person suffering from this high-risk trauma may be of crucial importance in influencing the level of social and personal adjustment.

One person in every 400 in Kansas, in April of 1964, was receiving aid to the disabled, amounting to an average amount per month of $96.74. A wide variety of illnesses and disabilities, with varying degrees of increased risk of mental and emotional illness and social dysfunctioning, would go to make up this group.

The category of public assistance referred to as general assistance includes a heterogeneous group of persons experiencing a wide range of personal and family misfortunes and diseases. In April, 1964, 8,739 persons in Kansas received general assistance, averaging $31.69 per person. It is with this group that a consistent and well-implemented rehabilitation philosophy is most essential, where interagency collaboration is most needed and useful, and where training and skill of the welfare worker is most put to the test.

All told, in Kansas, in April of 1964, there were 73,110 persons receiving some form of public assistance: about one in every 30 citizens. The directors and workers in the 105 welfare departments in Kansas had some sort of contact in the lives of these individuals, whose risk of mental and emotional illness would be presumed to be higher than for the population at large.

About 2,000 individuals in Kansas, during April, 1964, received assistance from the medical care for the aged program, and in so doing went through a transaction with the welfare office that might serve either to support and boost self-esteem and feelings of self-sufficiency, or undermine such attitudes.

In addition, 3,467 children were provided child welfare services during April, 1964, involving a wide range of child-protective services, adoptive studies, supervision of foster homes and institutional care, and so forth. Licensing and supervision of boarding homes and day care homes for children would be a part of the spectrum of child welfare services in most states.

In some states, as well, licensing of nursing homes and other group living situations for the aged, as well as other services for the aging citizen, would be provided by state and county welfare departments.

Welfare personnel may have responsibility for preparing a social history prior to admission of patients to state hospitals. The role of the county welfare department in aftercare services for patients, following discharge, varies between states. The county welfare office is the only source of help available in all parts of the country to persons in need of social services and financial aid. Only in the large metropolitan centers are

there casework agencies and mental health clinics organized
to give special help to people who have emotional and psychological problems. In the rest of the country, the public
welfare agency, whose basic function has been to administer
financial assistance, is being increasingly called upon to
render a wide variety of social services to the entire community. The service amendments to the Public Assistance
Titles of the Social Security Act give legislative recognition
to the role of the social services that will "promote the well-
being of the nation by encouraging the state to place greater
emphasis on help to strengthen family life and help the needy
families and individuals obtain a maximum economic and
personal independence of which they are capable" (Amendments to the Social Security Act, 1957).

An examination of any public welfare caseload reveals a
substantial amount of mental illness, character disorder, alcoholism, mental deficiency, delinquency and crime, and
neurosis and psychosis. These disorders are long-term and
are accompanied by all the problems of any prolonged illness
or disability—the high cost of care, family breakdown,
economic need, and loss of personal esteem. They are some
of the underlying reasons for large caseloads in a period of
economic well-being, and for the disintegration of family
life with its attendant fostering of personal and social malad-
justment in children reared in such an environment (Robinson et al., 1960).

But despite the importance of, and need for, welfare services, why should mental health professionals in community
settings extend themselves to provide consultative assistance?

First of all, because almost none of the workers in county
welfare departments are adequately trained by current professional standards.

According to Robinson and co-workers (1960), in 1950,
only 4 per cent of the workers in county welfare departments
at either the state or local level had had two years of training

in a graduate school of social work; 18 per cent had had less than 2 years of graduate work; and 78 per cent were without any graduate social work training at all (p. 82). While there has undoubtedly been some improvement during the last 16 years, all too often trained social workers only move *through* the public welfare field, and pass on to terminal positions in other areas of social work rather than in the public welfare agency. There seems little likelihood, without major changes in the field of social work as well as in the general social milieu, that within the foreseeable future, public welfare departments, or child welfare services, will be staffed with a majority of fully trained individuals.

One continuing and pressing need in the development of public welfare services, then, is for the provision of inservice training for untrained or partly trained professional persons carrying such major responsibilities at the community level. Psychiatrists, psychologists, and social workers in the community mental health center can all participate in soundly planned inservice training programs for county welfare workers.

However, in such inservice training relationships, as well as consultative activities which will be discussed later, several facts should be borne in mind:

1. The welfare worker, whether at the state or local level, is by and large insufficiently trained for the responsibilities that he is asked to assume. It is also not unusual for him to be poorly paid, and to be subject to a personnel and supervisory system that can only increase personal and professional insecurity. Because of this, he is vulnerable to feelings of unworthiness and inferiority, and prone to interpret helpful comments from more fully trained individuals as critical, condemning, or in some other way unhelpful.

2. State welfare personnel may experience the same feelings of inferiority as enumerated for their county welfare counterparts. In addition, many of them will have relatively

limited field experience themselves, since the rapid expansion of welfare programs resulted in extremely fast promotion of fully trained personnel to supervisory and administrative positions, without sufficient periods of practical experience and seasoning to allow them to have a firm and secure professional identity. Feelings of uncertainty as to whether they have anything to offer their supervisees, unsureness about the security of their own positions, inability to give or receive support from other members of the state-level staff, may all render the supervisory personnel suspicious of offers of assistance, and fearful of criticism and usurpation by mental health consultants.

3. The concept of welfare has become tinged with all manner of social, moralistic, and political overtones in our society. It is rare for the welfare worker to hear a kind word about the program, either from his clients, from politicians, or from professional persons in other fields. Whether individuals who stay in such a field may tend to do so because of some liking for, or predilection to, mistreatment, or whether they become trained and habituated to such mistreatment by years of exposure, is open to question; but it does seem likely that many workers in the welfare field have difficulty in recognizing, accepting, and allowing relationships to persist in which they feel that they receive esteem and affection rather than disparagement and rejection.

4. Because the clients of welfare are often marginal and rejected citizens of our society, subjected to all manner of scapegoating and prejudicial mistreatment at the hands of the dominant and "righteous" majority, the social worker may come to identify with their plight in life. Feeling as if he himself were badly treated and rejected, stigmatized and expelled, he may become suspicious, litigious, cautious, and as skeptical as are his impoverished clients, that anyone else might care about what happens to him.

In addition to inservice training, the mental health professional can play an important role by providing consultation services. In line with preceding comments, however, an orderly and careful procedure is necessary in establishing such contacts. Initial contact should be made with the field representative or other representatives of the state, and the general desirability of such a service discussed. Then—or on some occasions, perhaps prior to the contact with the state representative—beginning discussions should be held with the director of the county welfare department. Only after considerable exploration of needs and issues, and with careful attention to the metaphorical communications given by the welfare representatives, should some type of consultative activity be structured.

As in all relationships, it is probably wise to in some way give recognition and support to the higher status of the director of the welfare department. Periodic individual consultations with the welfare director, in addition to group or individual consultations with rank and file welfare workers, should be insisted upon to enhance his prestige and status. Unless this is done, he will generally feel that his workers are "learning more than I know," and will soon tend to feel that the presence of the mental health professional is disruptive, and is encouraging arguments and disagreement with him on the part of his staff.

Mental health workers should be aware, at all times, that the primary personal identity of the welfare worker, as well as his ascribed status in the community, is usually considerably lower on the socioeconomic and prestige hierarchy than is that of the mental health worker. In many communities, the welfare worker may also be more closely aligned in background and personal identity with the rural population than with urbanites. All of these factors must be weighed in determining the structure of the consultative relationship, in order to allow sufficient formality and distance, so that the welfare worker may feel unthreatened and may protect and enhance his personal and professional esteem by the consultation process.

The suspicion of the welfare department, like the suspiciousness of the poor man, is not without considerable basis. Who offers the welfare department, or the poor man, something for nothing? Charity carries with it, always, the price tag of loss of self-esteem and personal debasement. As with the pauper, the welfare department will almost routinely insist that the services be given without charge, and will cite poverty, mistreatment, and general woefulness as the reason for this need. Mental health workers should think twice before succumbing to the guilt-provoking qualities of this appeal. If a decision *is* made to provide services without charge, it should definitely be on a time-limited, demonstration, or trial basis.

As the trial comes to an end, there should be a series of graduated increases in demands upon the welfare department to support the cost of the service, so that the agency may be helped to assume an identity of self-reliant independence, just as the individually disadvantaged and dependent individual must be helped. That is, after a certain period of time, the agency should be given the choice of either reducing consultation time by 25 per cent, or paying 25 per cent of the cost of full continuing service. After an additional period, the percentage can be increased to 50 per cent, and so forth. All of this should be made explicit in advance, not only with the local agency, but with the state welfare department, and/or with the local governmental structure responsible (if the welfare department is set up on a county unit basis).

If the mental health center is looking for a way to have dramatic results and to make a strong impact upon the community, which will be recognized and esteemed by power and opinion-setting figures within the social structure, the welfare department is not the place to turn. If it wishes to make a needed, but little esteemed contribution to the health of the total community, and to cope with large and continuing difficulties, then a cooperative relationship with the welfare department should be considered.

SUGGESTED READINGS

Bemmels, V. G. (1964), Survey of mental health problems in social agency caseloads. *Amer. J. Psychiat.*, 121:136-147.

Bowers, S. (1949), *The Nature and Definition of Social Casework*. New York: Family Service Association of America.

The Consultant Psychiatrist in a Family Service Agency (1956), Group for Advancement of Psychiatry, Report No. 34, New York.

Harrington, M. (1963), *The Other America: Poverty in the United States*. New York: Macmillan.

Maas, H. S. & Gold, R. F. (1959), *Children in Need of Parents*. New York: Columbia University Press.

Schechter, M. D. et al. (1964), Emotional problems in the adoptee. *Arch. Gen. Psychiat.*, 10:109-118.

Schottland, C. J. (1958), The mental health implications of social legislation. *Amer. J. Orthopsychiat.*, 28:115.

Vasey, W. (1957), *Government and Social Welfare*. New York: Henry Holt.

Weller, E. G. (1957), *Building Sound Staff Development*. American Public Welfare Association.

IX

Consultation with Educational Agencies

If mental and emotional illness may indeed be prevented by specific interventions during childhood, and/or positive mental health be promoted by experiential factors during personality growth and development, then the school system is an obvious focus for community mental health activities. The school is the one institution in our society where all individuals congregate at predictable points in their lives, and for predictable periods of time that comprise a significant percentage of the total phenomenal world of childhood and adolescence.

The importance of the school in providing mental health services is highlighted by the fact that the Joint Commission on Mental Illness and Health published a separate monograph devoted to the subject (Allinsmith and Goethals, 1962).

It is important, however, in discussing mental health programs in schools, that particular attention be devoted to differentiating between the promoting of specific value systems or world views, and preventing emotional illness. When the mental health practitioner participates in an agency of society, such as the school, which is charged at least partly with promoting normative value systems, the individual-centered approach of mental health professionals may be jeopardized. Conformity is not synonymous with mental health, tractability with maturity, or subservience with freedom from mental illness.

The school may make important contributions in the areas

of primary, secondary, and tertiary prevention of mental and emotional disorder, and the community mental center may participate in either cooperative, consultative, or assistive roles in many of these activities.

PRIMARY PREVENTION

Curriculum planning and development should receive attention in appraising the school's contribution to the primary prevention of mental and emotional illness in children. There is, in fact, no general consensus concerning the proper purpose or content for the public school curriculum, nor the relationship between the curriculum and mental health. The publication of the Joint Commission on Mental Illness and Health points out that there are five main viewpoints expressed about mental health and the curriculum: "These five clusters of opinions advocate respectively: (1) A focus on traditional subject matter; (2) An emphasis on life adjustment; (3) The seeking of a healthy personality for every child; (4) The improvement of society through increased maturity of individuals; (5) Neo-fundamentalism, in which teachers are enjoined to stick to instruction and schools are urged to resist their burgeoning non-academic functions" (Allinsmith and Goethals, 1962, p. 37).

Rather than entering into this extremely complex area of general curriculum, its purpose and development—about which no consensus has developed—attention will be devoted to areas of curriculum *content* that may have potentialities for primary prevention, such as sex education and human relations training.

At times it appears as if the public system is involved in a conspiracy against teaching children about human beings. The child is taught a great deal about things, and about animals of one sort or another. In our supposedly emancipated and scientific society, effective education about human sexual functioning is extremely rare in the public schools. In many communities in our nation, merely to raise the topic would evoke stormy and bitter community-wide debate. When sex education does eventually sneak into the curriculum, it is characteristically introduced quite late, not infrequently taught by unqualified instructors, and usually handled in an abstract, intellectual, and overgeneralized fashion.

The potential role of the mental health professional, in relationship to sex education in the schools, may be multifaceted. If the community has no organized sex instruction in the schools, he may play a role as a responsible citizen, as well as a professional person, in attempting to make the community aware of this deficiency in the educational system. If, because of his efforts or the efforts of others, sex education is introduced into the schools, he can play a useful role in assisting the school administration in its provision of inservice training opportunities for the teachers who will be presenting material about human sexual behavior, physiology, and reproduction. These inservice training experiences should provide opportunity for free expression of feelings on the part of prospective teachers, for group discussions aimed at minimizing anxiety and conflict, and should also allow for the exclusion of certain teachers from the sex education program because of their inability to be emotionally comfortable with instructional materials dealing with sex. In a well-developed and ongoing program, the mental health practitioner provides periodic consultation with the administration concerning the overall sex education program, or with groups of teachers concerning their experiences, operational anxieties, or questions about the management of the sex education experience for the child. Or he may participate in the actual educational process itself, by presenting material about the interpersonal and emotional aspects of sexuality, and/or by leading small discussion groups of students.

Human relations training has, in recent years, become increasingly prevalent in college curricula. Such educational experiences are almost entirely lacking in the public schools, however. It is strange that the study of human beings and human behavior should be handled in such a dispirited and mechanical way within the public educational program, although this perhaps is only a reflection of the general superficiality governing human understanding and interpersonal relationships within American society. A number of authors have commented upon how little the causal approach to human behavior is utilized in the public school curriculum:

> When we examine the discussion in an ordinary civics book of such a problem as crime, we would find a description of how the police force is constituted, its functions as ascribed by law, methods for detecting and apprehending the criminal, and information on the system of courts, training schools, and prisons. At times we would also find a short discussion indicating that crime is often associated with economically underprivileged conditions.
>
> Such an approach treats crime primarily as a surface phenomenon. . . . This same pattern was found for the other social studies. Styles, for example, found in an analysis of human behavior in 15 social studies readers used in elementary schools that less than 1 per cent of the selections treated human behavior in a dynamic way. Much of the treatment was of the surface variety [Ojemann, 1961, pp. 382-383].

Ojemann has developed a program for the continuing education of teachers to assist them in teaching an understanding and appreciation of behavior dynamics.

> Concern with the dynamic nature of behavior or a 'causal approach' involves an appreciation of some probable consequences of these alternative methods under specified conditions. . . . A 'causal individual,' is, as here defined, one who is sensitive to the probable future consequences of behavior, as well as how behavior develops from the past [p. 379].
>
> . . . the data we have cited provide some evidence that the child can be guided toward a more causal orientation to the social environment. Furthermore, those children who have acquired to some degree such an orientation show many of the characteristics that increase the probability of the individual's being better able to deal with the stresses presented by the environment [pp. 393-394].

It will be the rare school system that will be able or ready to introduce a program of human relations training for teachers, preparatory to teaching the causal approach to human behavior in the classroom through improved curricula materials, as well as through special structured human relations training groups within the school. It is also the rare mental health worker who has sufficient knowledge about, and comfort in, working within the educational milieu, and who is also highly knowledgeable and experienced in human relations training activities, to exercise decisive leadership in the development of such a program. In those mental health centers having a staff sufficiently large enough for differentiation, a desirable plan might be to designate one staff member to learn and develop skills in working within the educational milieu, and also to assist him in obtaining ongoing training in human relations and group dynamics theory and techniques, so that a long-range program of coordinated planning and development with the school system may ensue. The mental health center should be a co-participant, playing an initial role in stimulating interest, supporting and encouraging experimentation, and continually reasserting the need for preventive measures within the school system in order to prevent mental and emotional disorder as well as promote positive mental health.

The relationship of high school courses in psychology and in marriage and the family, to the prevention of mental and emotional illness is certainly moot. However, a minimal requirement of such courses is that they should not present gross misinformation, stimulate unrealistic fears, or contribute to lack of understanding of psychological processes or interpersonal behaviors. The mental health professional, in many instances, would be shocked to discover how antiquated the texts used in the public schools are, and how instruction is, at best, desultory and, upon occasion, actively destructive. As a professional person, the mental health worker has a right, if he behaves with tact and consideration, to call to the attention of top-level school administrators any inadequacies in the timeliness or accuracy of texts and other instructional materials. Comment upon instructional *methods* is another matter, however, and he cannot intrude into the classroom situation without a specific invitation from the school administration.

Services for High-risk Trauma as a Technique for Primary Prevention

The school has ample opportunity to prevent emotional illness by offering services to students suffering from high-risk disabilities, thereby warding-off the crippling emotional reactions which may accompany the trauma. Many programs such as vision screening, hearing screening, and intelligence testing are designed to identify children with sensory deficits, with retardation, or with specific disabilities such as reading disability. The intent is to afford, as early as possible, specific remedial measures in order to minimize or limit the disability; and, when necessary, to reduce demands upon the child in accordance with his limitations. Many school systems have excellent programs for identifying disabilities in children, and for minimizing the risk of emotional illness as a secondary complication. However, school programs characteristically tend to exclude the parent, and careful attention should be given, in many situations, to productive involvement of the parent in a counseling and collaborative relationship focusing on the child's needs and disabilities.

Crisis Intervention as a Technique for Primary Prevention

Life situation crisis intervention offers many opportunities for preventive mental health activities in the school system. The birth of a sibling, the death of a parent, divorce, any of a number of personal crises within the life of the child, may result in temporary stress and psychological decompensation. The classroom teacher, if she is well trained, experienced, and sensitive, may be of inestimable help to a child at such crisis points, and may genuinely contribute to the primary prevention of mental and emotional illness. The mental health worker can play a particularly useful role through consultation services to the classroom teacher, in order to help her understand more fully the child who is experiencing a life situation crisis, as well as to understand and cope with her own feelings, and thus free herself to behave in a more supportive and constructive manner.

The Educational Milieu

The community mental health worker can potentially play a role in screening and selection of teachers for employment in the local school system. If the school system can develop a consensus about the particular personality traits that are regarded as necessary for a classroom teacher, and if there were a surplus of teacher applicants so that careful selection could be done, the mental health worker could play an active part in teacher selection. However, in most educational systems, the criteria for the personality of the teacher are extremely vague and often contradictory, and shortages of properly trained teachers generally tend to insure against rejection unless it is for the most gross inadequacies.

The mental health professional may contribute to the education of teachers, either in college or through inservice training programs within the local school system. While it is inexact to think that the professional mental health worker has any special or great knowledge about education simply because he is interested in, and knowledgeable about, human behavior, it is accurate to assume that within every basic teacher curriculum there are places where mental health workers can contribute important and significant information, insight, and understanding concerning normal and abnormal child behavior, recognition and referral procedures for disturbed children, and group dynamics within the classroom. While the offer of the mental health worker to participate in teacher education, either within the college or in the inservice program of the local school system, will not always be met openly and with joy by educators, it is a task that needs doing. The community mental health worker should make tactful but persistent attempts to improve upon the classroom teacher's ability to clearly perceive behavior and feelings in children, to understand motivations, and to adopt an appropriate and constructive role for herself in relation to the individual child and to the class as a whole.

In some school systems, the director of the mental health center, or one of his staff, may be able to successfully develop a collaborative or consultative relationship with the superintendent of schools, which will allow for mutual discussion with regard to the mental health implications of a broad range of matter, such as personnel policies, administrative procedures, program planning, and curriculum planning. Where this is possible, the mental health center will be able to make its greatest contribution to the largest segment of persons within the community, at the most impressionable stages in their life cycles, and consequently make the greatest contribution to the mental health of the total community.

SECONDARY PREVENTION

The major emphasis in secondary prevention of mental illness within the school milieu, lies in the recognition of maladaptive behavior as indicative of psychological stress. Recognition should lead to the institution of prompt diagnostic and remedial procedures. The classroom teacher sees many problems that fall into this category. A few actual case histories, in the words of teachers, follow:

Case I

Frank is a boy of average or better intelligence. He is 11 years old and is the second child in a family of six. He has an older sister and two younger ones. His father is a mechanic in a local garage, his mother stays at home to care for the family. They have a small but comfortable home and the children appear to have most of the things that other children in their income bracket have.

My acquaintance with Frank dates back to his first year in our school. He was beginning to exhibit actions that are not associated with the usual behavior of first grade children. He disturbed the others; he climbed and walked on top of the desks. If his teacher reprimanded him, he bit and kicked her. His work was poorly done, when and if he chose to do it.

One day when Frank was especially obstinate and mischievous, his teacher tried to put him in his seat and he proceeded to crawl up the water pipes which were exposed in that particular room. The principal called Frank's father and he came to school. He said that the child behaved well at home and he could not understand the child's actions.

When Frank was in the second grade and in my room, his behavior was similar to that of his first year. He was loud, talked out any time he wished, and worked only when he wished. His work was slovenly and poorly organized.

One day when things were going badly for Frank and the teacher, he opened a window and screen in the classroom, and threatened to jump out. There was a little ledge on the outside wall under the window and he stood on that.

We persuaded him to come back into the room and he finally did.

Frank is now in the sixth grade and every teacher who has him as a student says that he is a problem, to the teacher at least.

Case II

Louise is the middle child in a family—she has a sister 3 years older, and a brother 2 years younger than she. She could be called a tomboy—much prefers outdoor work on the farm to housework. She does help with farm tasks as she is 14 years old. The 12-year-old brother is as large as she is, and also does a considerable amount of work.

Family background shows very high intelligence—one paternal uncle of Louise has won national recognition, and other relatives are in very responsible positions.

There have been deep religious convictions—Protestant—on both sides of the family, resulting in sincere routine Sunday School and church attendance, and various related activities. This has all been in a seemingly wholesome atmosphere—nothing too radical or fanatical.

Three years ago, when 10 and 11 years old, Louise seemed to become very disturbed. Up until that time, she did exceptional school work. When in the third grade, even, she could stand in front of the class and conduct a recitation in a very efficient manner. She knew how to ask questions, and she was confident of all the answers required of third graders, and more.

It happened that within a comparatively short time, before her disturbed condition, several relatives on both sides of the family passed away. Louise gave the impression, even in the classroom, that she was fearful of death. That seemed strange, because everything in the family's routine, and in the handling of the children, had seemed to be so sensible and wholesome.

She withdrew more and more, and would not eat in the lunchroom with the other students. She brought her lunch, eating it alone in the room; preferring it that way. For quite a period of time, she called her mother by telephone every noon.

Finally, for a while, her mother came to school each noon and ate with her. Gradually, Louise started eating again with the others, but had lost weight, was very nervous, and still wanted to withdraw to herself.

Gradual progress was made, with companions and teachers being kind and as understanding as possible. Schoolwork again improved.

She is ready for high school now, but is still something of a small problem. She does have a keen mind, and probably should be in a school with every modern advantage and with specialized departments. She does not want to be bothered with too much detail—she can work that out for herself, usually. While the average students are having a point explained, which she may already know, her mind is going on farther, or daydreaming in some other field. She usually has a book handy, and if allowed, will pick it up and read until she thinks she needs to 'join' the class again.

Many times she can arrive at arithmetic answers without working step by step. However, she does make mistakes, especially when she is in one of the depressed moods, which she still does have occasionally. If a mistake is checked, she will make a notation to the effect that she got mixed on the figures, but that she understands it now, giving the teacher the impression that she doesn't need to bother to explain. At times, no explanation is necessary, but at other times, it is.

Everything seems to work out pretty well now, if the teacher 'goes along' with the moods in an understanding way, but, at the same time, sees that a reasonable amount and quality of work is done. Pushing and demanding definitely do not get results at some times. More often than not, now, Louise is happy and just one of the crowd. She can also be so light-hearted and mischievous that a reprimand is needed. This, she seems to accept.

Everyone is glad about the progress, but is wondering if she does have an unusually brilliant mind which needs special handling. Considering the fact that she had been disturbed, it was commendable that almost entirely on her own initiative, she received an honorable mention in history on the Emporia Scholarship Tests this spring.

Case III

Stephanie is a very brilliant, creative, and artistic little girl—in the sixth grade last year. Various IQ's on her record range from scores of 139 to 145. Her scores on achievement tests were exceptionally high in every area. She is an attractive child, and will be a beautiful young lady. She has beautiful features, fine bone structure and superb posture.

Her problem . . . ? She had absolutely no friends among her peers, and the term used by most of the faculty to describe her was 'obnoxious.' I have never known a child who could generate such animosity so easily.

Stephanie was always talking; usually telling someone what to do or what they had done wrong—she was most officious. If she worked with a committee, she always took over, whether she was chairman or not. She never asked for anything—she demanded it. She walked up to a teacher on the playground and gave the teacher her large purse and said, 'Hold my purse.' It was her tone of voice as much as what she said that people resented, though she could be most sarcastic and witty at the expense of others.

Evidently she thought rules were made for everyone but Stephanie, although she thought others should abide by them, and was the first to report even the slightest infraction of rules made by any of the boys. The boys openly detested her. There were two girls who sometimes tried to be friends with her, but she would get them into trouble, or she would want the one girl to be mad at the other.

Everywhere she went she was disliked; the ladies in our cafeteria, the secretary in the office, the librarian—everyone knew her and disliked her. The gym teacher asked her if she didn't get tired of being in trouble and she replied, 'Oh no, I really enjoy it. I like to be different.' I knew this was not so, though. She wanted friends and praise like anyone does. I praised her for her poems, original stories, pictures, etc., that she did so well, and she would perk up like a wilted plant that has been watered well. However, she didn't do much for the other teachers that would merit any praise. She was seldom on time, was always forgetting materials. She borrowed a pen from one of the teachers, and then took it to the library and just left it on a table.

I liked Stephanie—I had her in my home room and had a better opportunity to know her—though I did not like the way she acted, much of the time. She came from a divided home. Her father was a college instructor in the East; her mother was a chemist. Stephanie had an older and a younger sister. The father had her two younger brothers. I tried to help Stephanie by talking with her privately; she liked to visit with me after school, and we had discussions in the girls' health class about getting along with others, etc.

I finally decided to call the mother in to talk about psychiatric help. I debated about this because after all she didn't lie, cheat, steal, etc. . . . I didn't think of her as mentally ill, but as having a personality disorder which would certainly interfere with her happiness and her ability to progress in any field of work.

Her mother was most eager for her to receive some professional help. She stated that Stephanie had been arrogant and demanding since she had been a very small child, and that she had had the same trouble (being disliked) in previous schools.

I am surely hoping that she can get some good help.

Case IV

Betty, age seven years, an only child, of average intelligence, slight body build, inclined to droop shoulders.

In school Betty is quiet and follows the room activities with her unhappy, hungry-looking eyes. In spite of her ability, Betty does below average work, does not complete work on time, forgets easily and shows little interest in formal or informal school activities. Seldom, if ever, does she volunteer a response. When something amusing happens in the schoolroom, Betty does not laugh with the other children, neither does she cry easily.

In play, at the least provocation, Betty hits or scratches her classmates. Although she does not take active part in play, she follows the group around and does not go off by herself. The little children are very forgiving and try to include Betty in their group activities. Betty remains with them, but is not a part of them.

The teacher tried to draw Betty into active participation in both school work and play, using smaller groups and inviting a few others with Betty to stay after school to prepare the room and materials for future activities. The other children chattered about school and home, but Betty remained silent.

One day Betty had scratched members of a small group and all ran to the teacher. The teacher dismissed the group except for Betty whom she drew to her and asked, 'Betty, why do you hurt the other children when they would like so much for you to play with them?' At this Betty threw her head back, jumped up and down and screamed loudly, 'OK, I'll tell you. I hurt them because I hate everybody. I hate everybody because no one loves me. I know no one loves me because even my father and mother don't love me!' Then she told that she never got to be with her parents. Both parents left for work before Betty was up in the morning, she ate breakfast after her mother called her by phone from work and told her to hurry to school. At noon Betty returned from school to eat lunch alone, after school she was to sit quietly in the house and watch T.V. until her parents returned from work. She was given her dinner and sent to bed. On Sundays her father took her to Sunday School and Betty was told to stay for church after which the father came for her to take her home for lunch. After the meal Betty was taken to a show and told to see it over and over until she was called for.

A conference was called but the father did not come because it was not worth his time. The mother came but did not take time to sit down. She admitted that Betty's report was correct and asked what more could Betty expect. Betty was getting her Sunday School and church and any other child would be happy to see a show over and over. The mother explained that the father worked at two jobs and she also worked away from home so that they could move to a 'better' part of the city. An appeal to give Betty love and companionship was answered by, 'We are not going to spoil her, anyway, when do you think I would get the house cleaned and the washing and ironing done?'

The consultant from the mental health center may assist in the proper recognition of such cases of maladaptive behavior through direct consultation with the classroom teacher, with the school principal, or with special personnel such as school psychologists or counselors. The administration plays a crucial role in setting the climate within the school about deviant behavior. All too often the educational bureaucracy has a policy of: "Don't rock the boat, and whatever you do don't annoy the parents." In such a system, the teacher who is sensitive to problems in children, who attempts to encourage parental concern and involvement, who tries to make the school experience supportive and constructive for the troubled child—is often seen as being, herself, some kind of troublemaker. The administration in such a system prizes the teacher who never has children with emotional problems, who never makes referrals, who never asks for services from the school psychologist, who never involves the parents in any save the most formal and cursory conference. Anyone who has worked in a mental health center with children is familiar with school situations of this sort. In looking back through the cumulative record of the child, evidence of emotional problems and behavioral disturbances is often recorded from kindergarten on, for the years prior to actual referral to a mental health facility. As an overall average, it probably takes between two and three years after the appearance of overt difficulties, within the "typical" school system in our country, before clear identification of the child as a problem child, and referral for diagnostic evaluation at a specialized facility, occurs. It is likely that many of the referrals, when they are actually made, are done in the late spring just prior to the end of school, so that the teacher can inform the parents and hope that they will not make a fuss before the end of school.

In other instances even greater courage and fortitude will be called for on the part of the school administration. Some parents are, of course, unable to admit that their child is experiencing difficulty. In the event that his personal adjustment is rapidly regressing or there is behavior disruptive to the classroom, it may be necessary for the school principal to make psychiatric consultation a necessary condition for continuance of the child in school. Laws in most states make this a possible course of action, but many school administrators are reluctant to exercise their authority and assume so much responsibility for the well-being of the individual student.

Specialized personnel within the school system play a vital role in the secondary prevention of mental and emotional illness. Working relationships between the mental health center and specialized personnel should be close, mutual, and provide for considerable informal communication around the focus of specific problem cases. To the extent that the mental health personnel enhance the status and prestige of the specialized personnel within the school system, relationships will probably flourish; to the extent that they derogate or undermine the position of specialized personnel within the school, the relationship will deteriorate.

School psychologists are rapidly increasing in numbers, and are gaining wide acceptance within public schools. While their professional identity is still unclear, their training sometimes grossly inadequate, and their role poorly defined, the mental health worker in the community would do well to accept school psychology as a fact of life, and to devote himself to determining how he may contribute to making the profession and practice of school psychology more prestigious and effective.

There is no quicker way to alienate specialized personnel within the school system, as for example, the school psychologist, than to avoid requesting information concerning specific children when they are referred to the mental health center for evaluation. Formal policies and channels for requesting copies of psychological reports, guidance testing, achievement testing, and classroom observations should be established between the administration of the mental health center and the school.

Social workers are relatively rare in schools, but in some areas have an established role and identity. As with school psychologists, a central task involves the careful and tactful delineation of respective roles between these personnel and those within the community mental health center.

The school nurse has a particularly amorphous role. She may have almost no impact, or she may be an extremely influential figure within the informal communication and prestige network of the school. In establishing inservice programs in conjunction with the school, and in providing ongoing consultation programs to the school, the nurse is often bypassed. She should not be.

Most schools rely upon the private practitioner of medicine to provide medical care as needed for the schools. However, specific physicians in some systems provide specialized services in terms of screening or examinations. Communication between the mental health center and the physician should be established and maintained.

Speech and hearing therapists and correctional reading teachers have an excellent opportunity to observe maladaptive behavior and to play a secondary prevention role. Ongoing consultation between the community mental health center and these personnel should be planned.

Techniques Related to Secondary Prevention

Many schools conduct a preschool health survey. Rarely is psychological status or mental health evaluation included. There is an increasing body of evidence to suggest, however, that practical and brief survey techniques, utilizing largely naturalistic observation by skilled clinicians, can identify many problems prior to entrance into school. Careful planning will be necessary in order to set up such mental health screening programs, as well as to arrive at decisions concerning the utilization of such findings. That is, should the classroom teacher be made aware of such potential problems and continuing consultation offered to her? Or, as a result of the screening, should the parents be involved in a conference and recommendations made by the mental health worker for an evaluation?

Inschool screening and casefinding procedures have received attention for many years. A whole variety of paper and pencil techniques, sociometric procedures for use by teachers, and so forth have been experimented upon within the school system. Studies by Eli Bower and his associates to demonstrate the feasibility of casefinding procedures within the school, conducted by the teacher, have been the most carefully designed and carried out. It is clearly possible, that with proper training and preparation, a schoolwide system for detection of early emotional problems and disturbed interpersonal relationships can be developed. It will undoubtedly be many years, however, before most school systems are willing to assume sufficient responsibility for the emotional well-being and personality growth of their students, to institute such programs, or to actively commit the school to utilizing its resources towards the correction of difficulties that are discovered.

Secondary prevention may be feasible through the utilization of such techniques as "Worry Clinics" for high school adolescents. Worry Clinics have been conducted in many areas of the country by Associations for Mental Health, and seem to have a great popularity with housewives. No careful studies have been done to assess their usefulness or lack of usefulness, but experimentation within the school system in making voluntary experiences such as Worry Clinics available for adolescents, would not be amiss. These programs usually consist of one or two short presentations on the general topic of worries, emotional tensions, and so forth, followed by a series of small discussion groups led by professional persons in which participants in the Worry Clinic may discuss problems such as dating, relationships with parents and vocational choice problems.

Secondary prevention through the recognition of maladaptive behavior may also be promoted directly in the school system by PTA-sponsored programs related to adjustment problems of children and adolescents. Here material may be presented concerning the normal range of behavior, and opportunities given for parents to ask questions concerning the significance of certain types of behavior in their children. Or, even more effective are ongoing discussion groups sponsored by the PTA, in which the parents may meet regularly

with a professional person to discuss the developmental problems of some specific age group.

One problem in all such procedures is that through the
process of self-selection, it is usually those parents who least
need such counsel, who become the most active participants.
(It's not the sinner who goes to church.)

There are opportunities for a whole variety of other special
programs which may contribute to the secondary prevention
of mental and emotional illnesses in the school system. Vigorous and imaginative experimentation is called for—the time,
interest, and resourcefulness of the mental health center staff
are the only limitations.

Tertiary Prevention

While not all children who need education also need the
services of the mental health professional, all children who
need psychiatric care also need educational services. The
educator is much more important, in the final analysis, to
the mental health professional, than the other way around.

Many school systems are developing classes for the emotionally ill, as well as classes for the educable and trainable
mentally retarded. Such classes for emotionally disturbed
children offer a superior educational experience by a teacher
who has specialized in the education of the emotionally disturbed. In such small classes, demands upon the child can
be adapted to his ability; allowances made for the fluctuation
of his capabilities related to his emotional health and ill
health; special activities provided to allow for the constructive release of drives, and the resolution of conflictual impulses—in general, the development of a climate which mini-
mizes competition and maximizes acceptance and support.

For the seriously mentally ill, this would seem to be a
valid model. However, some problems may arise for less
seriously ill children, who have been placed in situations
where the mentally and emotionally ill have been segregated

from the general society, as for example, in state hospitals. Is it wise to put five ill children together, or to have one ill child in the class with 19 relatively normal children? Do the ill children "learn how to be sick" from each other? Do they learn "symptoms" from each other? Do they suffer stigmatization as a result of being in "the nut's class"? When they leave their regular class does the class close ranks behind them, and are they permanently excluded from their peer groups? The staff of the community mental health center may be of service to the teacher of special classes for the emotionally ill, as well as to the school administration, by continually appraising such matters related to program development, and by encouraging rapport between the individual child and the individual teacher.

Community mental health centers and schools are often at odds about the participation of the school in the treatment program of the child if he is a patient of the community mental health center. Mental health professionals tend to feel that the school's curiosity is inordinate and inappropriate; and school personnel feel that the mental health center staff is being secretive and not involving them as professional equals. The school may, if allowed, contribute to the tertiary prevention of mental illness by providing a wide range of information about the child's adjustment within the school, for use by the mental health center in the initial evaluation. The school may also provide periodic progress reports as a child progresses in treatment. And, if the school and center are both willing and able, the school may participate in the treatment program of the child by appropriate environmental manipulation, and/or by inducing attitudinal changes on the part of the classroom teacher.

It is the exceptional mental health center that is able to realize the full contribution that the school may make to the treatment program of the child. Admittedly, some parents will not wish communication between the mental health center and the school, and without their permission it obviously cannot occur. However, if the mental health center staff is convinced that the school may collaborate and genuinely contribute to the treatment of the child, and if it conveys this attitude to the parents, it will be extremely rare for a parent to refuse the mental health center permission to obtain information about the child from the school, to obtain progress reports, or to communicate specific information— i.e., so long as the parents are assured that the personal details which are irrelevant to the treatment of the child will not be made known to the school.

The school system may contribute directly to the tertiary prevention of mental illness, by the assignment of teachers with adequate training in special education to teach in a children's day hospital within the community mental health center. For those centers that develop special programs for certain groups of the mentally retarded, the school system may be able to provide special educational assistance as well.

SUMMARY OF PRECEDING DISCUSSION

This chapter says, in essence, that opportunities for collaboration between the community mental health center and the public educational system for the betterment of the mental health of the community are almost unlimited. Seldom is this potential achieved. Rigidification of roles, suspiciousness, institutional antagonism, status and prestige insecurity, competition—all contribute to keeping mental health workers and educational workers from attaining real closure.

The first step, then, in improving relationships between the community mental health center and the school, and in maximizing the contribution of the school to the community mental health program, lies in the development of channels of communication between the mental health agency and the schools. The initial contact should occur between the direc-

tor of the community mental health center and the superintendent of schools. In time, and after discussion, the governing board of the mental health center and the school
board should be involved in discussing relationships between
the mental health center and school. With top-level administrative and board sanctions, progress can then be made
towards developing mutual communication channels, collaborative ventures, and consultative activities.

COLLEGES AND UNIVERSITIES

This chapter has focused upon the public school system
and has ignored an equally important area of education: the
junior college, college, and university. Yet, the community
mental health center can make a real contribution in providing for mental health services for colleges (Whittington,
1964). Only the minority of colleges and universities within
this country can be expected to develop their own mental
health service.

The leaders of tomorrow are in our colleges and universities today. The degree to which they are successful in coping
with the demands and making use of the opportunities of
this educational experience will determine how useful they
will be to our society in the future.

Unfortunately, many university administrators have not
benefited from the experiences learned in the military service
during the last war. Military men also used to view psychiatric services as unnecessary luxuries and frills. However,
they became increasingly aware of the role that psychiatric
services could play in maximizing the potential of the manpower that they had available. The motto of the Navy medical corps sums this up very neatly: "To keep as many men
at as many guns as many days as possible."

Similarly, the effectiveness of our educational program is
seriously weakened, in many instances, by the interference
of emotional and mental disorders. When a student becomes

emotionally disturbed, learning ability is impaired seriously; in fact, the ability to concentrate, to learn, and to retain knowledge is one of the earliest functions to be affected by any emotional or mental disorder. This effect is not limited to the student who is directly involved. Anxiety and behavior disturbance definitely have a "contagious" effect in close group living situations. One emotionally disturbed student, or a socially deviant one, living in the wing of a dormitory can significantly affect the emotional well-being, and consequently the ability to benefit from the educational experience, of many students living in that wing.

In the final analysis, all the great outlay of money for buildings, educational materials, and highly qualified faculty comes to naught if the individual student is unable to make use of this opportunity. For too long we have satisfied ourselves with vague platitudes about "lack of motivation," and have given a variety of "reality" explanations to the high dropout rate of students in college. Perhaps even more significant than the dropout rate is a relative underutilization of the learning opportunity by many students who manage to graduate.

Now, we cannot propose that psychiatric or mental health services can really cure all problems of education, make all students scholars, or guarantee that everyone will graduate from college. However, it has been clearly demonstrated that mental health services in the university can and do make a significant contribution to the educational milieu.

The availability of mental health personnel allows many other people involved in caring for the personal and human needs of the student to operate much more effectively. The Dean of Students, the Deans of Men and Women, dormitory counselors, counseling psychologists working in educational clinics and in guidance bureaus, faculty advisors to individuals—all can and do make use of the advice and consultation of the psychiatrist and his colleagues in psychology and social work.

For those colleges unable to maintain psychiatric or mental health facilities within their student health service, contractual relationships can be arranged with the community mental health center which serves the total community within which the college is located. The staff of these mental health centers would have to be augmented sufficiently to provide services to the university and services to the individual as follows:

A. Services to University

1. Consultation with president and other administrative officers regarding mental health implications of programming; regarding specific problems of students and their families; and consultation regarding behavior problems of faculty, proper administrative action, etc.

2. Collaboration with student personnel services

   a. Regular consultation with deans of students, and of men and women, regarding specific problem cases, overall program goals and implementation, etc.

   b. Participate in inservice training of dormitory counselors.

   c. Aid, when requested, in interpreting students' problems and needs, and limitations of university's responsibility to the parents.

   d. Provide regular consultation to nonmedical, second echelon mental health services operating on campus (counseling bureau, psychological clinic, etc.); assist director of personnel services in evaluating effectiveness of such agencies, assist president in evaluating need, budget requests, staffing pattern, definition of responsibility, suitable inservice

training role, potential for accredited clinical training, etc.
3. Consultation services to faculty
   a. Concerning need of individual students for pro-
      fessional assistance.
   b. To help faculty be supportive, "friendly coun-
      selors" to students in need of this rather than pro-
      fessional help.
   c. As a resource person in giving lectures, leading
      discussions, obtaining specialized guest lectures,
      etc.
   d. As a part-time teaching associate in an academic
      department: psychology, sociology, social work,
      political science, home economics (child develop-
      ment), education, etc.
4. Consultation services to Student Health Service.
   a. Patient-centered consultations upon referral.
   b. Assistance in preadmissions examinations, psychi-
      atric screening of selected cases.
   c. Staff development
      1. M.D. education regarding psychiatric aspects of
         illness.
      2. Nurse education: nursing care of the emotion-
         ally ill.
      3. Education about preventive role of all health
         personnel in college setting.
   d. Hospital services to patients while in university
      hospital.
B. Services to Individual Patients
   1. Intake interview and brief evaluation without charge
      to bona fide students paying health fee.
   2. Intake interview without charge for faculty members
      and/or faculty families.
   3. Treatment services on basis of sliding fee scale, based
      on ability to pay.

There are also very sound administrative reasons for recommending such a merger. In a college setting, there are many vacation periods during which the staff time is under-utilized. There is a two-week Christmas vacation, two-week spring vacation, a complete month's vacation in the summer, and two months during which the caseload is much smaller than during the regular school year. Likewise, there are slack periods in most of the community mental health centers, which tend to occur in the early fall, and which consequently place a heavy demand for services on the university mental health facilities. In other words, *by combining these two functions, there would be a leveling out of caseload which would allow for the most efficient use of staff time.*

It would also enhance the process of community involvement on the part of the colleges, which has been recognized as being of increasing importance by so many college educators. In other words, the college would become an integral part of the community by using another one of its resources, just as it relies on the community for water, electricity, and many other services. Here the college would be contracting, in effect, with an agency of the community, to provide mental health services for its students.

SUGGESTED READINGS

Ackerly, S. S. et al. (1958), Extension of a child guidance clinic's services to the schools. In: *Orthopsychiatry and the School*, ed. M. Krugman. New York: American Orthopsychiatric Association.

Cohen, T. B. (1963), Prediction of underachievement in kindergarten children. *Arch. Gen. Psychiat.*, 9:444-450.

Erikson, E. H. (1950), *Childhood and Society*. New York: Norton.

Rabinovitch, R. (1959), Reading and hearing disabilities. In: *American Handbook of Psychiatry*, ed. S. Arieti. New York: Basic Books, pp. 857-859.

Slavson, S. R. (1958), *Child-Centered Group Guidance for Parents.* New York: International Universities Press.

Smith, W. G., Hansell, N., & English, J. (1963), Psychiatric disorder in a college population. *Arch. Gen. Psychiat.*, 9:351-361.

Whittington, H. G. (1964), *Psychiatry on the College Campus.* New York: International Universities Press.

X

The Clinical Program of the Community Mental Health Center: General Considerations

From the outset, we are confronted with the dichotomy between the ideal and the attainable, as has been the case elsewhere in this book, and as will pertain in any consideration of community mental health practice. In this particular discussion, primary attention will be given to the attainable; but without, we hope, supporting a cult of mediocrity. While achieving the attainable, we should—in clinical services, as in other aspects of community mental health—pursue the ideal.

We must first examine problems of prevalence and incidence of mental and emotional disorder, if we are to decide what we can realistically hope to achieve in a population of given size, with available financial and professional resources.

Mental and emotional illness, often being chronic conditions, must be looked at from the standpoint of prevalence as well as from that of incidence. That is, to plan a realistic treatment program in the community we need both adequate information concerning the number of persons experiencing mental or emotional illness at any one point in time, as well as knowledge concerning the incidence of the development of new illnesses or of symptoms during any given period of time. The literature in this area is scanty, and leaves much to be desired in terms of answering, definitively, these questions of prevalence and incidence.

However, the midtown Manhattan study of mental and emotional illness can perhaps be used to give us some rules of thumb or bench marks against which to predicate the ensuing discussion of the clinical program of the community mental health center (Srole et al., 1962).

In an attempt to answer questions about prevalence, the research design embodied a home survey sample, utilizing the interview method, with the interview protocols being graded by independent psychiatric raters as to the degree of sickness or health of the person interviewed. The study in Manhattan revealed much higher prevalences of psychiatric illness than our previous estimates had suggested. For example, 23.4 per cent of the population was found to be definitely impaired; that is, to have marked or severe symptom formation or to be incapacitated. The following table summarizes the findings of the Home Survey Sample:

TABLE 1

Home Survey Sample (Age 20-59), Respondents' Distribution on Symptom-Formation Classification of Mental Health

Well	18.5%
Mild Symptom Formation	36.3%
Moderate Symptom Formation	21.8%
Marked Symptom Formation	13.2%
Severe Symptom Formation	7.5%
Incapacitated	2.7%
Impaired *	23.4%
N 100%	(1,660)

* Marked, Severe, and Incapacitated combined

It is not within the scope of the book to discuss all the other morbidity studies that have been reported in the literature. However, general experience would indicate that at least 10 per cent of the population, at any one time, is probably suffering from some form of mental or emotional illness

resulting in some significant degree of morbidity or inca-
pacitation. In the discussion that follows, then, we should
bear in mind that we may have to reduce the prevalence
figures by half, and that the discussion of the clinical program based upon the midtown Manhattan studies must, at
this point, remain tentative.

When one begins to look specifically at an area to be
served by a community mental health center, he is faced
immediately with an acceptance of considerable ignorance
about what the mental health center is purporting to treat:
how many patients, with what sorts of illnesses, with what
sort of incidence rates of new illness, and so forth. In planning for a new community mental health center, then, it is
important to find out as much as possible about the characteristics of the population. For example, variables that have
been isolated as affecting the prevalence rate in the midtown
Manhattan Study include age, sex and marital status, socioeconomic status, generation in U.S., rural/urban origin,
national origin, and religious origin. As we will discuss later,
many of these same variables will also influence the rate of
treated illness, which we must remember is quite different
from, and lower than, the rate of actual morbidity.

Now, for the purposes of discussion, let us assume that a
basic team of one psychiatrist, one clinical psychologist, one
psychiatric social worker, and one secretary-receptionist,
establishes a community mental health center in a population
of 50,000 persons. For the typical Kansas community, we
could expect the demographic characteristics appearing in
Table 2 to be discernible.

The first task of the director of the new center, then, would
be to compare data for his population with that for the state
as a whole. By so doing, he would be able to isolate special
characteristics of the population that would require special
reflection in programming for his area. As an example, if
he were establishing a community mental health center in

Table 2

Demographic Characteristics of a "Typical"
Kansas Community *

AGE

Preschool (1 to 5 years)		13.5%
School (6 to 17 years)		21.9%
Adult (18 to 64 years)		53.6%
(65 years)		11.0%
Live Births		22.5 : 1,000
Marriages		7.6 : 1,000
Divorces & Annulments		2.5 : 1,000
Illegitimacy		31.4 : 1,000 live births
Deaths		10.0 : 1,000
Suicides		11.5 : 100,000
Per Capita Valuation		$2,079

INCOME

Per Capita Mean		$1,912
Households	$0-2,499	26.0%
	2500-3999	19.1%
	4000-6999	31.7%
	7000-999	10.8%
	10,000	12.4%

STATE HOSPITALS: RATES PER 100,000

First Admissions	64.3
Readmissions	42.2
Discharges	104.4
Resident Population	158.3

JUVENILE INSTITUTIONS: RATES PER 100,000

Admissions	10.0
Discharges	9.7
Resident Population	12.1

INSTITUTIONS FOR RETARDED: RATES PER 100,000

First Admissions	15.4
Readmissions	—
Discharges	6.8
Resident Population	90.3

PENAL INSTITUTIONS: RATES PER 100,000

Admissions	61.2
Discharges	47.9
Resident Population	171.6

* Mean or Average Rates.

Wyandotte County, Kansas (the location of Kansas City, Kansas), he would discover that the divorce and annulment rate is above the state average (3.2 compared to 2.5), that the illegitimacy rate is greatly above the state average (53.8 versus 31.4), that the per capita valuation is quite low ($861 as opposed to $2,079), and that the income breakdown by household is skewed in the direction of middle-class and upper-middle-class income levels (52.9 per cent earning between $4,000 and $9,999 a year, as opposed to 42.5 per cent for the state on the average with per capita income of $1,825 as opposed to $1,912 for the state). He would also discover that the readmission rate to the state hospitals is higher than average for the state (56.5 versus 42.2), and that the admission rate to institutions for juvenile offenders is markedly higher than for the state as a whole (24.8 admissions versus 10.0, and 27.2 resident population versus 12.1). In other words, the indications are that the amount of support which could be derived from a tax upon tangible property would be relatively limited, since there is a very low per capita valuation. In contrast, there would be a fair number of families earning sufficient income to pay a substantial portion of their treatment expenses. However, there are high illegitimacy and juvenile delinquency rates, suggesting that perhaps there are pockets of lower socioeconomic families having a high prevalence of social disorders. This would lead the director of a new center in that area to recognize the need for a more detailed demographic study, using census tract data to outline the specific demographic and social and psychiatric disorder characteristics of various sections of a large and rather heterogeneous urban population.

In contrast, if one were establishing a community mental health center in adjoining Johnson County, a rather different profile would emerge. The director would discover that there are fewer old people in the population than for the state as a whole (5 per cent over 65 as opposed to a state average of

11 per cent); that there are lower rates for marriage (4.5 versus 7.6), divorce and annulment (1.8 versus 2.5), illegitimacy (11.2 versus 31.4), deaths (5.5 as opposed to 10.0), than for the state population on the average. He would also discover a very high per capita income ($3,012) and a very high family income level (35.1 per cent of the households earning $10,000 or more a year). Likewise, he would discover that first admissions to state hospitals (27.3) are below the average for the state (64.3). The readmissions (32.3) and resident population (62.4) rates are also low. The mentally retarded admissions (10.8) are below the state average of 15.4. As for the law offenders, juvenile institutions admissions are low (7.6 versus 10.0) as are penal admissions (39.5 versus 61.2).

It is thus apparent that the respective psychiatric and social profiles for Johnson and Wyandotte counties are markedly different. Hence, rather than apply any one standard model of the "ideal" mental health center for two such dissimilar need configurations it would be most logical to evolve different kinds of programs utilizing different services and requiring personnel having varied backgrounds, training, and experience.

In developing a plan, the initial step is to carefully study and understand the particular characteristics and problems of the population which is to be served. Here in effect, we are only applying the clinical model of the individual case study to planning for the development of community resources.

Let us assume, for the purposes of this discussion, that a team comprised of psychiatrist, psychologist, and social worker establishes a community mental health center in a "typical" Kansas community of 50,000 people. How many potential patients are there in the community on the day that the clinic begins operation? If we interpolate the results of the midtown Manhattan survey the following findings become manifest:

TABLE 3

*Prevalence of Symptomatic Mental
Illness in Community of 50,000*

	RATE	NUMBER
Well	18.5%	9,250
Mild Symptom Formation	36.3%	18,150
Moderate Symptom Formation	21.8%	10,900
Marked Symptom Formation	13.2%	6,600
Severe Symptom Formation	7.5%	3,750
Incapacitated	2.7%	1,350
		11,700 Impaired

Thus on the day that the team opened the clinic, there would be, as a minimum, at least 11,700 potential patients in the community of 50,000, if we include only those with marked and severe symptom formation, and those incapacitated. Now, from experience in Kansas between July and December of 1963, involving community mental health centers with different staffing patterns in all the many areas of the state, we can anticipate that one team in an average year, will carry to termination somewhere between 200 and 250 patients or cases. If we assume the most optimistic estimate of 250 cases carried to the point of termination per year, it would take this team 46.8 years to treat, *in the manner that most patients are now being treated,* all of the individuals who were suffering marked or severe symptom formation, or who were incapacitated in the community on the day that the clinic was established. There are no really valid and reliable studies of incidence rate showing the frequency of development of new psychiatric illness within the community, but we can assume that with such high prevalence rates, probably more than 200 new cases of recognizable illness are being generated in a population of 50,000 within a year. In other words, as we presently see psychiatric treatment, and as we structure our treatment programs, it would seem very difficult for a team of three professional people for 50,000 population to even maintain present levels of morbidity within the community, much less to roll back the tide of mental and emotional illness which exists in an endemic form in the usual American community—unless a significant portion of the ill individuals experienced spontaneous or socially-induced cures.

If we move from this theoretical discussion to look at the experience of various communities, we must ascertain how many patients are actually in treatment at any one time.

Turning first, again, to the midtown Manhattan study, we can compare it with the New Haven Study as follows (Hollingshead and Redlich, 1958):

TABLE 4

*Treatment Census (Age Inclusive), Prevalence Rates of
Midtown Outpatients (per 100,000 population)
by Type of Service with Comparable New Haven
Psychiatric Census Rates*

	Midtown (May 1, 1953)	New Haven† (Dec. 1, 1950)
Clinic	168*	67
Office	620**	157
Total	788	224

* Estimated by Midtown Study social workers to be about 95 per cent complete.

** Corrected by estimation for noncooperating therapists but not for underreporting by cooperating therapists.

† Estimated by New Haven investigators to be about 98 per cent complete.

Translated to a community of 50,000, at any one time we would anticipate that the clinic would have, in treatment, somewhere between 34 and 84 patients, providing that private psychiatric practice were well established in the area. In most rural Kansas communities, and in other areas of the country as well, mental health centers would carry practically

the entire outpatient load, however, since private treatment
resources are not readily available.

Or, to look at the entire question of treatment experience,
we might ask ourselves what percentages of the patients with
various degrees of incapacity are actually in treatment at any
one time? Again, we turn to the midtown Manhattan study,
and find the following figures:

TABLE 5

Home Survey Sample (Age 20-59) Impaired Respondents'
Distributions on Patient-history Classification by
Impairment Grades

	Impairment grades			
Patient history	Marked	Severe	Incapa-citated	Combined Impaired
Current outpatients	5.0%	4.0%	11.1%	5.4%
Ex-patients	18.3	22.6	24.4	21.3
Ever patients*	23.3	29.6	35.5	26.7
Never patients	76.7	70.4	64.5	73.3
N—100%	(219)	(125)	(45)	(389)

* It must not be inferred that respondents who were ever patients were
necessarily considered by study psychiatrists as being in an impaired state
of mental health. On the contrary, of the sample's 40 current outpatients,
19 were not so regarded, and of 182 ex-patients, 99 were not so considered.

With the leadership and encouragement of the National
Institute of Mental Health, and particularly Anita Bahn of
the Biometrics Section, efforts have been made in recent
years to establish psychiatric case registries. For example, in
Monroe County, New York, a case register has revealed the
following prevalences of psychiatric treatment (Gardner,
1963): In all types of psychiatric services, they discovered 850
individuals in psychiatric service as of January 1, 1960 and
an admission to psychiatric service during 1960 of 850 per
100,000 population. For outpatient services, referred to as
clinics in their study, 310 patients per 100,000 population
were inservice as of January 1, 1960, and 580 patients entered
service in psychiatric clinics during the year 1960. Trans-

lated to our population of 50,000, we might, at any one time, expect the clinic to be carrying a total caseload of 155 persons, and during the year, to admit 290 new patients.

What types of services do these individuals receive? Again, the information provided by a case registry, this time in Maryland, provides the most accurate data that we have at the present time for children's cases (Bahn et al., 1962). All children were estimated as being under treatment in outpatient facility for a mean of 2.8 months. However, almost 60 per cent of the patients terminated treatment within a month after admission, and by the end of six months over 80 per cent of the patients had been terminated. The expected deviation of treatment was found to vary by age groups, by sex, by race, and by location of the clinic, and by diagnosis.

The mean number of interviews for all cases was between five and six. The type of service varied markedly depending upon the diagnosis. For example, 40.5 per cent of psycho-neurotic disorders were treated, 30.7 per cent of transient situational personality disorders, 24.5 per cent personality disorders, 19.4 per cent of psychotic disorder, 12.7 per cent of brain syndromes with convulsive disorder, 7.3 per cent of other brain syndromes, 1.3 per cent of severe mental defectives, and 4.3 per cent of mild, moderate or other defectives.

Depending upon the location of the clinic, the mean number of months under treatment for adults varied from 3.2 to 4.7 months (Bahn, pp. 407-442). The estimated mean number of interviews for patients under 15 years was 2.8, and for those 15 years and older it was 4.0. The median number of interviews varied between three and five depending upon sex and diagnostic classification. The percentage of patients accepted for treatment also varied on the basis of sex and diagnosis; between 45.8 per cent and 71.4 per cent of admissions were accepted for treatment. For every disorder, patients who withdrew from clinical service with or without notifying the agency constituted the largest disposition category, accounting for two-fifths of the patients. One general conclusion of this study was that in Maryland, clinics played only a minor role for alcoholic illnesses and patients with degenerative disorders of the nervous system. A contrasting point of view is taken by the author who sees the length of service, together with the high admission, treatment, and improvement rates for the psychotic, as indications that outpatient clinics in Maryland played a significant role in the care of this group of seriously ill patients. About half of the involutional, affective, paranoid and schizophrenic reactions, and about two-fifths of other psychotic disorders are treated in the clinics—many of them for an extended period of time. Twenty-five per cent to 30 per cent of the patients in this psychotic group are referred to state hospitals for further care.

The picture that begins to emerge, then, is of an extremely diverse range of services offered to a very heterogeneous group of patients, with most of the therapeutic transactions being brief in duration and limited in number of contacts.

In 1962 the total number of clinics varied from a low of one clinic in the Virgin Islands, to a high of 363 clinics for New York State (U.S. Department of Health, Education and Welfare, 1962b). At that time there were 1,656 known outpatient clinics in the United States. Likewise, the total number of professional people working in outpatient clinics varied from a low of six in the Virgin Islands to a high of 5,137 in New York State. For the nation as a whole, there were 7,828 psychiatrists, 3,424 clinical psychologists, and 4,403 psychiatric social workers working in outpatient settings. However, about one-half of the psychiatric social workers and one-third of the clinical psychologists were employed full time in an outpatient clinical setting, whereas only about 12 per cent of the psychiatrists were employed full time.

Psychiatrists provided 96,310 staff hours per week; clinical psychologists, 67,697 hours a week; and psychiatric social workers 113,281 hours per week. During this same year, there were 2,211 psychiatrists working as trainees in outpatient clinics, 556 clinical psychologists, and 633 psychiatric social workers.

Also, the rates of patients in treatment or evaluation varied widely by geographic area (U.S. Department of Health, Education and Welfare, 1962a). Rates varied from a low of 157 patients per 100,000 population in the east-southcentral portion of the United States, to a high of 691 per 100,000 population in the middle Atlantic states.

The relationships between adult and child patient rates also varied in different portions of the country. For example, in the middle Atlantic states, the rate of treatment for children under 18 years of age was 894 per 100,000 as compared to 591 per 100,000 for individuals 18 years of age and over. In most of the areas, the relationship was reversed, with more adults being treated than children. This was most striking in the Virgin Islands, where 486 adults per 100,000 population were in treatment, as compared to 250 children per 100,000 population. For the total United States there were approximately 404 individuals per 100,000 in treatment in 1962, with rates of 403 per 100,000 population for children under 18 years of age, and 404 for individuals 18 years of age and over. The number of new admissions per 100,000 population for the United States averaged 160 per 100,000 population, with an average of 191 per 100,000 for the population under 18 years of age, and 143 per 100,000 for the population 18 years and over. However, these admission rates varied widely from a low (among states reporting complete statistics) of 22 per 100,000 for New Mexico, to 467 per 100,000 for Hawaii. Likewise, the number of patients under care per 100,000 population varied widely. The average for the entire country was 322 per 100,000 population, with 350 per 100,000 being under 18 years of age and 306 per 100,000 being over 18 years of age. The rates on clinics reporting complete statistics varied from a low of 43 per 100,000 in New Mexico, to a high of 1,165 per 100,000 for Hawaii, of total patients under care.

Now, all of these varying patterns of staffing and service are bound to affect the program that is developed by the staff of a new community mental health center. Whether these figures also reflect variations in prevalence and/or incidence of mental or emotional disorder is unknown at the present time. However, increasing knowledge about the interrelationship between the organization or disorganization of community life, and interaction between social process and interpersonal and intrapersonal development and functioning suggests that there may be significant differences in incidence, prevalence, and type of mental and emotional illness between various regions and communities, just as differences have been demonstrated on the basis of age, sex, socioeconomic background, and so forth.

The developing clinical program in the community must inevitably take into account the perceived needs of the community, as represented by the governing board of the mental health center. The perceived or recognized needs may or may not reflect accurately the problems of highest prevalence, but in a locally organized and supported mental health center must influence the development of the clinical program.[1] That is, the staff may have an interest in some special problem such as alcoholism or mental retardation, but if this is not seen as pressing or important or of high priority by the governing board of the mental health center, the staff often cannot develop an effective program in that area. One study of the staff and board attitudes concerning the priorities of

[1] A parallel in physical medicine comes to mind. Statistically, poliomyelitis has been a disease of only moderate public health significance, and yet has attracted public interest and found support far beyond its "real" significance.

various kinds of problems indicated that, contrary to frequent impression, staffs and governing boards do not differ significantly in their attitudes (Houda and Wiene, 1961). It was found that the staff and boards both gave high priority to the treatment of emotionally disturbed children and the caring for individuals experiencing their first mental or emotional breakdown. In contrast, they tended to give a low priority to the care of the mentally retarded child, to providing long-term intensive treatment, to conducting surveys of community needs, and to treating individuals who have previously been hospitalized.

Increasing attention has been given to the special social and technical problems involved in providing outpatient mental health services for lower-middle-class and lower-class socioeconomic groups. There has been general recognition by representatives of labor organizations that outpatient mental health services, as presently structured, do not adequately meet the needs of laboring-class individuals. Various factors relating to financing, accessibility, and treatment modalities have been recognized as important. For example, it is necessary that services be available at times other than during the normal working week if a significant number of hourly wage earners are to be offered services. While the white-collar and professional worker can find time free from his job to consult with the center during the day-time working hours, this is often not equally feasible for the blue-collar worker. Also, there has been increasing professional recognition that particular kinds of therapeutic skills, not emphasized in the "standard" treatment model, will be necessary to afford successful service to lower socioeconomic groups.

It is still difficult to assess what the long-range impact of the increasingly wide and sophisticated use of the tranquilizing and psychic-energizing drugs will have upon community psychiatric practice. Certainly, they have contributed to the increasingly short hospitalization of patients and their rapid discharge into the community. This is interrelated with the previously reported findings from the Maryland study, that many psychotic individuals are, in fact, being treated in community mental health centers at the present time. In practice there would seem to have been, in the judgment of the author, some lag in full utilization of medication in the treatment armamentarium of the typical community mental health center. Certainly, the degree of importance of medication in the treatment program of a community mental health center has definite implications for the design of the service, and the staffing pattern to be adopted. The best available facts concerning prevalence of mental and emotional disorder, professional and financial resources available for treatment services, and the "typical" type of treatment afforded in community mental health centers, would all suggest that the use of medication probably has an increasingly significant role to play in the community mental health services. To the extent that chemical modification of behavior becomes of increasing importance, so may the redefinition of many community mental health services as particularly medical, rather than social or psychological, services be forthcoming. It is preferable to view the medical, educational, interpersonal, psychoanalytic, communication, and sociological models of mental and emotional illness and treatment as complementary; but the agency of the future should be expected to integrate *all* of these insights into theory, practice, organization, and administration to provide treatment and preventive services at the community level.

SUGGESTED READINGS

Blum, R. H. & Ezekiel, J. (1962), *Clinical Records for Mental Health Services*. Springfield, Ill.: Charles C Thomas.

Confidentiality and Privileged Communication in the Practice of Psychiatry (1960). Group for Advancement of Psychiatry, Report No. 45. New York.

Gardner, E. A. et al. (1963), All psychiatric experience in a community. *Arch. Gen. Psychiat.*, 9:369-378.

Gardner, G. E. (1951), Appraising the contribution of the mental hygiene clinic to the community: I. In psychiatric treatment, training and research. *Amer. J. Orthopsychiat.*, 21:74-82.

Hollingshead, A. B. & Redlich, F. C. (1958), *Social Class and Mental Illness: A Community Study*. New York: Wiley.

Leighton, D. C. et al. (1963), *The Character of Danger, Psychiatric Symptoms in Selected Communities*. New York: Basic Books.

Reiff, R. & Scribner, S. (1963), *Issues in the New National Mental Health Program Relating to Labor and Low Income Groups*. New York: National Institute of Labor Education.

Rosen, B., Bahn, A. K., & Kramer, M. (1964), Demographic & diagnostic characteristics of psychiatric clinic outpatients in the U.S.A., 1961. *Amer. J. Orthopsychiat.*, 34:455-468.

Srole, L. et al. (1962), *Mental Health in the Metropolis: The Midtown Manhattan Study*. New York: McGraw-Hill.

XI

Intake and Evaluation

Intake is essentially an inappropriate term. It emphasizes the transitional nature of the transaction by which the individual is "taken into" the clinical facility. As such, it underlines and reinforces the dichotomization between the treatment setting and the community as a whole. So many of our efforts in recent years have been directed to breaking down distinctions between the treatment institution, as an agent of the community, and the community as a whole, that it is unfortunate that no one has come up with a more popular euphemism to describe the process of initial contact with the patient.

Because of the very real logistical problems in providing services to the ill segment of our population, the whole process of admitting a patient to a treatment facility has become imbued with considerable feelings of urgency, importance, anxiety, and guilt on the part of the clinicians involved. Rather elaborate discussions of this process of initial interview and admission to the agency have, in many instances, contributed little to our understanding of the process. Much of the literature has been devoted to discussing various kinds of "intake policies," all of which have been attempts to deny or push away the logistical realities, to allow mental health centers that are not comprehensive to function comfortably, and to protect and isolate the staffs from the reality of community needs as well as their own personal and professional inadequacies involved in meeting these needs.

The only type of "intake policy" that really makes a great deal of professional and social sense, is the open intake policy. That is, the center functions to meet the needs of the ill and troubled people in the community, and can only meet these needs if these persons are seen promptly for initial interview, evaluation and treatment.

Some agencies have experimented with accepting new patients or clients only by referral from other community caregivers (Rooney and Miller, 1955). An approach of this nature may be seen as having considerable rational underpinning, for the following reasons: when the new team of three professional people moves into a community of 50,000 people, it faces an enormous backlog of problems and cannot, in all truth, hope to directly meet the needs of all these troubled people. In the decades before this new specialized facility was available, with its highly trained and expensive staff, many persons in the community were attempting to meet, and partly meeting, the needs of mentally and emotionally ill individuals in the community. To be entirely honest, the staff of the mental health center should say to these people, "We cannot and do not want to assume responsibility for all the ill persons in the community. Rather, an important part of our function is to help you become more effective in your continuing attempts to assist them with their problems." With this approach, accepting intakes by referral from these caregivers serves a very useful function in terms of reinforcing their importance in the community; affording an opportunity to modify their attitudes and to provide them with new information concerning mental and emotional illness; and also in providing a readily accessible path by which patients seen for consultation or evaluation may be referred back to community caregivers for continuing treatment.

Probably the least rational and most destructive approach is the "intermittent intake." In this system, the staff members

allow the waiting list to build up to the point where they feel
that they have a year or two of work ahead of them, and then
close down intake while waiting to complete the evaluation
for these individuals.

The waiting list, itself, is probably the greatest psychological bugaboo to all of us working in community mental health
settings. A long and guilt-provoking waiting list seems to
be the albatross hanging around the neck of each community
mental health practitioner.

Is the waiting list inevitable? General experience would
seem to indicate that it is, but perhaps this should be qualified. It is important, first of all, to pinpoint one unconscious
psychological distortion that frequently creeps into this
problematic matter of the waiting list. That is, a patient or
family does not become ill exactly at the point at which they
are seen in intake, placed on the waiting list for intake, placed
on the waiting list for evaluation, or placed on the waiting
list for treatment. The mere fact of being on a waiting list
does not make them any sicker than they would have been
if they were in the community and *not* on a waiting list. In a
very real sense, having a few of the many community people
who are known to be ill, on a waiting list for some kind of
service or other, is undoubtedly a step in the right direction.
However, because each of us is subject to pressures toward
perfectionism, punished frequently and irrationally by our
unconscious superegos, we cannot avoid the feeling that by
keeping someone on a waiting list, we are performing a disservice. We are confronted here, as everywhere in community
mental health practice, with the irreconcilable conflict between the immediately attainable and the distant ideal.

Nor, in the judgment of this author, is the waiting list an
inevitable feature of community mental health practice. It
is unavoidable only if the staff of the community mental
health center adheres to some model, ideal, or desirable
evaluation and treatment procedures, and does not accept the

logistic realities of the situation at hand. Faced with thousands of casualties, it would be inappropriate to adopt surgical or medical procedures that could, at best, provide care to only a few hundred. Rather, the traditional medical approach to such a battlefield or epidemic problem would be to adopt that form of treatment which offers the most likelihood of affording some material assistance to the greatest number of individuals. One would not be satisfied with intensive and prolonged treatment that provided a very great improvement for only a small number of the casualties, nor would one approve of a treatment that was so superficial and incomplete that it afforded no substantial help to any of a large number of casualties "treated." To phrase this another way, the basic problem is how to "cut the coat to fit the cloth," and still have a garment that provides some degree of warmth against the elements. If the mental health center staff tries to see all potential patients, without providing any amount of substantial service to any, not only do they perform an injustice to the patients, and to themselves, but, ultimately, to the community, because they do not stimulate motivation for providing additional resources which would afford appropriate services to troubled citizens.

If, on the other hand, the community mental health center staff pursues a policy of excellence and perfection in the face of an extremely heavy demand for services of moderate adequacy, it falls into the trap of meeting its own professional and narcissistic needs at the expense of those patients who are unable to get any treatment at all, and at the expense of the community which establishes and supports the center to provide generally available service of moderate adequacy.

It would seem desirable to have some logical frame of reference upon which to make decisions concerning the immediacy of intake, and to delay intake for those patients in whom a spontaneous or socially engendered remission seems likely. It would also seem desirable to have some procedure that could be used by persons conducting the intake interview, to assist them in making judgments concerning emergencies, needs for hospitalization, and so forth.

Most essential is the mandate, which would be supported by most experienced community clinicians, that all patients must be seen within 48, and preferably within 24, hours following the time of their initial contact with the clinic. Only by this initial interview, whose goal it is to delineate the urgency of the problem and to decide whether an outpatient evaluation is indeed appropriate, can the staff be assured of assuming a role that is both humane and scientific. Some of the criteria that should be taken into account in the intake process are as follows:

1. How great is the *subjective discomfort* experienced by the individual? If it is severe and constant, this would tend to give a higher priority to a prompt evaluation and treatment program, whereas, if it is minimal or mild, a lower priority might be assigned. The judgment of subjective discomfort is a complex, multifactorial, intuitive decision made by the clinician and can only offer any hope of accuracy if it is arrived at through face-to-face interviews.

2. The amount of *discomfort or harm inflicted* by the patient is a crucial variable. Not only must we consider if the patient is possibly suicidal or murderous, but the intake should also ascertain whether the patient is likely to be physically assaultive toward some individual in his environment. Particular attention must be given to the well-being of children, especially in view of the increasing prevelance of the "battered child syndrome." The psychotoxic effect of the individual should also be studied: how many individuals in the immediate environment of the potential patient are being subjected to serious emotional trauma as a result of the patient's illness, while the patient may be awaiting evaluation and/or treatment?

3. *The trend of the illness or psychosocial decompensation*

should be carefully evaluated. If it is rapidly progressive, a very high priority should be given to immediate evaluation and planning for treatment. If, on the other hand, the trend of the illness or of the psychosocial decompensation seems to be improving, it would seem desirable—in the interest of economy and in the face of the logistic realities—to allow a period of observation to see if the client is able through self-healing, or through nonclinical assistance, to return to his state of premorbid adjustment.

4. *Chronicity* should be given a considerable weight in determining the evaluation priority for a prospective patient. For example, an illness that is only a few months in duration should have a higher priority, in all likelihood, than should an extremely chronic illness.

5. *The degree of community concern* about the prospective patient is particularly important. For example, if the community or agents of the community are fearful of, and punitive towards, the individual because of his disturbed behavior, this would be an indication that evaluation and treatment should be attempted as soon as possible. On the other hand, if the community is generally accepting of the individual, and perhaps even supportive of him, this would allow somewhat more leeway in planning for evaluation and treatment.

6. The person conducting the intake interview must decide *how crucial it is that the prospective patient maintain his coping ability.* For example, a wife with young children, or a child patient, would have a higher priority on the basis of a need to maintain adequate coping ability. On the other hand, a self-sufficient bachelor or maiden, living alone, might have a relatively low priority in terms of immediacy of maintaining coping ability.

7. The *attitudes of significant relatives* must be critically appraised. For example, if total rejection will inevitably result in a continuing development of the illness, or psycho-

social decompensation occurs, evaluation and immediate institution of the treatment program is desirable. If, on the other hand, significant relatives are supportive, accepting, and willing to maintain helpful relationships with the patient despite symptomatic behavior, the mental health center staff has wider discretionary rein.

8. The patient's *motivation for treatment,* while difficult to assess, will naturally enter into judgments concerning the urgency of need. Our general model holds that typically, the longer a patient suffers with his illness, the greater will be his motivation for treatment. While this may be a valid hypothesis, it will not hold if, while his illness is steadily worsening, he is subjected to harassment, rejection, or punitive behavior on the part of clinicians. For many patients, an active attempt by clinicians to reach out and be helpful *despite* the patient's attempt to reject such help and to sabotage a treatment relationship, can be genuinely useful in reinforcing his motivation for treatment. In other clients, attempts to override fearfulness and rejection of treatment by being "giving," will only arouse suspicion and further retreat from, and diminution of motivation for, treatment. The judgment as to which approach is likely to be more useful must rest with the individual clinician, based upon his training and prior experience.

Some mental health centers may wish to develop an intake planning schema and attempt to apply some of the above judgments in order to formulate a priority list for patients awaiting treatment. Such a schema could be used as a self-training and inservice training device, rather than as a rigid instrument. That is, it may have some usefulness in helping the staff attempt to evaluate certain variables upon which hinge decisions concerning evaluation priorities; but it should not be used as a substitute for human judgment and reason based upon experience.

The unconscious model upon which the community mental health center bases its entire clinical program will have an all-pervading influence upon the intake and evaluation process. For example, if the group consensus is that mental and emotional illnesses are chronic conditions, strongly conditioned and even "caused" by antecedent events that occurred mainly within the first five years of life, and which may be corrected only by prolonged psychotherapy involving the use of interpretation, transference, and analytic methods, the model for evaluation becomes a very stereotyped and demanding one. The evaluation must involve, if this model of treatment is used, an extensive associative anamnesis, psychological testing, and a very detailed and elaborate diagnostic synthesis, with particular importance being given to psychosexual fixations, the relationship between regressive aspects of personality dysfunctioning and aspects relating to personality fixations, the impulse defense configurations, and so forth.

If, on the other hand, the treatment processes are seen as being predominantly crisis-centered and as helping an individual cope with interpersonal and/or intrapersonal dilemmas in his current life situations, the evaluation process must be focused much more upon current reality, and upon a much more careful investigation of current familial interactions, social functioning, job performance, and interpersonal behavior patterns of the individual. Such a focus is much more likely to be current reality- and ego-centered; with goals that deal more with restoring the individual to his "premorbid state of functioning," rather than attempting to make him a "mature, genital individual."

An alternative model for treatment is to provide symptomatic relief. A careful evaluation of the symptomatic constellation, including the degree and extent of autonomic nervous system dysfunction accompanying the psychological disequilibrium, would have heavy importance. Use of medication, supportive parameters in the interpersonal transaction between patient and clinician, and a focus upon return to the premorbid level of adjustment would all have validity in such a system.

The *triage* or battlefield model for evaluation and treatment has some usefulness, in view of the epidemic nature of mental and emotional illness. In mass casualty situations, an attempt is made to sort casualties into three general categories. Those who are so seriously wounded that they have a very low survival rate, with or without treatment, would be sorted into an untreated category, and an attempt would be made only to relieve their pain and to provide humane care during their terminal hours. At the other extreme, those patients who have a very high likelihood of surviving without treatment would be sorted into a category in which they would be left mainly to fend for themselves and to provide self-help, or to receive assistance from nonclinical personnel. The intermediate category whose survival rate would be materially enhanced by treatment, and morbidity significantly reduced by treatment, would be the focus of the major share of attention on the part of clinicians. In the community mental health setting, a case can be made, at least at the present time, for the application of a somewhat similar model to the evaluation and treatment process.

THE EVALUATION PROCESS

The evaluation of the psychiatric patient should be a functional rather than a ritualistic endeavor. The function should be to assist the staff of the mental health center in understanding the patient's illness and in planning a treatment program that affords optimum likelihood of success. The proper aims of the evaluation process do not include narcissistic enhancement of either the individual or the agency, nor competition with rival agencies to determine which is the "best" or "most thorough" agency.

The issue of relevance must firmly be held in the foreground in structuring, implementing, and appraising the usefulness of an evaluation system. Many systems for very careful and exhaustive collection and ordering of data have great usefulness in the training process, and in clinically-based research involving small numbers of patients. However, it is often difficult to see how the bulk of the data is used in arriving at decisions that influence, in any significant way, the choice or application of treatment, or the eventual outcome of the treatment process.

There are some issues that have particular relevance for the community mental health practitioner, and which should be answered by the evaluation process. Some of these are as follows: Will the patient get well by himself? Will the patient probably not get well either by himself or with prolonged treatment? How much effort, time, and skill is the treatment process for this patient likely to entail? Is this patient inflicting emotional trauma upon other persons in his environment? That is, is he "a carrier" of emotional and mental illness? Is this patient likely to physically harm himself or other individuals in his environment, particularly children? Is this person a crucial attitude-setter in the community, or related in a significant way to such a person, so that successful treatment of his illness may result in a constructive modification of community attitudes concerning mental illness and mental health services? Should this patient be hospitalized immediately? Can this patient be safely and effectively evaluated in an outpatient setting? Can he be successfully and safely treated in an outpatient setting? Are there organic determinants involved in the illness?

Prognosis, of course, is always extremely difficult to evaluate, and yet it is involved in many judgmental priority decisions that are made by community mental health staffs in their day-by-day functioning, and upon which they base decisions concerning whether individual patients will or will not be offered treatment within the context of the community. In other words, part of the battlefield model of evaluation creeps in here. Some of the variables that have been reported in the literature as having a relationship to prognosis are as follows:

1. *Premorbid adjustment.* The general consensus is that the better the premorbid adjustment, the better the prognosis for remission either with or without treatment.

2. *Duration of symptoms.* The longer the duration of illness, the poorer is the prognosis, either with or without treatment, for return to premorbid or healthy adjustment.

3. *Precipitating event.* The general impression is that the more severe and prolonged were the stressful event or events which immediately preceded the onset of the illness, the better is the prognosis for remission of symptoms with treatment and/or removal of the precipitating stresses.

4. *Affect.* In general, clinicians tend to associate blandness or flatness, or marked inhibition of the range and intensity of the affective life of the individual with a poor prognosis—whereas free affective reaction to psychic conflict is equated with a better prognosis.

5. *Motivation for change.* This is an extremely difficult variable to evaluate, but—often because of narcissistic needs of the therapist—it may assume an inordinately large role in judgments concerning prognosis and acceptance for treatment.

6. *Ego-strength.* This is a multifactorial, intuitive appraisal which can be made by the experienced clinician with some degree of reliability and validity. In general, great ego-strength has been associated with a good response to treatment and poor ego-strength with a poor response to treatment.

7. *Psychological mindedness.* This variable, also because of narcissistic needs of clinicians in many cases, receives a great deal of attention. Often it only amounts to the

clinician's asking whether the patient is like himself, in which case he feels more able to establish rapport, to empathize with and to assist the patient.

8. *Likableness.* This is seldom given much importance in determining prognosis, but has considerable relevance if we assume that processes are occurring outside of the therapeutic situation which also influence the adjustment of the individual. If a person is likable or able to establish some kind of good relationship with other individuals, despite psychiatric illness, he is much more likely to be met in his social and interpersonal world with support, friendliness, and reassurance than is one who is unlikable or irritating or disagreeable in some way. Only if we somehow encapsulate the treatment process from the real world of the patient can we leave out such variables as this in appraising prognosis.

9. *Psychosexual fixations.* It requires a clinician with considerable depth of training and breadth of experience to be able to make really valid and reliable judgments concerning psychosexual fixations. However, in the literature we tend to find the occurrence of many oral mode fixations associated with poor prognosis; whereas, at the other extreme, primarily phallic-oedipal fixations have been associated with a generally good prognosis for remission with psychotherapy.

10. *Faith in psychotherapy.* Generally, the clinician tends to equate great faith and belief in psychotherapy with good prognosis. I am sure that clinicians with considerable experience, however, have found that this is not always true, and that patients who are openly scornful of, and resistant toward, psychotherapy can often benefit most from it—just as the vociferous agnostic may become the most rabid church member.

11. *Externalization.* In general, if a patient tends to see his problem as largely or entirely external to himself, and uninfluenced by his own behavior, feelings, and attitudes,

prognosis for improvement, either with or without psychotherapy, is relatively poor.

All of these attempts to judge and assign weights to the
various aspects of prognosis may be incorporated by some
mental health centers into a Prognostic Rating Schema which
may prove itself useful as an inservice training or self-develop-
ment tool for the clinician desiring to improve his own
prognostic skill.

CRITERIA FOR HOSPITALIZATION

One function of the community mental health center, even
in its clinical program, is to attempt to educate other community caregivers toward a more sophisticated and effective
functioning with mentally and emotionally ill clients. It is
particularly crucial, in terms of the overall community
mental health program, to assist these other caregivers in
understanding some of the criteria which call for hospital
evaluation and treatment of mentally ill persons, as opposed
to the usual outpatient evaluation and treatment.

The attached work sheet may have some usefulness in
assisting relatively inexperienced intake workers at a mental
health center in evaluating the need for hospitalization, so
that immediate psychiatric consultation may be obtained; it
may have even greater usefulness in communicating with
other community caregivers about criteria for hospitalization. In other words, it would be advantageous for all concerned, if the community mental health center could convince physicians, ministers, welfare workers, etc., that they
have, at their disposal, a logical, consistent, and systematic
way of determining an individual's need, or lack of need
for immediate hospitalization. Such a check list form may
serve a useful role in terms of writing reports to other community caregivers, and allowing for mutual discussion of the
individual case, which will hopefully upgrade the quality of
diagnostic and management skills.

(For Experimental Purposes Only)
CRITERIA FOR HOSPITALIZATION

	Weight	No 0	Slight 1	Moderate 2	Extensive 3
1. Is there evidence of active suicidal preoccupation, in fantasy or thoughts of patient?	2				
2. Have there been recent suicidal attempts or active preparations to harm self (i.e., buying gun, etc.)?	4				
3. Has the patient threatened to hurt someone else physically?	2				
4. Have aggressive outbursts occurred toward people?	4				
5. Have aggressive outbursts occurred toward animals? Objects?	2				
6. Has antisocial behavior occurred?	1				
7. Are there evidences of impairment of such functions as reality assessment, judgment, logical thinking, and planning?	1				
8. Does the patient's condition seem to be deteriorating rapidly despite supportive measures?	1				
9. Are these physical or neurological conditions which require the rehabilitation facilities of the psychiatric hospital?	2				
10. Do pathological, social, or family situations exist that require isolation of the patient?	1				
11. Are emotional contacts of the patient so severely limited that the "push" of a structured hospital program may be helpful?	1				

Score of 12 or more: Hospitalization for evaluation mandatory.
Score of 8-11: Outpatient evaluation probably feasible before deciding on hospitalization.
Score of 7 or less: Outpatient treatment probably feasible.

SUGGESTED READINGS

Ackerman, N. W. (1958), *The Psychodynamics of Family Life*. New York: Basic Books.

Bahn, A. K., Chandler, C. A., & Lenikan, P. V. (1962), Diagnostic characteristics of adult outpatients of psychiatric clinics as related to type and outcome of services. *Milbank Memorial Fund Quart.*, 15:407-442.

Korner, H. (1964), Abolishing the waiting list in a mental health center. *Arch. Gen. Psychiat.*, 121:1097-1100.

Wilder, J. F. & Coleman, M. D. (1963), The "walk-in" psychiatric clinic: some observation and follow-up. *Int. Journal Soc. Psychiat.*, 9:192-199.

XII

The Treatment Program

In 1960, of 211,085 patients terminated by mental health centers reporting to the Outpatient Studies Section of the Biometrics Branch of the National Institute of Mental Health, only 75,517 received diagnosis *and treatment* services; 81,658 received diagnosis only, 16,297 psychological testing only, 37,613 other services only. Of 105,525 patients under eighteen years of age, only 25,362 were afforded diagnosis *and treatment* services; of 105,560 patients eighteen years and over, 50,155 were afforded diagnosis and treatment services. In Table XIII of the same publication (National Institute of Mental Health, 1961), of 25,297 patients under eighteen years of age treated, on whom condition and diagnosis at discharge was recorded, 18,739 were felt to have been improved after treatment. Of 49,881 persons eighteen years and over receiving treatment, on whom condition at discharge was recorded, 31,929 were felt to have been improved after treatment.

In other words, of all patients only 36 per cent received diagnosis *and treatment* services; 38 per cent diagnosis only, and 8 per cent psychological testing only; whereas 18 per cent received other services only. Only 23.1 per cent of patients were seen for ten or more interviews. The percentage of patients receiving treatment services for those under eighteen years of age varied from a low of 7.2 per cent for cases of mental retardation, to a high of 47.7 per cent for psychoneurotic disorders; 33.1 per cent of psychotic disorders, 19.9 per cent of brain syndrome, 38 per cent of personality disorders, and 40.4 per cent of transient situational personality disorders in children were offered treatment services.

In contrast, for adults the percentage of cases receiving treatment services ranged from 19 per cent for mental defectives to a high of 59.3 per cent for personality disorders; 48.1 per cent of brain syndrome patients received treatment services; 58.7 per cent of psychotic disorders, 59.1 per cent of psychoneurotic disorders, and 54.3 per cent of transient situational personality disorders were treated.

From looking at these statistics alone, then, it would seem that only a small portion of the total caseload of outpatient psychiatric centers is offered formal treatment services, and that far from all the patients offered treatment are felt to be improved by the staff. It would seem that from the flood of patients descending upon psychiatric outpatient and community mental health services, only a minority enter the pipeline referred to as "treatment," are afforded services which are generally quite brief in duration, infrequent, and only partially successful.

If, indeed, such a treatment program materially or greatly benefits a large number of its recipients, we might be inclined to think that psychiatric outpatient treatment is extremely effective, that the majority of the patients seen are not particularly ill, or that most psychiatric illnesses are self-healing and undergo spontaneous remission.

In truth, good judgment and experience would seem to support none of these contentions. Most psychiatric illnesses seen in community mental health settings are moderate to severe in intensity, relatively chronic in duration, do not seem to improve spontaneously in the majority of instances, and are treated by procedures that are neither particularly efficient nor effective.

In other words, once again we are confronted with the

broad gap between the ideal and the present reality. The present reality is that most of the individuals seen in public outpatient settings, including community mental health centers, receive precious little assistance in the formal treatment program. Is it really worth the effort? Clinicians, both in and out of community mental health settings, repeatedly ask this question of themselves and each other. So few of the patients pass through the treatment services, and treatment is so abbreviated, that it is difficult for professional people to believe that patients *have* been materially benefited. A large amount of this fretting is solid, realistic, humanitarian and scientific concern for suffering people. A not insignificant portion of it, however, may have a more neurotic basis. In medicine, and in disciplines that sometimes unconsciously model their identity upon medical practice, the highest prestige and greatest rewards have gone to the individual treating the most seriously ill persons. It is striking how much manpower, energy, scientific know-how, and money are expended helping people prolong their lives to the extreme limits of human durability; while in contrast, how little effort, time, money, and knowledge are expended at the other end of the life cycle in prenatal, perinatal, and postnatal care for the newborn. An aspect of this culturally-conditioned snobbery rubs off on the mental health professions, and we tend to ascribe the greatest importance and highest prestige to treatment activities that expend the most time and energy on the most seriously ill and least treatable cases with the poorest prognoses.

Is it more useful, glamorous, and prestigious to cleanse minor wounds and bandage them so that they will not develop infections, or should we allow them to fester until it becomes necessary to perform surgical incisions and drainage because an abscess has resulted? This is not a new dilemma for medicine; it was not too long ago that we felt, for example, that in trauma, infection was an inevitable and desirable process. As a matter of fact, suppuration was once referred to as "laudable pus," in the belief that infection and pus formation were essential parts of wound healing. It is only in relatively recent times that we have decided that in trauma, early cleansing, debridement, provision of adequate drainage when necessary, and the stringent use of aseptic technique can and will prevent infection in the majority of wounds.

We are just at the point in psychiatry where activities that are aimed at intervention at moments of crisis, and provision of services that are essentially designed to prevent further regression in personality functioning and to forestall deterioration of social and psychological adjustment, are beginning to acquire prestige. In American society, for example, public health activities involving the prevention of disease have, to this day, not acquired the aura of prestige typically given to the essentially curative procedures, which are ultimately much less efficient, effective, and economical than are preventive activities.

MODELS OF TREATMENT

It is not the intention of this book or this chapter to scrutinize the treatment process as it is practiced by the individual clinician. The actual process is little affected, in the final analysis, by the milieu in which it takes place, and we must assume that the trained practitioner brings with him to a community mental health setting, a relatively standard set of skills and techniques appropriate to his profession.

However, it is less usual for the clinician to have always before him, a clear idea of the model upon which he bases his treatment activities. Thus, some general discussion of various models upon which treatment is predicated may be in order at this point.

I. The Classical Medical Model

In its truest form, this model presupposes the action of some noxious agent upon the healthy organism, resulting in symptoms and signs as the expression of a disease process. It also assumes that these symptoms and signs have characteristic clusters that are referred to as syndromes, which may be utilized in the process of diagnosis. By eliciting and studying symptoms and signs, delineating the syndrome, and making a diagnosis, a rationally based treatment plan can then presumably be designed. The treatment plan must take into account the causative agent—whether it be infectious, toxic, degenerative, metabolic, traumatic—the effect it has had upon specific tissues and organs in the body, the resultant derangements in physiological and biochemical functioning of the organism, the characteristic course of the illness over time, and what is known about specific corrective measures for the illness. Diagnosis, therefore, has a central place in this whole scheme of things, and is an essential part of the treatment process. Underlying this entire model are concepts of disease specificity, syndrome uniqueness, rational and specific treatment, and predictable course of illness.

II. The Psychoanalytic Model

The psychoanalytic model is rooted in the biological and medical tradition. It assumes specific causative agents, in this instance assumed to occur in the interpersonal milieu of the patient as a child, influencing the development of a "personality organ system." This process is subsumed under the general title of "psychosexual development." It applies essentially the embryological model to personality development, and assumes that certain toxic events at particular points in the development or unfolding of the personality have specific and relatively predictable consequences.

In such a model, the concept is—as in the classical medical

model—that one must diagnose the particular syndrome, and by virtue of that diagnosis be able to retrospectively discern the agent or agents leading to such a syndrome. The model further holds that there are specific treatment processes by which the "psychological clock" may be turned back, by which personality development may be in effect undone and redone, and the embryology of personality development gone through again by the intensive treatment process of psychoanalysis.

III. The Interpersonal Model of Treatment

This general model maintains that interpersonal events are important not only in the development of the personality, but also in day-by-day personality growth, and functioning. It agrees with the psychoanalytic model to the extent that the earlier a crucial interpersonal event occurs, the greater is its effect on personality development likely to be. However, the interpersonal model is based much more on learning theory, rather than on a developmental or embryological theory. The treatment process is partly a relearning of appropriate modes of interpersonal behavior, to some extent by "corrective emotional experience" in a structured situation, rather than a process that attempts to essentially excise diseased personality "tissue," undo personality development, or remake the personality.

IV. Communication Theory

As applied to treatment, this theory would hold that behavior is essentially a communication from the individual to others in his environment concerning his needs, fears, conflicts, and aspirations. It would maintain that behavior persists so long as it is effective in achieving results that tend to meet the needs, or the perceived needs, of the individual, and that it is discontinued when it is no longer necessary to meet these needs, or results in consequences which are not desired by the person. In other words, symptomatic behavior is abandoned when it is no longer necessary for the communication of deeply felt needs, fears, or conflicts to significant other persons in the environment, or when symptomatic behavior brings additional or incidental consequences which are more undesirable than are the desired consequences.

V. The Social Model

This model emphasizes that the individual is always caught up in a matrix of interpersonal and social transactions, which defines for him the limits of acceptable behavior, acceptable modes of meeting his needs and expressing strivings; defines for him the rules of a wide variety of relationships; and even defines expectations for the roles of sickness and health for the particular society. Treatment based on this model would emphasize the transactions occurring between the patient and his peers as being of equal or even greater importance than transactions occurring between the patient and the treating individual.

Now, these vignettes of the various models that may underlie treatment activities are oversimplified and overdrawn. Also, as one explores them carefully, it becomes apparent that none of them is really mutually exclusive of any or all of the others. In any one illness, one can often find aspects that can best be described and understood following one or another of these models. We are hopefully past the day when each system, and splinter subdivisions within each major system, shall have their champion or champions, and shall be at war with all the others. The experienced, mature, well-trained, competent clinician must be conversant with, and able to use appropriately, each of these models of treatment in governing the therapeutic program set forth for the individual patient.

As a matter of fact, if there is any one thing that characterizes treatment programs as they develop in comprehensive community mental health centers, it is their eclectic
nature, the vigorous and unbridled mingling of different
schools to develop an amalgam of treatment activities having
very diverse theoretical bases, but all of which are used to
help varying patients.

It would be appropriate at this point to look at some of
the specific activities, in addition to individual psychotherapy,
that are practiced to an increasing degree by comprehensive
community-based mental health centers.

Family Therapy

Many authors have advanced theory and practice in family
diagnosis and treatment in the last decade. As one moves
towards the family model it becomes increasingly necessary
to add to and enrich the psychoanalytic model of treatment
with insights based upon communication theory, sociology,
interpersonal theory, and small group dynamics.

To quote Nathan Ackerman,[1] the family therapist attempts
to alleviate emotional distress and disablement and promote
the level of health of the family group and its individual
members by

> . . . solving pathogenic conflict and anxiety within the matrix of
> the interpersonal relationship; by raising the level of mutual comple-
> mentation of emotional needs; by strengthening the immunity of the
> family against critical upsets; by enhancing the harmony and balance
> of family function; by strengthening the individual member against
> destructive forces, both within him and surrounding him in the family
> environment; by influencing the orientation of family identity and
> values toward health and growth.

While based in traditional psychodynamic theory concerning the practice of psychotherapy, family therapy emphasizes a number of attributes and techniques used by the
therapist that are ordinarily not prominent in individual

[1] Mimeographed paper.

psychotherapeutic practice. In such a relationship the therapist tends to be more active, to be more emotionally involved with the family group, to serve as a personal and active instrument of reality testing, to serve as an educator and as a model of mentally healthy functioning within the family, and to support active coping and resolution of conflict within and between individual family members.

GROUP PSYCHOTHERAPY

The initial promise of economy held forth by group psychotherapy is seldom realized in practice. However, there are many other justifications for the use of group techniques in community mental health practice. The adolescent individual, and to some extent the young adult, is often particularly amenable to group psychotherapeutic techniques. In fact, for certain adolescent behavior problems group therapy is clearly the technique of choice, and individual psychotherapy is fraught with such technical hazards, that it is seldom successful.

The treatment of alcoholic problems, and perhaps even more importantly, the treatment of the wives of alcoholics, can proceed with at least equal and probably greater success in group therapy settings.

For the chronically and seriously ill individual discharged from the hospital into the community, group therapeutic methods offer, in addition to insight-giving and supportive elements, crucial assistance with resocialization and interpersonal "training." As a matter of fact, in perhaps any patient group where stigmatization and exclusion from social processes is a predominant feature of the psychosocial decompensation—such as aging persons, welfare clients, illegitimately pregnant women, sexual offenders—group techniques may have a special justification as being especially useful in the treatment program of the agency.

Group techniques also have a wide variety of usefulness in

portions of the agency program that are not strictly therapeutic. For example, human relations techniques for school
teachers; process-oriented learning experiences for school administrators; parent education groups, in which all or a part
of the members may be the parents of emotionally disturbed
children; groups made up of young married couples that
discuss the adjustment problems of early married life, without the development of any overt marital problem or symptoms being necessary as a ticket for admission—these are
only a few of the additional uses to which group techniques
may be put.

DAY HOSPITALS

Increasing interest, experience, and research on the role
of the day hospital have demonstrated that this kind of
program may serve as a substitute for full-time hospitalization for children and adults, and as a supplementary parameter to outpatient therapy. Much of this information and
experience is still in the formative and developmental stage,
has not been written down, but has been reported at such
meetings as the First National Day Hospital Workshop in
Kansas City in September of 1963. The general consensus
is that day hospital treatment is an efficacious and practical
way of meeting the treatment needs of many individuals.
For example, experience at the new Fort Logan Mental
Health Center in Colorado had revealed that for every
patient needing 24-hour hospitalization, two and one-half
patients can be treated entirely with day hospital treatment.
Participants at the First National Day Hospital Workshop
believed that at least 50 per cent of the state hospital patients
could be treated successfully in day hospital settings. Experience in the San Diego Day Hospital indicated that 65
per cent of the individuals treated in their day hospital had
a psychotic diagnosis, while about 50 per cent of the total

group had a diagnosis of schizophrenia. At the San Diego facility, the mean length of stay was 57 days.

In England, planning under the National Health Service had been predicated on the feeling that 20 to 30 patients seems to be the optimum size for a day hospital. Extending the day hospital beyond this, even with the establishment of multiple units, is thought to weaken some of the unique effects of small group functioning that the day hospital maximizes. England is planning, at the present time, to establish 20 day hospital slots for each 200,000 population. Fort Logan Mental Health Center, in contrast, is planning 40 day hospital slots for every 75,000 population.

The San Diego Day Hospital has had experience with over 700 admissions since its establishment in 1960. In 6,000 square feet of space, it treats about 30 patients on any one day, with a staff consisting of 3 psychiatrists, 2 clinical psychologists, 1 research psychologist, 2 psychiatric social workers, 1 occupational therapist, 1 psychiatric nurse, and 2 psychiatric technicians. Modalities include milieu treatment, individual and group psychotherapy, family psychotherapy, psychodrama, and chemotherapy. Seventy-five per cent of their patients receive drugs at one time or another.

General experience has indicated that the day hospital has offered a reasonably economical type of treatment, and should definitely be included in planning for comprehensive community mental health services. Staffing problems are somewhat less acute with day hospitals than for the usual outpatient settings, since only 30 per cent of the professional staff hours in day hospital settings are accounted for by psychiatrists, psychologists, and psychiatric social workers. In other words, psychiatric nurses, aides, and ancillary therapists of various types can be effectively used within the day hospital setting.

PSYCHIATRIC UNITS IN GENERAL HOSPITALS

While the establishment of special treatment units for psychiatric patients in general hospitals is not a new concept, it is only in recent years that such units have become widely distributed geographically. Experience indicates that 20 to 24 beds is an ideal size for a psychiatric unit. The authors of the American Psychiatric Association's publication entitled *Standards for Hospitals and Clinics* say, "Any community that can support a good 150-bed or larger general hospital can usually support a psychiatric service in their hospital." General experience indicates the desirability of having a hospital-employed social service department, at least on a part-time basis, and available psychological services, occupational therapy, and activity therapy are essential elements of the program. The American Psychiatric Association recommends the following minimal personnel rates for psychiatric units in general hospitals: 1 registered nurse per 5 patients, 1 attendant per 4 patients, 1 occupational therapist per 100 patients, and 1 activity therapist per 30 patients.

The authors of another publication (Bennet et al., 1956) state that 3 or 4 attending psychiatrists can adequately handle a 30-bed psychiatric unit and still each have a half day free for office practice. However, they recommend that there should be two psychiatric residents and an intern available, and that the psychiatric unit should give psychiatric nursing instruction to student nurses. The authors emphasize that it is not feasible or financially practical to set up a unit smaller than 10 beds. It is their impression that 80 per cent of the patients recover fully or partially, and that only 5 to 10 per cent must be transferred to a state hospital for further treatment. They, as other authors, agree that there are some fee collection problems, but emphasize that the units are financially self-sustaining and have the highest percentage occupancy of any unit in the hospital.

The usefulness of psychiatric units in general hospitals, despite the relatively small number of beds, is pointed out by the fact that while 2 per cent of the beds in general hospitals in Michigan are psychiatric beds, these beds handle more than 51 per cent of all the mental patients and 62 per cent of all the first admissions during the year (Waggoner, 1962). In 1958, tax supported mental hospitals discharged 150,000 patients while units in general hospitals (which comprised 2 to 3 per cent of the beds) discharged 180,000 patients.

In planning for the comprehensive range of services in the community mental health center, therefore, it seems very desirable to plan for the development of at least a 20-bed psychiatric unit in a local general hospital, which will have open staff privileges, and which can be used by psychiatrists on the community mental health center staff, as well as psychiatrists in private practice in the community.

NURSING HOMES

Nursing homes have a very real contribution to make to a comprehensive community mental health program. Some states, among them Kansas, have developed programs that actively encourage local nursing home care of discharged but not fully recovered mental hospital patients. For example, in Kansas there are 450 nursing homes, with a total of 12,869 beds, of which 1,447 are occupied by patients who have been discharged from state psychiatric hospitals. Of the total number of patients, 2,282 have diagnoses of mental, psychoneurotic or personality disorder; 2,432 have diseases of the nervous system and sensory organs, and 2,959 have ill-defined conditions of senility.

It would be desirable, in developing the comprehensive community program for mental health services, therefore, to have adequate nursing home beds available to provide for sheltered living situations for those with chronic emotional illnesses who cannot be rehabilitated sufficiently to assume independent or semi-independent living within the community. The mental health center can play a useful role in providing consultative services to these nursing homes.

NIGHT HOSPITAL

The night hospital serves the same general functions as does the day hospital in bridging the gap between full-time hospitalization and full-time community living. Certain patients are employed during the daytime, but need the treatment activities and structure of a hospital during the evening hours. The patient can sleep in a secure situation and can participate in milieu and recreational therapy; upon prescription, he may avail himself of group and individual psychotherapy facilities.

THE WEEK-END HOSPITAL

This is a creative innovation that has been tried in some locations such as the VA Hospital in Topeka, Kansas. It provides a useful type of service in sparsely populated areas, where day and night hospital programs are not suitable for many individuals. There would seem to be a fair number of persons who are able to function fairly adequately vocationally and interpersonally during the week, but who could derive great benefit from the structured milieu and group psychotherapy programs offered in a week-end hospital. This type of arrangement is perhaps particularly suitable for the working male, whose self-esteem and social identity are so much dependent upon his vocation that it would be desirable to assist him in continuing to work as much as possible.

VOCATION REHABILITATION AGENCIES

State vocational rehabilitation agencies, assisted by federal monies and consultation, have developed active rehabilitation programs for the physically ill, and are increasingly expanding their efforts in the direction of rehabilitation of the mentally retarded and mentally ill. State vocational rehabilitation agencies may directly operate such facilities as "half-way houses" and sheltered workshops; may provide vocational rehabilitation counselors to work with the state hospital staffs and/or with the community mental health center staffs; or may provide consultative and financial assistance to the local agencies in providing local vocational rehabilitation services, such as counseling, half-way house activities, and sheltered workshop programs.

A sheltered workshop is a small nonprofit enterprise operated for the primary purpose of rehabilitating persons who have either physical, mental, emotional, or social handicaps or disabilities. There have been sheltered workshops in various locations in this country for many years, but it has only been in the past decade or so that these enterprises have expanded to the extent that a sufficient body of experience is now available to point up their potential usefulness in a program of comprehensive community mental health services. The intent of the sheltered workshop is to provide remunerative employment in a setting approximating normal industry as closely as possible, so that the workshop may serve, wherever possible, as a bridge leading the worker-clients back to normal vocational life at that time when they are medically, psychologically, and socially ready for such job placement. In addition to this transitional role, sheltered workshops can, and probably should, provide a situation of continuing employment for those who are unable to participate on the free job market, and who can make a significant vocational contribution only in a sheltered and protected environment.

In order to best serve the needs of psychiatric patients, the workshop should have close administrative and functional ties with a community mental health agency, where ongoing consultation and involvement with psychiatrist, clinical psychologist, and psychiatric social worker are possible. Only by such a teamwork relationship between the clinician and the rehabilitation personnel, can the needs of a full range of patients be met with optimum effectiveness.

CLUBS FOR FORMER PATIENTS

Social clubs for patients returned to the community from state hospitals have been developing under a variety of auspices for a number of years now. They help patients relearn social skills, and provide support and reassurance to the patient who is often estranged from the community following his hospitalization.

Some of these clubs have been developed with links to specific hospitals or community treatment settings. However, it has seemed desirable, insofar as is possible, that they be developed as autonomous units which tend to encourage the eventual assimilation of the patient into other social groupings in the community, rather than foster his continuing participation in a "patient subculture."

The citizen volunteer can be particularly useful in this effort. A number of mental health associations directly provide volunteer services to chronic mental patients who have returned from the state hospital to the community; while the final success of these programs has not been evaluated, this seems to be a direction that should be explored in any community program for comprehensive community mental health services.

FAMILY CARE

Many patients no longer need full hospital treatment nor day or night hospital facilities, but do need continuing care, supervision, and support. If relatives or friends are not available, or if therapeutic reasons contraindicate return to relatives, family care may be given in private homes which are selected, supervised, and subsidized by the parent agency, which can either be the public mental hospital, local county welfare, or voluntary health and welfare agency. Such home placements may serve either as a transition towards independent community living, or as a more or less permanent sheltered living situation, as an alternative to continuing hospitalization.

HOME AND EMERGENCY TREATMENT

Relatively little has been done systematically in the United States in terms of providing, on a community-wide basis, readily available emergency and home treatment services. Experience with this modality of treatment in the Netherlands, justified originally on logistical and reality grounds, has shown itself to be a very flexible and effective therapeutic modality. In the Netherlands, for example, there is a team of mental health personnel, under psychiatric direction, which is available on a 2-hour basis for mental health emergencies, often in collaboration with law-enforcement officers.

Research explorations of such an emergency and home treatment mode of service have been conducted at the Boston State Hospital and the Boston Municipal Hospital Center in this country. Experience to date has indicated that a readily available emergency psychiatric service will materially prevent the accumulation of a long waiting list, will afford effective treatment for many patients, and will forestall hospitalization for some individuals whose condition would otherwise deteriorate.

COUNTY WELFARE

The role of the county welfare department has primarily been one of dispensing financial and other material assistance to poor and needy individuals, but this situation may be changing in our country. In some states, such as Kansas and Minnesota, the county welfare departments have been assigned roles in preadmission evaluation of patients being admitted to the state hospital, and in the preparation of social casework histories for hospital use. County welfare offices have also been assigned responsibility in these states for providing supervision, upon request, of patients returning to the community. Such arrangements, where staffing patterns make this practical, may also provide casework for significant relatives, both prior and subsequent to the individual's return home, in order to modify the pathogenic milieu which may have precipitated the patient's illness. In another section of this book, potential modes of interrelationship between the community mental health center and the welfare department are explored.

Summary

If any summary is possible from such a wide-ranging survey of the many aspects of a comprehensive clinical program for mental health services, it would be that a community mental health center does not exist in isolation, but should be nestled in, and enmeshed with, the whole matrix of other helping agencies, all contributing towards meeting the needs of mentally and emotionally ill individuals in the community. We have barely scratched the surface, as far as innovation and experimentation are concerned, and the years ahead provide rich opportunities for us all in terms of exploring new patterns of service for ill and troubled people.

Suggested Readings

Bahn, A. K. & Thrall, C. A. (1964), Inpatient psychiatric outpatients and change with treatment. *Ment. Hyg.*, 48:217-242.
Friedman, R. T., Becker, A., & Weiner, L. (1964), The psychiatric home treatment service: preliminary report of five years of clinical experience. *Amer. J. Psychiat.*, 120:782-788.

Greenblatt, M. et al. (1963), *The Prevention of Hospitalization*. New York: Grune & Stratton.

Katz, M. M. & Cole, J. O. (1962), Research and drugs and community care. *Arch. Gen. Psychiat.*, 7:345-359.

Linn, L., ed. (1961), *Frontiers in General Hospital Psychiatry*. New York: International Universities Press.

Mechanick, P. & Nathan, R. (1964), The community psychiatric hospital. *Arch. Gen. Psychiat.*, 10:284-291.

Nielsen, J. (1963), Home visits by psychiatrists. *Compr. Psychiat.*, 4:442-460.

Psychopharmacology and community mental health services. Supplement to Sept. 1962: *Amer. J. Pub. Health*, Vol. 52.

Scarpette, F. R. et al. (1964), Problems in a home care study for schizophrenics. *Arch. Gen. Psychiat.*, 10:143-154.

Stubbs, T. H. (1960), Progress of intensive treatment program for brief general hospital treatment of the mentally ill. *J. Med. Assoc. of Georgia*, Vol. 49, No. 1.

XIII

Persuasive Communication

By Susan Ellermeier *

Why on earth is this chapter included in a book on community psychiatry? And what possible use can it be to you, practicing in a community mental health center?

There are many reasons for including this chapter, and its usefulness to you will depend on how you wish to utilize it— on the application of the principles of persuasive communication to your interactions with co-workers, newspaper reporters, community groups and leaders, community caregivers, and the amorphous "general public."

Just what is persuasive communication, and how is it different from ordinary conversation? Persuasion is not *different*—it's a *tool* used in communicating. It's not a hard-sell promotion gimmick—it's a way of making your words work effectively for you. You use it every day to alter opinions and produce desired reactions, perhaps without realizing it. Everyone does. We live in a world of persuasion; gone are the authoritarian ways of getting people to work with and for you. Now you *persuade* people, by making sure that they know and understand what you're communicating, and

* Miss Ellermeier has been serving as the Informational Council for Kansas Community Mental Health Services for the past four years. The following two chapters on persuasive communication and mental health education were contributed by Miss Ellermeier at the personal request of the author who hopes that they will inspire self-examination and further study for those community mental health practitioners who are devoted to communicating ideas in an effective and functional manner.

by knowing yourself that they must *believe* in your communication before they can act favorably on it. You define a task or your goal; you explain your motives; you relate the message to the public you want to reach. You are positive, but not pushy; you bring the goal into the familiar, the concrete; and you state clearly the benefits of the desired action. In short, you instill a person, your audience, or the public, with the desire to work with you in meeting your goals.

For example, chances are you don't order Junior to mow the lawn or clean the garage. You probably point out to him that this is a job that needs to be done, and persuade him that it's in his own best interest—and, secondarily, in the interest of the family—that he do it. You may even reinforce his motivation by pointing out several advantages which will accrue when he completes the job.

And you don't tell your wife that you can't afford a second car, and let it go at that. You *persuade* her that a second car would be more trouble than it's worth—that the capital outlay, maintenance and operating expense would demand cutting down on other expenditures. You explain your ideas to her, and bring her over to your way of thinking.

Employers use persuasive communication. Very seldom will a conscientious boss order that a task be done. It's more likely that he'll explain to his employees that the task is important, tell them why it is needed and what use will be made of the work, and point out benefits to the agency and the employees. He instills them with the desire to go along with his way of thinking, and to get the job done.

Teachers use persuasion. So do lawyers, hard-headed businessmen, parents, lobbyists, and leaders of some "cause." And so can you, if you want to.

But do you want to, or do you feel that this whole chapter is a pitch to change you into a salesman? Why should you bother with persuasive communication? You're in a community to do a job—not to manipulate people into thinking the way you think, or acting the way you think they should.

Persuasion won't do these things—but it will help you to communicate effectively with important groups and individuals.

Do you feel that persuasive communication is beneath you, demeaning, that it will injure your prestige and self-esteem? Persuasion is, and will do, none of these things. It's familiar to you in your personal and family life, and it doesn't hurt you there. It is equally harmless—and as potentially useful to you—in your business dealings as it is in your home life.

Or do you reject the use of persuasion in your business world because it's useless in therapy? Persuasion may very well have no place in your work with patients, but it can be a very effective tool in your work with others. However, you must be convinced that persuasion can be useful, learn to use it, and apply it every chance you have.

For example, you may want to start a program of consultation to school personnel. Will you simply assign the task to a staff member and assume that he will carry out the program thoroughly on his own initiative? Or will you fully explain to him why you think it's important to consult with the schools? Will you tell him about the goals and possible results of the program, about the importance of consultation and his contribution to it, and about the benefits of this program to school personnel, students, the mental health center, and to himself? If you want the interest, sincere involvement, and desire to carry the program out well, you will probably do the latter—and *persuade* your staff member to consult with the schools.

Or let's suppose that you need volunteers to work in a day treatment program you're establishing. Do you go to the local mental health association and ask for them? Well, yes—but the *way* you ask for help has a great bearing on

the kind and amount of help you will get. You can tell
the association about the program, the patients in it, and
the goals and advantages of treatment in the community.
This is good—it's important too. But what have you done
to make people *want* to volunteer their time?

In addition to telling people about the goals and advantages of day treatment, you'll want to discuss concretely,
the kind of work a volunteer would be doing, explain why
his help is needed, and point out the benefits of working
in the program. It may take more time, but you'll end up
with volunteers more genuinely interested in the welfare of
patients and the success of your program. Active participation augments and reinforces persuasive communication.
People must be given concrete ways by which they can help
improve the mental health of the community. And the
more personal a message is, the more effective it is likely to
be.

Or let's suppose that your mental health center is not
receiving any referrals from the physicians in town, and you
want to do something about it. Will you speak formally at
the next meeting of the local medical society, and berate
members for not using your services? Not if you're smart.
Instead, do a little informal fact-finding work on your own.
Go to see the physicians—in their offices—not to find out
what the problems are, but simply to get acquainted. In
your conversation, you may find that the older, more well-
established physicians don't have patients with mental health
problems—but they see many people who are alcoholic, or
are frequently absent from work. Perhaps the younger practitioners suspect you of practicing socialized medicine, or of
wanting to "take over" their patients. There may be some
who don't even know that the center exists. Whatever the
problems are, you'll have a better idea of what you're up
against—and you'll have an opening for discussing the services and goals of the mental health center, and for indirectly

persuading physicians that you can help them in treating their patients. You'll probably be asked to speak to the medical society too, as physicians become aware of the potential and actual help you can be. And encourage the physicians in thinking that the idea to utilize the services of the mental health center was theirs—not yours. Publicity or recognition is not what you're seeking.

You're holding a conference on aftercare for ministers in the surrounding ten counties, and you think it's worth a pretty large story in the daily newspaper. You go to the editor and tell him so—and then wonder, after the conference is over, why your shining efforts went unheralded. Can it be that you've violated one of the basic principles of the newspaper world? Remember that the editor and reporter are professionals in their field, just as you are in yours. *Never* misjudge their ability to evaluate news by telling them that your story is important to the paper and the community. If a story has news value, the editor knows. Don't try to club him into running it. The most effective approach to take is to write the story yourself (but keep in mind that, if used, it will undoubtedly be rewritten), and then go talk to the editor about your conference. Tell him when and where it's going to be, who's coming, what you plan to do, and what you see as the results of the conference. Your object is simply to keep him informed—not to talk him into running prepublicity or covering a session of the conference. If the editor *is* interested in a story, you can give him yours as a "fact sheet," and invite him to attend the conference. Don't push. Remember that what you see as *important* may not be *interesting* to the audience you are trying to reach.

All of these examples illustrate, in varying degrees, some of the principles of persuasive communication. First you must know your audience (which may be a roomful of people, or just one person) as completely as possible. Are they

already familiar with the subject you're going to discuss? If
so, how much do they know, and what more do they need
and want to know? You must establish communication on a
common ground, so that your audience understands, without
question, your stated goal and your reasons for communicating it.

And remember—what you think they *need* to know may
not be what they *want* to know. Don't get caught talking to
local law enforcement officials about the causes of mental illness, when they'd much rather be hearing about procedures
of referring a patient to the mental health center, or about the
special handling of alcoholics. It's a waste of your time and
theirs, and—worse yet—you've lost an opportunity to *really*
communicate.

What is the attitude, background, interest, and experience
of your audience? Will it be favorable to your message, or will
there be resistance? If you anticipate resistances or fears,
either spoken or nonverbal, they must be overcome or your
message—and your goal—will not be received.

If your audience is a group or organization, you must know
the accepted way of dealing with it. In some cases, a group
approach is best; in others, you'd be better off talking to
individual members. Your message must be appropriate to
each group—what is persuasive to one may be seen as chal-
lenging or threatening by another.

If your goal is abstract, make it concrete. Make it familiar
and specific to your audience. Relate your goal to the interests of the audience. Bring it "close to home." Give
examples, and dramatize your ideas.

Your listeners will want to know *why* you are speaking to
them (in effect, what your angle is), and what benefits they
will derive from listening to you (what's in it for them).
Even if they don't verbalize these questions, you must answer
them.

And, aside from the content of your message, what do

people hear? If they agree with your message, it probably comes through relatively intact. People tend to select communications that are favorable or that agree with their predispositions. But if they disagree or are neutral, they can generate a lot of "internal static" which prevents even the simplest, clearest message from getting through and producing the desired effect. An audience that's undecided about your message will probably ignore it, unless communications about it are highly available to them. Those who disagree with your message will tend to misperceive and misinterpret it in such a way as to make it compatible with their prior convictions.

Intelligent people tend to be more influenced by logical arguments in persuasive communication—and they tend to be more critical. Persons with low self-esteem are more predisposed to persuasion, and tend to respond quickly to gain the approval of the communicator.

Communications are most effective when they tell people what they want to hear. But if the goal of your persuasive communication is to change opinions and attitudes, you must offer a strong incentive for bringing about an acceptance of the new opinion you propose, and for rejection of the old. The content of your message may be learned, but it will not be accepted without adequate motivation—social approval, safety, or similar "reward." An appeal to fear, or a threat, is not effective in creating and sustaining a new attitude unless that threat is minimized and you can reassure your audience and alleviate its anxiety. Don't provoke anxiety without offering "a way out," or the power of your threat will be lost. Your audience will reject your statements, become aggressive, or develop a new defensive avoidance to what you say.

Remember that any time you communicate with people, there's going to be a loss of information, and misunderstanding. Thus, your message should be simple and redundant.

If there are two contradictory "sides" to your message, it is generally more effective if you present both sides to a more educated audience, and only one—the argument you support —to the less educated. In the long run, presenting both sides of the argument is usually more effective when your audience is exposed to subsequent contradictory communica- tions, or when the audience initially disagrees with your communication. When your audience agrees with you, and is not exposed to contradictory communications, it may suf- fice to present your side only. But facts alone are not enough in persuasive communication. You must explain, define, and interpret them. Make the facts meaningful to your audience.

Several studies on communications efforts have been made to determine the relative effectiveness of placing major argu- ments at the beginning or the end of the communication. These studies have shown conclusively that neither method is invariably effective—effectiveness depends on the condi- tions in which the communication is presented, the pre- disposition of the audience, the type of material presented, and so forth. In general, it is usually effective to begin with major arguments when the audience is not interested or not highly motivated to accept your communication. If your audience is attentive, familiar with, and concerned about, your communication, incentives are usually increased when the strong argument concludes the communication. In either case, state your conclusion explicitly—especially if it deals with complicated issues.

Another stumbling block to persuasive communication— one which you must anticipate—is that people probably do not see you the way you are. They may have preconceived, stereotyped, distorted expectations of mental health profes- sionals. Does your public "see" the psychiatrist as aloof, imperturbable, introspective? Is he truly judgmental, critical of all communications and behavior? Does he leap to "ob- vious" conclusions which are not so obvious to the un- initiated? And the clinical psychologist—is he cold, analytical, unfeeling, ungiving, self-centered? What about the social worker—a thin-lipped, scurrying, nosey do-gooder?

Perhaps *these* expectations are not typical of your community, but others—equally distorted—may be. One thing you can anticipate, pretty much at face value, is that you will be seen by the "business world" as being impractical, definitely not production-oriented.

And don't assume that the community supports you and the mental health center wholeheartedly. Even though the center may be financially supported through local funds, psychological support may be nonexistent or negative. And even though your professional colleagues extol the benefits of psychiatric treatment in the community, important members of *your* community may privately think it's much better to isolate the mentally ill, and may be biased and hostile toward your efforts to carry out a comprehensive program.

How can you cope with this mass of unfounded, but nonetheless real, negative attitudes and misperceptions? Don't discount them as being biased or unfounded. Even though completely groundless, these expectations exist and have a powerful influence on all your communications. If your audience sees you as being knowledgeable and intelligent about your subject; if you are seen as an "authority" or "expert"; if you are admired, sincere, trusted—then your communications will have a greater effect. If you have the approval of respected community leaders, are an effective speaker representing a well-regarded community agency, without a deliberate intention to manipulate, then your influence upon your audience will be more positive, and the audience will be more receptive to your communication. But if you are not viewed in all these favorable lights, what can you do about it?

One important step is to *keep visible*. When invited, speak to community groups, even though you're not sure your presentation will have an impact. Let people see you and talk informally with you. If you're not an experienced public speaker, become one. Join the local Toastmasters group, or participate in speech training seminars offered by national drug companies and other organizations.

Call upon other caregiving professionals and agencies routinely—law enforcement officials, medical personnel, ministers, social service agencies, school personnel, and others. Find out what kinds of services they offer, and what kind of assistance they would like. It may be that some of these caregivers see you in opposition or competition with them. In that case, do *not* make suggestions. Don't offer to work with them or tell them how you might help. Don't argue with them, or try to convince them that you're one big happy family of helping services. Any "agreement" you gain in this way will last until you walk out the door. Instead, appreciate their programs, understand their problems (if they have any), and tell them a little about your program. Try to see things from their points of view.

As time goes on—as you maintain your contacts with these caregivers—you will undoubtedly discover ways in which *they* can help *you,* in providing needed services for a particular patient, or in working with you to establish a new service, such as a nursery school for children of working mothers. When you demonstrate that you value their professional competence, and that you can work together as professionals in your respective fields, they will be much more likely to come to you with specific problems, and to want your help and suggestions. It's a simple principle—when you trust others, they trust you.

Call upon key people often—city administrators, physicians, judges, community leaders, newspaper editors, and others. Initially, you won't have a clearly defined goal— except to get acquainted and to *mutually* communicate. Let the others do most of the talking. Be a good listener. Find out the nature of prevailing community attitudes toward the mental health center (and perhaps toward yourself, as a mental health practitioner). Find out what these people expect from the mental health center. Are their expectations reasonable? Or are their demands too great, and have they built in unseen frustration and dissatisfaction? Are they accepting, supporting, or antagonistic and biased? If there is no prevalent community attitude (or attitudes) which reveals itself through your conversations with these people, widen your scope of contacts. There are other opinion setters —perhaps not in official administrative or caregiving positions—in every stratum of society. Find out who these people are, and get acquainted with them. Don't be a back-slapper, but do make yourself known to them, and make it clear that they are known to you. These people are vitally important to your program. They must have given at least tacit approval to its establishment, and it's up to you to strengthen that toleration into endorsement.

Don't overestimate the power of the mass media (particularly newspapers) in informing people or in effecting any kind of a desired change. The media are important, but they do not wield the kind of influence that many attribute to them. Media can support social action, and they can confer status on projects by publicizing the efforts and participation of community leaders. But they don't directly change individual beliefs, attitudes, and behavior.

Consider, too, that when you communicate your story to the editor or reporter (taking the newspaper as an example), it may be misunderstood, misconstrued, or substantially edited. The headline assigned to your story may not accurately reflect its content. Newspapers try to be fair and honest in their reporting, but they are not above mistakes— and they must often cut your story or assign it to a back page when space is limited.

Then consider who receives your communication, once it is printed or broadcast. Studies have indicated that there is a direct relationship between educational level and media readership: more educated people rely on print media, and the less educated on sound and picture media. More perceptive people tend to glean more information from the mass media. The more influential members of a community —the opinion-setters—are more exposed to mass communications than are members of the community at large; and the media help present material from which the opinion-setters develop their expertise and form opinions.

Thus it can be seen that those to whom your mass media communications are most available and meaningful, are those who influence the opinions of others. This is not to say that others don't read or hear your story, but it is not likely to produce the desired effect *until* it has been reinforced by one or more recognized opinion-setters—people who are trusted, and who are in better positions to receive more communications than average members of the group.

Ideally, you should communicate with the opinion-setters in two ways—through your direct contacts with them, and through the mass media. Each communication reinforces the other, and the opinion-setter (through his contacts with the group for which he *is* an opinion-setter) reinforces the effect of your mass media communication with a larger public. It's a complex network of formal and informal communications, but once it's working for you, you'll be able to reach a large number of people effectively and meaningfully.

When you're communicating with a group, remember that individual members are strongly influenced by, and adhere to, the group's standards and expectations of conformity; the more each member values his membership in the group, the more his personal attitudes and opinions will resemble the group's consensus, and the higher his resistance will be to your communication—especially if that communication conflicts with the group's standards. Group leaders will appear to be less anxious to conform to group standards, but in practice tend to conform more to those standards because of group expectations. An analysis of the group's influence on individual members' opinions is vital in attempting to change opinions or produce desired action through communication.

Whenever possible, encourage recognized community leaders to participate in specific projects, and to repeat your communications to their reference groups. This has several advantages: their public support of community projects will encourage general community support; reformulation of your ideas in their own words reinforces their own acceptance, and it has a greater influence on their reference groups than the same communication from you.

One of the principles of persuasive communication, which has been discussed in several ways, is: Don't approach organized groups or the "community at large" (through the mass media) too soon. Attend and speak at meetings, of course, *if you're asked*. But don't initiate speaking engagements. At first, establish a trusting relationship with key people in the community—caregivers and opinion-setters. A formal presentation to a group is often seen as a "bill of goods," and a story in one or several mass media can too easily be ignored. A "shotgun" approach is seldom effective.

Meet people. Go to their offices. And don't wait until you have need of their help with specific projects. Through your informal, nondemanding contacts, you will build a foundation of trust, acceptance, and support from important community leaders.

In all your contacts and transactions with individuals and groups, be open and trusting. If people feel that you are confident, they will have more confidence in you.

Don't challenge or criticize. Be positive, encouraging.

When you ask for suggestions, be willing to consider and use them. Show respect for the opinions of others.

Do keep a planned goal uppermost, but be willing to change the means of reaching that goal if necessary.

Present only one idea at a time. Don't overwhelm people with a mass of projects or suggestions. Allow time for a new idea to be accepted. Don't push it.

Cooperate in planning meetings, conferences. Help people. You'll have built up some good "social credit" which you may want to use later.

Praise the efforts of others, if you can do it honestly. Don't be lavish, or confide to others that the idea was poor to begin with. Be sincere in your appreciation.

When others work with you in a project, share the credit. Don't hog the spotlight, and don't adopt an advertising or self-seeking attitude.

Seek to *inform* people—not to *educate* them.

Another important principle of persuasive communication is—*communicate*. Keep it up. Don't stop. Don't initiate an all-out campaign for a psychiatric unit in the local general hospital, and then drop from sight when the goal is accomplished. Keep people informed about how the new unit is working out, how many people were seen there last month, what the average length of stay and per day costs are. Keep people informed about *all* activities of the mental health center.

And if your communication efforts are aimed toward producing a change in attitudes, or toward effecting a desired action, don't be discouraged if you can't see immediate results. You may not want them; a quick overt response may be made without inner conviction. But, on the other hand, don't discount altogether, early responses to your communications; public expression of agreement with you will influence inner acceptance.

Repetition is one of the key factors in persuasive communication. For every exposure your audience has to communications that contradict or compete with yours, the lower will be its desire and ability to retain your message—and reten-tion is necessary if the goal of persuasive communication is to be met. Opinion change depends on retention of your communication, as well as on the motivation to accept it.

There are several media through which you can communi-cate. This chapter has discussed, by and large, just one—direct, face-to-face contact. This is, of course, the most effective. You can see your audience, and it can see you. You can fairly well determine your audience's reactions; you can alter your message if it seems advisable, repeat your ideas, and answer questions. But don't overlook the wide variety of other media which exist—or potentially exist—in your community. They can be broken down into three general categories; print media, broadcast media, and visual media, which, in some cases, overlap the first two categories. (These media, and suggestions for using them, are discussed in the following chapter.) How you use these media will depend on your knowledge of working with them, the specific publics you want to reach, and the goals of your communica-tions. Some can reach your entire community; some, your general area of the state; and others, specific groups or publics within your community.

One general thing can be said for them all, however. Through them, you can communicate *persuasively*. If you know the background, attitudes, and interest of your audi-ences; can tell them, in language they can easily understand, the things they need and want to know; and can point out benefits to them for receiving and accepting your communi-cation, you're well on the way. By communicating *persua-sively* and consistently, you can present your message in such a way that your idea is not only accepted, but desired and acted upon effectively.

SUGGESTED READINGS

Berelson, B. & Steiner, G. E. (1964), *Human Behavior: An Inventory of Scientific Findings*. New York: Harcourt, Brace and World.

Hovland, C., Janis, I., & Kelley, H. (1953), *Communications and Persuasion*. New Haven: Yale University Press.

— et al. (1957), The order of presentation in persuasion. In: *Yale Studies in Attitude and Communication, Vol I*. New Haven: Yale University Press.

Partridge, H. (1944), *How to Make a Speech and Enjoy It*. National Publicity Council for Health and Welfare Services, New York.

Visual Persuasion—The Effect of Pictures on the Subconscious, McGraw-Hill Series in Marketing and Advertising, 1961, New York.

XIV

Public Information and Mental Health Education

By Susan Ellermeier

Whether you are aware of it or not, your mental health center has an *image* in the community.

You may think "image" is a word, a thought, for a mental health professional to avoid; that it's Madison Avenue "shop talk"; a fancy word implying that something undesirable and untrue is being foisted upon, and blindly accepted by, an unsuspecting public. This is simply not so. "Image" is a perfectly acceptable word which, in the simplest sense, means the *personality* of a successful organization, business, or agency; or the public's spontaneous idea of a company. It is the *total* relationship of a company to its community. There are no successful organizations in existence without an image. Even the inconspicuous grocery store around the corner, and the local weekly newspaper, have images. On the other hand, did *Collier's* have a consistent image? Did Edsel?

Many things contribute to the image of a company—the appearance of its building and its furnishings, the type and quality of its product or service, the impression of its staff members and employees on the community, the contacts the company has with its various publics, the effectiveness of the service in meeting a legitimate need, and so forth.

You may not think that building or considering a corporate image is a particularly appropriate role for a mental health center, but be assured that it is the single most important aspect of your program which you must appraise and with which you must work. It is the foundation upon which all your services will be established, offered, and used. The center's image in the community affects the confidence placed in it by the public, the patient referrals you receive, the credibility and acceptance of your communications efforts, and the welfare and mental health of the community served by the center. You cannot ignore it; nor can you disregard its effect upon everything you do, or plan to do.

And, just as the image affects everything done by the mental health center and its staff, so do all the activities of the center, its board, and its staff affect its image.

Just what is the image of the mental health center in your community? Is it seen as an agency just for the poor, or for those with only mild emotional disturbances? Is its function understood by the community, or are people under the impression that the center will eventually replace other, established community services? Are your services fully used and appropriately requested? Or do people come to you for services that are not offered? Or are there too many demands placed on the agency and individual staff members? Can the staff and board interpret the agency's functions to the community, and answer questions about the center? What is the public's reaction to the physical facilities of the center, its staff members, volunteers, board members? Does the board adequately represent all different segments of the community served? What sort of relationships do you have with key groups in the community—caregivers, opinion-setters, professional and civic organizations, community decision-makers, newspapers and radio stations? Is the mental health center a subject of familiarity, controversy, indifference, hostility, fear, prejudice? Are you receiving legitimate referrals from all reasonable sources? If not, why? Is the community really aware of the mental health center, its function, its philosophy? Are expectations of service too great, or wrong?

Answering questions like this can help you evaluate the community's image of the mental health center. Perhaps none of these examples would be appropriate for your mental health center or community; perhaps all of these questions, and many more, need to be answered in order for you to fully appraise the community's idea of the center. These questions are offered only as samples, to guide you in finding the type of facts you need to know.

Where can you go to find these facts, to answer these questions? Right in your agency is the best place to start. Call the center from an outside phone; listen critically to the sound of your receptionist's voice. Is it pleasant, calm? If Dr. So and So is not in, does she tell you where he can be reached, let you know when he's expected to return, or offer to return your call when he's in the office? Does she give the kind of information that's needed, correctly, without confusing or overwhelming the caller?

What do your files show? Does your correspondence indicate a large number of complaints, incorrect referrals, criticisms? Do minutes of board meetings indicate real information-sharing, or are they bogged down with routine business?

Do you have a file or scrapbook of newspaper clippings? What is the attitude of the press? Is there any way you can find out how many people read those stories, and how much they learned and retained?

What sort of people make up your waiting list? How many? How long must people wait for service?

Talk to people. Why aren't you getting referrals from the schools? Why was your budget request cut this year? Why does the county welfare department make so many incorrect referrals? Why are the logical sources of support indifferent? Why don't your staff's public speaking engagements get the results you hoped for?

When you've answered the questions you need to know, and studied the facts you've uncovered, you will have analyzed many things—the people you serve, actually and potentially; your staff and board, and the ways they contribute to the image of the center; the services you offer, and the way those services are received and used; and the public's reaction to the entire program of the mental health center.

Once you feel you know the image of the mental health center in the community, what are you going to do about it? Do you like it, and will you plan to go along with things the way they are? Or are there misconceptions, negative attitudes you would like to change? Do people really understand the function and philosophy of the center?

You can make the image of the center whatever you want it to be, if you plan work for it consistently—both inside and outside the agency. One of the most important and effective (if used persuasively) tools you can use in working toward a successful corporate image of your center is that of communication.

There are two major and specific parts of your overall communication program. One is public information about the agency, and the other is mental health education. In many instances, the goals and methods of these two communications programs are the same, or very similar. Informing important publics about the functions, services, and purpose of the center often increases their understanding about mental health and illness; working with others in an educational program about mental health can, if you wish, also serve to inform them about the mental health center.

Mental health education and public information often cannot be separated from each other in communications efforts. And many times both are an integral part of your professional consultation activities with other community caregiving persons and agencies.

Public information is more than the simple dissemination

of information. It is an integral part of administration, programming, and policy-making of every public agency. It is
not a crusade to get people "stirred up" about something.
It is the *earning* of support, and the knowing how to use that
support to effect necessary changes.

An effective public information program must first have
a goal. Your goal may be to increase patient referrals from
the other helping agencies in the community, to change
negative community attitudes, to establish a new needed
service in conjunction with the mental health center, to
amend or pass a new law during the next legislative session,
or to insure adequate financial support. Whatever you set
as your public information goal, don't just "pull it out of a
hat" because you think it's worthwhile, or can be achieved
easily, or because it's something you can work on if and when
you have spare time. Public information is not a "catch as
catch can" program. It is one of the most vital services you
offer because it will directly influence whether or not people
understand, accept, and use your services—correctly—at the
time they are needed.

Go back to your image-defining survey. Perhaps it showed
that your relationships with schools, welfare agencies, and
other caregivers are not really *bad*, but that they're not so
good either. Or perhaps the ministers and physicians don't
really understand what services you offer, and so haven't
been calling on you for help. In that case, you'd want to
strengthen your relationships with these groups, and inform
them of your services. You might also want to increase your
consultation time with them, or help them determine correct
referrals to you.

Perhaps your waiting list showed a large number of former
hospital patients who need structured aftercare services.
You might want to work closely with a church or civic group
to establish a social club for these people.

Perhaps your fact-finding uncovered a surprising amount

of community indifference; people knew about the mental health center, but they hadn't thought about it much one way or the other. In that case, you'd want to familiarize them with the functions of the mental health center, the services it offers, and its philosophy.

After your public information goal has been defined, you then must plan ways of informing the relevant publics so that they will know, understand, believe in, and act favorably toward meeting that goal. This part of the public information program raises two very important questions which must be answered before any planning or action takes place. First, precisely *who* is the public you want to reach? Second, *how* do you go about informing it?

There are literally dozens of publics upon which you will want to focus many or all of your public information efforts: your governing board, the professional staff and other employees of the mental health center, your patients and potential receivers of your services, the community decision-makers, the group opinion-setters, the other caregiving agencies and professionals in the community, various professional and civic organizations, your professional colleagues, the state mental health authority, taxpayers and voters, and a host of others.

And what about the people who make up these publics? How old are they? What are their attitudes toward the mental health center and toward the mentally ill? How much do they understand? What do they need to know? Will they resist your message? How much money do they make, and how do they make it? What is their educational level? Are their occupations medicine, law, industry, teaching? Is the group one that might have a "vested interest" in mental health services, such as the mental health association, a church group, or the PTA? Is it a group that has no obvious tie to mental health services, such as a fraternal organization, or a women's club? Is it openly supporting, politely indifferent, or hostile? The more you know about the publics whose cooperation you seek, the more successful your public information efforts will be.

And the second big question you must be prepared to answer is how to effectively and efficiently reach these defined publics with your message. A very important point must be made here: a good public information program involves much more than publicity in the recognized media—radio programs, newspapers, and so forth. Traditional publicity should be used too, when it is indicated. But a public information program can and does involve every contact made by every staff member, board member, employee and volunteer of the mental health center, with every person, organization, agency, and segment of the community.

What are some ways of informing people, other than using the traditional publicity tools? Many groups can be reached, informed, and motivated by working *with* you on a project—by actively participating in it. For example, the mental health association or a local church group may help you establish, and eventually manage alone, a social club for former hospital patients returned to the community. The PTA or Rotary Club may cooperate with you in starting a summer camp for mentally retarded or emotionally disturbed children. Through your working contacts with these groups, you will naturally inform them about the purpose and operation of the mental health center in the community, about the kinds of services you offer, and about the importance of, and need for, a wide variety of helping agencies and services.

But what if the local school system asks *your* help in planning and carrying out a conference for teachers, to help them understand the emotional needs of children? You may think it's a fine idea, but hesitate because it doesn't fit in at all with your public information goal. What should you do? Accept, by all means. Help, and find out more about the structure of the school system. Establish a working relationship with school administrators and personnel, find out what they think of your services, learn about guidance and counseling in the schools, and perhaps open the door for securing the school's support and help in your agency's projects. Plan for your public information program, but don't let that plan be so inflexible that you disregard opportunities for furthering your agency's overall goal—to improve the mental health of the community.

Or you might work with the community welfare agency in finding foster homes for children. When you work *with* other groups and agencies in this way, you actually achieve several objectives: you have an opportunity for finding out more about specific publics important to your agency, you help accomplish the immediate goal, you set the precedent for working together in other areas, and—hopefully—members of the cooperating group will talk with others about this project, your help, and the things they learned about the mental health center. Your contacts and conversations with others *do* have results that extend far beyond the immediate point of contact and concern. And you can capitalize on this free word-of-mouth publicity, if you're aware of it, and want it to work for you.

Another means of reaching a specific group is to speak formally at one of its meetings. This offers a good opportunity for face-to-face contact, for letting the group ask questions and discussing the mental health center or a proposed project or goal, and for meeting staff or board members of the center. Too, the local mass media may cover the meeting and carry a report of your presentation.

Let's suppose you've just published your annual report, and distributed it to the board and staff, the local media representatives, and relevant community groups. You think it shows real program growth and has implications for securing more money and starting a new service next year, and you want to see the report used to the fullest extent. Perhaps you saw a record number of patients, recorded a lower per patient cost, established the effectiveness of group therapy, or worked more hours consulting with community caregivers than last year. You've kept the community informed of the accumulating facts and figures (through your contacts with decision-makers, community groups, opinion-setters, care-givers, and so forth) all year long, but now you want to really wrap the year's work up by letting the community know what a good job you've been doing. First of all, stop and consider: will all these statistics honestly be important and useful to the community? Will they, in fact, be important to any specific group within the community? Some—like the mental health association—might be interested. So might the local decision-makers—those in authority positions in the community—and the state mental health authority. And so will many other groups, if you first break down and inter-pret those statistics so that they're meaningful to those groups.

The caregivers will want to know what services were given to the patients they referred to the center, and how many received services. They will want to know how many hours of your consultation time their staff received. If you saw a large number of employees from the town's industrial plant, you might want to talk to the plant manager about it, and suggest a program of consultation with shop foremen. If an unusually large number of adolescents were referred to the center, you might want to call a meeting of the juvenile judge, law enforcement officials, and school personnel to discuss a community youth program.

There are many ways in which you can put your annual report to very good use—ways other than a blanket report of patients seen, cost per hour, and so forth. There are also ways of obtaining written publicity from your annual report, by working with and through such media as are available to, and recognized by, defined groups.

For example, suppose that your report showed that the amount of time spent in consultation with physicians, or with the courts, had gone up over last year. Wouldn't this be of interest to the medical or legal profession in your community? Does the local medical or bar association have a newsletter? Here's a possibility for a story, if you talk to the newsletter editor.

And talk to the local association president about it. If he supports the consultation program, and feels that its results are worthwhile, he might think it's worth a story in the state association's journal. If you know this man well enough, and think he feels positive enough about the program, you might suggest the story—but let him write it, or at least make sure that the story goes in under his name. This is an excellent opportunity for you—here would be a story written by a recognized and accepted member of a professional organization, telling other members throughout the state about the merits of local mental health services. You personally might get little gratification from a story like this—but it's the story that counts, not you as an individual staff member of a mental health center.

If you already have a consultation program set up with personnel of the local industrial plant, you might run a story in the plant's house organ, reporting the results of the program. Plant employees will be likely to read, in their own newsletter, an article discussing how the mental health center directly affects them. It is likely that they would skip over a similar article in the local daily newspaper.

And if few mental health centers in the state are actively consulting with industry as you are, a story describing your program will almost certainly be of interest to them. Do staff members of the centers have a statewide organization? Can you be on the program at the next regular meeting? Does the state mental health authority publish a newsletter or magazine? Can your story be published in a future issue?

A good medium to use in informing publics about your agency is visual tools—charts, graphs, pictures, and so forth. These can be used effectively in displays, in conjunction with spoken presentations, in booklets, and on television. Comparisons of this year's caseload with last year's, the numbers of children and adults seen at the center, or the effect of the mental health center upon hospital admissions can be seen quickly. Visual aids can help you get an idea across (which, when discussed verbally, may be complex and confusing to the layman) in simple, easily seen terms. To be effective, visual aids should be attractive, colorful, and simple—definitely not intellectual. Of all the media available to you, visual aids have the most appeal. Nearly everyone—intelligent and well educated or not—will take time to look at a picture or simple bar graph. And, while the graph alone won't tell the whole story, it will plant an idea, create an impression.

So do the old standbys—newspapers, radio, and television. Monthly news coverage of some aspect of your program—the number of patients seen, the expansion of services, the employment of a new staff member—will probably not be remembered in detail, but they will serve to keep the center in the public's eyes, and help create an impression that your agency is active, reliable, and offers needed services. Don't assume that articles carried by these media will, by themselves, accomplish your task. On the other hand, don't overlook them in planning and carrying out your public information program. Even though they can't change opinions or fully inform important publics, they can influence and reinforce other communications you have had with the publics you need to reach.

In utilizing the potential of mass media in the community you serve, it is important that you work closely with the editor, reporter, and news director. What kind of news do they want? Does the paper or station have "slow" days when news about the center would receive higher priority? For the daily newspaper, Monday is usually a slow day. So is Friday. Remember that the major purpose of these mass media is to report *news*—all kinds of news. An overseas war crisis, or a major flood in a neighboring state, may make the news of your growing patient load or your new occupational therapy program relatively unimportant by comparison. Don't rely exclusively on your community's mass media, but keep them informed continuously, and work with them in determining what type of news articles are appropriate, and when they should be submitted for most favorable consideration.

Let's assume that there is a real need for a day treatment unit in the community, and that additional funds are required in next year's budget in order to provide necessary staff and services. How should you go about asking for these funds? If it's the state or community which provides your operating funds, naturally you'll want to discuss the program, and the needed financial support, with financial administrators. But first you'll want to lay groundwork in the community—to build up a backlog of support for your request. This is the time that the importance of continuing informative contacts with community leaders and opinion-setters will be brought home to you. Through your consistent, nondemanding contacts with them, you will have already gained their familiarity, understanding, acceptance, and support for the mental health center. Hopefully, they have conveyed their opinions and attitudes to their reference groups, and the center has support from all quarters of the community. Now, you'll want to begin telling these community leaders about the expanded services you envisage, the need for them, and the need for funds with which to support the program. Don't emphasize the need for money— instead, stress the importance of the program, and its advantages. Talk in terms of people who could be helped, if such services were available locally. When your proposed program gains the support of community leaders, caregivers, and opinion-setters, their understanding and fund-raising activities will come automatically and will be conveyed to their reference groups. You'll want to reinforce this understanding and support through regular stories in the local mass media— again, not emphasizing the need for money, but rather the need for expanded services. When the time comes to approach financial sources with a request for funds, important people and organizations in your community will be familiar with your request, and will support it.

Maintaining contact with important community leaders is the cornerstone of a good public information program. The acceptance and support that you can gain from them—and through them, from the community at large—is the best (and often only) effective antidote to unfavorable publicity about the center, or to any existing community opposition to mental health movements.

A good public information program often must contain elements of mental health education. The goal of public information may be to help relevant publics become aware of the services offered by the mental health center. In working toward meeting this goal, you will probably indirectly assure your publics that the mentally ill are not to be feared, or shunned, or pitied, and that treatment in the community is logical and desirable.

Mental health education, on the other hand, is more "pure." This part of your communications program does not necessarily involve information about your agency, but it *can*. For example, you may be conducting for teachers, a series of conferences on the "problem child" in the classroom. While the emphasis of the conferences is on the causes of behavior problems, and the ways of handling them, it will probably be entirely appropriate to discuss how the mental health center could be of help to the teacher in dealing with particular children, or how many children with similar problems are seen at the center.

Why should mental health education be important to you and to your agency? One reason is that it's probably endorsed by your governing board, and seen by the members as an important function of the mental health center. Another reason is that you can help produce favorable and accepting attitudes upon which to base the expansion and the optimum and correct use of your services. One of the overall goals of mental health education is to create, motivate, and direct favorable attitudes towards accepting and helping the mentally ill, and towards promoting mental health.

The steps in planning for a mental health education program are much the same as they are for the public information program. What is the goal of your mental health education program? Who are the people you're trying to reach? And how can you best reach them with those messages you wish to get across?

Mental health education can have two different emphases: education *about* mental illness, and education *for* mental health. The former is geared toward bringing the concept of mental illness to a level which can be understood and not feared by the average person. It means education about the causes of mental illness, its effects, and different kinds of treatment. Education for mental health means teaching about human behavior and dynamics, healthy interpersonal relationships, family life, and so forth, in order to increase self-understanding and to further healthy attitudes. Your goal with some groups or publics will be to bring mental illness into the realm of understanding and acceptance; for others, it will be to help promote community mental health through healthy practices, attitudes, and behaviors.

Both kinds of education are important—to the community and to the mental health center as well. Both seek to dispel ignorance, to improve the circumstances of the mentally ill in society, to promote early treatment when necessary, and to increase general knowledge and understanding.

What sort of people make up the specific publics that you're trying to reach with a mental health education program? How old are they? What are their attitudes, opinions, beliefs? What is their level of education? What do they want and need to know? What do they already know? How much of what they know is correct?

You're probably familiar with several studies conducted during the past 20 years which have shown that people are *un*informed, not *mis*informed, about mental illness. Attitudes toward the mentally ill, while not entirely negative, are generally distrustful and fearful. The more informed segments of the public are younger, and have a higher degree of education. There is a high positive correlation between exposure to information about mental health and "correctness" of opinions. At all educational levels, people who gained information through several sources were more knowledgeable than their educational peers. Stories and programs in mass media are infrequent and generally distorted. People are unable to recognize symptoms of mental illness unless behavior is bizarre and inappropriate. It is not known what impact community mental health centers have had on public opinions and attitudes, but demonstrated local treatment of the mentally ill has probably greatly furthered public understanding of mental illness; the current trend toward community mental health services has at least made us aware that community attitudes are vitally important in the treatment, rehabilitation, and acceptance of the mentally ill into community society.

What about the people in your specific community groups? Are these survey results typical of them? How much do you really know about the groups you need to reach? Probably, quite a bit—in the light of your own informal survey which helped you define the image of the mental health center in the community. In addition to determining community attitudes toward the mental health center, you should have been able to learn much about community attitudes toward the mentally ill, and about the extent and accuracy of the community's knowledge of mental health and illness.

When you begin to work with specific groups, however, you'll want to analyze in depth the characteristics of their opinions, knowledge, and their need to know. This will help you determine both the content of your educational program, and the media through which you should work to transmit the necessary communications.

When you're ready to plan for your mental health education program, just what are the tools you can use to communicate with your publics? There are many different ways of working with them. The conference, or seminar, is one medium. Through a conference you can conduct inservice training for staff members of the mental health center. Your goal might be to learn about techniques to use in group therapy; you might ask for consultative assistance from the state mental health authority, or from a state mental hospital. You'd also want to conduct an inservice training program for volunteers working in special projects of the mental health center, such as an occupational therapy class.

Other agencies in the community—the county welfare department, or a day care center for children—might ask your assistance in planning and carrying out inservice training for staff and volunteers.

You might want to schedule, with the cooperation of the local ministerial alliance, a series of evening seminars for ministers, to discuss and learn about effective counseling.

Public speaking, of course, is a very effective tool in mental health education. In the course of a year, you, your staff, and your governing board may very well speak to every civic and professional organization in the community, from a regular meeting of a women's church group to the annual meeting of the local bar association. Remember, though—it is much easier to teach factual information than it is to change attitudes and opinions. In all your contacts with these groups, you must communicate *persuasively*, if that communication is to have effective and long-lasting results.

There are several tools you can use in conjunction with public speaking. One is the film. An increasing number of good films are available on a variety of mental health-related subjects: healthy child growth and development, planning for and utilizing community mental health services, treatment of mental illness, and such related areas as alcoholism, juvenile delinquency, and mental retardation. Films must be carefully selected for each group, previewed before showing, and, to be maximally effective, discussed by the group after viewing. Don't show a film simply to take up time— show one for a specific *purpose* and make sure that the film you select will not only fulfill that purpose, but will be understandable, meaningful, and informative to the audience. Films, and suggestions for using them, are available from your state mental health authority. In most states, films may be borrowed free of charge; a catalog or listing of films is usually available too. Your local mental health association might also maintain a small film library which could be made available to you.

Pamphlets, too, cover a wide range of subject matter. Like films, they must be selected carefully to help present your communication in the most effective way to your specific audiences. In addition to distributing pamphlets in conjunction with public speaking, you may wish to use them in several other ways. You or the local mental health association might maintain a display rack in the waiting room of the center. Encourage both the mental health association and the association for retarded children to display pamphlets in physicians' offices, in the county welfare department, and in other social service agency offices. Use pamphlets in displays and exhibits. Pamphlets are available free of cost from the state mental health authority and may also be purchased from the state associations for retarded children and for mental health. Drug and insurance companies also furnish good mental health pamphlets, usually without cost.

You might also want to write and print yourself a small pamphlet or folder describing the mental health center—the services offered, the fee schedule, the hours of operation, and so forth. As a general rule, publish, yourself, only those things which are not available from other sources. It's a waste of your time and energy, as well as the center's funds, to write and design a pamphlet which duplicates one already available, usually at lower cost.

Still another tool is the exhibit or display—in a public office, in the center's waiting room, in a school, at a conference or other meeting, in a wide variety of locations. You may even want to participate with the local mental health association in planning a display for the county fair. Plan the display carefully. Make it simple and easy to understand. If possible, you might want to incorporate a supply of inexpensive pamphlets which your target group can look over while at the display.

Suppose that you were considering a "mental health checkup" at the preschool roundup, as part of your mental health education program. Teachers in a local school have been coming to you for help in dealing with several children who have learning and behavior problems, and you think poor school adjustment may be creating, or at least contributing to, definite mental health problems. What implications does a program like this have for mental health education? What educational tools would you use, and how would you initiate the program?

Your first step, of course, would be to discuss it with your staff, to gain its opinions and suggestions. Your governing board, too, must be involved. Does it see this as a legitimate function of the agency? If your staff and board support the program, you would then want to contact the school administrator. Does he recognize the need for a program like this and does he think the checkup would meet that need? Will he support the program?

Then, the school personnel—teachers, nurses, guidance counselors—must be contacted. You'll want to discuss the program and its implications with them, solicit their suggestions, and discuss how they will help in conducting the roundup.

After planning has incorporated all useful and feasible suggestions, and the roundup has been scheduled, you'll want to begin using standard tools of publicity and education. Prepublicity in newspaper and radio should be augmented by a staff or board member and a school representative, speaking at a regular meeting of the PTA, and by a direct mail announcement to mothers of preschoolers.

At the roundup itself, you'll probably want to again explain the procedure to participating mothers. Your publicity efforts should not be geared exclusively to the where and when of the roundup; your direct mail, speaking engagements, and mass media publicity should also contain an explanation of *why* the roundup is being held, and what may be gained from it. You will want to tell all relevant publics that adjustment to school is difficult for some children, that intellectual and emotional development of the child affects his adjustment, and that this program is being offered to help parents assess their child's readiness for school. Publicity should stress the maintenance of mental health, not the detection of mental illness.

Also at the roundup, you'll want to distribute pamphlets on healthy child growth and development, and perhaps to display an exhibit which depicts different areas of adjustment to the school setting.

And don't neglect post-publicity after the roundup is over.

Go back to all the groups and people you contacted before the roundup and tell them what the results were. Tell them how many mothers participated, what sort of problem areas were uncovered, and what sort of solutions were decided upon. Talk to local media representatives about the roundup, and submit stories to them. You'll be reaching not only those who supported the program actively, but you will also be informing those mothers who did not participate, as well as those who are potential participants of next year's program. A comprehensive mental health program reaches all the relevant publics, and it reaches many individuals many times, in many different ways.

Mental health education is one of the most important functions of the community mental health center. Its value, and the needs for it, are as great as the value and need for clinical treatment and therapy. As part of a wide spectrum of helping services and agencies in the community, the mental health center is not alone in its obligation to mental health education. Even though the center may be viewed as the "mental health expert" in the community, the professional staff, volunteers and board members cannot alone conduct an effective educational program, just as they cannot conduct an effective public information program alone. Both programs must involve the active participation of all community leaders, opinion-setters, caregivers, civic and professional organizations, and recognized media if they are to be effective, meaningful, accepted, and acted upon by the community.

And, just as they cannot conduct these programs alone, you shouldn't attempt to conduct them yourself. The logical person to carry out these programs for you is a public information specialist, or mental health educator who is trained or skilled in communications. Too often the director and staff do not have the time required for this important function; neither do they nor the governing board have the experience or background to do the job properly. The trained public information specialist, on the staff of the mental health center, can help the agency plan and can carry out a comprehensive program of public information and mental health education. He can interpret the agency to the community and enlist the support of its many publics —the basis of knowledgeable, unfaltering long-term support in times of crisis. He can keep the agency continually advised about its public image, and can help the agency develop effective, mutual communications with community publics. He can also plan special events (such as a conference or an open house) for the center; establish a speakers' bureau; maintain a professional library; be a resource for mental health materials of all kinds; plan visits to the center by the mental health authority, legislators, and others; develop exhibits for various meetings; and in general bring the mental health center and its functions "close to home" in terms of its supporting publics.

The public information and mental health education programs of the community mental health center require skillful, patient, and long-term planning, if they are to help create an impression that will last and assure sustained and consistent support. The importance of these programs cannot be overlooked or short-shifted. These programs cannot be conducted in a half-hearted way if, and when, time permits. They are an integral part of the mental health center's program, and they must receive the same careful planning and attention that is devoted to every other phase of the center's operation.

SUGGESTED READINGS

The following are publications of the National Publicity Council for Health and Welfare Services, New York:

Bright, S. *Public Relations Programs—How to Plan Them.*
Church, D. *The Public Relations Committee—Why and How It Works.*

Crosby, A. *Pamphlets that Pull.*

Demorest, C. *The Board Members' Manual.*

Hall, R. *Taking Hold of Television.*

Kleinschmidt, H. E. *How to Turn Ideas into Pictures.*

Lane, J. & Tolleris, B. *Planning Your Exhibit.*

Routzahn, M. *Better Board Meetings.*

Simpson, G. *Working with Newspapers.*

Stein, H. *Measuring Your Public Relations.*

Tolleris, B. *Annual Reports—How to Plan and Write Them.*

Trecker, H. *Building the Board.*

Auerback, A. (1963), The anti-mental health movement. *Amer. J. Psychiat.,* 119:705-712.

Cummings, J. & Cummings, E. (1957), *Closed Ranks.* Cambridge, Mass.: Harvard University Press.

Group for the Advancement of Psychiatry (1960), *The Psychiatrist and His Roles in a Mental Health Association,* Report No. 44. New York.

Halpert, H. (1965), Public relations in mental health programs. *Public Health Reports,* 80:195.

Matthews, R. A. & Rowland, L. W. (1960), *How to Recognize and Handle Abnormal People: A Manual for the Police Officer.* New York: National Association for Mental Health.

Miller, M. H. & Halleck, S. L. (1963), The critics of psychiatry: A review of contemporary critical attitudes. *Amer. J. Psychiat.,* 119:705-712.

Public Information—Essential for a Dynamic Mental Health Program, Conference November 27-29, 1962. Omaha: Nebraska Psychiatric Institute.

Stepanek, C. & Willie, C. (1961), A community mental health project in New York State. *Public Health Reports,* 76:979.

Stern, E. (1957), *Mental Illness: A Guide for the Family.* New York: National Association for Mental Health.

XV

The Governing Board

There is an ever-present gap between the democratic ideal and democratic reality. All citizens are neither created equal, nor do they become equal in abilities or opportunities with advancing years. Neither may every adult citizen participate directly in the operation of every democratic institution. The day of the town hall meeting—which in small communities most nearly approximated the ideal of equal participation—is a thing of the past. With urbanization, increasing population, increasing complexity and diversity of social life and increased availability of technological knowledge, the model of citizen participation in government becomes more and more broadly interpreted, and less frequently a specific reality.

The citizen governing board has been used in America to strike a compromise between the democratic ideal, social reality, and organizational expediency. Any public enterprise, under our system of government, employing tax funds, and affecting the public health, safety, morals or welfare, *must* have mechanisms for responding to public wishes and public needs. However, any such enterprise must also have the support and direction of informed and caring members of the community, rather than uninformed and indifferent members. And any organization, if it is to thrive and prosper, must have stability and constancy in direction and control.

The citizen governing board, selected from individuals who are reasonably knowledgeable and concerned about

266

mental health matters, and representing a broad cross section of the community, may combine the virtues of public representation, knowledgeable guidance, and stable direction.

The size of the governing board, its representation, terms of office, and responsibilities vary widely. The composition and method of appointment may be established by law or by custom. The board may be elected, appointed by some other elected official or officials, or self-appointed and self-perpetuating. The responsibility of the board may be advisory, directive, or inspectional in nature.

In Kansas, for example, composition of the governing board of a community mental health center is partly defined in the legislation governing the organization of community mental health centers. At least seven members, representing all counties supporting the center, and from a cross segment of socioeconomic and occupational levels of the community, should constitute the board under Kansas law. The mental health centers are organized as direct units of county government, and the board members are appointed by the county commissioners—elected representatives of the people—for overlapping three-year terms. If the mental health center is organized as a nonprofit corporation, the board is self-appointed and self-perpetuating; generally a system of overlapping three-year appointments is utilized.

The duties of the governing board may be many and varied, and will depend upon local needs and problems. Basic duties of all governing boards of community mental health centers will probably consist of the following:

1. Election of board officers from its membership.

2. Formulating and establishing policies for operating the center and employing personnel.

3. Annually reviewing, evaluating, and reporting community mental health services to the board of county commissioners (or to whomever else accountable).

4. Preparing and submitting the annual plan and budget and making recommendations thereon.

5. Fund raising.

6. Selecting and appointing the administrator.

7. Housing the center.

8. Community and public relations.

The administrative director of the mental health center is responsible and the staff of the mental health center has a specific responsibility to the director. The board, in turn, is responsible to the community.

These complex relationships must be clearly understood and respected by all board and staff members and must be interpreted consistently and frequently to the community at large. Differences of opinion may arise regarding program emphases, such as the number of patients to be seen, consultation services to other community caregivers, fee policies, and so forth. The reconciliation of differences calls for close working relationships between board and staff. The success of determining reasonable and effective policy, and of resolving differences, is to a large extent dependent upon the process of successfully defining areas of responsibility between board, director, and staff.

The governing board may be assisted in its decision making, policy formation, and administration by a number of committees. Basic committees should consist of the following:

1. The executive committee should consist of the officers of the board plus the immediate past president.

2. The finance committee should consist of several members of the board appointed by the chairman. This committee shall consider all matters pertaining to the finances of the organization, including auditing its accounts, preparing and submitting of budget to the board, and recommending measures to insure the continued financial stability of the organization.

3. The personnel committee should likewise be appointed by the chairman of the board, and shall prepare and recommend to the board, personnel practices and policies, consider all matters related to personnel administration, and select and recommend a professional staff administrator whenever this position is vacant.

4. The public relations committee shall be appointed by the chairman of the board, and should be responsible for acquainting the public with the work and needs of the center through whatever media may be available and desirable.

5. The housing committee, also appointed by the chairman of the board, shall assist in procuring and replacing the physical equipment of the center and securing adequate physical facilities for its location.

6. The nominating committee, normally consisting of three members appointed by the chairman, shall suggest nominees for vacancies on the board and for officers of the board.

In addition, the governing board should have available, a professional advisory committee to assist in decision making, policy formulation, and administration. Members of the professional advisory committee should *not* be board members, but should be appointed to the advisory committee membership by the chairman of the board. They are persons who (by reason of position, qualifications or profession) have a particular interest in the work of the mental health center. The advisory committee's function is to continually inform the governing board of community needs and effectiveness of the mental health center services, and to help the board in making decisions and establishing policies. Upon request of the governing board, the professional advisory committee can help in the establishment of personnel policies and practices, staff salary ranges, patient fee schedules, recruitment policies, staff qualifications, etc.

Advice in deciding how to allocate professional staff time to allow for maximum efficiency between direct clinical services, consultation to community agencies and professional caregivers, and participation in community and area planning for comprehensive mental health services, can also be given to the board and staff by the professional advisory committee.

BOARD-STAFF RELATIONSHIPS

As mentioned previously, the first step in board-staff relationships lies in the clear and unequivocal definition of mutual responsibility and authority. The board should deal with the staff of the center, and regulate the operations of the center, through the administrative director of the agency. Likewise, the staff of the center should express their grievances or opinions to the governing board through the director; the governing board is well advised not to let the staff bypass the director in discussing and solving problems. The staff should be encouraged to talk over problems and work out solutions with the center director, rather than bring these difficulties up directly with the governing board.

At meetings of the governing board, which normally should occur monthly, or at least no less than nine times a year, the administrative director of the center shall have responsibility for acquainting the board with the current operations of the center.

At each meeting, the director of the center should inform the board of the activities of the staff during the preceding period. Often, the basic document can be a copy of the monthly workload summary report, which in most states is submitted to the State Mental Health Authority for use in compiling reports requested by the National Institute of Mental Health.

An additional effort should be made to acquaint the board with consultation activities of other community caregiving groups, as well as with any activity in the area of mental health education, research, planning, and so forth. Reports of these activities should be presented in a brief tabular form, similar to the monthly workload summary for direct clinical services. In addition, however, there should be a narrative description—both written and verbal—explaining the meaning and significance of some of the activities.

As a general rule, the board should be advised as to all aspects of clinic operation, whether any specific need or request is involved or not. Moreover, it is wise that the majority of communications between the director and the board *not* be around the focus of problems or needs. Individuals have many reasons for serving on governing boards. One motivation is the desire to enhance their self-esteem and their sense of personal and social worthiness. The director must be sensitive to this need, and if all board meetings deal with problems, challenges, difficulties, etc., the director will not be meeting the basic motivational needs of at least some members of the governing board: to have the feeling that they are doing a good job and are good persons.

At the other extreme, if no problems are ever presented, no policy decisions ever requested, the board will equally tend to suffer in its own eyes, and will not feel useful or really worthwhile. The director, then, must walk a narrow path between overwhelming the board with too many difficulties or, at the other extreme, not giving it sufficient problems on which to work. For some experienced and competent directors, it may even be difficult to find problems for the board, since the director will be able to solve most of the difficulties himself. The better part of valor, however, may often lie in asking the advice of the board, even at the risk of having it decide upon a course of action which, in the eyes of the director, is not optimal. He can still follow the board's direction, and if things do not turn out well can use the difficulty or failure as a tool for continuing board development and inservice education.

There will be many tactical problems that may prove difficult for the director in deciding how to best implement a necessary strategic decision: not to allow the board to become involved in professional decisions, or to intrude upon the internal operations of the agency. These responsibilities belong to the director and the professional staff, and the board should not be permitted to direct ongoing operations, direct day-by-day activities, or to assume unwarranted authority and responsibility in regard to the management of specific cases. However, the director should be certain that this battle about staff prerogatives and professional autonomy be fought only around issues that are clear-cut, where professional consensus and support would be unanimous, and where a united and determined stand can be made by the entire staff in case the board were to push the issue to the limits. It would be a mistake, for example, for a new director to refuse to discuss with the board *any* details of *any* specific clinical cases—as some directors have done—on the basis that this would be violating privileged communication. The board has a natural and generally constructive curiosity about the clinical operations of the center. When the board is being informed about specific cases, it is possible to disguise the material in such a way that it will not be aware of the identity of the individual, and yet can gain at least some understanding of the nature of psychiatric work. Again, it is essential for the self-esteem of the board, that it be aware of the general nature of the work done by the center; while on the other hand, if allowed to learn the identity and the details of problems of specific and identifiable persons, it will suffer guilt and anxiety about what would eventually be recognized as unwarranted inquisitiveness.

Problems Arising Between Governing Boards and Staff Members

None of the professional disciplines is adequately prepared for assuming the directorship of a clinic and conducting relationships with the governing board, as current training sequences are structured. The medical tradition of the autonomy of the physician and the sacredness of the patient-doctor relationship, as well as the psychologist's tradition of scientific objectivity and scrupulous honesty, are handicaps in dealing with governing boards. There is much in social work theory and practice that should theoretically be appropriate to the social worker's role in these dealings, but there is perhaps insufficient preparation in the area of taking stands on professional issues and disagreeing with governing boards. The social worker often seems to feel that if "the relationship is good" between the director and the governing board, then everything will go smoothly; and that conflict, disagreement, and struggle are a symptom of "poor communication." There are times when governing board members, as professional persons, will be acting in destructive and harmful ways as a result of personal illness, long-standing grudges, extreme political convictions, or ignorance and stupidity. While the basic model, that good communication and an understanding of the relationship between the board and the director will result in harmonious and effective operation, is valid, there can be difficult times for even the best boards and the best directors.

Because of the importance and difficulty of the relationship between the director and the governing board, and because of the lack of training on the part of many directors, attention has been given in the staff development program of Kansas Community Mental Health Services towards helping directors increase their skills in relating to the governing board. At a seminar held in 1962 for directors of mental health centers (Lawrence, 1962), a considerable amount of time was spent in discussion of sample cases, submitted by directors, of problems in relation to the governing boards. The following are representative of some of the problems that were presented as prototypical and worthy of discussion:

Case 1

Following conclusion of the first year of the mental health center operation, the county commissioners received a statistical report of the clinical services rendered. Although the staff and center board have recognized that a visit before the Board of County Commissioners might be desirable, this plan was never implemented. Several weeks later, when consideration was being given to the levying of the tax for another year's operation, the board chairman informed the staff that the county commissioners were questioning whether or not the professional staff was 'actually helping people,' and had not found the statistical report especially helpful. They felt unable to judge whether the service was really being utilized and whether the staff was serving other than 'welfare clients' who were already being provided for through the county welfare office. The request was made through the center board chairman that the commissioners be given a list of patients served, in order that they themselves could attempt to make some judgment of the effectiveness of our treatment. However, the staff objected to divulging patient names on the basis that this is confidential information.

The Board of County Commissioners retaliated with the following reasons:

1. They, as elected officials, are representatives of the people—responsible to the taxpayers for efficient and equitable expenditure of local tax funds.
2. A record of all names of public assistance clients is made available to them, where not only county, but also state and federal funds are utilized.
3. All names of referrals made to state institutions are readily available, as well as any business concerning the county.

Staff Decision: The staff continued to believe that divulging patient names would be a violation of professional ethics. In order, however, not to alienate the source of financial support, it was decided to acquiesce and grant permission for the county commissioners to examine the clinic card file if the staff were notified in advance.

This permission was granted after weighing the staff's personal knowledge of these individual men, and feeling relatively sure that this privilege would not be used. This proved to be true.

Next year the center will be adding additional counties to the mental health center operation. Should a similar request be made by other county commissioners, the original solution to the problem would not be appropriate. The staff recognizes the inadequacy in board education, but even as it becomes 'more sophisticated' could this not continue to be a problem worth considering?

In discussing this particular case, center directors felt that the board of county commissioners was expressing genuine interest in the center activities through its demands for patient names, but that the content of the demand itself was inappropriate. It was felt that attention should be given to finding an adequate and appropriate means to inform the board and the county commissioners about activities of the center without divulging patients' names. It was felt that more information was needed as to what services were actually being provided, and that the names would no more fulfill their need for more information than empty statistics had previously done. The discussants felt that the difficulty of the county commissioners in understanding center operations is understandable because psychiatric methods of care are fundamentally more intangible than the activities of the regular medical center, where one can see concrete evidence of bandages, pills prescribed, and operations performed. It was felt that the staff should present programs at board meetings to explain different practices and activities, and to present disguised cases, simplified and dramatized for effect. The specific interests of the board should be taken into account in the programming of such demonstrations. The staff should become more active in speaking engagements and other public relation activities throughout the community, in order to stress that the center, staff, and its clientele are integral parts rather than isolated fragments of the community. Participants felt that if the county commissioners insisted upon obtaining the names of patients, the director of the center should appear before them, with the permission of the chairman of the governing board of the center, to explain personally, the sensitive nature of divulging names. He might diplomatically express his confidence in the present commissioners but cite hesitation in setting a dangerous and unnecessary precedent.

Case 2

During the formation of a Mental Health Center there was a great deal of intense interest and activity among the community leaders in developing this facility. Upon the formal incorporation of the center, professional staff were employed to carry out the day-to-day operations of the center. Up to this time the citizens' group was very active, speaking to civic and service clubs in the area, discussing the need for such a community facility, and gaining community support and understanding. The board members were directly involved in program planning and special needs of the center. Board meetings were held at least every other month with frequent executive committee meetings in between.

Since the employment of the full-time professional staff, interest and activity have waned. Meetings are called infrequently, and members elected to positions of responsibility have not had the energy, interest or drive to maintain the previous activity. Meetings are now called only on the initiative of the paid Director. Major policy decisions are side-stepped by the board, leaving them to be made by the Director. Although it cannot be said that the board members have completely lost interest in the center's functioning, they seem to take the attitude that, 'We have started this center and have worked hard in doing it. Now that we have a full-time director, let him do the job.'

The board is composed of twenty-eight members. The decision to have a large membership was made originally to get as complete a cross section of the community involved as possible. Members are from the medical profession, attorneys, teachers and ministers as well as from the business and banking community and interested lay citizens. The executive committee consists of a chairman, vice chairman, treasurer, secretary and two others. This committee makes the majority of the decisions and calls full board meetings infrequently or as required by the center's by-laws.

In their discussions, center directors felt that the feelings of the board members were understandable, and it was natural that, as community leaders who contributed a great deal of effort to establish the mental health center, they should feel that their task is complete, and should express hope that the staff provide excellent services to follow up their own efforts. It was felt that an important problem involved continuing education of the board about the actual activities of the center. In addition, considerable discussion centered upon the size of the board, as to whether twenty-eight members was too large or not. It was pointed out that there were two different kinds of functions in relation to the center:

1. To render practical advice to the center.
2. To promote community interest in, and understanding of the mental health center.

A small, relatively homogeneous 'working' board may serve the first function most efficiently. A larger, more heterogeneous board may be able to serve the function of community education more effectively. Careful attention should be given, in such a large board, to its internal organization and its committees, such as the executive committee, in order to combine the advantages of a small board for practical guidance, and a large board for effective and broad community education.

Case 3

One area of confusion and potential difficulty that arose with a mental health board concerned the action to be taken with unpaid fees. Due to the accounting system, it is necessary to secure from the board, a written authorization to charge off such bills as uncollectible debts. In one of the recent business meetings several board members, including the president, felt that individuals who owed money to the center but yet were known as having financial resources in the community should not be allowed to 'escape' their obligations. It was felt that the accounts of these several patients should be turned over to an attorney for appropriate action, including litigation if necessary. This suggestion was viewed with concern by the staff of the center, in that it was seen as professionally inappropriate. It was argued that legal action which would imply public notoriety would of necessity violate the confidential guarantees of these or any other patients' relationships with the center. The lay board, acting on what otherwise constitutes sound business principles, felt that patients should not be so easily able to avoid their financial obligation to the center. The question of an actual lawsuit was finally dropped. However, the issue of having an attorney act on the center's behalf to collect unpaid fees is still under discussion.

In discussion, it became clear that the subcultural values of governing board members, and those of at least some members of the mental health professions, are at variance. However, there was also wide variation *within* the professional group as to whether the center should aggressively attempt to collect fees. In general, psychiatrists seemed to feel most comfortable with insisting upon the payment of incurred obligations by patients, and did not feel that such payments need necessarily be out of current income but rather could be viewed as a capital investment or expenditure. On the other hand, social workers seemed the least comfortable in insisting upon payment of fees, most prone to making excuses for their clients, and most likely to object to the aggressive fee collection policy of the governing board. Both of these groups were relatively homogeneous, whereas psychologists, while occupying a generally intermediate position, had a wider range of variance within their profession. In general, no consensus was reached by the mental health center directors concerning this particular issue.

Parenthetically, it might be mentioned that this was taken as indication of an area in which considerable agreement and dissension existed within and among the professions, and served as a focus for future staff development seminars for the professional staff persons in community mental health centers in Kansas. In other words, the problem was at least partially defined as being a professional problem, that had to be resolved in some workable way by the professional disciplines themselves, prior to any hope of successful resolution of differences between professional persons and the governing board.

These three cases may be sufficient to give some indication of the many types of problems that can develop in relationships between the director of a center and his governing board. As with psychotherapy and other complex interpersonal transactions, only through supervised experience can the director hope to develop real proficiency in staff-governing board relationships. This is one area in which ongoing consultation from a senior, experienced clinician, who has worked with governing boards successfully for a number of years, can be of invaluable help to the new director of a community mental health center. He should not expect himself to have been prepared for this type of relationship by his training, nor by his preceding experience in psychotherapy. While there is great carryover from his understanding of human motivation and personality functioning, as well as small group dynamics, there are special skills and principles involved in relationships between the director and his governing board which must be gained by study and supervised experience.

There is one overriding principle that should be kept clearly in mind in all dealings with the governing board: *to deal manipulatively with the board is to court disaster.* While secrets will sometimes have to be kept from the board (in the sense that it is not told everything, or involved in all decisions), attempts at blatant manipulation of the board usually fail. Attempts to court favor with one faction or another of the governing board, to involve only the chairman in decisions without informing the rest of the board, to supply information to only certain members of the board, to talk about one board member to another, and so forth, is the height of folly. No matter how confused or stupid the board may *seem*, functioning collectively—even if it prefers to talk about the prices of hogs or the latest basketball game, rather than the mental health center—it is not, in the final analysis, stupid, weak, or disinterested. The board members are complex people with multiple and diverse motivations for serving on the board, with antecedent intrapersonal difficulties that they bring to the situation, as well as intrapersonal difficulties that arise during the course of board functioning. They have strivings for power and prestige, and at the same time fear power and eminence, respect mental health professionals and at the same time distrust and fear them; want to do a good job and at the same time are unwilling to commit themselves sufficiently. They are, in other words, typical human beings, with conflicting motivations and pervasive ambivalences. But, if the director is to build a genuinely useful relationship with them, he must treat them with respect, compassion, patience, and forbearance. They are neither dictators nor pawns, patients nor fools, but are simply human beings trying to get on with the business of society for reasons that are, in the final analysis, intensely personal and idiosyncratic. While their language, interests, and values may differ from those of the director and staff of the center, their motivations and their basic human behaviors undoubtedly differ very little from his own.

SUGGESTED READINGS

Cape, W. (1965), *Handbook for Mental Health Center Governing Boards*. Lawrence: Governmental Research Center, University of Kansas.
Cartwright, D. & Fader, A., eds. (1960), *Group Dynamics, Research and Theory*. Evanston, Ill.: Row Peterson.
Houle, C. O. (1960), *The Effective Board*. New York: Association Press.
Routzahn, M. S. (1952), *Better Board Meetings*. New York: National Publicity Council for Health and Welfare Services.
Sorenson, R. (1954), *How To Be a Board or Committee Member*. New York: Association Press.
Visher, J. S. (1960), The problem of community pressure and the mental hygiene clinic. *Psych. Quarterly Supp.*, Part 2, pp. 1-12.

XVI

Program Evaluation

From time to time, it is necessary and desirable that communities evaluate the present status and future goals of their local mental health services. This need for evaluation and planning is not unique to the mental health field, and is a well accepted operational principle in many fields of industry, social enterprise, and merchandising. The local citizens who serve on the governing board and the professional staff that works at the centers are of necessity identified with their program, involved in it personally and professionally, and limited in the degree of objectivity that they can bring to bear in evaluating their own operation. It seems particularly desirable, then, to have available a service of Program Evaluation, to assist centers in gaining an objective view of their present operations and future plans. If such outside evaluation is not available, it is possible for the governing board and staff to conduct a self-evaluation.

There are several assumptions built into this evaluation protocol which we should make explicit at this point.

I. We do not assume that there is any "right," "model," or "universal" mode of organization, staffing, or functioning that best meets the mental health needs of all communities. Rather, we believe that the community mental health center must be based upon the problems, wishes, and resources of the community in which it exists.

II. We view a community mental health center as a growing social organism which has a discernible life history. Just as in evaluating the performance of a growing human being, then, we would not expect a new mental health center to be as large, as fully differentiated, or as versatile as a mental health center in "middle age."

III.   In evaluating a center, it is very difficult to make valid judgments about the most crucial variable in determining its effectiveness: the personal and professional ability and competence of the individual staff members. We are aware of no way to appraise this scientifically.

IV.   We assume that an invitation by a governing board to evaluate the program of their mental health center indicates a readiness to hear unfavorable as well as favorable comments, and to evaluate them in the spirit in which they are offered; and also signifies the strength to implement changes when and if they are necessary and possible. Additionally, we assume that the evaluation process is a mutual endeavor between board, staff, and evaluating team, during which free and frank interchange must go on in both directions.

V.   The evaluating group must stand ready to assist the board and staff of the community mental health center in making whatever program modifications upon which they decide, following the evaluation. These changes may not necessarily be in line with the recommendations; decisions about the role and function of the community mental health center must be left with responsible agents of the local community. The role of the team is to assist them in accomplishing their goals, so long as these goals are generally congruent with acceptable psychiatric practice.

The actual process of data collection outlined below requires that a team be at the site from one to two days. Each member of the team should be assigned responsibility for certain areas of the evaluation. In consultation with the director of the mental health center, each team member sets up a series of appointments and procedures that will be necessary to assist him in evaluating each area of the center's functioning. Following the data collection phase, the members of the program evaluation team should meet together to integrate their findings, and then should meet with the staff of the community mental health center to discuss preliminary findings and suggestions. Following this discussion, the evaluation-team staff should prepare a comprehensive report of the evaluation process, including recommendations for change, and have it typed in sufficient quantities to provide several copies to the governing board of the local community mental health center, with an informational copy to the director of the mental health center. The report should be confidential, and is the property of the requesting or evaluated agency.

The following areas of functioning should be evaluated as a minimum:

Organizational Structure

The survey team should attempt to understand the formal structure by which the community mental health center is organized, and by which business is conducted. Particular importance should be placed on a set of written by-laws which have been voted upon and accepted by the governing board of the mental health center. There should also be a formal board policy stating the functions of the center and delineating the duties and responsibilities of each staff member. The team would want to know the staffing plan, and whether the present staff approximates that which was originally desired by the board. The fee policy, its underlying philosophical basis, and how workable it is, should all be studied. Written personnel policies which govern the conditions of employment of each staff member are especially important. A written contract or agreement for each of the staff members is desirable, outlining the reciprocal privileges and obligations of the staff members and the governing board. The adequacy of the financial base for providing adequate service to the population-at-risk should be carefully appraised.

Administrative Considerations

A personnel record should be kept for each staff member, indicating his qualifications, conditions of employment, salary increments, accumulation of sick and vacation leaves, dates of required physical examinations, attendance at meetings designed to increase his usefulness to the center, and annual evaluation of his effectiveness in the employment situation.

Inspection of the administrative records on patients should be conducted to determine the accuracy of records kept on times of visits, purpose of visits, billing procedures, collection procedures, etc.

The evaluator should determine how complete and accurate a record the staff keeps of its various activities; since this is a particularly important phase of administration, such information must be available to the board to assist it in evaluating the effectiveness of the staff members. The daily schedule should be examined to determine staff time utilization.

Particular attention would be paid to the security of the clinical records, both in terms of physical security during the hours that the clinic is unoccupied, and also in terms of procedures required for the release of information.

The staff members of the clinic and the governing board should be covered by adequate malpractice and liability insurance.

An accurate and complete record, in scrapbook form, should be kept of all news coverage that has occurred over the years. This will allow the staff and the governing board to evaluate the effectiveness of the public information program, and to pinpoint areas that need fuller interpretation to the community.

Statistical recording and reporting should follow NIMH and state mental health authority standards and should include a statistical report of terminated outpatients and a monthly caseload statistical report.

There is no uniform method of determining cost per patient hour. We would suggest a common procedure: from the total operating cost, that part of the cost designated by the board to be attributable to "public health," "community consultation," "mental health education," or "preventive mental health practice" activities should be subtracted. That is, such activities as consultation with the counselors in the local schools, consultation services to the probate judge or his parole officer, to the county welfare office, etc., should not be charged against the individual patient expenses. We suggest that *at least 30 per cent of the total staff time be devoted to such community consultation activities,* and that 30 per cent of the tax monies, in consequence, should be subtracted from the total budget of the center. Additional budget allotments for administration, research, etc., should also be established. The remainder of the operating budget should be divided by the total number of patient hours, to get the gross cost per patient hour.

Budget procedures will be discussed in Chapter XXIV.

Staffing

Rigid criteria for a uniform staffing pattern cannot be established. Rather, the evaluators should attempt to determine whether the disciplines represented on the staff are those which allow the center to achieve its avowed purposes. established by the governing board as representatives of the community.

In evaluating the salary structure, and such fringe benefits as hospitalization and retirement plans, the team should determine if the governing board of the center is demonstrating a long-range commitment to each staff member, and is instituting salary and personnel policies designed to encourage a permanent stay in the community. The salary would, of course, have to be competitive with others in the state and with comparable situations out of state; however, studies in industry and many other settings have demonstrated clearly that salary is not the primary consideration determining an employee's commitment to the employer, or his devotion to the job. Salary is only one of the ways by which the board can demonstrate concretely its esteem for staff members. It is important in setting up salaries, in our judgment, that there be a schedule of raises or series increments, written in advance by the governing board, so that the staff person is in a position to know the long-range conditions of his employment. It is discouraging for staff members to have to "haggle" with the board each year for a salary increase. The hospitalization and retirement plans, likewise, are ways of encouraging staff members' permanent commitment to the community.

A staff development plan is also an excellent way to tangibly demonstrate the board's commitment to investing in the professional staff members. Educational leave and expenses for professional meetings, consultation, sharing time spent in personal analysis and/or analytic training, and the encouragement of teaching affiliations demonstrate to the staff that the board has a continuing vested interest in, and concern for, their growth as individuals and professional persons.

An annual physical examination should be a required condition of employment.

Governing Board

All community interests, both favorable and unfavorable, should have adequate representation on the board, as should various ethnic, socioeconomic, and cultural segments of the community.

In addition to determining the board's devotion to responsibility, the evaluation should determine whether the governing board has a clear concept of its responsibilities and obligations, and whether this concept is reflected in an adequate system of committee organization which allows the governing board to accomplish its responsibilities. Minimum committees should be personnel, finance, housing, and public information; the functioning of each should be appraised.

In conversations with the governing board and the staff members, the team should try to appraise the adequacy of communication between the board and the staff, between the board and county and city officials, and between the board and the community.

Clinical Functioning

This is a difficult area to appraise adequately. Guidelines in this area will be in a state of flux over the next few years.

In evaluating the intake policy, all individuals should be seen promptly (within 48 hours at the maximum) following their appeal for assistance.

If a waiting list has developed for evaluation or treatment, the team should investigate what steps the staff and board are taking to correct it. One solution is to add additional staff; however, there are other solutions which can be considered.

In examining the evaluation philosophy, the evaluators would want to know the conceptual framework within which the staff views mental and emotional illness and health, and how this framework is reflected in a systematic way of collecting and evaluating various kinds of observation data from the patient.

The treatment priorities, and whether these priorities are in line with the stated purposes of the center as formulated by the governing board, should be studied.

Clinical records should include as a minimum, the following: basic descriptive data concerning the patient; a summary of the evaluation process, including diagnosis, treatment recommendations, prognosis, and outcome; a record of the physical examination; a record of any psychological tests; a brief summary of the treatment process; and a termination note. If medication is administered, there should be a record of the dosage, duration of administration, and results of the medication. At the point of termination, there should be a concise statement concerning the future prognosis of the patient and the responsibilities for future care which the mental health center should assume. There should also be a record of all communications with family members or other caregiving persons in the community.

Any operation, whether it be industry or mental health, should have ongoing evaluative or "house" research in order to study its operations systematically and continually, to appraise its effectiveness, and to determine what modifications may be necessary to improve its functioning.

The comprehensive community mental health center should offer a full range of treatment modalities, including social casework, casework treatment, counseling, individual, family, and group psychotherapy, pharmacotherapy, milieu treatment activities (occupational therapy, recreational therapy, etc.), day treatment programs, and the use of community resources to modify environmental stresses and supports.

There is considerable consensus about the appropriate roles for the various disciplines in terms of clinical functioning. By and large, professional people feel that the needs of the widest range of patients can be met most adequately by a basic team consisting of psychiatrist, clinical psychologist, and psychiatric social worker.

The particular skills and experience of each of these professional members should be integrated into the functioning of the team as a unit; staff responsibilities can be divided to preserve diversity of function while maintaining unanimity of purpose and direction.

The fee structure will be considered again under clinical functioning, in terms of its effect on clinical practice. No matter what the fee policy is, there should be sufficient flexibility to allow each clinician to adjust the fee to best meet the needs of each patient.

Consultative Functioning

Increasing experience and sophistication in the area of community or public health psychiatry has convinced professional people that direct clinical service to patients is alone insufficient to meet the needs of the community. Recent prevalence studies indicate that there are at least 5,000 and, more likely, 10,000 potential patients resident in a community of 50,000 at the time a mental health center opens. If the team sees the usual level of about 200 patients a year, it will take them at least 25 years to see the initial caseload, if no one else becomes emotionally or mentally ill over that period. The staff is faced with an enormous backlog of unmet needs, which cannot in the foreseeable future be met by direct clinical services. One important role of the community mental health center, then, is to provide consultation to the existing "helping" agencies in the community in order that they may more effectively and adequately serve the mental health needs of their clients. The evaluation team, then, should attempt to understand the philosophy and policy of the center regarding mental health consultation, and to study the consultation programs with the public schools, probate court, county welfare office, district court, public health personnel, physicians, colleges and universities, and other agencies in the community that provide services to those who are experiencing difficulties in living.

As with the clinical program, a good consultation program should include evaluative research, to estimate the weaknesses and strengths of the program, and to appraise the needs for modification.

As mentioned in another context, we believe that at least 30 per cent of the staff time of a comprehensive community mental health center should be devoted to consultative functioning.

Mental Health Education

In accordance with the recommendations of the Joint Commission on Mental Illness and Health, mental health education should probably not be the primary responsibility of the three members of the basic psychiatric team. Rather, they should be available as resource people to the local mental health association, the association for retarded children, local councils on children and youth, and other agencies that have accepted the responsibility for general public education about matters of mental illness and mental health. However, if the board feels that mental health education should have a high priority in the total community programming, we would recommend that a mental health educator be employed, and assigned responsibility in this area.

Public Information Program

The mental health center is an agency of the community and frequently a unit of government. For these reasons it has a definite responsibility to keep the taxpayers and the citizens of the community informed of the potentialities, problems, needs, and future plans of the mental health program. It is important that this public information program be totally realistic, and that expectations not be elevated beyond the level which psychiatric science can promise, or beyond the level which local resources will permit.

Consequently, the team should appraise the implementation of the public information program through media and community groups, and also attempt to evaluate community attitudes. In essence, the public information program tells about the functioning of the community mental health center; it is different than the mental health education program. Mental health education attempts to give general information about personality growth and development, emotional illness, emotional health, and so forth.

The public information program concerning the activities of the mental health center, in contrast, is focused specifically upon the activities of that facility; consequently, the public information program is primarily the responsibility of the governing board and, secondarily, of the professional staff of the center.

Research

In addition to program evaluation research which has been mentioned in another context, better developed centers should also be conducting basic research into areas such as the relationship between social forces and personality dysfunctioning, implementation of public mental health programs, and various special problem areas such as delinquency, alcoholism, and aftercare of the psychotic patient.

Training

The manpower shortage is a dilemma that continues to plague all in community mental health service activities. For this reason, it is imperative that all mental health centers, as soon as possible, begin to plan for, and implement training of, the various disciplines. Not only should psychiatrists, clinical psychologists, and psychiatric social workers receive training in mental health centers, but possibilities should be explored for training mental health nurses, counseling psychologists, "mental health workers," mental health educators, and community mental health organizers.

Other Considerations

Community mental health centers do not substitute for the private practice of psychiatry. Consequently, one responsibility of the governing board and staff of the community mental health center is to actively encourage the establishment and growth of private psychiatric practice in the area.

Communication between the community and the staff should be mutual; the staff should participate in a variety of community activities not directly related to the work of the mental health center.

Morale is a very difficult factor to objectify, but one that is relatively easy to assess after several hours of talking with the board and staff of the community mental health center.

Program evaluation should be an evolving and collaborative endeavor. A certificate may be issued after the evaluation. It should state whether the center is approved, the type and duration of certification, and should specify type of community mental health center.

In summary, the program evaluation is one tool of administration, to assist the community mental health center's board and staff look at current functioning, institute improvements, and plan effectively for future development.

SUGGESTED READINGS

APA Committee on Standards and Policies for Hospitals and Clinics: Emerging patterns of administration in psychiatric facilities (1964). *Psychiatric Studies & Projects,* Vol. 2, No. 9.

Group for the Advancement of Psychiatry (1949), *An Outline for Evaluation of a Community Program in Mental Hygiene,* Pub. No. 8. New York.

Ross, M. (1962), Psychiatric clinics—standards, practices, and trends. *Mental Hosp.,* 356-60.

Standards for Hospitals and Clinics (1956). Washington, D.C.: American Psychiatric Association.

XVII

Special Problem Areas: Aftercare

The term "aftercare" has been in use at least since 1879, when The Reverend H. Hawkins, Chaplain of the Middlesex Asylum at Colney Hatch, England, wrote a paper having that title. The Reverend urged that the indigent poor who had been in asylums needed help to bridge the gap between the asylum and the outside (Muth, 1961). An Aftercare Association was formed in 1879, and is still in existence, in Great Britain.

In the United States, the first paid aftercare worker was employed by the New York State Charities Aid Association in 1906. In 1913, social workers were employed by Danvers and Boston State Hospitals. By 1914, 11 New York State hospitals employed social workers (Muth, 1961).

The development of aftercare proceeded slowly; usually, services were provided by the hospital in which the patient had been resident. Since World War II and the reawakened interest of the public in mental illness and health, much attention and much effort has been expended in the development of community-focused social psychiatry. Aftercare services are part of this development.

The Kansas Experience: An Illustration

In 1962, 1,164 patients were readmitted to our three general state psychiatric hospitals. By 1975, on the basis of population growth alone, 1,549 patients (of a total 3,270 admissions) will be readmitted patients. Also, if the present pattern of bed utilization remains constant, and first admission and readmission rates neither increase nor decrease, population growth, alone, will necessitate a 700-bed increase in the capacity of the hospitals. A reduction of this readmission rate could realistically obviate the need for growth in bed capacity of the hospitals, could save in current budget expenses, and could benefit the well-being and social functioning of many discharged patients.

During 1962 and 1963, Kansas Community Mental Health Services sponsored two conferences on Aftercare of the Psychiatric Patient in Kansas. Participants noted that there had been an enormous increase in the number of readmissions to Kansas state psychiatric hospitals. Between 1952 and 1962, the hospital readmissions climbed from 226 a year to 1,164 in a single year. The individual state hospitals and the Division of Institutional Management have been well aware of this problem, which mirrors changes that have occurred in many sections of the country associated with a more rapid treatment and prompt discharge policy. The first state-wide conference on Aftercare was designed to focus attention on the problem, to involve responsible citizen leaders and professional people from various settings, and to hear reports of differing approaches to the problem of aftercare. The delegates heard about the New York program of state support of aftercare clinics; about the suitability of types of brief-contact aftercare as a satisfactory alternative to 50-minute psychotherapy; about the role of the comprehensive mental health center; and about ways for intelligently and effectively utilizing local facilities of all sorts to assure adequate treatment.

In this first state-wide meeting, as well as in the subsequent follow-up meeting in the Kansas City area, all participants commented upon the considerable discrepancy existing between the idealized and official administrative plan in Kansas and the practical reality. One discussion group concluded,

"The general conclusion seemed to be that, presently, follow-up tends to be a hit-and-miss situation with a little done by several different group-welfare departments, public health nurses, Topeka State Hospital Outpatient department, mental health centers, and physicians." Another discussion group decided, "The process of referral of patients by hospitals to community agencies is somewhat uncertain. More clearly defined lines of communication are necessary. . . . The community agency to be responsible for the returned patient is not clear." Another group stated, "The group discussed the high readmission rate of former patients in Johnson County, and pointed out that poor hospital-community communications and the failure of community agencies to take active responsibility in providing aftercare to discharged patients might contribute to readmissions."

In all of these meetings, considerable confusion developed concerning the actual statutory responsibility of the county welfare departments for aftercare services. Initially many of the discussants seemed to have the impression, somehow, that all patients returning to the community were almost the "property" of the county welfare department. There was also a generally held belief that all patients are referred to the county welfare department for aftercare; this proved repeatedly to be grossly inaccurate. In fact, the Institutional Manual for County Departments of Social Welfare states: "to participate and assist in casework planning and placement . . . *as requested.*" Also, it became increasingly clear that the definition of the role of the county welfare department should be redefined in a way more in keeping with the actual potentialities of the average county department, both in terms of staff training and staff time availability. Most of the discussion groups advised that "county welfare offices act as a clearing house or central source of information regarding patients' discharges . . ." Or, as another group said, "After considerable discussion, it was agreed the responsibility for triggering community action rested in local departments of social welfare." In line with this attempt to redefine the role of the local department of social welfare as *a coordinating and clearing-house agency, rather than an agency providing all service directly,* one group said, "Someone pointed out that cooperation and coordination between all interested groups, rather than attempting to fix the responsibility upon one agency, is needed in order to provide the best services, although some central agency was needed for leadership and planning."

Most of the discussion groups seemed to believe that there were definite problems in terms of the hospitals' communicating to local agencies about discharge planning for individual patients. One group stated this as follows, "It was recommended by Group II that a plan be worked out immediately for routine notification to local courts and departments of welfare regarding people released from mental hospitals. It was suggested that the notification include a statement of the referring person or agency, the date of release and status of the patient, and responsibility for notifying the referrer of the patient's release to be assumed by the department of social welfare." In elaborating upon this recommendation, the same group said, "Several commented that the only time discharge information is received is when a placement or financial assistance is needed. Mental health clinics are likewise 'in the dark' unless the hospital requests services."

Other groups felt that a primary problem, which was very difficult to surmount, involved the geographic remoteness of some of the state hospitals from the population concentration that they served.

Several groups were of the opinion that it is difficult to maintain chronically ill patients on medication following discharge from the hospital. It was felt that patients with tenuous motivation and severe illness were not likely to remain on their medication if any significant financial sacrifice were required. One group said, "Concern was expressed for the patient discharged on drugs and not referred for follow-up." Another group recommended, "That some state and/or county agency subsidize medication for patients released from state hospitals."

Many groups recognized the potentially crucial role of the family physician in terms of supervising medication and providing minimal aftercare services for the vast majority of patients, particularly in the less thickly populated western portion of the state. One of the discussants at the state-wide aftercare meeting recommended, "Selection of a group of trained medical doctors to be given a modified psychiatric training program in state hospitals to increase the number of personnel who could treat patients in the community for less acute psychiatric conditions."

This rather detailed description of one state's groping attempts to improve a crucial area of patient care is presented because it is probably typical, and because in these discussions, a handful of recurrent themes developed which perhaps have some general applicability:

1. Assumption of Local Responsibility for Coordinating Aftercare Services

The overwhelming consensus was that this could and should be done—in Kansas—by the county director of social welfare. It was, however, emphasized clearly that the county welfare department could *not* be expected, with its present staffing plan, to provide direct casework services to a significant number of patients and/or their families. Rather, the role of the local director of welfare was seen to consist of coordinating existing services, and being aware of the availability of various services so that appropriate referrals could be made upon request of the state hospitals.

2. Adequate Communication between the Hospital and the Community Was Felt to Be Lacking

It was recommended that a standard release form be prepared, which would be a necessary "ticket" for the patient to be discharged from the hospital. That is, the basic demographic data will be completed by the county welfare department when the application for admission is processed, and will be forwarded to the hospital. In addition, they will get written permission from the patient and/or his next of kin to send out this information at the time of discharge. This form would also be accompanied by a standard letter, and would be sent out on the day of the patient's discharge to the family physician, the welfare department, the probate court, the mental health center in the district, and the minister (if appropriate).

3. Assumption of Clinical Responsibility

a. For making discharge plans. It was brought out in the discussions that the responsibility for making a specific prescription for aftercare services rests with the hospital. That is, the hospital should prescribe for each patient, at the time of discharge, what type of treatment he should ideally receive after he returns to the community. It is then the responsibility of the community to implement this prescription, and to modify it over a course of time if appropriate.

b. For implementing aftercare services. While the role of the county welfare department in coordinating and planning local services, and stimulating their development and utilization, is indisputable, the county welfare department does not carry a primary responsibility for actually providing the clinical services of aftercare. *This is a medical responsibility, and must be assumed by a medical agency within the community.* It would seem desirable that the selected community mental health center be the logical agency.

4. Relocation of Hospital Facilities

Relocation of some of the services of the existing state hospitals nearer major population centers would seem desirable.

5. Medication

Many of the discussion groups felt that some financial support for medication was necessary since about one-half of discharged patients are taking medication, the discontinuation of which frequently precipitates readmission.

6. The Development of New Resources

It was the consensus that the family physician must be involved more actively in providing day-by-day aftercare services for his patients. Proposals were made for setting up a periodic inservice training program to train a selected group of general practitioners throughout the western part of Kansas. In return for this training and a small honorarium, these practitioners would agree to keep open a half day a week of their time to treat psychiatric patients of all types, including patients discharged from state hospitals, charging them upon ability to pay. A similar program in Nebraska has proven to be quite successful.

WHAT ARE THE NATIONAL EMERGING PATTERNS OF AFTERCARE?

Social workers and public health nurses are the two largest groups involved in aftercare. The involvement of social work is traditional, stemming from the responsibility of the hospital social worker to maintain contact with the patient's family. It was natural for this group to take leadership in the expanding aftercare programs.

In states other than Kansas, the enormity of the problem

and its social and humanistic urgency, have led to diverse
and creative programming for aftercare services. Minnesota
has legislation which places the responsibility for aftercare
in the local welfare department. The welfare department,
on request, maintains ongoing contact with the patient.
Minnesota has provided an extensive training program on
a regional basis for welfare workers and more recently has
included public health nurses. The training occurs over a
period of several months in three separate sessions; one
session is held at the state hospital serving the region.

California has for some years provided follow-up care
through a separate Bureau of Social Services in the Department of Mental Hygiene. This bureau stations social
workers on a regional basis in relation to specific state hospitals. Their sole job is follow-up care either in their office
or by home visits.

New York provides follow-up care by sending out social
workers and other personnel from the hospitals to population centers, by visiting patients in their homes, and through
providing special aftercare clinics in the large cities. In
Illinois, hospital social workers provide the aftercare services
in outpatient clinics operated by the hospitals. Patients are
also referred to community clinics. A report based on ques-
tionnaires to states, indicates that the pattern of follow-up by
hospital social service is followed in Pennsylvania, Maine,
Connecticut, New Jersey, and Indiana.

Public Health Nurses

The use of public health nurses in aftercare is spreading
rapidly. The nurses themselves are very much interested,
since they already provide service to families who may have
problems associated with mental illness or emotional disorders. The nurses all have a basic preparation in nursing
and many have specialized training in public health.

Georgia was a pioneer in the use of public health nurses.

In 1953, a procedure was worked out with the one state hospital to refer all patients who would accept referral to their local county health department. Georgia is fortunate in having a local health department in every county. The local court which committed patients was also asked to notify the health department so that families could be contacted early. Orientation, consultation, and a visit to the state hospital was provided to the nurses.

Tennessee instituted a similar program in 1958. In two counties, it was found that 74 per cent of the families having a patient at the state hospital, were already known to the public health nursing service.

Alabama established a program using public health nurses in 1958. Similar programs are reported for Colorado, Florida, Kentucky, Maryland, Michigan, and other states.

An interesting study has been going on in Hartford, Connecticut, where the Visiting Nurses Association made an agreement with the State Department of Mental Hygiene to follow-up patients released from the state hospital. They found that the average aftercare visit took 42 minutes as figured by one method, and 66 minutes as figured by another. The cost of a visit was $5.96, compared to $5.88 for a cancer visit, $6.55 for a cardiovascular arteriosclerosis visit, and $3.82 for a postpartum visit. An interesting change in agency practice was the establishment of voluntary visits occurring after hours or on weekends. During a 12-month study period, 312 patients left the hospital. Of these, 21 per cent refused aftercare service and 73 per cent accepted. More than two visits were made to 63 per cent of the latter group and less than three visits were made to 10 per cent (Ozarin, 1962).

Physicians

A recent study in Kansas (Sigler, 1963) demonstrates that private physicians—most often general practitioners—are the most frequently utilized resource (35 of 56 patients receiving community services). Yet, physicians were almost never involved in predischarge planning. In addition, the average physician will have only 2-4 patients returning to his care from the hospital each year; these small numbers, his lack of involvement in planning for discharge, frequently inadequate medical school preparations for assuming such responsibility, and his participation in the general cultural tendency to reject the mentally ill—all impair the general physician's potentially very great usefulness in aftercare. Patients will seek him out; it is the responsibility of the mental health profession to help him be more effective.

The Community Mental Health Center

Hopefully, the preceding discussion has demonstrated the complexity of aftercare, the need for careful planning, for community assumption of responsibility, for fixation of agency accountability, and the necessity to involve many disciplines: social service, volunteer, vocational rehabilitation, public health, the ministry, employment security, and medicine. The community mental health center can play a crucial role in planning and coordinating aftercare services on a community-wide basis; in affording consultation and inservice training to other caregiving persons; and in affording direct services.

Yet, in all honesty, community mental health centers do precious little! In Minnesota, in Fiscal Year 1961, 9 per cent of the patients at one center were from state hospitals; in Indiana for Fiscal Year 1962, 2 per cent were referrals from state hospitals. A study of 649 patients released from state hospitals showed only 18 per cent had contact with professional personnel during the first month or two back in the community (Freeman and Simmons, 1961).

The previously cited Kansas study (Sigler, 1963) revealed that about one-third of the patients in the sample found it necessary to return to the hospital during the two-year period following their release. One-fourth of the patients made no use of community facilities. *Only five of 56 patients used a local mental health center; 12 a private psychiatrist.*

The role of the comprehensive community mental health center, then, rests largely with the future. What sorts of services should be available for the discharged patient at the local mental health center?

1. The supervision of ataractic medication is certainly necessary. In many areas, over half of the patients discharged from the state hospital are receiving medication. This may be supervised directly by center psychiatrists, or indirectly, by psychiatric consultation to the family physician, who will continue to regulate dosage.

2. The "minimal contact clinic" is a logistically feasible method for supervising medication, assessing adjustment, and providing psychotherapeutic support. This practice of ego-oriented psychotherapy utilizes "institutional transferences" heavily, abandons the 50-minute hour, and emphasizes the supportive aspects of the clinician's interaction with the patient (MacLeod and Middelman, 1962).

3. Public health nurses with psychiatric training and experience may participate in the aftercare program, either as employees of the mental health center or "on loan" from the local health department. The versatility, flexibility, and home-visitation skills of public health nurses make them valuable members of the aftercare team.

4. Social casework services should be available for the patient and/or his family as needed.

5. Group counseling and supportive group therapy can be useful to many, although not all, returning patients.

6. A social club, utilizing the skills of volunteers, is an extremely important part of the resocialization process in the community.

7. Day and night hospital services would be useful in the hospital-community transition for many patients, and

would often forestall rehospitalization at points of relapse.

8. Vocational rehabilitation, employment services, and sheltered workshops all would expand the usefulness of the mental health center to the seriously ill person.

9. Financial assistance, medication, child care services, homemaker services, religious services, adult education—all these and more will be needed if optimum rehabilitation is to be offered each discharged patient.

The future leaves much to be accomplished. Up until now, because of inadequate discharge planning, we have been sending patients from our hospitals into communities which are too ill-staffed and ill-trained to care for them: it has been like sending a cured pneumonia patient out into a snowstorm in his underwear. We can, must, and will do better.

SUGGESTED READINGS

Andrew, G. & Smith, E. (1963), *Program Implication of One Project for Psychiatric Patient Aftercare*. Lansing: Michigan Departments of Health and Mental Health.

Freeman, H. E. & Simmons, O. G. (1963), *The Mental Patient Comes Home*. New York: Wiley.

Laverty, R. (1960), *The Utilization of Local Facilities in the Supervision of Psychiatric Patients*. Red Bank, New Jersey: Monmouth County Organization for Social Service.

Pishkin, V. & Shunley, J. T. (1963), Trial visit adjustment index. *Arch. Gen. Psychiat.*, 9:471-476.

Proceedings of the Institute on Rehabilitation of the Mentally Ill (1962). New York: Altro Health and Rehabilitation Services.

XVIII

Juvenile Delinquency

A community mental health worker should avoid involvement with the juvenile delinquent unless he is prepared to examine closely, some of his own basic operational assumptions. Yet, juvenile offenses are frequent, concern the community, and can scarcely be omitted from a comprehensive, community-wide program designed to meet human needs.

In 1958, between one and a half and two million youngsters under 18 years of age were dealt with by the police for misdemeanors (U.S. Department of Health, Education and Welfare, Children's Bureau, 1960). The national rate of reported juvenile court actions had doubled in the decade between 1948 and 1958. Of the total offenses in 1958, about 20 per cent of the arrests of juveniles were for serious offenses. While urban areas have seemed to contribute more to juvenile delinquency rates than rural areas, in the last few years the rate of increase in juvenile delinquency has been greater for predominantly rural areas and small towns. Juvenile delinquency appears more often in the lower socioeconomic strata of society, but occurs in all socioeconomic groupings —although community means of coping with such deviant behavior may be differentiated along socioeconomic lines.

Before becoming involved in a community-wide effort for the control of juvenile delinquency, mental health workers would do well to consider the following questions:

1. Is delinquent behavior symptomatic of a psychological disturbance, or mental or emotional illness? The statement in

the above-cited report to the Congress tries to be explicit on this point:

> The relationship between delinquent behavior, as defined above, and psychological disturbance, character disorder, and actual mental illness, is particularly important to clarify. Psychological difficulties of youth and delinquent behavior are related and overlapping areas; but they are not the same thing. Psychological disturbance is a cause for only a portion, and it must be said an undetermined portion, of all delinquency. Some delinquency is 'normal' in that it develops out of identifications which children make with their own neighborhood or special groups within it. There are groups that are rebellious and defiant towards the norms and life patterns which the majority in the adult community sets for itself and proposes as models for children and youth. Immediate rewards in the psychological satisfaction of acceptance by their peers lead children and youth under such conditions to participate in what in fact may be delinquent behavior on a basis that is quite understandable in terms of the individual's sense of personal worth [p. 2].

To mental health professionals, this somewhat facile avoidance of the basic problems involved in the relationship between emotional illness and delinquent behavior is less than satisfying. However, upon closer scrutiny the entire concept of "illness," as related to all kinds of deviant behavior, is equally unsatisfactory. The illness model, when applied to behavioral deviations, is of questionable usefulness.

Perhaps it is only necessary to reassert our belief that all behavior is purposive—even if not effective—and is determined. We might go on to say that causation of behavior is multiple, with interweaving of biological, psychological, and sociocultural factors. Motivations are both conscious and unconscious. Behaviors, whether they deviate from the norm or fall within it, whether they are seen as illness or health, normality or criminality, persist because significant rewards accrue—primary or secondary gains—or because alternative behaviors are not available to the individual as a result of deficient ability, inadequate learning experiences, or personal experiences that have made certain behaviors, for which innate ability exists, unutilizable (avoidance conditioning).

The community mental health worker, in other words, may contribute to an understanding of the particular set of motivations and behaviors adopted by the individual delinquent. Whether this understanding—composed, as it ideally should be, of information about the biological, psychological, and sociocultural parameters of behavior—will be particularly useful in planning a treatment and/or rehabilitation program, is another question entirely.

2. Are the mental health center and the individual community mental health worker agents of the individual, or agents of society? In providing diagnostic and treatment services for many patients, this issue is not a particularly cogent one. However, when participating in a community program for delinquency control, its valence increases considerably. To what extent does the mental health worker serve to promote the normative societal values, with their associated moralistic and religioethical connotations? To what extent is he an agent of the police department, or probation officer? To what extent is he an agent of the individual patient? Of the patient's parents? Of the school?

There are no easy answers to these questions, and each mental health worker will have to come to some kind of peace with himself. To the extent that his values closely approximate those of the nurturant society, the conflict will be less sharp. To the extent that he repudiates, as does the delinquent, certain of the value systems of society, his own conflict and personal uncertainty will be greater.

3. Can a patient or client who does not want treatment be helped? Can one successfully help someone who is forced to see a community mental health worker? Much of the training, professional behavior, lore, and tradition of clinical psychiatry is based on the concept of an unwritten contractual arrangement between a willing patient and a willing therapist. No third party is involved, no direct or overt coercion is invoked, and the contract may be canceled at any

time. Reciprocal obligations are clearly defined, acceptable behavior is specified, and goals delineated.

This neat conceptual model rarely applies to the juvenile delinquent.

4. Can the individual mental health worker deal with patients from socioeconomic levels widely divergent from his own, and with subcultural groupings with which he has no familiarity by direct experience? It is easy to be unprejudiced and nonjudgmental when one is dealing with individuals like oneself. It may be somewhat more difficult when one's clients neither look, talk, act, nor feel as the mental health worker looks, talks, acts, or feels.

5. Can primarily verbal and permissive therapy be effective with nonverbal and impulse-ridden clients? The flexibility of the mental health worker will be put to the test by juvenile delinquents more than by any other group. If the worker must, for a variety of reasons, always be "a good guy," and never adopt behaviors that are judgmental, directive, controlling, or punitive, he may find himself unable to work with the juvenile offender. Being a nice guy at all times, and being consistently nondirective and loving, is in some ways a luxury that one can afford when one is dealing primarily with middle-class neurotic patients.

WHAT CAN THE MENTAL HEALTH CENTER DO?

First of all, the center, and particularly the mental health education staff, may participate actively in a community-wide effort to stimulate interest and enlightened concern on the part of nontreatment agencies in the community, such as the school system, the churches, recreational facilities, employment agencies, and so forth, in the problems of juvenile delinquency. The attempt should be to substitute knowledge for ignorance, planning for panic, compassion for retribution.

In addition to the involvement of opinion-setters and

caregivers of the community in examining the problems of juvenile delinquency, and planning for improved services, the mental health center can participate either as a leader or co-participant in efforts to integrate all community services to provide comprehensive, continuous, and available services for the potential and actual delinquent. A wide variety of special treatment and remedial activities could potentially be involved. For example, juvenile delinquency and reading disability are highly correlated, and remedial reading services hold much potential as an important contribution to a community-wide delinquency program. Adequate opportunities for initial work experience, vocational training, and vocational counseling are also needed. A community mental health center should be willing to participate in planning for the integration of these programs.

Third, the community mental health center can and should offer direct diagnostic and treatment services. Many centers find it advantageous to differentiate between two kinds of services: the first, following the traditional clinical model, defines the mental health center and its staff as agent of the patient, and evaluation and treatment of the delinquent and his family is fully confidential; in the second, the community mental health center is an agent of society, and evaluates the juvenile in order to consult with agencies of the communities such as the court. In some centers, when interagency relationships become well-defined, and as community mental health practitioners become more comfortable about their "in-between" roles, increasing freedom may develop to experiment with services that combine both the patient-centered and society-centered approach. However, the beginning community mental health worker, and the relatively new center, are probably well advised to initially differentiate their services very sharply, using such distinctions as a technique for educating other community caregivers—such as the court—about the special quality and nature of the clinician-patient relationship in psychiatry.

And, the community mental health center should stimulate interest in, and participate with, other agencies of the community, in developing a wide variety of services to alleviate some of the underlying social causes of much deviant behavior. An immediate focus of concern would be "hardcore," "multiple problem" families, which contribute many delinquents, mentally and emotionally ill individuals, illegitimate pregnancies, school dropouts, welfare clients, and venereal disease cases to the caseloads of all public agencies within the community. Such services must impinge upon the potential delinquent even before his birth. Aggressive reaching out to insure adequate prenatal care for mothers in low socioeconomic groups in order to prevent prematurity, brain damage, and increased prevalence of mental retardation is related to a comprehensive community program for the prevention of delinquency. Provision of prenatal classes, public health nursing services, well baby clinics: all are related to the maintenance of a healthy mother-child relationship. If our theories about human personality development are at all valid, this cannot help but be related to the future behavior of the individual child within his social milieu.

Preschool enrichment experiences for children from socioculturally or psychologically deprived or alienated environments would also be important in preventing future delinquency.

All studies have indicated that aggressive and brutal behavior in adults has usually been preceded by their own brutal mistreatment in childhood at the hands of parents or parent surrogates. The child learns well by experience, and seems to introject the example of brutal mistreatment. Because of this, as well as because of the other types of psychological and physical damage that may be inflicted upon the child, the community must pay particular attention to the areas of child abuse and mistreatment, as well as child neglect. Increasing clarity and strength in state legislative enactments, more vigorous enforcement at the local level, and more involvement of social, educational, and mental health institutions in concern about the plight of the battered child are necessary. All too often, professional persons in mental health disciplines and the social service areas need, for a wide variety of personal reasons, to hold to the belief that human beings are innately good, and that evil and aggressive behavior occurs only in the face of frustration. This may be perfectly true, and is certainly a workable clinical model, so long as it does not lead to a Pollyanna-like need to deny or minimize the existence of cruel or vicious behavior. Unfortunately, it is not uncommon to find that with an apparent conscious unawareness, mental health clinicians and workers in social agencies seem to look away from examples of child abuse and "pass the buck" to some other agency to handle the problem. Not infrequently, the problem receives no attention, and permanent psychological and/or physical trauma to the child results.

The provision of a full spectrum of services in the schools is essential for delinquency prevention. Reading clinics, speech therapy, special classrooms for behavior problems and emotionally ill children, the full gamut of special education facilities, school psychology, social work, and counseling and guidance service, special vocational sequences— these are a few of the contributions that the school can make to the community program to minimize delinquent behavior problems.

Law enforcement agencies have an inescapable responsibility in the field of juvenile delinquency. In the previously mentioned report of the Children's Bureau it is stated:

> However, the agencies are understaffed. For example, few police departments in cities under 25,000 and only half of those between

25,000 and 50,000, have officers on their staff that specialize in work with juveniles. Many detention homes and training schools are poorly staffed and overcrowded, and some 100,000 children per year are held in jail awaiting court trial. The number of juvenile probation officers has increased only 46 per cent between 1952 and 1957, as contrasted with an 82 per cent increase in juvenile delinquency. . . . The existing staffs of a number of the agencies are, for the most part, inadequately trained. Police chiefs agree that officers who specialize in work with juveniles should have more training. Other groups also need more training. The generally accepted goal, recognized by the relevant professional organizations, is for all probation officers, for example, to have completed graduate social work training. However, at present only 10 per cent of this group has achieved this level. Many other social agencies inevitably become involved with problems that have a bearing on delinquency, and their staffs, too, need more professional competence [pp. 8-9].

In relationships with law enforcement agencies and the courts, it is most important that the mental health center not participate in either a conscious or unconscious conspiracy to deny the shortages and inadequacies that exist in these agencies. That is, a little bit of consultation or diagnostic service from the community mental health center will not make up for the fact that there are inadequate juvenile personnel—either in numbers or training—inadequate court personnel, or inadequate detention home facilities. The mental health center may decide to work in a consultative relationship even if serious deficiencies in court and law enforcement agencies exist, but a clearly defined role for the consultation process should be upgrading of existing services, and the relationship should be terminated after a reasonable length of time if efforts to upgrade services quantitatively and qualitatively are not forthcoming. To do other than this would be to participate in a conspiracy to cover up and gloss over rejection of the juvenile delinquent by the community and its agencies.

Youth groups, such as the Boy and Girl Scouts, and public recreation services may *potentially* make a rich contribution to delinquency control. However, as is true for most community services, the value system of such organizations, and the cultural backgrounds of the personnel, are usually strictly American middle-class. Children most in need of organized social activities and supervised recreation may be specifically, even if covertly or unconsciously, excluded.

The public health unit, welfare services, and child welfare services have specifically assigned, special responsibilities for a segment of the community which contributes a large proportion of delinquent children. It may well be in partnership with these services—inadequately staffed though they may be—that the community mental health center can best develop collaborative and consultative relationships leading towards delinquency control.

Whether the community mental health center can make a significant contribution to the primary prevention of juvenile delinquency may be somewhat in doubt; that it can make a contribution to the secondary prevention of juvenile delinquency, at least in many individual cases, is extremely likely; and that it can assist in the tertiary prevention of continuing deviant behavior is certain. Delinquent children who are sent to state industrial or training schools return, almost invariably, to a family that has received no professional assistance during their absence, and to communities that often have "closed ranks" behind them. Their initial sense of rejection can only be heightened by return to a school where they are viewed with even greater suspicion than previously, to a neighborhood for whom the title of "troublemaker" has been confirmed, and to a family which is annoyed, inconvenienced, and embarrassed by the delinquent's behavior as well as the secondary social reaction against it. A community mental health center should—after prior planning with the state training school—be able to make available casework services for the parents of children who have been sent to industrial or training schools, and family or individual psychotherapy for parents can be provided where indicated. Such treatment will not be easy, and will be neither universally accepted by parents nor uniformly successful. The delinquent child, upon his return to the community from a training school, or while on probation or parole, may or may not be willing to accept and benefit from treatment services in the community mental health center. Proper training and experience are by no means universal in the training programs of any of the three professional disciplines. Specifically, group therapy techniques, which seem to offer the greatest likelihood of success for many delinquent adolescents, have, in many instances, not been mastered by the practitioner in the community mental health center.

Can the community mental health center contribute to a community-wide program of delinquency control? Yes, but the task will be difficult, the outcome uncertain, and the price in personal discomfort and effort on the part of community mental health center staff considerable. Whether the goal is sufficiently important and the price sufficiently reasonable, will in the final analysis be decided by the staff of the individual community mental health center. This realism should be tempered, however, by recognition that the community and its specialized agencies have heretofore not been doing an outstandingly successful job in coping with delinquent behavior. Consequently, the community mental health center should be able to proceed with the conviction that its efforts will not make things materially worse for either the community or the individual delinquent, and may even result, with patient and genuine effort, in improvement.

Suggested Readings

Block, H. A. & Flynn, F. T. (1956), *Delinquency*. New York: Random House.
Glueck, S., ed. (1959), *The Problem of Delinquency*. New York: Houghton Mifflin.

Hodges, E. F., Jr. & Tart, C. D., Jr. (1963), A follow-up study of potential delinquents. *Amer. J. Psychiat.*, 120:447-453.

Kahn, A. J. (1963), *Planning Community Services for Children in Trouble*. New York: Columbia University Press.

Michaels, J. J. (1964), The need for a theory of delinquency. *Arch. Gen. Psychiat.*, 10:182-186.

Report to the Congress on Juvenile Delinquency (1960). Washington, D. C.: U. S. Dep't of Health, Education & Welfare.

Vedder, C. B., ed. (1954), *The Juvenile Offender, Perspective and Readings*. New York: Random House.

XIX

Addictive Diseases

Addiction to alcoholism and narcotics are ancient problems for society; in recent years there has been an increasing incidence of addiction to barbiturates, amphetamines and other drugs. In varying degrees, the addict is a source of worry to himself, his family and friends, the community and its institutions (neighborhood, church, industry, traffic safety, law enforcement), caregiving agencies, individual citizens, and sometimes, to mental health professionals.

In addicted persons, as well as in others with serious and disabling illnesses that are troubling to society, we can see the "game of disposition" played out most blatantly.[1] All caregiving agencies—whether they be social welfare, general physicians, mental health centers, vocational rehabilitation services, or whoever—prefer to serve those with highest status in the community, with conditions that are not noisy or troublesome, and whose prognosis for recovery is good. To the extent that clients occupy lower socioeconomic positions in the community, are stigmatized, have illnesses that are noisy or frightening, and have prognoses that are less than favorable, they will tend to be shunned and scorned by all caregiving groups. A "game" then develops, to "pass the buck" and get rid of these clients, using a variety of devices or alibis. The agency may define its role operationally so as to exclude certain types of difficulties,

---

[1] Dr. David Vail and his associates of the mental health program of Minnesota have developed the concept of the game of disposition at some length, and I am indebted to them for this idea.

without explicitly excluding them. For example, a clinical system that is based upon a long wait for intake interview, a long wait for evaluation, and another long wait for therapy would effectively dispose of those individuals who have difficulty in delaying gratification and who act impulsively and rapidly, if not wisely, when uncomfortable. As simple a factor as the location of the agency may also determine patient clientele. For example, if the agency is located in an upper-class neighborhood, at considerable distance from public transportation, and on the opposite side of town from slum and lower socioeconomic areas, it will effectively be able to discourage many clients of lower socioeconomic status.

The community mental health center may decide to have a clinical program for alcoholics, or for a variety of reasons may decide to exclude alcoholism from its program. It is to be hoped, however, that whatever decision is made will be on the basis of rational planning and conscious decision, rather than through rationalization and denial.

A great deal of energy and not a few words have been devoted to defining alcoholism. By and large, the question as to who is alcoholic and who is not is relatively easy to decide for everyone except the alcoholic himself, and in some instances his immediate family. Alcoholism has been defined as an acquired, chronic and progressive condition of adult life involving the compulsive intake of excessive amounts of alcohol, and leading, in time, to psychological, social, and physical disabilities. It would seem that recognized alcoholism in males as opposed to females occurs in a ratio of about 6 to 1, and is diagnosed most of the time in adults between 35 and 55 years of age. Alcoholism has been found to be high in prevalence in urban areas, connected with certain occupations, and more frequent in certain ethnic groups. However, it is very difficult to determine the true magnitude of alcoholism, since there exist neither objective and unequivocal criteria for diagnosis, nor uniform statistical reporting. One report (Jellinek and Keller, 1952) has indicated a prevalence of 2.4 per cent of the total population, or about 7 per cent of those who drink. Since 6 out of 7 of known alcoholics are adult males, the estimated prevalence of alcoholism in the male population twenty years and over is around 7.5 per cent. Alcoholism is, therefore, not only a serious personal and public health problem, but is also economically important, of concern to industry, and related to crime and accident rates.

It is beyond the scope of this chapter to describe the pharmacology and physiology of alcohol, the characteristics of the alcoholic syndrome, or to summarize studies of psychopathology and other aspects of etiology and epidemiology. Rather, we will pose the deceptively simple question of, "What can the community mental health center do about the problem of alcoholism?"

Activities may consist of direct clinical services; alcohol education; consultation services to other community caregivers; and research into the causes, prevention, or treatment of alcoholism and/or its sequelae.

ALCOHOL EDUCATION

There has been no really sound demonstration that education about alcohol and alcoholism, conducted in any context and by any method, significantly affects incidence or prevalence of alcoholism, and/or various sequelae. However, neither has there been any convincing evidence—in fact, there has been some rather convincing counterevidence—that a liberal arts education has a significant humanizing or broadening influence on the individual student. Much education is, at the present time, accepted largely upon the basis of faith, and supported by basic societal values.

The goal of alcoholism education has become, increasingly, one of presenting known facts about alcohol to young persons at various phases in the educational process: its effect upon the body, the causes of alcoholism, and the consequent effects of excessive use of alcohol. This "scientific" or dispassionate approach to problems of alcohol education stands in marked contrast to the polemical, evangelical, moralistic and punitive educational approaches of only a few decades ago.

The introduction to a recent book delimits the problem as follows (McCarthy, 1964):

> The responsibility for assisting young people in the socialization process is shared by the home, church, and the school. Questions regarding the use or non-use of alcoholic beverages represent only one of many issues to be faced in the process of moving from adolescence to young adulthood. . . . The public schoolteacher, however, has an unselected student population. Reflecting as she usually does a middleclass background, she often brings to the class-room conflicting personal attitudes towards drinking. Yet she must attempt to deal objectively with material to be studied and particularly with the questions that students will raise, often questions for which there are no simple answers.

The role of the mental health center in participating in the program of alcoholism education may be either direct or indirect. That is, the center may employ a health educator or mental health educator, and conduct a series of workshops and educational programs for various community groups about alcohol and alcoholism. Or perhaps a more effective approach will lie in collaboration between the community mental health center—either through the mental health educator or some other professional person or persons—and a number of churches, schools, and other community groups (such as YMCA, Scouts, Boys' Clubs, Settlement houses, etc.) interested in conducting programs of alcohol education. The role of the mental health center staff may be consultative and/or collaborative. The mental health center may assist in planning, preparation of the course outlined, and development of curriculum materials and visual aids. The center may provide special inservice training for potential teachers, or may actively provide teaching staff to assist in various programs of alcoholism education.

Any course in alcoholism education should provide basic, scientifically valid information concerning alcohol as a chemical, and the nature of various alcoholic beverages. As well, information should be presented concerning the metabolism of alcohol and the effect of alcohol upon physiological and psychological processes. Information should be given concerning drinking patterns and customs in the United States, as well as social problems associated with the use of alcoholic beverages—such as disturbances in family relationships, crime, economic difficulties, and accidents. Consideration should be given to alcoholism as a syndrome, with a description of characteristic stages of development, methods of treatment, public attitudes, and the role of Alcoholics Anonymous. Particular attention should be given to the many communications within our society which indicate that alcohol is good, stylish, socially acceptable, and "smart." Critical study of alcoholism as presented in such media as the movies, advertisements, humor, etc., should be emphasized throughout the course sequence, as a way of highlighting the complex and often conflictual nature of social and personal attitudes about alcohol and its use in our society.

CLINICAL PROGRAMS

Alcoholism, no matter what its etiology or etiologies, as it occurs clinically is both a physical and psychological disorder.

Basic to any program of alcoholism treatment, therefore, are adequate facilities in the local general hospital for treatment of the acutely alcoholic patient. Not all hospitals accept alcoholics on a par with other ill individuals, even today; and often they do not receive, even after admitted, entirely adequate care. Water and electrolyte balance, nutritional status, and treatment of neurological and psychological reactions to withdrawal should receive careful medical supervision.

The second phase of treatment of the alcoholic should begin, ideally, while he is still in the hospital. Studies have indicated that if the initial contact is made with the alcoholic patient while he is still hospitalized, the follow-up rate for continuing in therapy is markedly higher than if he is only referred by the hospital staff to an outpatient facility at the time he is discharged from the hospital. This conforms with several known facts about human beings. First of all, sick persons who are relatively helpless are more suggestible than those who feel that they are functioning independently and competently; suggestions and instructions that are given to the alcoholic while he is still acutely ill and in the hospital, then, would be expected to result in more compliance. Secondly, the alcoholic, like all human beings, responds to positive demonstrations of affection and concern. While he may eventually frustrate these offers of help, at least an initial expression of interest by the staff of the outpatient facility —by visiting him in the hospital and soliciting his participation as a patient in the outpatient treatment—yields a higher treatment rate.

There is voluminous literature on the psychodynamics of the alcoholic personality, and proper treatment modalities. Although it is not the intention of this chapter to make a detailed survey of this complex, extensive, and often contradictory literature, two questions will be raised for consideration as they relate to the program of alcoholism control:

1. First, perhaps more emphasis should be placed on aspects of primary and secondary prevention in providing services to the alcoholic and his family, rather than on tertiary prevention through the treatment and rehabilitation of the alcoholic himself. Attention to the needs of the spouse and of the children of the marriage may yield a richer reward

in terms of prevention of emotional illness and mental disability than "all out" therapeutic efforts directed only toward the alcoholic himself. Cooperation with a variety of community caregiving agencies would be necessary to achieve this aim. For example, during periods of acute family crisis, foster home care or summer camp placement for some or all of the children, might be the most effective preventive measure available. At other times, temporary separation of husband and wife, requiring temporary support of the family through welfare channels, might be a desirable expedient. In other words, emphasis might be shifted from viewing the alcoholic as the center of attention—a position he characteristically manages to achieve—putting him in his proper position as only one member of a family group, whose needs should not be allowed to take precedence over those of the wife and children, even though his behavior is temporarily more distracting or imperative.

2. Might there be a role for a subprofessional alcoholism counselor in a community program for alcohol control? Professional people tend to veer away from involvement with the alcoholic patient because of the unpredictable and often inordinate demands made upon their time and personal resources by this kind of patient. Scrapes with the law, jail, family fights in the middle of the night, concerned telephone calls from fellow members of Alcoholics Anonymous, etc., are only a brief sampling of the types of annoyances and disruptions to which the professional staff may be subjected. In a public agency, the availability of trained but subprofessional alcoholism counselors, whose major responsibility would be to cope with as many of these alarms and disruptions as possible, and to attempt to help the alcoholic deal with the secondary complications he has stirred up in his environment, might allow the agency as a whole, to be more effective in its interactions with the alcoholic, as well as in making him a more acceptable patient to the

individual professional person. The trained alcoholism counselor would be responsible for mediating between a variety of agencies that provide partial services to the alcoholic, such as the family physician, the general hospital, the staff of the mental health center, ministers, public health nurses, welfare departments, law enforcement agencies, the courts, etc.

There has been a tendency in many states to establish a separate alcohol commission, with a separate system of clinics. While such a system may have something to say in its defense in terms of the development of special demonstration or research facilities, such syndrome specialization in the field of mental health has not generally been associated with the maintenance of high standards. Neither is it logistically feasible in sparsely populated states and rural areas, where a single system of outpatient facilities may best serve the needs of persons with a variety of syndromes or conditions.

CONSULTATION PROGRAM

Many other agencies are involved in and concerned about the problem of alcoholism within the community. Courts and law enforcement agencies, welfare departments, attorneys, general physicians, public health departments, and ministers all have a role to play in the management of the sequelae of the alcoholic syndrome.

The alcoholic is a particularly difficult client. He evokes attitudes that are ambivalent and conflictual, often moralistic, sometimes punitive, or again indulgent. He may be laughed at, scorned, despised, or pitied—but seldom really understood.

As in all consultation processes, initially, the mental health consultant must attempt to understand the role of the agency to which he is offering consultation. His responsibility is to help the agency perform more effectively, the task that has been assigned it within the community. He should not attempt to make policemen into counselors, ministers into psychotherapists, or judges into mothers. Rather, in response to specific requests for consultation, he should attempt to define, with the prospective consultee, the exact nature of the assistance desired, whether he may meet the need expressed, and how the consultative process might best be structured and carried out.

There are certain basic principles and convictions that most mental health workers will carry to this task. It is probably best not to disguise these, but to make them explicit. For example, most mental health workers' basic belief system about alcoholism probably runs along the following lines: Alcoholism is a symptom, and has primarily psychological causations. As a symptom, it provides both primary and secondary gratifications. More or less predictable interpersonal, social, economic, and psychological complications result from prolonged overuse of alcohol. The alcoholic drinks because he is unable to stop; his action is not under conscious control, no matter how much it may seem to be. Punishment has been ineffective as a treatment modality, as has argumentation, exhortation, and reasoning. The wife and other family members of the alcoholic are involved in his condition, and may play either a constructive or a destructive role. Physical, psychological, and social therapeutic and control measures may all be necessary at various points in the course of the alcoholic syndrome. None of these measures—neither psychotherapy, imprisonment, prayer, Alcoholics Anonymous, "Antabuse" or tranquilizers —are a unitary or universally successful solution. None is a panacea, nor inherently better or more prestigious than any other method of intervention.

Within this basic frame of reference, then, the task of the mental health worker is to guide—if the consultee finds it possible to accept the majority of these basic premises and work comfortably within this frame of reference—the consultee to a fuller understanding and a more effective use of his agency in assisting the alcoholic individual, the family of the alcoholic, society, and the institutions of society in coping with the problematic behaviors resulting from the alcoholic way of life.

OTHER ADDICTIVE DISEASES

Addiction to narcotics is a much less frequent problem than is alcoholism. It is estimated that in the United States about 3.3 per 10,000 population are addicted to narcotics. A single mental health center team serving 50,000 population, then, would thus be expected to treat only about 16 narcotic addicts as opposed to 700 alcoholic addicts in the population. Etiology, prevention, and treatment of drug addiction is, if anything, even more complex than is true of alcoholism. Because of the highly specialized nature of the problem, and the relative scarcity of narcotic addiction, discussion is not felt to be appropriate to the present volume. Similarly, habituation and addiction to dexadrine, barbiturates, and tranquilizing agents occur in the population, and will occur sporadically in the patient population of a community mental health center, but will not be discussed in this volume.

SUGGESTED READINGS

A. A. (1952), *44 Questions and Answers About the Program of Recovery from Alcoholism.* New York: The Alcoholic Foundation.
Handbook of Programs on Alcoholism: Research, Treatment, and Rehabilitation (1959). New York: Licensed Beverage Industries.
Jellinek, E. M. (1963), *Government Programs on Alcoholism: A Review of Activities in Some Foreign Countries.* Ottawa: Mental Health Division, Department of National Health and Welfare.
McCarthy, R. G., ed. (1964), *Alcohol Education for Classroom and Community.* New York: McGraw-Hill.
Manual on Alcoholism (1962). Washington, D. C.: A.M.A.
Narcotic Drug Addiction (1963), Mental Health Monograph 2. Washington, D. C.: U. S. Department of Health, Education & Welfare.

National Conference on Alcoholism (1963). Washington, D. C.: Department of Health, Education & Welfare.

Program Planning for Alcoholism in a Metropolitan Community (1962). Committee on Alcoholism, Health Council, United Community Fund of San Francisco.

Thompson, G. N., ed. (1956), *Alcoholism.* Springfield, Ill.: Charles C Thomas.

Todd, F. (1964), *Teaching about Alcohol.* New York: McGraw-Hill.

Wallerstein, R. S. et al. (1957), *Hospital Treatment of Alcoholism* New York: Basic Books.

XX

Mental Retardation

Community mental health practitioners have a definite role to play in providing services for the mentally retarded. Physicians, pediatricians, neurologists, psychiatrists, clinical psychologists, and social workers have made contributions to the understanding of mental retardation, and to treatment and rehabilitation procedures, of significant scope and depth. Too often we participate in guilty and masochistic self-condemnations, and join with parent groups in denouncing ourselves for having "neglected the mentally retarded." The mentally retarded *have* been rejected and neglected by our society, just as other marginal, handicapped, or "weak" individuals have been overlooked by a society which stresses competitiveness, self-reliance, and independence. In this regard, the mental health professions are noteworthy because they have swung against the tide and have attempted to provide services to the retarded and their families.

Mental retardation is a large descriptive category. The use of such a unitary term involves some of the same dangers that are inherent in speaking about mental illness as if it were one condition. Greater sharpness in describing and defining etiology, degree, and type of limitation is necessary.

As a complex problem with biological, cultural and psychological factors, mental retardation is not the property of any one group. Many professions in our free and pluralistic society have a necessary, legitimate, and continuing interest in providing services for the retarded. Competition between these various groups is most likely to be a mainspring of significant new advances in knowledge, as well as in care and treatment. Only if this competition and rivalry is harmful, wasteful, or results in the actual neglect of the retarded, should it be criticized.

EXTENT OF THE PROBLEM

There are estimated to be 5.4 million mentally retarded at the present time out of a population of 179,000,000 (U.S. Department of Health, Education and Welfare, 1963). Each year, 126,000 infants are born who will be mentally retarded. Approximately 0.1 per cent will be retarded so severely that even as adults they will be unable to care for their own needs of daily living; 0.3 per cent of all births will remain below the 7-year intellectual level; while the remaining 2.6 per cent are those with mild retardation who can, with special training and assistance, acquire limited job skills and achieve a measure of independence.

Mental retardation is thus a problem of great social and public health importance because of its prevalence, potential severity, and chronicity. Those who are affected, either directly or indirectly by mental retardation, comprise almost 10 per cent of the population.

It is beyond the scope of this book to give detailed attention to the various classifications of mental retardation, or to discuss, in any depth, its etiology. In only about a fourth of the cases of mental retardation, however, can brain damage be demonstrated, from a variety of causes such as German measles during pregnancy, infectious diseases, Rh blood incompatibility, toxic agents, metabolic disorders, trauma, or diseases due to abnormal chromosomal groupings (such as mongolism).

For about 75 per cent of those diagnosed as retarded there is no demonstrable organic brain pathology. These persons are, by and large, those having relatively mild degrees of retardation, arising from a wide variety of factors. Parental neglect, sociocultural deprivation, psychological illnesses, mild and undiagnosed brain damage—these are a few of the many possible causes of mental retardation.

It is important to note that as modern medical care has improved, infant mortality has declined in the United States, and the survival rate of the mentally retarded has increased. Mental retardation will, therefore, increase in prevalence as infant mortality continues to decrease, and as medical care for childhood and adult retardates continues to improve.

There are 210,000 mentally retarded patients in residential institutions in the United States, but despite this, the waiting list continues to grow and the average waiting time for admission is three years. While an increasing number of local school systems have special education programs, it is estimated that special educational services are available for only about 20 per cent of the known retarded children of school age. Likewise, vocational rehabilitation services for the retarded through state vocational agencies reach only 3 per cent of the mentally retarded.

In other words, the need is great, the resources are few, and the likelihood that the community mental health center will be called upon to play a role in providing services for the mentally retarded and their families is great. What kind of service?

PRIMARY PREVENTION OF MENTAL RETARDATION

Improvement of prenatal care and obstetrical procedures would not generally fall within the purview of the community mental health center. As a member of the medical society, the psychiatrist may contribute some small influence toward continued upgrading of such services. The psychiatrist, as well as other staff members, may also, as enlightened citizens, increase the level of public awareness and support of improved public health services. Public health prenatal clinics for socioeconomically and culturally deprived segments of the community offer the best single hope of reducing the incidence of mental retardation in the general population, and should be vigorously pursued in all communities. Because of widespread concern about "socialism" and lingering moralistic and puritanical attitudes towards the poor and underachieving segment of our population, special efforts in community education and mobilization of community sentiment for improved public health services, including prenatal care and public health nursing services, are necessary in many communities. In this endeavor to improve the general level of social responsibility in community life, mental health center staffs may play a significant role.

Some states are developing genetic registries for conditions such as phenylketonuria, for which definite genetic causation is known. The community mental health center may contribute by directly supporting such endeavors, by providing names of known patients seen during evaluation, and by assisting in general community and medical education towards the acceptance of such innovations in public health services.

The mental health center can also play a role in primary prevention related to the individual case. For example, the seriously mentally ill woman may often neglect, if she becomes pregnant, to receive adequate prenatal care. One responsibility of community mental health center workers, whether physicians or not, is to insure that disabilities caused by mental illness in one generation do not impair the chances of the next generation to be able to cope adequately with the world. Professional persons should assume responsibility for insuring, insofar as it is humanly and professionally possible, that the mentally ill pregnant woman, as an example, receive adequate prenatal and obstetrical care, including in-home supervision by a public health nurse to insure that the patient follows any special dietary or medication regimes prescribed.

The encouragement and support of special prekindergarten, enrichment experiences for children from socioeconomically, culturally, and/or psychologically deprived or alienated families, should be given a high priority by the staff of the mental health center. Because of rigid social attitudes about the sacredness of family life, a tendency to view children as the property of the parents, and a sometimes morbid concern about civil rights and individual liberties, it is not unlikely that neglect of children may be easily tolerated and rationalized by the community. As responsible citizens and professional persons, the staff of the community mental health center should help members of the community look clearly at needs for improved day care programs for preschool children. If necessary, such programs may have to be organized under local governmental auspices, although sponsorship by church or other nonprofit groups would be preferable in most communities, and more acceptable to the public.

In addition to neglect and lack of stimulation, a significant number of children in the community are psychologically and physically abused by their parents. It is rare that this abuse is entirely unknown. The more usual sequence of events is that some citizen becomes concerned about the problem and reports it to one or another community agency, but generally the report is not followed up by action. There would seem to be a conspiracy in most communities to deny that parents can treat their children brutally, and a tendency to "look the other way" when such reports are received. Through special workshops and seminars, as well as through consultation activities to all caregiving agencies, the mental health center staff may contribute to a greater conscious awareness of the problem of child abuse as well as increase their willingness and ability to protect children.

SECONDARY PREVENTION

In programming for secondary prevention of mental retardation and consequent disabilities, increasing attention has been given to the concept of a "fixed point of reference." The mentally retarded child has disabilities that require the services of the physician, psychologist, educator, social agency, vocational rehabilitation agencies, and vocational training services, and sometimes psychiatric and other mental health services. Because of the complex needs of the mentally retarded, and the usual fragmentation of such services in our complex society, the parents of many mentally retarded are frequently buffeted back and forth from one agency or individual to another, and tend to feel lost, confused, and bewildered. Discontinuity and fragmentation of care may result. It would seem desirable, then, to have in each community some designated agency that has a responsibility for coordination of services and will act as a clearing house for information about available services, as well as provide channels for orderly referral and systematic communication between agencies about specific cases. In some states, such as Minnesota, such responsibility has been assigned to the county department of social welfare. It could with equal efficiency be assumed by the local health department, the special education department of the local school, the vocational rehabilitation agency, or the mental health center.

Casefinding, to allow for early diagnosis and prompt institution of remedial measures, is of vital importance. All too often, however, recognition of retardation occurs only after the child enters public school. In cases where psychological and social deprivation or trauma are of particular importance, five or six years of age is quite late. Where the primary deficit may be organic or prenatal, such a delay in recognition of the special learning problems of the child may result in distortion of the mother-child relationship, which may lead to secondary complications resulting in an overlay of psychological disability further impairing the individual retarded child's ability to cope successfully with his environment.

The physician, pediatrician and general practitioner alike, are keys to early recognition of mental retardation. Physicians are the only knowledgeable group within our society who predictably will have frequent contact with practically every child between birth and five years of age. To the extent that he is informed about mental retardation, responsible in his attitude about it, and realistically optimistic about rehabilitative and educative measures, the physician will be an effective casefinder; to the extent that he is ignorant, does not assume responsibility, and/or is pessimistic about the prognosis of the mentally retarded, he will be an inadequate or indifferent casefinder.

There are other potential resources in the community for preschool casefinding. The public health nurse, in her family visits, can play a vitally important role in detecting mental retardation. She often deals with families who have particular difficulty in recognizing or taking appropriate action about a mentally retarded child. The teachers of preschool and nursery programs, likewise, need special training and skill for recognizing and effecting appropriate referrals for definitive diagnosis of the retarded child. It is possible that, with a good inservice training and consultation program, many ancillary casefinders could be developed: Sunday school teachers, playground supervisors, county welfare workers, and so forth.

If the retarded child reaches school without recognition, it is essential that the degree and exact nature of his mental retardation be determined as early in his school career as possible; and that a continuous, coordinated, and comprehensive program of special education services be offered.

The mental health center may provide, or participate in

the provision of, a comprehensive evaluation for the mentally retarded child. Such an evaluation should include a complete physical examination, with special attention to the existence of additional handicaps which occur frequently in the retarded such as impaired hearing or vision, poor muscular coordination, or physical deformities that may require corrective measures. A comprehensive neurological evaluation including electroencephalogram should be performed in all cases of mental retardation. The psychological evaluation should provide not only formal testing of mental abilities, but an appraisal of personality attributes, part-process functioning, and the developmental stages of various integrative patterns. In many cases, a psychiatric evaluation in addition to psychological testing will provide valuable additional information. Depending upon the age of the retardate, the evaluation should also include educational and vocational aptitude and ability testing. The social casework evaluation should consist of a careful study of social adequacy and functioning of the individual retardate himself, as well as evaluation of family dynamics and interrelationships between the retarded individual and other members of the family. As a result of these evaluative processes, a comprehensive diagnostic formulation, a long-range plan for special training and education, as well as necessary therapeutic or rehabilitative measures, should be evolved, including definite fixation of accountability and responsibility on specific agencies to provide continuing supervision and coordination of the entire program, or specific parts of it.

It is not within the scope of this chapter to discuss in detail the specific educational and therapeutic services that may be offered to the mentally retarded. In addition to the retarded child, many parents and families need special assistance at one or another point during the life of the retarded child. This may consist only of short-range counseling, or it may involve individual or family psychotherapy if severe relationship or adjustment problems result from the impact of the retarded child upon one or the other parent, or upon the family unit. In addition, community resources should be available to assist the family at points of crisis in caring for the severely retarded child. For example, homemaker service should be available in the event that the mother becomes ill. Day-care services for the severely retarded are likewise important. Often families can cope with continuing care of the severely retarded child if they have available some foster placement for the child during periods when the family is traveling, or when it requires relief from the burden of care for the child.

TERTIARY PREVENTION

The prevention of disability from mental retardation depends upon early and accurate diagnosis, continuous and comprehensive care, and the availability—preferably in the community—of the full spectrum of services: medical care, special education services, vocational guidance, training, and sheltered workshops, recreational opportunities, mental health services for the retardate and/or his family where necessary, and public health services.

For some of the severely retarded, lifelong institutional care may be the only feasible solution. Such care may be custodial, but without the usual implications of neglect. Humane custodial care should provide the best available nutrition, personal stimulation, comfort, and cleanliness. There is no reason for the segregation of the severely retarded, either with or without physical disabilities, into special state hospitals for the retarded. Such segregation results in serious problems in personnel morale, and tends towards a steady lowering of standards of competency and adequacy of service. Rather, flexible financial arrangements should be made available within each state so that the mentally retarded individual, requiring long-term hospital care, may receive

such care within his home community. Equivalent care can
be provided as cheaply by public nonprofit medical facilities—hospitals, skilled nursing homes, convalescent homes
—as it can by large state hospitals and training schools.
*State institutions can be cheaper only by providing less
adequate care.* This fact should be spelled out clearly and
repeatedly, and the core problem of financial support should
be highlighted whenever state-wide planning is done in the
area of services for the mentally retarded.

Some retardates may benefit from special institutional services for training and education during adolescence and
young adulthood. These services should be as close to the
community, and as integrated within the community as possible. Removal to a state hospital and training school may
be necessary because of lack of community resources, but
can seldom be justified on the basis that care in such an
institution is preferable to giving it in the community.

EDUCATION AND INFORMATIONAL PROGRAMS

The mental health center has a responsibility to disseminate
information to opinion-making groups concerning mental
retardation, in order to stimulate an increased level of public
awareness. Such groups as women's clubs, youth organizations, health and welfare organizations, a variety of service
groups, colleges and universities, religious groups, and parent-
teachers associations are all important audiences.

Information programs for professional groups within the
community should be sponsored by the mental health center.
Physicians, educators, recreational personnel, county welfare
workers, public health personnel, ministers, judges and attorneys should all be included in such educational and informational programs.

PLANNING AND COORDINATION OF SERVICES

The mental health center may also play a responsible role
in encouraging community or regional planning to provide

the full spectrum of services for prevention, diagnosis, treatment, care, training, education, counseling, rehabilitation, employment, and research in the field of mental retardation, as well as in providing an adequate legal and financial structure for such services, and promoting recruitment and training of necessary personnel.

The mental health center should be involved in such endeavors as a co-participant, and should not assume total responsibility or authority, but rather should assume with peers—including the members of the Association for Retarded Children—such activities for planning and coordination of services. No one agency or profession can, at the present time, provide really adequate services for the mentally retarded; and proper humility is, in this case, well supported by reality.

SUGGESTED READINGS

Group for the Advancement of Psychiatry (1919), *Basic Considerations in Mental Retardation: A Preliminary Report,* Report No. 43. New York.

— (1963), *Mental Retardation: A Family Crisis—The Therapeutic Role of the Physician.* New York.

Holtgrew, M. M. (1961), *The Role of the Public Health Nurse in Mental Retardation.* St. Louis: St. Louis University.

Massland, R. L. et al. (1958), *Mental Sub-Normality—Biological, Psychological, and Cultural Factors.* New York: Basic Books.

Perry, N. (1960), *Teaching the Mentally Retarded Child.* New York: Columbia University Press.

The President's Panel on Mental Retardation: *Mental Retardation, a National Plan for a National Problem* (1963). Washington, D. C.: U. S. Department of Health, Education & Welfare.

XXI

The Role of the State Mental
Health Authority

Generalizations about the State Mental Health Authority are easy to make and hard to defend. Many factors will influence the organization, purpose, administrative philosophy, and functioning of the State Mental Health Authority.

But perhaps, before discussing some of the variables that determine the character of the State Mental Health Authority, an historical explanation about the term itself is in order. In 1946, the United States Congress passed the Community Mental Health Act, which provided for a series of grants-in-aid from the U. S. Public Health Service to the various states, to assist in the development of community psychiatric services. This program represented the adoption by the federal government of procedures for stimulating the development of community guidance clinics which had been supported by private foundations, such as the Commonwealth Fund, prior to the Second World War. In part, it was an outgrowth of our experience in the war: psychiatric casualty rates were very great despite high rejection rates for psychiatric disability. There developed a heightened public awareness and sense of governmental responsibility concerning mental illness. The original legislation specified that, unless otherwise designated by the state, the state health department should become the Mental Health Authority for the purpose of receiving and administering federal funds. In some states, then, the state department of health did become the Mental

338

Health Authority; whereas in other states, the mental hospital authority, division of mental diseases, or some other separate unit of state government was designated as the responsible state agency. This is the origin and official meaning of the term "Mental Health Authority."

In other dealings with the public health service and its constituent agencies, state agencies have been designated as the Mental Hospital Authority, the Community Mental Health Center Construction Authority, the Construction Authority for Community Facilities for the Retarded, the Mental Health Planning Authority, and the Mental Retardation Planning Authority.

In some states all of these functions are subsumed under one agency, in other states under two or more; while in some states planning activities are carried out by interdepartmental committees or organizations.

Each state brings with it to the mental health endeavor, as is true for all social enterprises, a characteristic and unique history, into which are woven economic and ethnic variables; characteristic shared attitudes resulting from particular experiences of the state or the region; a style of life determined and influenced by geography, climate and economic endeavor; and unique historical events related to the dominant and continuing influence of strong families and competent individuals. As one travels about the country, the amazing heterogeneity of our social and political life is borne home to even the casual observer. While certain basic principles of democratic government and social cooperation run through the entire fabric of our national life, institutions and mechanisms by which these principles are, theoretically at least, instituted, vary greatly from state to state, and indeed from region to region within one state.

Jurisdiction over the community mental health program of the state may be clearly defined by law, adequately financed, and supported by licensing provision in states where the central government is strong. Or, the entire responsibility of the State Mental Health Authority may consist of consultation to local units of government, and assistance in the development of local mental health centers.

Some of the functions that the State Mental Health Authority may serve can be summarized as follows:

1. To encourage and aid in the establishment of community mental health resources by: a. The promulgation and dissemination of standards and operating guides as to (1) staffing (2) fees (3) principles and techniques of operation. b. The mobilization of public and local state legislative support. c. The recruitment of personnel. d. The planning for location, staffing, and financing of such centers.

2. To insure, insofar as possible, the maintenance and necessary expansion of community mental health resources by: a. Sponsoring inservice training programs for clinical staff. b. Continuing education and maintaining a climate of public and legislative support for the mental health program at a state and community level. c. Providing short-term staff, technical, and financial assistance to clinics at the point of distress. d. Setting up workshops for clinic boards to provide for inservice training of new board members, and promoting a climate of readiness to respond to the proposals of individual clinic staffs.

3. To promote the effectiveness of the mental health program by: a. Promoting cooperation and mutual education among the various caretaking agencies and professions within the state: interdisciplinary liaison. b. Supporting new applications of clinical techniques by demonstration projects, such as emergency psychiatric clinics, suicide prevention centers, preschool mental health checkups, etc. c. Designing and supporting field projects for such activities as improved secondary prevention of mental illness by refined casefinding and early treatment, the development of alternatives to hospitalization such as day and night hospitals, etc.

4. To effect long-range, realistic state planning, in cooperation with federal, state, and local government, and public and private agencies and groups, to insure orderly growth of the full spectrum of integrated mental health services.

5. To participate in postgraduate medical, psychiatric, clinical psychological, and social work education in order to supply current knowledge about, and concepts of, community mental health practice.

6. To inspect and license, as provided for under law, the operation of public and/or private mental health agencies of various sorts.

7. To administer, as provided by law, state financial grants-in-aid to assist local communities and private nonprofit groups develop various types of mental health services.

Now, the exact emphasis and priority of development of various aspects of the State Mental Health Authority's responsibility would necessarily and rightly vary from state to state. The underlying philosophy about the program necessarily exerts a strong influence upon the establishment of priorities.

Programs are based upon ideas. Each administrator brings to his task a characteristic group of experiences, attitudes, emotional sets, and ideational constructs. The program that evolves from his leadership inevitably reflects his personal view of the world, and his concept of the people that inhabit it with him. In Kansas, for example, community mental health services were established in a manner congruent with state history and philosophy. The State Mental Health Authority's role has been consistently defined by the legislature as facilitating and consultative to local units of government. Out of this program a number of more or less consensually held views about the proper function of the State Mental Health Authority and the discharge of administrative responsibility developed among the staff of the state community mental health services.

For example, the decision was reached that the administrative structure of community mental health services in Kansas should reflect the values of the mental health subculture. The state staff was impressed with how seldom, in our own mental health institutions, the values of the mental health subculture are reflected in the administrative framework. We seldom treated each other the way we believe patients, and indeed all human beings, should be treated. Despite many disagreements, psychiatrists, psychologists, social workers, and ancillary professions involved in mental health services do hold allegiance to a common core set of values.

Central to the shared subcultural values is a conviction of the worthiness of the individual. There are many attitudes among professional people condemning judgmental and critical attacks upon the weakness of the patient, and supporting attempts to help him function more effectively and maximize his own potential. It seemed to us that similar behaviors should be encouraged and supported in relationships between the State Mental Health Authority and the community mental health agencies.

Likewise, in a setting where the clinician is in contact with more than one patient at a time, there is a companion mandate that one must not show preference for one patient over another merely because he meets the clinician's personal needs. Likewise, we thought that this impartiality should govern our relationship with the several mental health centers of the state.

A third conviction holds that patients behave the way they do because motivations are multiple, highly complex and largely unconscious in origin, and that the responsibility to help the patient understand his motivations and modify his behavior rests largely with the therapist. We felt that similar responsibility rested with State Mental Health Authority personnel in their dealings with the directors and staffs of the individual mental health centers.

Some of the employees of the State Mental Health Authority, as they assumed their new responsibilities, found themselves tempted to behave in ways that were not congruent with this set of values. By going to work for a state agency, many of us experienced a loss of stature in the eyes of our colleagues, and became labeled as administrator, state employee, enemy of private practice and free enterprise, or free loader upon the taxpayer.

Colleagues in various disciplines and various settings complained about the low quality of services offered by community mental health centers, inadequate qualifications of the staff, the usurpation of leadership and authority by social workers and psychologists, and the generally deplorable state of community mental health services. As self-esteem took a beating, our staff members tended to become increasingly defensive, and had to cope with, in retrospect, a *predictable* series of temptations.

We were first of all tempted to identify with the aggressor, and to join the critics of the centers by feeling, talking, and acting scornfully and punitively toward the less qualified staff members of the mental health centers. We were also tempted to favor those individuals, especially psychiatrists, who tended to bring recognition for "high quality" community mental health services. In other words, we were strongly drawn to single out "favorite" members of the community mental health team, and to scorn the "less desirable." We came to recognize that we were tempted to leave out the most important question: Which individuals, regardless of discipline, were contributing the most to their patients and to their communities? Instead, we were being caught up in all the prestige issues, were succumbing to peer group pressures, and were losing sight of the goal of our activities —that of providing readily available, inexpensive, minimally adequate mental health services to the citizens of all Kansas communities.

In general, members of the mental health disciplines tend

to reject the authoritarian approach to life. It is thus ironical that many mental health agencies are set up in a rigid hierarchical authoritarian manner. Most mental health workers tend to be reasonably trusting of other human beings, and to see potentialities for growth and self-realization in most people. It is therefore a paradox that the personnel of many agencies treat their colleagues with distrust, and utilize supervisory practices that clearly indicate a lack of confidence and a belief that professional colleagues cannot ask for, and utilize, help in dealing with clinical problems. Supervisory systems tend to be rigid and imposed from above, rather than structured in such a way as to allow the subordinate to seek consultation when he needs it. The clinician who would never insist that a patient enter into psychotherapy, with complete compartmentalization can insist that a subordinate enter into regular supervisory sessions with him, whether or not the colleague expresses the wish or need for such supervision.

Our beliefs and actions have been relatively consistent in demonstrating our conviction that community mental health services should not be organized in a hierarchical and authoritarian manner. We are determined to try deliberately to minimize distinctions between the disciplines, and have avoided having any meetings or functions which involve members of only one discipline. In addition to demonstrating a model of healthy and productive team functioning among the disciplines on the state level staff, we have attempted to reinforce this model of team functioning by involving all disciplines in any activity for which we are responsible.

The fact that we have refused to take a stand as to which of the disciplines makes the "best" administrative director of mental health centers has caused considerable concern among our medical colleagues. Psychiatrists may prove themselves best suited for this position of leadership and responsibility. It is the hope of the author that this should prove to be so. However, it is clearly the responsibility of the psychiatric profession to select, train, and equip its members to assume and exercise leadership and this commensurate responsibility. Psychiatry has no guarantee to leadership by right of professional birth. To guarantee psychiatrists this kind of authority regardless of their training, their ability, their judgment or their experience would be grossly unrealistic and in violation of basic mental health principles. For example, we do not see the parents who guarantee their son a "soft living" regardless of his performance in college or business, or the parents who give their son new automobiles as fast as he wrecks them as "loving parents." We see them as indulgent parents who do not have confidence in their child's strength and ability. Our basic assumption has been that if psychiatry, indeed, is the discipline that has the most depth of footing, soundest philosophical and scientific orientation, and the keenest and most valid sense of responsibility and leadership, then psychiatry will in fact assume and exercise effective leadership for community mental health services.

This is a radically different viewpoint from that held by many states, who define community mental health services quite rigidly as medical facilities that must be directed by a psychiatrist. Our position would *not* be that psychological centers or family casework agencies are the same as a psychiatric clinic or a comprehensive community mental health center. The psychological and social casework agency can meet the needs of only a portion of the total spectrum of mental and emotional illnesses. So long as they realistically define their role, however, we would have no quarrel with these nonmedical organizations, although, if the needs of the total spectrum of patients are to be met, it is not an ideal situation.

While we have gradually discarded the authoritarian model in the operation of the community mental health program in Kansas, and have grown away from any convictions of omniscience and omnipotence—as we also have in treatment services—we have come to see how effective the peer group is in modifying and controlling individual behavior. While we have abandoned structuring the administrative framework in an authoritarian manner, and likewise have eschewed legalistic solutions to social and professional problems, we have not abandoned the wish to exert leadership or the desire to influence the course of developing services. Rather, we must discover avenues other than authoritarianism and legalism in our attempts to effect needed changes. It has been and continues to be our conviction that the only truly effective control over the behavior of professional people, working in heterogeneous and isolated settings, lies in the covert and overt pressures and opinions of their peer group.

One mechanism for allowing such internal self-regulating devices is the development of an association of directors of community mental health centers, and/or an association of staff members of community mental health centers. Such an association of directors in mental health centers in Kansas has been established, and is playing an important role in determining policy, resolving professional issues, and cooperating in planning for comprehensive long-range services.

The governing boards of community mental health centers likewise have a heavy and shared responsibility for the development of services across the state. It would be desirable for the governing boards to participate together in an association of mental health center governing boards, to allow for extralegal regulatory devices, and the establishment of policy, as well as to provide an organization for effective lobbying activity. For example, one approach to the problem of unreasonable competitive bidding among centers for professional staff would be to pass laws setting rigid pay ranges. However, these laws would invariably become effective out of date, and could not be flexible enough. Another solution would be to encourage the association of governing boards and mental health centers to establish a code of ethics outlining acceptable limits for competition, to set some pay ranges which can be agreed upon, and to establish regulation of recruitment activities in this way. It is our conviction that this mode of self-regulation is, over the long haul, the most effective and most constructive.

Now, all of these attitudes and opinions have not been manufactured out of whole cloth; they have been our attempt to cope constructively with the realities of the situation in Kansas. In Kansas, each of the local mental health centers is entirely autonomous, governed by a local governing board, and supported by a local tax levy. In other words, the structuring of mental health services in Kansas is wholly congruent with the general social climate. In general, it is our conviction that psychiatric services should be designed to conform as closely as possible to the norms of the nurturant culture rather than attempting to impose a set of psychiatric values that may be divergent from the values of the larger culture.

Just as we are committed to a system of decentralized and locally autonomous, community-based mental health services, we are also committed to a state mental health program that is congruent with our pluralistic and open society. We believe, for example, that local government should do only that which individual citizens cannot do for themselves; the state government should do only that which local government cannot do; and that the federal government should do only that which state governments cannot do. In adhering to this philosophy, the opportunity of assuming and exercising local responsibility and authority must be given consistently to citizens living in the communities and counties of our state. We believe, also, that there is an area for public enterprise and an area for private enterprise in providing mental health services, as in any other segment of our national life. We do not see community-based mental health services as supplanting or competing with private psychiatric practice. Mental health centers are urged to set an upper-income level, beyond which patients are referred to private practitioners.

In other states, with differing resources, a different philosophy of government and of social responsibility, with a different history and a different beginning, community psychiatric services might be structured and administered in quite different ways. The intent of the foregoing comments, therefore, is not to say that this is the only way, or the right way to organize and develop community mental health services.

Rather, we should like to emphasize that the establishment of administrative structures should be the end point of a process of rational problem solution. The purpose for which the new service is established, and the goals which are set for it should be spelled out as clearly as possible. An attempt should be made to move from the careful study of the social innovation, its goals, purposes, and methods, to an understanding of the broader social context within which the institution is born. Added to that should be a careful study of the social forces that support and oppose various possible program elements.

Out of such a careful study, rational decisions can be made concerning the organization of service, administrative arrangement, staffing, and program emphasis.

The overall intent of the State Mental Health Authority should be to provide mental health services for the prevention, treatment, and rehabilitation of mental and emotional illness: *to achieve the attainable, to pursue the ideal,* and *to move forward as pragmatic idealists.*

The mission of the agency must always be kept clearly in mind. The more sharply the mission is defined, and the more rigidly it is circumscribed, the more likely can a plan of action be evolved which will lead to the attainment of objectives. To the extent that the Mental Health Authority becomes involved in attempting to bring about modifications in basic social structures or value systems of the nurturant society, it will fall heir to conflict, disillusionment, and failure.

SUGGESTED READINGS

Belknap, I. (1956), *Human Problems of a State Mental Hospital.* New York: McGraw-Hill.

Greenblatt, M., Levinson, D. J., & Williams, R. H. (1957), *The Patient and the Mental Hospital.* Glencoe, Ill.: Free Press.

McInnes, R. S., Palmer, J. T., & Downing, J. J. (1964), An analysis of the service relationships between state mental hospitals and one local mental health program. *Amer. J. Public Health*, 54:60-68.

Schwartz, M. S. & Schwartz, C. G. (1964), *Social Approaches to Mental Patient Care.* New York: Columbia University Press.

XXII

The State Mental Hospital

How do we really begin to logically discuss the state mental hospital? A consideration of this institution immediately raises such images of isolation, neglect, and dismal failure that the initial reaction is to turn away in dread and avoidance.

In discussing the state mental hospitals, the late President John F. Kennedy in his message to Congress on February 5, 1963, stated:

> There are now about 800,000 such patients in this nation's institutions—600,000 for mental illness and over 200,000 for mental retardation. Each year nearly 1,500,000 people receive treatment in institutions for the mentally ill and the mentally retarded. Most of them are confined and compressed within an antiquated, vastly overcrowded, chain of custodial institutions. The average amount expended on their care is only $4.00 a day—too little to do much good for the individual, but too much if measured in terms of efficient use of our mental health dollars. In some states the average is less than $2.00 a day.
>
> This situation has been tolerated far too long. It has troubled our national conscience—but only as a problem unpleasant to mention, easy to postpone, and despairing of solution. The Federal government, despite the national impact of the problem, has largely left the solutions up to the states. The states have depended upon custodial hospitals and homes. Many such hospitals and homes have been shamefully understaffed, overcrowded, unpleasant institutions from which death too often provided the only firm hope of release.

The Joint Commission on Mental Illness and Health devoted a considerable part of its effort to a study of the state mental hospital system, and recommendations for its reform. In discussing the causes for the deterioration in the state system, the Joint Commission arrived at the following conclusions:

> Unfortunately, moral treatment declined with the rise of large state hospitals, due to a combination of circumstances that cast the mentally ill under an ill star for a century to come. The first circumstance stemmed directly from the force of Dorothea Dix's crusade. When legislatures declared the indigent insane to be wards of the state, the town or county operating alms houses and jails were happy to transfer their burden to the newer and larger state hospitals and thus save further local tax expense. State facilities rapidly became loaded with chronic patients with a poor outlook for recovery.
>
> Secondly, this overcrowding was aggravated by the enormous foreign immigration during the last half of the nineteenth century. In fact, the decline of moral treatment in New England appears to have coincided with the wave of immigration following the Irish potato blight and famine of 1845. Native Yankee physicians, complaining bitterly of the influx of 'foreign pauper/insane,' found it difficult to extend their brotherly love to fellow Anglo-Saxon alien cousins (Bockover, 1956). There even were pleas that Yankee and Irish patients be segregated. Our state hospital system never has recovered from this original overcrowding and these facilities never have kept abreast of continued population growth.
>
> The new found dignity obtained for the mentally ill by rational humanitarians suffered another blow when Dr. John P. Gray of the Utica State Hospital, as new editor of the *American Journal of Insanity,* became spokesman for American psychiatry. Gray maintained that mental patients were really physically ill with a brain disease. He rejected the psychological implications of moral treatment and the concept of mental disease. . . .
>
> Lastly, the geographically isolated state hospital offers little challenge to the medical student from the standpoint of teaching, research, or private practice. As modern medical education evolved, doctors received their basic education and first practical experience in medical schools and affiliated teaching hospitals, with the older men and the young men working in a stimulating competition, perpetuated to test the truth, discard the tried but untrue, test out new theories and techniques. . . .
>
> Thus, state hospitals found themselves without influence in recruitment and replacement. From a distance, the average medical graduate saw them as particularly repelling institutions. The bulk of energetic young doctors—it has been generally observed—turn to areas and techniques in which they believe they can do something tangible for patients, or otherwise satisfy themselves in careers as

teachers and scientists [Joint Commission on Mental Illness and Health, 1961].

The Joint Commission set forth many recommendations for modification and improvement of the state hospital system. Some of these recommendations have received support from Congress, through such mechanisms as the Hospital Improvement Program and increased federal support for Inservice Training Programs in state hospitals. Other recommendations have not as yet received governmental support, and a number of the conclusions have been subjected to harsh criticism from some corners of the psychiatric and other mental health professions.

The intent of the present chapter, however, is not to review in detail the state hospital program as such, but rather to investigate the relationship between state hospital programs and community mental health services.

Can some of the patients now hospitalized in state hospitals be successfully treated in community settings, in outpatient treatment, day or night hospitalization, or brief hospitalization in general hospitals? The vast weight of the evidence would indicate yes, and estimated percentages would vary from a low of 25 per cent to a high of 75 per cent of patients now hospitalized in state hospitals.

Would such alternative forms of treatment be equally effective? The weight of evidence appears to indicate that it would, but studies of the evaluation of the psychiatric treatment are sufficiently rare and unconvincing in all areas to make such comparisons difficult at best.

Will the proper development of community mental health services do away with the need for state hospitals? This is a much more complex question.

If the query may properly be interpreted as meaning— "Could, through proper and intensive treatment and rehabilitation activities, all mentally ill persons be socially restored so that they can function independently in the community?"

—the answer, by most authorities, would be *no*, not with our present state of knowledge about etiology and treatment.

If the question is—"Can the present spectrum of services offered in state hospitals be offered under the auspices of community organizations?"—the answer would be *yes*. Whether the treatment might be more effective, the cost greater or lesser, the long-range results better or worse, cannot be said in all honesty, or with proper respect for the dictates of science.

No matter what else is involved, the basic case for the maintenance of the state hospital system in our country is essentially economic. So long as the practice of medicine is based upon the entrepreneurial, fee-for-service, private practice model, there would seem to be little likelihood, with present available knowledge concerning the treatment and rehabilitation of the mentally and emotionally ill, of doing away with all forms of state participation in the cost of services. A beguilingly simple, and apparently economical solution to the discharge of state responsibility, is to provide services in a state owned and operated hospital. However, this is only one possible mechanism for the discharge of state financial obligation. State subsidized insurance plans, and/or distribution of state tax revenues to local government and private nonprofit organizations, provide alternative methods for state participation in financing the cost of psychiatric care, without becoming involved in the direct provision of services. Under such a system, the responsibility for the care of all mental and emotional illness—including long-term custodial care—might be achieved through a system of decentralized, locally based and locally administered, governmental and private nonprofit facilities, which would receive state financial assistance to bear the partial or total cost of treatment for those citizens unable to support privately the cost of their own treatment or custodial care.

In reality, it will probably be a long time before radical

realignments of services and payment procedures will come about, in most states of our union. Many states will have to decide whether to even *attempt* to upgrade state hospital services; or whether to leave the state hospitals much as they are, and prevent new admissions by developing intensive treatment units in general hospitals located in communities about the state.

Some states are already well along in upgrading state hospital services, and are determined to develop intensive treatment units in such hospitals as well as to effect the discharge of as many patients as possible through rehabilitative efforts.

Because of the heterogeneity of state hospitals and state programs, perhaps it would be appropriate to take Kansas as an example, and describe experiences and current developments in that state, with which the author is most familiar.

In 1948, a broad base of citizen awareness concerning the deplorable situation in all the state hospitals of Kansas led to necessary and long-overdue reform. With enlightened professional leadership and strong legislative support, the state hospitals were changed from custodial institutions, staffed by untrained and incompetent personnel, to well-staffed treatment, training, and research institutions. Patient populations have been reduced by half; admissions have increased many fold; and length of stay has been radically shortened in all of the institutions. This was accomplished by expenditures to provide more hospital personnel and physicians per 100 patients than exists in any other state, and by the enlightened and forceful pursuit of a program summed up in the words of Dr. Will Menninger, as "brains before bricks."

An early administrative innovation divided each state psychiatric hospital into sections, which eventually came to function as semiautonomous hospitals sharing certain central services. This has resulted in a marked increase in staff morale, in staff efficiency, in facilitation of communication, and in improved clinical results.

A logical extension of this section plan involved the assumption of responsibility by each section for a defined geographic area of the state, in reality making each hospital a community-oriented, small, semiautonomous state hospital.

Two other elements of the state plan in Kansas have contributed to the marked upgrading in state hospital services. First, the county welfare departments were involved, as a policy decision, in obtaining preadmission social histories before admission of the patient to the hospital; and, upon request, in planning and supervising aftercare services for the returned mental hospital patient.

Second, as a matter of policy, the discharge of patients no longer benefiting from active treatment in state hospitals into nursing home situations for humane custodial care was implemented. At present there are approximately 1,400 patients in nursing homes in the State of Kansas who were formerly patients in the state mental hospitals, or state hospitals and schools for the retarded.

Now, in a state such as Kansas, where we have already succeeded in reducing patient populations, upgrading staff, and introducing administrative innovations which allow for community-oriented services providing continuity of care for the individual patient, the question arises as to what changes are necessary or desirable in order to further integrate the state hospital system with the developing network of community mental health services? Perhaps we might look at other examples of medical services, to help us in considering some possible interrelationships.

For example, in the field of hospital services, there is a definitely interdependent relationship between various types of general hospital facilities. The majority of the hospitals in Kansas are small community hospitals, which provide adequate nursing, diagnostic and medical services for most patients residing in or near the community. For a few patients, transfer to regional, comprehensive medical centers in the larger urban areas may be necessary, for complex diagnostic and therapeutic procedures. For a small minority of the cases, transfer to the medical center of the state university's medical school may be necessary in order to afford highly specialized or complex diagnostic and thera-peutic procedures, or procedures requiring expensive spe-cialized equipment that is not widely available in state medi-cal centers. In other words, all of these hospitals are inter-dependent, and are links in the chain of evacuation and rehabilitation which begins in the office of the family phy-sician. They are not competitive in the usual sense of the word, and no one of them can survive and provide really good service without the existence of the others. For exam-ple, the small community hospital cannot provide the best medical care for patients with rare or inordinately complex diseases. Each is dependent upon regional comprehensive medical centers, and the university medical center to supple-ment its available services. The university medical center, likewise, is dependent upon local hospitals in at least two ways. First, if patients are referred appropriately and early in the course of their disease, the probability of effective therapeutic results at the university medical center increases. Secondly, the likelihood of a good therapeutic result at the university medical center is enhanced by adequate follow-up care, so that treatment and rehabilitation may continue upon return of the patient to his home community.

In studying the interrelationship between the state men-tal hospital and the community mental health center, the author will be attempting to ask what sorts of modifications in the organization, staffing, and program of the state men-tal hospital would enhance and reinforce elements of inter-dependency.

The traditional role of the state hospital superintendent, in relationship to medical responsibility, should be periodi-cally under review. There can be little question that a senior physician must hold final and full responsibility and authority for the treatment program. Whether he need necessarily be invested with full responsibility for the entire operation of the hospital is a separate question. Experimentation in England, and in Minnesota, with a system of co-directorships—a trained hospital administrator serves as associate superintendent of the hospital—has been successful. This model frees the medical superintendent from the routine administrative matters that may eat into his time and energy to such a great extent. The medical director of the hospital would then be able, and expected, to make more direct use of his clinical skills as a clinical consultant, teacher, planner, and leader.

Table 1 outlines a possible organizational scheme for purposes of redesigning services offered by the state mental hospital, in keeping with the rapid expansion in community mental health resources.

The medical director of the hospital would be directly responsible for the operation of clinical services, extramural consultation services, intramural consultation services, and research and training. In Table 1, it is proposed that four operating sections exist: two would be general psychiatric sections and receive all types of psychiatric patients from one-half of the defined area served by the hospital. It is proposed that two sections have specialized functions, one for children and adolescents, and one for the residential treatment of alcoholics. The chiefs of these sections would answer directly to the medical director of the facility.

Parenthetically, it should be emphasized that the organizational plan proposed does not necessarily dictate that all of the units, or all of the services must necessarily be situated in one location, or in one cluster of buildings. It would be quite possible to have the actual clinical sections located in different areas of the hospital district, under one common medical director for the hospital. The "hospital" would then

TABLE 1

Proposed State Hospital Reorganization

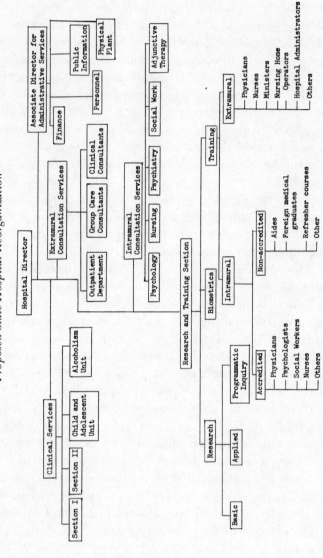

be defined as an organization of services, rather than as a specific building or group of buildings existing in one geographic location.

Double control of operating personnel would be eliminated, and a direct line of authority from the medical director of the hospital to the chief of each section substituted. The director's staff would include senior clinicians in the areas of psychiatry, psychology, social work, adjunctive therapy, and nursing. They would serve as consultants to personnel on the operating sections, and would also be responsible for recruitment and inservice training of personnel. However, there would be no direct line relationship between the consultants in the various disciplines and the operating members of that discipline on the section.

The extramural consultation service would provide assistance in various forms to community mental health centers in the area served by the hospital. The outpatient staff could function both traditionally, by making preadmission evaluations and providing aftercare services for patients, as well as by being available as clinical consultants to assist the staffs of community mental health centers upon request. Because of the increasing tendency to place many patients in nursing homes and other group living situations, another component of extramural consultation services would be group care consultation, provided by psychiatric nurses and/or psychiatric social workers. It would also be desirable to develop specialized clinical consultants within the extramural consultation services, to provide expert case-centered consultation, and inservice training for the mental health centers in that area in such specialized fields as mental retardation, child psychiatry, alcoholism, adjunctive therapy, medicolegal problems, and so forth.

The research and training section would combine the standard biometric operations of the hospital, along with research in both the basic and applied areas, as well as ongoing programmatic inquiry to evaluate the effectiveness of the total program of the hospital. The training division of the research and training section would include both intra- and extramural training programs. Intramural programs would consist of accredited training in psychiatry, psychology, psychiatric social work, psychiatric nursing, and perhaps other disciplines. Nonaccredited training would consist of basic and advanced aide training, special training for foreign medical graduates, etc.

The extramural training program would, in conjunction and cooperation with the community mental health centers, provide a wide variety of nonaccredited educational experiences for significant caregivers within the community, such as physicians, nurses, ministers, nursing home operators, and hospital administrators.

The associate director for administrative services would be responsible for public information programs, finance, personnel, and physical plant operations.

It would also be desirable for each hospital to have a regional advisory council, consisting of key lay and professional leaders and opinion-setters in the hospital area, who would meet regularly and advise the hospital on a wide variety of program questions. Or, a more highly developed system would be one whereby the hospital would participate in a regional health and welfare planning council, where lay and professional leaders from the area of the state would attempt to plan together for the *full* spectrum of health and welfare services for that area of the state.

Again, it might be useful to look to the medical model and ask if refinement might be possible in the internal organization and functioning of the state mental hospital. The general hospital and the university medical center have a wide variety of internal regulating devices to promote and insure the maintenance of high standards of care. For example, the tissue committee is responsible for examining all tissues removed, to render some judgment as to the appropriateness of surgery. In many training institutions, there are also regular surgical death conferences, in which an attempt is made to decide whether the death was or was not preventable.

Such self-scrutiny and peer regulation is notable by its absence in psychiatric settings. For example, one possible mechanism would be to develop a special staff committee which would review and present a teaching conference about each suicide occurring during hospitalization or shortly after discharge. Another staff committee might be constituted to review a representative sample of readmitted patients, and through a series of teaching conferences, encourage the staff to consider mutually, whether the readmission was a preventable readmission, and how hospital procedures and policies might be improved.

Many general hospitals are instituting a program for an internal medical audit, sometimes with the assistance of complex statistical data collection systems, in an attempt to evaluate, among other things, the effectiveness of various members of the medical staff. Attempts to develop such an internal audit system, to evaluate the effectiveness of medical and other professional staff, might be worthy of study by state psychiatric hospitals. For example, how do lengths of hospitalization and readmission rates of various sections and wards of the hospital compare? If differences exist, can they be correlated with differences in competency or administrative or clinical practices on the various units?

Also, if state psychiatric hospitals follow the admonition to extend staff privileges to physicians in the community, some mechanism must be developed for review of the credentials of particular applicants, supervision during the probationary period of staff membership, and acceptance to full staff privileges. If an open staff system is developed, a mechanism must also be evolved to allow for adequate communication between full-time and visiting members of the staff, and for involving visiting staff in decision-making processes—in other words, a mechanism very much like the staff meetings that are required in general hospitals accredited by the Joint Commission on Hospital Accreditation.

Observers of the training methods of psychiatry have commented that psychiatry is the only medical specialty which is taught almost entirely by hearsay. That is, in the characteristic training program, the resident reports on various kinds of activities with patients. A supervisor, on the basis of these reports, attempts to help the resident modify and improve his professional behavior. This air of secrecy and sacrosanct privacy has prevailed too long for the good of the mental health disciplines, and it is time—if we are indeed to be scientists as well as practicing moralists—that we turn the searchlight of self-scrutiny upon the whole range of clinical activities in which we engage. The state hospital, long subject to criticism from outside, would do well to take leadership in self-study and self-evaluation with an aim towards improvement.

SUGGESTED READINGS

Areawide Planning of Facilities for Long-Term Treatment and Care (1963). Washington, D. C.: U. S. Department of Health, Education & Welfare.

Areawide Planning of Facilities for Rehabilitation Services (1963). Washington, D. C.: U. S. Department of Health, Education & Welfare.

Bibliography on Planning of Community Mental Health Programs (1963). Washington, D. C.: U. S. Department of Health, Education, & Welfare.

Blain, D. et al. (1963), A long-range plan for mental health services in California. *Amer. J. Psychiat.*, 119:1027-1032.

Design of Facilities for Mental Health and Psychiatric Services: A Selected Bibliography (1963). Washington, D. C.: U. S. Department of Health, Education & Welfare.

Gaylin, S. (1964), Psychiatric planning at the community level. *Amer. J. Psychiat.*, 121:153-159.

Planning of Facilities for Mental Health Services (1961). Washington, D. C.: U. S. Department of Health, Education & Welfare.

XXIII

Planning for Mental Health Services

Four planning projects, all of national scope, have changed and are in the process of further changing the entire structure of mental health services in the United States.

In 1955, the Congress authorized, through the provisions of Section 304 (b) of Public Law 182, the establishment of the Joint Commission on Mental Illness and Health. A series of well thought out and cogently written monographs, covering practically the full range of mental health areas, and a final report entitled *Action for Mental Health,* have issued from the Commission. Between 1955 and the publication of the final report in 1961, a total of $1,584,027.21 was invested in this far-reaching project, which was designed to survey resources, and to make recommendations for combatting mental illness in the United States.

There have been many developments directly attributable to the work of the Joint Commission, others that were indirect outcomes, and undoubtedly more await us in the future. As examples, the federally-supported Hospital Improvement Program and the Inservice Training Program, currently available to all state mental hospitals, are attempts to implement proposals for upgrading state hospital services for the mentally ill.

In addition, the importance of planning at the state level for improvement of the total spectrum of mental health services was brought home by the activities of the Joint Commission, which had a salutary effect on mental health professionals and politicians alike, with regard to the usefulness of planning. The 87th United States Congress, thus, made an initial grant of $4.2 million to aid the states in initiating comprehensive mental health planning endeavors. The appropriation was intended, as stated in the guidelines, to develop a plan for "comprehensive community-based mental health services."

In part, this planning grant was an outgrowth of requests for such assistance from the several states. For example, in 1962 the Conference of State and Territorial Mental Health Authorities recommended:

> In the belief that all community agencies have a stake in the prevention of mental illness and the provision of adequate mental health services, it is recommended that the Public Health Service be requested to develop guidelines with the collaboration of the states for more complete utilization of all local community resources for dealing with the mentally ill, and to provide assistance to the states to implement such community planning.

In addition, the Governor's Conference in May of 1962 adopted a resolution which stated, in part, ". . . each state develop a comprehensive master plan for coping with mental disability by state and local, private and voluntary resources, and stimulate greater community initiative and provide a long-term basis for meeting this great human responsibility."

A number of forces, then, have been at work.

The federal guidelines for administering grants to the states insured a broadly based planning endeavor. The intent was to involve all groups and agencies, whether governmental or private, national, state, or local, which have an actual or potential role in the prevention, treatment, or rehabilitation of mental or emotional illness. The concerns that lay behind this demand for such broad involvement were basically the following: 1) Good planning, presenting scientifically and professionally valid recommendations, does not necessarily lead to action. Many states have book shelves filled with worthwhile study and planning documents, which responsible individuals have been either unwilling or unable to implement. Consequently, the federal guidelines stressed the importance of a wide base of citizen involvement, so that the necessary climate of public opinion would be attained for implementing changes, and so that citizens might be involved in actively supporting suggested changes. 2) Fragmentation of services to mentally and emotionally disturbed individuals occurs widely, and is often related to the fragmentation of responsibility and authority between agencies at the state, local, and national level. If all agencies were involved in planning, jurisdictional disputes could be identified and hopefully resolved, accountability could be sharpened, and continuity of care for the mentally ill individual could be improved.

Actually, interest in long-range planning is not new or unique to mental health. Planning has been an unpopular concept, but has crept into more than one area of our national life over the last several decades. The upsurge of interest at the present time is probably related to a number of factors. After the Second World War and the Korean War, there was a considerable period of readjustment during which time resumption of the ongoing life of the nation was the primary concern. The decades since the Second World War have also seen a rapid expansion in available knowledge about human behavior, and have been witness to extensive experimentation in methods of treatment and rehabilitation for mental and behavior problems—and, to a lesser extent, experimentation in prevention of emotional illness. Enormous growth in the number of practitioners in psychiatry, psychology, and psychiatric social work; rapidly mounting state budgets for mental health activities; a much broadened base of public awareness of and concern about mental and emotional problems—all have led to a welter of conflicting trends and tendencies, antithetical power groupings, and confusion about the proper course of development of mental

health services, while criticisms about the present state of
such services proliferated. In other words, the climate was
ripe for an emphasis on planning, and much activity had been
underway at both state and local levels, prior to the initiation
of the federal planning grant-in-aid program.

Also, the growing complexities of our increasingly urban-
ized and technologically complex society have necessitated
planning in many other fields. There seems to be an air of
general optimism about the future, a more hopeful feeling
that perhaps "the bomb" will not destroy us all, and that
with reason and compromise the world can be made a somewhat better place for human existence.

In 1961 the Senate of the State of California directed the
Department of Mental Hygiene to "prepare a comprehensive report reevaluating its present program and setting forth
a master plan for the conduct of its operations in the future."
This project was completed in one year's time, and reported
to the legislature on March 12, 1962. The frame of reference was clearly comprehensive, involving the full spectrum
of preventive, therapeutic and rehabilitative services, and
conceptualizing an active partnership between state and local
government, private practitioners, and nonprofit corporations and agencies.

In April of 1962, the Community Welfare Planning Council of San Diego, California, completed a comprehensive
study entitled "Study of the Coordination of Local Mental
Health Services in San Diego, California." This study focused
upon the network of services within the context of the
single community, and the foreword stated:

> This report, in itself, will not improve cooperation or coordination
> among the community mental health services. It will not magically
> improve the services for the emotionally and mentally disturbed. It
> does, however, present the basic facts, findings and conclusions re-
> garding mental health services in San Diego county. These facts and
> findings support certain recommendations. It is hoped that imple-
> mentation of these recommendations will lead ultimately to the es-

tablishment of a coordinated community treatment plan for the benefit of the citizens of San Diego county who desperately seek help for emotional and mental disturbance.

The Citizens Advisory Committee on Community Mental Health Resources for the State of Wisconsin submitted in July of 1962, a report to the State Board of Public Welfare entitled *Community Services to Mentally Ill, Infirm, and Retarded.* This study, likewise, attempted to examine the full spectrum of mental health services, and to make recommendations of an overall nature as well as specific proposals.

Undoubtedly there have been many other completed reports at the state, local, and regional levels, with which the author is not familiar. The above, however, give some indication of a wide-spread interest in long-range planning for mental health services, prior to the development of a federal mechanism for supporting and assisting such activities on the part of the several states.

Added impetus to planning, and willingness to expand the concept of mental health services to include preventive services, also stemmed from an increasing body of scientific information about the prevalence and incidence of mental and emotional illness in our society. Through such studies as those of the Rennie group in New York (reported in *Mental Health in the Metropolis: The Midtown Manhattan Study*) and by the Leighton group in Nova Scotia (reported in *My Name is Legion* and other publications) the sheer logistical difficulty of providing adequate treatment and rehabilitative services, both in terms of money and manpower, came to weigh with increasing heaviness upon leaders in the mental health disciplines. Gradually, interest in the prevention of mental illness and/or of disability—which so characterized the beginnings of the child guidance movement in this country in the early twentieth century—began to grow. This time, however, certain of the deterents to healthy development of preventive services, that plagued the child guidance movement, no longer existed. The process of legitimation of psychiatric endeavors has been pretty much completed by the middle of our century; general public opinion supports the idea that there is a need for services for mentally and emotionally ill individuals, and that the professions of psychiatry, clinical psychology, psychiatric social work, and other related disciplines, have legitimate social roles. While the process of validation is not entirely complete—that is, general public opinion does not necessarily support the general effectiveness of treatment measures—it is much further advanced than it was at the turn of the century. Also, there existed at the middle of our century, a considerable body of substantive knowledge, which although imperfect and limited, was entirely lacking when the child guidance movement first began to develop momentum. A large backlog of clinical experience has also accumulated, which if imperfectly documented and recorded, has at least influenced the development of psychiatric thinking.

There is ample evidence that treatment programs, with the manpower and resources which have been available up to the present time, have not made an appreciable dent in the prevalence of mental and emotional disorders within the population.

The federal grants for assistance in planning, therefore, were received with considerable enthusiasm on the part of most state mental health authorities. Each state prepared a proposal for mental health planning, and upon approval by the United States Public Health Service, recruited staff and began a state-wide mental health planning project on or about July 1, 1963, with support promised through June of 1965. Additionally, an 18-month grant-in-aid has been made to all of the states for similar planning for mental retardation services, to be conducted between July 1, 1964 and

December 31, 1965. Funds also became available, as of July, 1964, for federal participation in the construction of community facilities for the retarded and for comprehensive community mental health centers.

The following schematic summary (Figure 1), prepared by the National Association for Mental Health, outlines important features of the four state plans on mental illness and mental retardation. It is very difficult to generalize about the planning projects that have been undertaken, since they vary so widely from state to state. Such a study has been done by the Joint Information Service (Glasscote and Canno, 1963). The vast majority of the planning endeavors call for the creation of a state-level planning committee, which ranges from eight to 110 members in size, and includes representatives from governmental and nongovernmental agencies. In some of these states, as in Kansas, the state-level planning committee is an ongoing, legislatively sanctioned body for interdepartmental coordination. In Kansas, this group is called the Advisory Commission of the Division of Institutional Management and Community Mental Health Programs, and has representatives from a wide variety of state agencies and special interest and professional groups. Many of the states also have developed steering committees from this larger state-level planning committee.

The states have tended to approach the planning process from two vantage points: topical and regional. That is, they have set up study committees to develop, on a regional basis, a cross section of citizen and professional opinion concerning mental health needs and resources. In some states, these regional need and resource studies have been handled in a decentralized manner so as to encourage and promote grass-root citizen involvement. In some states, as in Kansas, the state Association for Mental Health has been involved in this process.

In addition, a wide variety of topical committees have been established, largely representational, to study topical

FIGURE 1

Four State Plans on Mental Illness and Mental Retardation

WHAT	COMPREHENSIVE MENTAL HEALTH PLANNING	PLAN FOR CONSTRUCTION OF COMMUNITY MENTAL HEALTH CENTERS (CMHC)
AUTHORIZATION	"Federal Grant-in-Aid to Support Comprehensive Mental Health Planning", authorized by 1963 Appropriations Act for Department of Health, Education, and Welfare	The Community Mental Health Centers Act (Title II, Public Law 88-164) requires that each state must prepare a plan before requesting construction funds for centers
PURPOSE	To help states develop comprehensive mental health plans in order to strengthen community mental health programs and improve the mental health of the people	To outline how, when, and where steps will be taken to provide adequate community mental health services for persons residing in a state
TIME TABLE	Planning is now under way. Proposals submitted by the states to the Federal government were approved in 1963 and planning began almost immediately. The initial allocation was for the first year only. Applications for second year funds are now being submitted by states. These must be received in time for review and approval by June 30, 1964. A State Interim Progress Report must accompany the request for second year Federal funds. A Program Progress Report is due by July 30, 1965. It may consist of the State Interim Progress Report plus a statement of subsequent planning activities and achievements.	The U. S. Public Health Service will issue by May 1, 1964, regulations to guide states in planning. NIMH and the Division of Hospital and Medical Facilities, Bureau of State Services (Hill-Burton) are cooperating in preparation of the regulations. The state plan must, among other things: * designate a single state agency to administer the plan * provide for a state advisory council * outline a program for construction of community mental health centers * point out the relative need * set minimum standards for maintaining and operating the centers * provide for review of the state plan, at least annually State's CMHC plans can be submitted after July 1, 1964. The deadline will be announced by the U. S. Public Health Service.
FEDERAL FUNDS	$4.2 million per year (for a total of $8.4 million) was appropriated in the Appropriations Acts of 1963 and 1964 First year planning grant funds of $4.2 million, are to be spent by June 30, 1964. Similarly, second year funds of $4.2 million, approved by June 30, 1964, are to be spent by June 30, 1965. Each state received a minimum of $50,000 for the first year. Each state whose plan is approved for the second year is eligible for a second minimum of $50,000. The exact amount allotted each state is determined by a formula which takes into account the population and the need of the state.	None for the planning process itself After the state's plan is approved, applications for construction funds may be made. State construction allotments have been established.
STATE MATCHING FUNDS	States were not required to appropriate any money for planning. To qualify for the Federal money, however, they had to show they would be spending at least as much for community mental health services as they would be receiving from the Federal government.	State is entirely responsible for financing of planning

RESPONSIBILITY	Federal responsibility:
	
	  Office of the Director, NIMH
	
	  Assistance and information to be obtained from Mental Health Program Director of HEW Regional Offices
	
	State responsibility:
	
	  State Mental Health Authority was designated to receive Federal money
	
	  Planning to be done by a state planning committee including professionals and representative community leaders
	
	  Planning staff has been hired in nearly every state
	
	Community involvement strongly urged
		Federal responsibility:
		
		  Primary responsibility for state plans will be in NIMH
		
		  Responsibility for reviewing project applications will be shared between NIMH for program aspects and the Division of Hospital and Medical Facilities, Bureau of State Services (Hill-Burton) for construction aspects
		
		  Information and assistance in preparing this state plan may be obtained from the Mental Health Program Director in the HEW Regional Offices
		
		State responsibility:
		
		  Governors have been notified of availability of construction funds and the necessity for preparing a state plan as a prerequisite for getting the funds
		
		  The governor is to designate a state agency to be responsible for preparation of the plan
		
		  This CMHC plan must be consistent with the state's Comprehensive Mental Health Plan

INFORMATION SOURCES	Detailed information on applying for Federal planning funds available to state government in NIMH publications:
	
	  "Guidelines for the Federal Grant-in-Aid Program to Support Mental Health Planning", January 22, 1963
	
	  "Preliminary Guidelines to Second Year of Federal Grant-in-Aid to Support Mental Health Planning", January 14, 1964
	
	  "Digest, State Mental Health Planning Grant Proposals, 1963", prepared by the NIMH Clearinghouse for Mental Health Information
	
	NAMH information on statewide mental health planning:
	
	  "Plans for Planning", published by the Joint Information Service of the NAMH and the APA
	
	  NAMH Planning Bulletin #1 describes the Federal planning program
	
	  NAMH Planning Bulletin #2 tells how MHAs should be involved
		Regulations to implement Title II, Public Law 88-164 will be issued by the U. S. Public Health Service by May 1, 1964
		
		NAMH information on construction of community mental health centers:
		
		  NAMH Planning Bulletin #3 describes the law
		
		  NAMH Planning Bulletin #4 discusses the community mental health center and the MHA's function in relation to it

COMPREHENSIVE MENTAL RETARDATION PLANNING	PLAN FOR CONSTRUCTION OF MENTAL RETARDATION FACILITIES (MRF)
"Mental Retardation Planning Grants" – authorized by Public Law 88-156 amending the Social Security Act by adding Title XVII; money appropriated in a supplemental appropriations bill passed January 29, 1964	The Mental Retardation Facilities Construction Act (Title I, Public Law 88-164) requires in Part C that each state must prepare a plan as a necessary step before construction funds authorized in Title I, Part C, are allotted to the states
To help states plan comprehensive state and community action to combat mental retardation	To outline how the states plan to provide adequate services for mentally retarded persons
Application for a grant for planning funds must reach PHS Regional Health Director in HEW Regional Office by April 30, 1964, to get funds earmarked for each state As soon as possible thereafter, states will be advised of uncommitted funds which are available. If a state does not get in an application for its earmarked funds before April 30, it has a second chance to apply for a share of the remaining funds before September 30, 1964. States which have already received their earmarked money may ask for more before September 30, 1964. Final report of expenditures due no later than March 31, 1966. Final report of planning activities due no later than June 30, 1966.	The U. S. Public Health Service will issue regulations by April 30, 1964, to guide states in operation of the program The state plan must, among other things: • describe a program for construction of facilities based on a statewide inventory of existing facilities and a survey of need • describe the relative need for projects • designate a state agency to administer the program • designate a state advisory council The deadline for applications for construction funds will be established by the designated state agency after state plans have been approved by Public Health Service
$2.2 million was appropriated in a supplemental bill for a two-year period ending June 30, 1965 $30,000 is earmarked for each state until April 30, 1964. These earmarked funds account for approximately $1.65 million. The remaining $550,000 plus any uncollected-earmarked funds will be available after May 1, 1964 (and before September 30, 1964) on a competitive basis to (a) states which want supplemental funds, and (b) states which failed to submit an application in time to get their earmarked funds. States must obligate funds by December 31, 1965	None available for the planning process itself After the state's plan is approved, applications for construction funds may be made to the designated state agency
States must match every $3 of Federal money with $1 in dollars or in cost of staff time, space, facilities, supplies, overhead expenses, contributed by state or local public or voluntary agencies	State is entirely responsible for financing of planning

Federal responsibility:
 	
    Mental Retardation Branch, Division of Chronic Diseases, Bureau of State Services, Public Health Service
 	
    Assistance and information to be obtained from PHS Regional Health Director in HEW Regional Offices
 	
State responsibility:
 	
    Governors are to designate a state agency to carry out the purpose of the planning. This agency may be any appropriate existing agency or any new agency of state government, which may be inter-departmental in character. The planning itself, however, should be inter-departmental and involve education, employment, rehabilitation, welfare, health, and the law.
 	
    Full participation by state and community agencies concerned with the needs of the mentally retarded (such as a broadly representative state advisory group) is required
 	
Community involvement strongly urged
	Federal responsibility:
	
	    Plans are to be submitted to the HEW Regional Offices
	
	    Responsibility for approval of plans resides in the Division of Hospital and Medical Facilities, Bureau of State Services, Public Health Service (Hill-Burton)
	
	State responsibility:
	
	    Governors were notified last November of the availability of construction funds and the necessity of preparing a state plan as a prerequisite for getting the funds
	
	    The governor is to designate a state agency to be responsible for the planning
	
	    This MRF plan should be considered an integral part of the state's Comprehensive Mental Retardation Plan

Detailed information on applying for Federal planning funds was made available to state governments in the PHS publication:
 	
    "Terms and Conditions Governing Mental Retardation Planning Grants to States"
 	
    NAMH Planning Bulletin #3 describes Public Law 88-156, which provides for statewide mental retardation planning
	Regulations to implement Title I, Part C, Public Law 88-164 will be issued by the U. S. Public Health Service by April 30, 1964

It is to be noted that mental retardation planning must be coordinated with relevant aspects of state mental health planning and planning for construction of mental retardation facilities	

areas, either related to specific conditions, general areas of activity (primary prevention, for example) or specific agency functions (such as outpatient facilities, inpatient facilities, etc.) .

Now, out of each of these state planning endeavors there will come a document or series of documents which will be referred to as "The State Mental Health Plan." It should differ, in at least three ways, from planning documents that have been prepared by states in the past:

1. First of all, it is designed to cover a ten-year period from 1965 through 1975. Most of the states have planned on an annual, or at most a biennial basis in the past.

2. It will involve consideration of the full spectrum of services, including prevention, treatment, and rehabilitation of mental and emotional illness.

3. It will have involved all major state and local governmental as well as nongovernmental agencies and special interest groups in the development of the plan. Because of this, it should be possible to arrive at a system of priorities for changes and expansions in programs, which will be based upon an index of need, as well as indications of the acceptability of certain modifications to vested power interests in the particular state. While the elements of comprehensive services in each state plan will undoubtedly be similar, the priorities for changing and developing services, and the administrative organization or auspices under which services are to be offered, will vary widely.

The planning process, whatever else it has accomplished, has been a growth experience for the mental health professionals involved. Most of us have been struck by the vigor and effectiveness of our pluralistic society, which so often seems chaotic and disorganized. We have been impressed with the knowledgeability of the average citizen, his sense of community responsibility, and the zeal and effectiveness with which he can pursue idealistic endeavors.

Many of us have also been equally impressed with the narrowness, fearfulness, and suspicion of vested interest groups in the mental health field. Characteristic mammalian behavior, such as the defense of territorial claims and other types of intraspecies competition, has become highlighted in the planning process—and rendered peculiarly curious because of the complex pseudopsychiatric rationalizations developed by mental health practitioners to justify essentially regressive and destructive behaviors.

One real planning dilemma has hounded all states: in our society no one individual or agency possesses sufficient power, authority, or resources to implement broad, sweeping social changes. Those who are necessary as allies in such a project are, more often than not, serving in different "armies." Authoritarian and hierarchical models of organization and administration break down completely when faced with the task of realistic planning in our complex society.

The system of checks and balances, built into our social fabric and very often internalized by the individual citizen, is tremendously effective. While this system prevents the accumulation of excessive power in the hands of any one individual or organization, it often makes difficult the accumulation of *necessary and sufficient* authority to implement needed social changes.

For this reason, there are two possible courses of action to be taken by a mental health professional person if he wants to implement changes:

1. He can develop a relationship with vested political and other powers in the state. Their genuine interest in the problem, political expediency, or mutual advantage may cause them to lend their power to the implementation of needed changes. This cannot be done, however, while at the same time preserving absolute autonomy for the mental health endeavor. Everything is gained at some price, and the price for political assistance is that political favors must

be repaid—when the forces in political power shift, the mental health program may come into disfavor.

2. Or, the mental health planner may seek a broad base of public support for a variety of improved mental health programs. This is a slower, more complex, and initially more frustrating course of action. The assumption is that in our complex society, the major part of government goes on with the *consent* of the governed, rather than through their active participation. The process of regional need and resource studies, public information meetings, and frequent personal appearances and speeches by mental health professional persons is designed, then, to develop a favorable public image, to involve the public in concern about the mental health program, and to garner sufficient support from the people for the implementation of programs. This base of public support will be expressed not only in general attitudes—to which all agents of government in our nation are quite sensitive—but also through specific legislators acting upon their awareness of general community feeling about mental health needs and programs. A course of action such as this, while more laborious, builds a stronger base of support for the long-range development of programs, provides some degree of immunity from the vagaries of political chance—and, in the judgment of the author, is the more effective and wiser course to pursue.

The whole field of planning is complex, and many other chapters of this book are related to important issues of the planning process. This is an area of human endeavor about which relatively little is known, and yet it lies close to the heart of a crucial problem of our times: how may social change be instituted and maintained?

It is the hope of the National Institute of Mental Health, in making the planning grants, that state mental health and mental hospital authorities will include in their programs, on an ongoing basis, a planning section. It would seem to the author that at least the following elements are necessary for an effective planning program:

1. Data gathering activities, to allow regular and orderly development of statistical data concerning various elements of the mental health program, as well as general social and demographic factors affecting mental health and mental illness.

2. Special study activities involving projects utilizing interview techniques, questionnaire techniques, time and motion studies—in other words, the full range of management and behavioral science investigative methods.

3. Data analysis activities to interpret the statistical and other data developed, concerning mental health programs, needs and resources. This would require a senior professional person, ideally with a solid background in the clinical area as well as proficiency in research activities.

4. A section for the management of institutional change should be staffed by a professional person who has an understanding of institutional and group dynamics, and of the proper structuring and implementation of planned social change.

These various skill areas are quite discrete, and often require different competencies and different personality organization on the part of the professional persons involved. Such a section could be called a programmatic inquiry and evaluation section, or a planning section, or a research and development section—the most important point is that no one of these functions alone, nor one professional person alone, can adequately perform the task of programmatic evaluation, and continual modification and reshaping of the long-range plan for mental health services.

It is too soon to tell exactly what the impact of all of these planning activities will be on mental health services in America. It is doubtful that services will be unrecognizable after all this activity. But it is equally doubtful if they will ever be the same again.

XXIV

Budgeting and Accounting

Money talks. At times, it seems to speak in more strident and persuasive tones than do the needs of human beings. But, whatever other problems he faces, the director of a community mental health service must come to grips with fiscal reality if his agency is to survive, to fulfill its functions, and to grow.

We live in a money-oriented, competitive, entrepreneurial society. The mental health center, in spite of its high tax subsidy, is not immune to pressures that impend upon us all in such a society.

Most importantly, the mental health program should not be an instrument through which the director strives to protest the basic ground rules of a capitalistic society. Protest he may, as an individual citizen, but if his agency is to thrive and prosper, he must accept—or at least not openly contest—the basic rules of social interaction. In our society, people pay for services and products. They have been raised to do this, expect to do so, and are likely to view with suspicion and often contempt, services or products that are "free." Governing boards, likewise, have been raised with the same values. Governing board members often, in fact, are representative of those groups in society that place the *highest* value upon the competitive, entrepreneurial, free enterprise system. Woe to the agency, then, that proclaims its intention to offer "free" service because sick people should not be expected to pay for their care—not only would organized American medicine rise to do battle at such a proclamation, but the major opinion-setters and power forces within the business and political community would do so as well.

The concept of anything being "free," is a very shaky idea at best. If the staff members were indeed to provide all or part of their services without any reimbursement, in a very real sense they and their families would be paying for the service. If, on the other hand, the client does not pay any fee and the cost of staff services is borne entirely out of tax funds, it is the citizens of the community at large, rather than the patients, who are paying for the service. Largesse with one's own funds is permissible, even if foolish; but with public funds, it is seldom looked upon with favor.

Before the director of the community mental health agency can secure and manage adequate financial support, however, it is necessary that fiscal policies be established by the governing board of the agency. Often major elements of these policies will be governed by federal, state, or local laws or regulations. Fiscal policies are necessary to fix authority and responsibility for the collection and expenditure of revenues; to determine the division of resources between various operating units; and to determine procedures by which an accurate record and public accounting can be rendered of the revenue collected, expenditures incurred, and services offered.

Within the framework of such general fiscal policies, responsibility falls to the director of the community mental health center for proper implementation. Processes of revenue administration, by which taxes are assessed, levied, and collected, and the management of treasury funds, which is concerned with the custody and disposal of public money, are seldom of direct concern to the director of a community mental health service. He is concerned, however, with budgeting, accounting, and purchasing operations.

The budget should be kept as simple as possible and yet

be in sufficient detail so that the expenditures are fully under-standable to the nonprofessional reader. In larger community mental health organizations, the budgets should be classi-fied by units of organization, such as day-hospital, outpatient clinic, mental health education, community consultation ser-vice, and so forth. Within each of these operating divisions, there should be a further breakdown by function, if this is appropriate. For example, if there were a separate pro-gram for alcoholism services, a breakdown might be along the following dimensions: alcoholism education, public health nursing, medical services, psychiatric diagnostic and treatment services, alcoholism counseling services, etc.

Expenditures should be further subdivided, under each operating division and function, in the following ways:

(1) Operating expenses, such as salaries, travel, supplies, repairs.

(2) Capital costs, and

(3) Fixed charges, such as interest on building bonds.

There should also be included, if consistent with fiscal policies, a contingency fund amounting to approximately 5 per cent of the total budget.

In setting up a budget, a number of forms are commonly employed. The general intent of most of these forms is to show (a) the expenditure over a preceding period of time equal to that for which the budget is being prepared; (b) the budget of the period during which the budget is being prepared; (c) any changes in the present budget period from that which had been anticipated in preparing the orig-inal budget; (d) expenditures of the present period, giving expenditures up to the time the next budget is being pre-pared; and (e) estimates to the end of the present period. The budget should indicate a comparison between the present and anticipated budgets in addition to any increases or de-creases in budgetary items.

The budget forms should also have a final column in which

the budget that has been adopted may be recorded. Sometimes it may be advantageous to have a column for the budget adopted by the governing board, and another column for the budget finally adopted by the taxing or legislative agency.

Tables 1 & 2 indicate rather typical budget forms. The budget is an excellent medium for communication between the director of the community mental health agency and its governing board. In a budget, the director is essentially trying to describe—in terms often not too familiar to the mental health professional person—what he and his people are trying to do, what sorts of tools or resources they need to accomplish this task, and what they will deliver in return for financial support. A narrative description of activities and positions should accompany the formal budget sheet.

A good accounting system provides both a financial record of all activities and transactions of the agency, as well as a running tally on the financial situation so that the director of the service may plan rationally for expansions or changes in service emphasis as needs arise. Minimum accounting records should consist of at least a general ledger, and a complete and detailed record of receipts and expenditures. It is desirable to employ a certified public accountant to assist the director of the agency in establishing the accounting system, instructing administrative personnel in its use, and annually auditing the accounts of the agency. It is desirable to keep the accounting system as simple as possible, while still allowing an accurate, understandable, and complete indication of all receipts and expenditures.

Cost Accounting

Cost accounting for mental health services is extremely difficult. Certain basic distinctions must be made between *unit of work, unit of production,* and *unit of raw material consumed.* Many cost accounting procedures do not make

PAGE NO. 1

TABLE 1

ANNUAL BUDGET
FISCAL YEAR 1966
ACTIVITY EXPENDITURE ESTIMATE

FORM DA 406

Agency No. 5 Name: Tri-City Mental Health Center

1. Object Code	2. Object of Expenditures	3. Actual FY 1963	4. Actual FY 1964	5. Estimated FY 1965	6. Requested FY 1966	7. Governor's Recommendation FY 1966	8. Comments Adopted Budget
	1. Total Salaries and Wages	46,200	66,200	78,500	81,900		
200	Communication	360	420	500	500.00		
210	Freight and Express	0	0	0	0		
220	Printing and Advertising	198	216	250	235.00		
230	Rents and Utilities	2,586	3,018	3,200	3,200.00		
240	Repairing and Servicing	0	0	0	0		
250	Travel and Subsistence	1,015	1,623	2,000	1,820.00		
260	Fees—Professional and Other Services	1,293	1,690	1,800	1,800.00		
290	Other Contractual Services	0	0	75	75.00		
	2. Total Contractual Services	5,452	6,967	7,825	7,630.00		
300	Clothing		0	0	0		
310	Feed and Forage		0	0	0		
320	Food For Human Consumption		0	0	0		

330 Fuel (Other Than For Motor Vehicles)			0	0
340 Maintenance Materials, Supplies and Parts			0	0
350 Motor-Vehicle Parts, Supplies and Accessories	105	197	200	250.00
360 Professional and Scientific Supplies and Materials				
370 Stationery and Office Supplies	395	182	200	175.00
380 Scientific Research Supplies			0	0
390 Other Supplies, Materials and Parts			0	0
3. Total Commodities	500	379	400	425.00
400 Equipment, Machinery, Furniture and Fixtures				
410 Livestock	3,800	1,900	1,250	785.00
4. Total Capital Outlay				0
600 Institutional or Departmental Debt				
7 Contingency Fund	500	2,500	3,000	4,155
7. Total Nonexpense Items	500	2,500	3,000	4,155
Total Activity Expenditures	56,452	77,946	90,975	94,895

PSYCHIATRY IN THE AMERICAN COMMUNITY

FORM DA 412

Agency No. 5 Name: Tri-City Mental Health Center

PAGE NO. 1

TABLE 2
ANNUAL BUDGET
FISCAL YEAR 1966
SALARY AND WAGE SUMMARY

1. Classification of Employment	2. Code No.	3. Salary Range	Actual FY 1963		Actual FY 1964		Estimated FY 1965		Positions Filled Sep. 1, 1964	Requested FY 1966		Recommendation FY 1966		
			4. No.	5. Amount	6. No.	7. Amount	8. No.	9. Amount	10. No.	11. No.	12. Amount	13. No.	14. Amount	15. Comments
Psychiatrist-Director	568	55	0	0	1	21,000	1	22,000	1	1	22,700			
Chief Psychiatric Social Worker	577	36	1	9,500	1	10,000	1	11,500	1	1	12,000			
Psychiatric Social Worker II	576	32	1	7,500	1	8,000	1	8,500	1	1	9,000			
Psychiatric Social Worker I	575	30	1	7,000	0	0	1	7,000	0	1	7,500			
Clinical Psychologist	587	47	1	12,000	1	13,000	1	14,000	1	1	14,500			
Psychometrician	584	32	1	7,000	1	7,800	1	8,500	1	1	9,000			
Receptionist-Secretary	593	25	1	3,200	1	3,600	1	4,200	1	1	4,200			
Clerk-Typist	590	20	0	0	1	2,800	1	3,000	1	1	3,000			
				46,200		66,200		78,700			81,900			

adequate distinctions between these three units as they apply to mental health practice, a situation which frequently results in misleading estimates.

The raw material of mental health agencies are individual patients. These patients are processed through individual or group contacts with professional staff members. Units of work may be expressed either as staff hours, or staff contacts. The end product of mental health activities in the community is the prevention, treatment, or rehabilitation of mental or emotional illness in individuals.

To divide the total expense of the agency, therefore, by the number of patients treated, and arrive at a cost per patient, does not really give the cost per unit of production. It gives the cost per unit of raw material, a patient needing treatment. Nor does dividing the total budget by staff hours provide an accurate estimate, since this is merely a measure of the cost per unit of work. The only really accurate measure of cost per unit of production may be attained by dividing the cost of the agency operation by the number of individuals who had a mental or emotional illness which was successfully prevented, treated, or rehabilitated. When the concept of service is broadened even further, to include indirect services such as consultation and mental health education, as well as research and training, cost accounting problems become even more complex.

As an example, an agency that has an average cost per case of only $50, as opposed to an agency whose average cost per case is $2,000, may not necessarily be more economical or more efficient. It may turn out, that only a few of the cases treated for $50 received any significant benefit from the service, whereas the majority of cases treated by the "more expensive" agency were significantly improved or recovered. Similarly, a staff that utilizes all of its time in direct treatment and receives low salaries may provide figures indicating that the "cost" is low; whereas a better trained or more experienced staff, which utilizes only part of its time in direct clinical services may have a much higher cost per unit of work. The first agency need not be more economical nor more efficient than the second, because the general quality of service provided may be low.

Evaluation of results and appraisal of the quality of service are therefore very important in evaluating the cost of an agency. Comparisons between agencies on the basis of numbers alone—such as cost per patient hour, cost per staff contact, cost per case—are extremely dangerous and lead to spurious conclusions by governing boards and lay citizens. For example, if an agency stresses the importance of economical operation, and considers economy to be a low cost per hour of staff service, the logical conclusion to a governing board—after hearing this kind of talk over a period of a few years—might be to decide that the best solution is to hire the cheapest staff persons available. This would initially result in the decision not to employ psychiatrists; a decision a year or so later to dispense with the clinical psychologist; and a decision a few years after that, to replace trained psychiatric social workers with lay social workers. A study of the history of welfare departments reveals in painful detail the logical outcome of any program that emphasizes quantity as opposed to quality, equates economy with cheapness, and does not stress high standards of training and professional competence.

In cost accounting, then, the constant frame of reference must be to use such cost accounts as a means of communicating with and educating the governing board. It is a metaphorical way of talking about the value of various kinds of services, and of discussing with the board, priorities between different programs.

In communicating with the governing board, for example, it may be useful to use a special breakdown of the budget, such as Table 3, in order to indicate the actual cost of con-

TABLE 3

Period Covered —————, 19—
to ————————, 19—

Cost Projection Estimates
Total Budget ————

A. % of staff time spent   Budget

in consultation ——————————— XT.B. = ——————————
with schools ——————————— XT.B. = ——————————
with courts ——————————— XT.B. = ——————————
with social agencies ——————— XT.B. = ——————————
with medical agencies ——————— XT.B. = ——————————
with rehabilitation agencies ——— XT.B. = ——————————
with other agencies ——————— XT.B. = ——————————

B. % of staff time spent in administration ——————— XT.B. = ———
C. % of staff time in mental health education ——— XT.B. = ———
D. % of staff time in direct clinical services ——— XT.B. = ———
E. % of staff time in research ——————————— XT.B. = ———

T.B. = Total Budget

templated services of various sorts. This is a way of telling the board about the different types of services that are offered, presenting in a concrete way the time involved, and illustrating the cost of each service. It is an important tool in calling to the board's attention a fact about which they constantly need reminding: direct clinical services are not and should not be the only function of a community agency.

Table 4 illustrates one method of demonstrating to the board the cost per unit of service for the various activities of the agency. The unit of service can be defined in a number of ways, but the exact definition should be made explicit for the staff and the governing board, and should not be varied from year to year. In many agencies, the unit of service is a 50-minute hour. Some agencies merely define it as a patient contact, in the case of clinical services, which may be either five minutes or two hours in duration. Consultation services may be broadened to include telephone conversations, or narrowed to include only face-to-face contacts of 30 minutes or longer. The National Institute of

TABLE 4

Period covered ————, 19——
to ————————, 19——

Annual Cost Accounting:
Gross Expenditures

Item	Budget *	÷	Units of Service	=	Unit Cost
A. Consultation Services ————			————		————
With Schools ————			————		————
With Courts ————			————		————
With Social Agencies ————			————		————
With Medical Agencies ————			————		————
With Rehabilitation Agencies ————			————		————
With Other ————			————		————
B. Administration ————			————		————
C. Mental Health Education ————			————		————
D. Clinical Services ————			————		————
E. Research ————			————		————

* Note: If actual annual expenses are significantly different than budgeted, difference should be pro-rated among budgeted items.

Mental Health has further complicated the definition of terms by asking for reporting of patient contacts: example, if five patients saw one therapist for an hour, this would be counted as five patient contacts rather than one therapist hour. At this juncture, each agency will have to develop its own vocabulary and standard frame of reference for defining units of service. In general, it should be kept in mind that lay people on governing boards need to be told in as many ways as possible, and as often as possible, that psychiatric services take time, and can not be done hurriedly.

Table 5 is an example of a further breakdown that may be helpful in indicating the actual portion of the service that is subsidized by tax funds. This is a way to demonstrate the differential responsibility assumed by the agency in paying for the cost of various services, and may help the board clarify policy concerning fees for services to other

TABLE 5

Period covered ———, 19——
to ———————, 19——

Annual Cost Accounting
Net Public Support ——

Item	Budget	Fee Income =	Net Cost	Units of Service =	Net Unit Cost
A. Consultation	———	———	———	———	———
With Schools	———	———	———	———	———
With Courts	———	———	———	———	———
With Social Agencies	———	———	———	———	———
With Medical Agencies	———	———	———	———	———
With Rehabilitation Agencies	———	———	———	———	———
With Other Agencies	———	———	———	———	———
B. Administration	———	———	———	———	———
C. Mental Health Education	———	———	———	———	———
D. Clinical Service	———	———	———	———	———
E. Research	———	———	———	———	———

agencies, upper income levels for clinical service, fee scales, and so forth.

One final word of caution which perhaps *should not* be necessary for mental health practitioners: money has many emotionally-laden meanings for the average American. Attitudes as to whether a professional person who devotes his life to helping others should be adequately paid, for example, are extremely varied. Governing boards often feel a heavy burden of social responsibility when they are spending public money, and are fearful of criticism from their peers. There is no time in his relationship with the governing board, when the director of the agency should be more patient and more attuned to helping board members deal with their own intrapsychic and interpersonal problems, than when he is presenting and justifying his budget. Unfortunately, it is often at that time that the administrator of the agency feels most under pressure, and least able to "listen with the third ear" and respond empathically and constructively.

In coping with this problem, the director must begin budget preparation and justification months ahead of the deadline, and involve his staff in discussing and preparing for the budget meeting, as well as in actually making the presentation to the board.

Surprises, demands, strident requests, and ultimatums have no place in the presentation of the budget request.

SUGGESTED READINGS

Aurnet, H. H. (1962), *Psychiatric Insurance*. New York: Group Health Insurance, Inc.

Insurance Coverage of Mental Illness, 1962. Joint Information Services of the American Psychiatric Association and the National Association for Mental Health, Washington, D. C., 1962.

XXV

Administration: Art and/or Science?

"Administration" is a derogatory word to many mental health professionals. Connotations include "the organization man," authoritarianism, rigidity, "the man in the gray flannel suit" and formalism. In the world of today, it is impossible to live entirely outside of organizations, and we all must struggle about our feelings concerning group pressures. These feelings are presented in many current art forms; a notable success was the musical *How to Succeed in Business without Really Trying.*

The basic issue, however, is the widespread concern that man should not be forced to sacrifice individual liberty and personal freedom, and with it a sense of personal worth and self-respect, because of the pressures and seductions of organizational life.

For mental health practitioners, these feelings may be even more troubling. The legacy of Freud would indicate, at least superficially, that society is a repressor of the individual, the source of neuroticism, and a constantly inhibiting force. This confusion is compounded by prolonged training emphasizing the importance of the individual one-to-one relationship between clinician and patient, and yet is conducted in large organizations characterized by impersonality, ritualism, and rigidity.

From this welter of discouragement and annoyance, we should tease out the basic purpose of administration, which is to assist a group of individuals accomplish certain goals

389

that are desired by the majority of the members of the group. Administration includes the establishment of organizational goals (the mission), methods of striving towards these goals, modes of deployment of resources to accomplish tasks oriented towards the goal; planning for staffing, recruitment of staff, assignment, evaluation, supervision, and coordination of staff activities; and directing the overall work of the agency and making decisions relating to proper means for pursuing agreed-upon goals.

In other chapters, attention has been given to the determination of the mission of a community mental health operation, the principles for pursuing these objectives, staff needs, supervision and training, and to relationships with governing boards and other responsible agencies. In this chapter we intend to discuss the organizational structure of the agency, and general principles of administration.

Responsibility and authority are two key concepts in organizing and managing any endeavor. In classic administrative theory, the director of the agency holds all authority and all responsibility for the entire operation. He delegates such authority and such responsibility to his subordinates as may be appropriate in pursuing the goals of the agency. A basic tenet, almost a commandment, has held that whenever responsibility is delegated, commensurate authority must be delegated. In practice, the proper management of responsibility and authority is the most important element of good administration. While a proper mastery of the concepts of responsibility and authority, and proper utilization of these concepts, is not sufficient for a good administrator, absence of the mastery of these concepts will almost certainly lead to difficulty.

Some social psychologists, and mental health workers as well, would question this concept of delegation of authority and responsibility. Such concepts as group decision-making, team cooperation, and blurring of disciplinary roles run counter to a neat system of orderly fixation of responsibility and authority. It is probably inappropriate to even pose the question as to what method of organization is *best*. To the extent that staff members generally have similar backgrounds in terms of length and complexity of training and experience, and hold similar aspirational goals, the implementation of entirely nonauthoritarian, nonhierarchical administration becomes more possible. To the extent that the staff is heterogeneous, nonauthoritarian administration becomes more difficult.

In the final analysis, as our world is currently structured, someone will, in reality, at least in any agency receiving tax or other public funds, be seen as holding the ultimate authority and responsibility. Whatever ground rules he may decide to set within his own organization, the basic reality that he has final power of veto, and thus of decision, cannot be obscured or denied if basic honesty is to be maintained within the administrative structure. Not all group decisions of the staff will necessarily be honored by the administrative authority, and to the extent that he allows staff to believe that all its decisions will be adhered to, he is participating in neurotic and regressive group processes.

At the other end of the continuum, usually, the more omnipotent and omniscient a role the administrator attempts to assume, the less omniscient and omnipotent will he be in reality. The chief problem of administrative authority lies in maintaining an adequate inflow of information concerning the operation of the organization. To the extent that the director is opinionated, unwilling to listen to the opinions of his subordinates, partial and punitive, cold and distant, inconsistent and arbitrary, his input of information will decrease. As employees tell him less and less that is valid, and more and more shape their comments to meet the administrator's predispositions and preconceived ideas, the less objective information will he have available for rational problem solving. In this way, a vicious circle is established: the administrator gets more and more anxious because he knows less and less about what is going on—he reacts in more and more authoritarian and arbitrary ways—less and less valid information comes to him—he becomes more and more anxious, and so forth. Two eventual outcomes are possible: the administrator may eventually destroy the organization or it will collapse of its own weight; or, the more usual outcome is that lower echelon personnel assume more and more informal authority while making more decisions on their own. Through informal group processes, the organization manages to limp along, but at considerable loss of efficiency and great cost of personal discomfort on the part of personnel and patients alike.

Span of control is a long-standing administrative concern. The standard dogma of the armed forces has been that the span of control is from three to eight persons, no more. Most organizations are set up so that one supervisor or administrator has no more than eight persons reporting to him. It is not unusual for mental health practitioners, because of certain problems with personal grandiosity, to forget the limitations of the human intellect and the human emotional system and to attempt supervisory relationships with 15, 20, or even 30 persons. It is rarely possible for one human being to maintain any kind of meaningful relationship with so many persons. By doing so, the administrator subtly derogates his importance, diffuses his impact, overextends himself emotionally and intellectually, and keeps very busy essentially supporting the development of a disorganized group, where power is systematically usurped by second echelon personnel. The "one big happy family" model simply does not work when the organization gets bigger than one big happy family. In fact, this communication model does not even work particularly well in many families, as we all know.

When the number of persons in an organization exceeds five or six, formal organizational structure becomes necessary. Certain persons must be assigned responsibility for specific tasks, must be held accountable for the proper performance of these duties, and must answer to the administrator. When the organization increases beyond 10, it is inevitable that authority and decision-making processes must be shared by the top administrator with one or more second echelon or intermediate administrators.

The attempt of one strong, determined, and even gifted professional person to maintain control and decision-making authority over a large mental health institution is a common organizational hazard in all mental health work. There is no better way for destroying the effectiveness of an organization or burning out the leadership abilities of professional persons.

A general principle of administration—which does not accept an entirely rigid and hierarchical system, nor at the other extreme, a completely nonauthoritarian group-oriented approach—is that decisions should be made as low in the organizational hierarchy as is possible. This requires considerable sophistication and skill among all supervisory personnel of the agency, who consistently must challenge their subordinates about the need or desirability of bringing decisions to the next higher level; they must consciously stimulate and support the development of individual initiative on the part of lower and lower echelons in the organization. The fear of many administrators, of course, is that this will somehow subvert their authority and consequently their control. Nothing could be further from the truth. A football team, for example, operates exactly on this principle: each player is expected to have highly developed abilities, and to act in the immediate situation on the basis of individual judgment and initiative; yet, the captain of the team has certain kinds of authority for determining overall policy. To the extent that the administrator is able to stimulate and develop truly autonomous behavior on the part of many persons in his organization, he will be able to develop a healthy social climate in which his leadership will be respected but not worshipped, his decisions will be followed but not blindly. Furthermore, in such a climate, he will be aware of the operations of his agency because fearfulness and distrust of him as an authority figure will be minimized—although in reality never entirely absent.

Organization should be, to the fullest extent possible, functional rather than formal. There is little justification, in the view of the author, for the organization of departments of psychology, psychiatry, social work, adjunctive therapy, nursing, and so forth. Rather, organization should be in terms of multidisciplinary teams which are devoted towards accomplishing certain of the subgoals of the agency.

The administrator must constantly be alert to situations where personnel are subjected to double control on double supervision. This is deleterious to morale, abrogates the basic principles of administration as well as of effective group functioning: deterioration of staff efficiency can be the only result. The natural power and prestige strivings of senior clinicians on the staff can be met in ways other than by appointing them chiefs of some subdisciplinary service.

For example, it is quite proper and appropriate that the chief administrator should have a staff to assist him in studying problems in planning, and in evaluating the function of the agency. These staff persons, not having a line relationship with other personnel, would influence the operation of the agency in many ways. Such a staff structure is paralleled to the organization of the armed services, where staff level officers are responsible for such operations as personnel, intelligence, materiel, etc.

Also, a wide variety of committee appointments is possible, allowing for necessary status distinctions between personnel and allowing them to participate in decision making.

Most important of these would be the executive committee, which would be charged with meeting regularly with the chief administrator to discuss certain aspects of policy and operations. Research committees, program evaluation committees, psychotherapy committees, committees on consultation activities, records committees, training and staff development committees—these are only a few of the many possibilities for sharing important operations of the agency with subordinate personnel, and allowing necessary hierarchical distinctions and prestige rewards without a frozen, self-perpetuating, stifling hierarchical organization.

The director of an agency has, in addition to administrative responsibility, two additional responsibilities that are somewhat difficult to define and evaluate.

The first of these is *leadership*. Concepts of leadership are based largely on current social models of "good leadership," and vary from time to time. Until relatively recently, the leader was one who forged ahead, and by a conspicuous show of valor and aggressiveness, spurred his followers on to higher and higher achievements. In recent years, the model of somewhat passive leadership has emerged, which in its extreme, results in the leader's assuming the responsibility only for implementing changes which the great majority of his followers want and push him into. The "Charge of the Light Brigade" was certainly foolish, we can see in retrospect. I suspect it will not be too many more years before we will also be able to see the passivity and essential shirking of responsibility of many "new style" leaders in a similar derogatory light. It is difficult to see how anyone can or should become director of an agency unless he has certain values that he wishes to implement. It rests with his good judgment and flexibility to determine which of his own personal values he may legitimately and successfully implement through his agency. To the extent that he has no values, either personal or professional, which he strongly wishes to implement, he will fail in the task of leadership. Leadership always has had, and always will have, certain elements of chauvinism, and the good leader always has had and always will have some charisma.

Another responsibility of the administrator is *ceremonial representation* of the agency. In fulfilling this responsibility, he must constantly indicate through attitude, word, and manner that he sees himself clearly as a representative of an enterprise involving many people, and is not seeking personal aggrandizement. The administrator must inevitably attempt to use his organization to accomplish certain goals, yet he can never allow himself to see or represent his organization as only an extension of his own person. He must also be willing, at times, to allow himself to be used by the organization, to be an instrument of the agency rather than vice versa. Such an ability to shift back and forth flexibly is, of course, very similar to the flexibility demanded of a good parent, or a good psychotherapist.

It is often desirable to have a pictorial representation or chart of the organizational structure of the agency. Such a chart may be set up either in terms of personnel, or in terms of functions. In the average mental health agency, at this particular stage in the development of our art and science, it is usual for professional persons to wear two or three different "hats." For example, the same professional person will quite likely be involved in such activities as outpatient evaluation and treatment, and consultation with certain community agencies. To the extent that such overlap occurs, a neat organizational chart on the basis of units, divisions, or sections is extremely difficult, and the more necessary does a functional chart become.

The coordination and control of the ongoing operation of an agency is extremely difficult. While the efficiency expert has been the object of many jokes, it is clear that frequent and careful reappraisal of most organizational functions is necessary in order to prevent the perseveration of unproductive behavior patterns. A question to be constantly asked at all levels, from the top administrator down, is: "Why are you doing that? Can you do it better?" No operation should be continued that does not intentionally serve the immediate and/or long-range goals of the agency. No data should be collected, as one example, that does not have an actual or potential usefulness in achieving the mission of the agency.

Although behavior patterns may persist indefinitely once they are established, it may also be extremely difficult to get new styles of behavior accepted by appropriate personnel. Follow-up, therefore, becomes an essential phase of administration, and should always come on the heels of planning and delegation of responsibilities. The administrator who follows up too quickly or too suspiciously may be seen as being a cruel tyrant by his employees. The one who never follows up may be seen as essentially indifferent to the actual results, and as only issuing certain ritualistic directions from time to time to assuage his own conscience. If the administrator does not follow up, he sabotages and destroys his own importance and that of his subordinates.

A subcommittee of the American Public Health Association, chaired by Jack Downing, M. D., has been struggling in recent years with proper methods of evaluating the operation of a community mental health program. Probably we are many years from having a method equal to that developed for public health departments by the American Public Health Association (1937).

The actual methods of communication used within the agency, and between the agency and outside organizations, require constant study. There are certain types of situations in which the only appropriate communication is a face-to-face conference, while in others a phone call will suffice; there are other situations requiring an informal memo, and still others that require a formal and detailed letter. Methods of communication must be geared to the task to be accomplished, and to the needs of the sender and the recipient. The careful administrator, however, will maintain a constant monitoring of a sample of the correspondence between representatives of his agency and patients, clients, and other community agencies. It takes only one staff member with a need to express his annoyance at the world, and some ability and willingness to do so through cleverly turned phrases in letters, to vitiate the best conceived public relations program, or to undermine the effectiveness of the most soundly planned service program. One general rule-of-thumb is that the more harsh or upsetting a communication potentially may be, the more value there is in scheduling a face-to-face conference during which time it can be discussed. This is only an attempt to transfer to administrative practice, those insights gained through clinical work as they pertain to the problems inherent in communicating with people on subjects about which they do not want to hear, or about which they are afraid to know either with regard to themselves or others. Just as we would not write a harsh, confronting letter to a patient or a relative—or should not—the same degree of empathy, insight, and skill should go into communications with other professional caregivers. We should treat our colleagues, and expect them to treat us, with the same sensitivity, empathy, and concern that we have for our patients.

SUGGESTED READINGS

American Psychiatric Association (1964), Emerging patterns of administration in psychiatric facilities. In: *Psychiatric Studies and Projects,* Vol. 2, No. 9.

Ewalt, J. R. (1956), *Mental Health Administration.* Springfield, Ill.: Charles C Thomas.

Gove, W. J., ed. (1962), *Administrative Decision Making.* Glencoe, Ill.: Free Press.

Group for the Advancement of Psychiatry (1960), *Administration of the Public Psychiatric Hospital,* Report No. 46. New York.

Myers, J. M. & Smith, J. H. (1960), Administrative psychiatry. *Amer. J. Psychiat.,* 116:649-651.

Pfiffner, J. M. & Presthus, R. V. (1960). *Public Administration.* New York: Ronald Press.

XXVI

Supervisory Processes

Supervision, consultation, and "psychotherapy control" are often used interchangeably. They should not be. A common element does exist in these relationships: one professional person engages in an interpersonal relationship with another, with the intention of modifying the behavior of the recipient. There are, however, wide variations possible within this general model.

First of all, they differ in terms of the *responsibility* of the supervising, consulting, or controlling person. In supervision, the supervisor is considered responsible and accountable for the behavior of the supervisee. In consultation, the consultant assumes neither responsibility for the behavior of the consultee, nor for the consultee's seeking needed assistance from the consultant. A psychotherapy controller, on the other hand, assumes some responsibility for maintaining regular, scheduled, structured contacts with the controllee, but does not assume direct responsibility for the behavior of the controllee in the psychotherapy situation (although there is a moral and indirect responsibility, whose exercise is complex, for the controller can always inform the supervisor if there is gross dereliction of duty or severe misconduct on the part of the controllee).

There are differences in *authority,* as well. The supervisor has authority over the supervisee, and may direct that he change his behavior, as well as invoke appropriate institutional sanctions if he does not modify his behavior in the desired direction. A consultant, in contrast, does not have authority over the consultee, cannot invoke organizational sanctions, and can only choose to terminate the relationship if the consultee's behavior is sufficiently deviant to make the consultant feel that, by continuing consultation, he is passively condoning harmful behaviors on the part of the consultee. Of course, in practice the consultant often exerts a much more powerful, indirect influence, since he characteristically has the ear of the supervisor and may indirectly invoke organizational sanctions. The psychotherapy controller has no direct authority, and cannot directly invoke organizational pressures. Characteristically, however, in a training situation he is asked to rate the performance of the controllee, and to evaluate his progress in learning particular skills; he thus, indirectly, has considerable authority over the kinds of training experiences, opportunities, and advancements that the controllee will be permitted within the organization.

A great deal has been made of different techniques in these various types of relationships. These differentiations are probably arbitrary, in reality exist more in theory than in practice, and are relatively unimportant as compared to the differentiation of the processes in terms of authority and responsibility. Whenever one human being confronts another, and engages in a dialogue concerning meaningful aspects of human experience, certain characteristics of the relationship are universal. These will be reiterated briefly, although undoubtedly their explication will sound trite and self-evident.

The establishment and maintenance of adequate communication is, of course, of paramount importance. Communication must be mutual, and must flow in both directions between the participants in the process. The communication must occur at both the intellectual or idea level (in both abstract and concrete realms) and at the level of feelings or affective experiences. Communication must address itself to both subjective and objective elements of behavior in the patient, supervisee (consultee, controllee) and supervisor (consultant, controller).

Goal or task-orientation must be maintained. The goals of the various types of relationships do vary to some extent. The goal of supervision is to insure that the supervisee behaves in ways that are seen by the particular agency as being appropriate and productive *behaviors*. The goal of consultation is to provide assistance to the consultee in utilizing his training and knowledge, through a better understanding of, and ability to cope with, his own emotional biases, conflicts, or blind spots. Psychotherapy control is usually conceived of as being a learning experience, which combines the elements of consultation mentioned above, with elements of formal didactic learning pertaining to the ideational basis of psychotherapy, emotional components of psychotherapy practice, and awareness of countertransference attitudes and behaviors.

Respect for the personal integrity and autonomy of both participants in the process characterizes successful relationships, whether they be supervision, consultation, or psychotherapy control. The supervisor (consultant, controller) should not seek to employ the supervisee (consultee, controllee) as an extension of himself. The supervisor cannot use the supervisee as a tool or instrument by which he accomplishes certain goals or purposes that he wants to accomplish. Unless the supervisee is involved in a collaborative process, is able to genuinely share and accept the goals of the supervisor, and then is given autonomy to move towards these goals in his own characteristic way, the process will be a partial failure. Provision of mental health services is sufficiently demanding, complex, and difficult, so that one individual cannot passively or compliantly carry out the directions of another in the free give-and-take of a treatment process. While these generalizations are particularly true with regard to governing the relationships between professional people—in fact, the essence of the concept of professionalism is contained in the preceding comments—they are to a considerable extent true in relationships between a professional person and a subprofessional worker or technician.

Understanding based on empathy is essential in all dyadic transactions. Empathy is not synonymous with indulgence, or with the acceptance of low standards of performance or of personal or professional behavior.

Just as a supervisor cannot successfully behave in an authoritarian and dictatorial manner, neither can he abdicate the essential responsibility which rests with him. One aspect of the supervisory responsibility, confused by inconsistent usage and unclear thinking, has been the concept of *medical responsibility*. In the judgment of the author, a psychiatrist should not allow himself to be labeled the medical director of an agency, nor to have it said that he has assumed "medical responsibility" unless the following conditions have been met:

1. He has control over the employment of all professional persons involved in the care of patients.

2. He has supervisory responsibility for all persons involved in the care of patients. While he may delegate a part of this supervisory authority to some other professional person of a different discipline, he cannot delegate his ultimate responsibility.

3. He must have authority to periodically review the caseloads of all clinicians involved in the care of patients, to evaluate their work, and to direct necessary changes or modifications.

4. He must determine the minimal standards for record keeping, including content, style, and criteria of adequacy.

5. He must evaluate and rate the work performance of all persons involved in the care of patients. This includes judgments concerning continuing employment, promotion, and salary of the persons involved in the care of patients.

6. He shall report directly to the chief administrator of the agency; or, in those cases where he is also the director of the agency, to the governing board.

7. He shall have final authority for determining which patients shall be accepted for evaluation and/or treatment by any staff member in the clinical program.

8. He shall have final responsibility and authority for recommending to the director of the agency (or if he is the director of the agency, to the governing board), needed personnel and budgetary requirements for the clinical program.

In any case, where the psychiatrist does not have this responsibility and authority within the agency, it should be clearly spelled out that he is *not* assuming medical responsibility, and is *not* the medical director of the agency. He may be titled a staff psychiatrist, or a psychiatric consultant, but he should not let himself become responsible, by implication and general consensus, for the total treatment program of the agency. Again, a basic principle of administration is highlighted: with the assumption of responsibility, commensurate authority must also be assumed.

This is not to say that psychiatrists should necessarily be critical of nonmedical practitioners, or feel superior to them, or should adopt a "hands-off" or "stand-offish" attitude. Rather, it *is* to say that medical practice has a long tradition and a heavy social responsibility, which should not be for sale to the highest bidder, nor pawned off in exchange for a tawdry and meaningless title. Psychiatrists, as other physicians, can and do work in nonmedical settings, and in agencies directed by persons other than physicians: schools, courts, prisons, hospitals, and military establishments are examples that come readily to mind. However, it should be pointed out that even within the military system, there have been safeguards set up to protect the patient, by insuring that the physician's judgment will not be arbitrarily overruled by nonmedical authorities: the medical officer may

refuse a direct order, if it is contrary to good medical judgment, and be immune from court martial proceedings.

Psychiatrists need not necessarily control, boss, or administer every agency providing services for troubled people.
But to the extent that they assume responsibility for the
operation of the agency or a portion of the agency, they
should insist upon and have commensurate and unequivocal
authority.

Suggested Readings

Administration, Supervision and Consultation (1955). New York:
   Family Service Association of America.
Ekstein, R. & Wallerstein, R. (1960), *The Teaching and Learning of
   Psychotherapy.* New York: Basic Books.

XXVII

Research in Community Mental Health

Research can be a rather scary word. It tends to denote elaborate methodology, complex equipment, detailed mathematical analysis, and abstruse language. The practitioner in the usual community mental health setting, bowed down with excessive demands, overworked and underappreciated, usually responds to the suggestion of research with at best a laugh, and more often with a sense of horror.

This is unfortunate, because the purpose of research is to simplify life rather than to render it more complicated. Research in the behavioral sciences is essentially disciplined observation which is then used to develop and test explanatory theories. In the community mental health field, research may be conducted by the individual case-by-case method, the correlation method, the survey method, or by the epidemiological method. The experimental model of the physical sciences has less applicability for our field, but certainly may be used with good cause for some aspects of a comprehensive community mental health program, such as mental health education, programs of casefinding and early treatment, and so forth.

What sort of research needs doing in community mental health? All kinds. Who should do it? A wide variety of behavioral scientists, including practitioners within the community mental health centers themselves.

Critics have speculated that the atrophy and loss of momentum in the child guidance movement occurred as it became solely pragmatic and technique-centered. Research, experimentation, and vigorous new thinking gave way to increasingly detailed elaboration of a very narrow theoretical base. The healthy balance between practice, research and teaching was lost, and the child guidance movement began to run downhill.

Will the same thing happen to community psychiatry? Most certainly, unless a spirit of vigorous inquiry and intellectual candor can be established and promoted in all of the disciplines currently developing community mental health endeavors.

The following are representative of the types of studies that warrant consideration:

1. *Programmatic inquiry* is a good beginning for the development of a research or self-study program by any community mental health agency, no matter how large or small, and no matter how experienced or inexperienced the staff may be in formal research procedures. In this research there is a high sense of ego-involvement among all members of the staff, and the project may become a shared responsibility and assume a central position in the functioning of the agency.

For example, the staff might set out to ask itself: "How do the various demographic characteristics of the patient population differ from the general population at risk?" It often will be possible, in such a study, to generate hypotheses concerning nonpurposive bias in patient selection, or in casefinding and referral channels within the community.

Or, a simple method may be developed for purposes of studying, in a descriptive fashion, the consultation activities of the community mental health center staff with various agencies and individuals within the community. With which community caregivers do they consult, how often, about what sorts of things, and how does all of this change over the course of time? The effort here would be to better understand the needs of other caregiving agencies and to develop an increasingly more sophisticated program of consultation.

Or, the staff might ask: "What about the patients who terminate against advice?" This could lead to a study of all unilateral terminations, to see whether there are meaningful differences between those patients who terminate against advice and those who do so upon mutual agreement. In the literature, severity of illness, ego-strength, whether the patient is referred by someone else or self-referred, and socioeconomic position are some of the variables that have been associated with unilateral termination.

Or, the staff might ask: "What about the patients who tween patients who are referred to us by other caregivers and those who come themselves?" Does the type of severity of illness differ? Are there socioeconomic or ethnic differences? Does the course of their evaluation and treatment in the agency differ significantly? Some of the long-standing stereotypes and prejudices of mental health workers, and the high value they place upon having patients self-referred, might be considerably undermined by such a study.

Or, the agency might decide to conduct a simple survey of consumer satisfaction, as is done by many other industries on a regular, routine basis, and ask all terminated patients to rate, through correspondence, the various kinds of services they received at the agency and the various staff members who provided such services.

2. *Studies of the social context of community mental health practice,* while somewhat more complex methodologically, have considerable relevance for the community mental health practitioner.

For example, the agency might set out to study the attitudinal changes that occur in key opinion-setters in the community over a period of years, as these attitudes concern mental illness, mental health, the role of the mental health center, psychiatric treatment, etc. By a relatively simple test and retest design, it would be possible to arrive at some hypotheses concerning the effect or lack of effect of the consultation and community education program of the mental health center.

Or, in a community where a mental health center is just being developed, it might be productive to study, over a period of time, the general public pronouncements—through newspapers, radio, sermons, etc.—concerning the community's view of man and human nature and the spectrum of people-centered attitudes: judgmental, normative, etc. Through a random sampling procedure, an item analysis could be made at specified time intervals to see if there were any indication of humanization, softening, or other change in the attitudes of significant opinion-setters in the community with regard to their fellow man.

3. *Studies of specific institutions* would help the community mental health center understand more about the mental health problems and potentials of various social institutions and thereby improve its own procedures in relating to such institutions. Here, the technique of naturalistic observation—at which the mental health practitioner should be expert—may be employed.

For example, what might a staff member of a mental health center, with the help of the school administration, learn about mental health problems and potentials in schools by spending two hours a week for a year observing randomly selected school activities? What might he learn about problems of forensic psychiatry by observing, on a regular basis, court procedures? What might he learn about welfare by spending a few hours in the welfare department office as an observer on a regular basis? In the public health department? In a physician's office?

4. *Evaluative research* is frequently the starting point for the mental health practitioner and is, by far, the most difficult task facing the researcher. The efficacy of psychotherapy

has been much discussed and much studied, yet a definitive answer has eluded the most skillful and "high-powered" research groups. In attempting to evaluate the clinical program, the usual mental health center would probably do best to keep its criteria at a relatively simple level. For example, how well do patients believe that they are getting along after a certain period following treatment in the center? How well do their families think they are doing? How well do their family physicians think they are getting along? Insofar as is possible, objective criteria such as rate of employment and annual income should be gathered.

The evaluation of the consultation program of the agency is, in some ways, even more difficult. Studies will, of necessity, have to be fairly gross at this point, and exploratory or hypothesis-generating in nature. One such research design might, however, involve providing consultative services to randomly selected classrooms within a school, and not providing such services to other classrooms. A variety of indicators such as absenteeism, academic achievement scores, referral rate to the community mental health center and other mental health agencies, ratings of the classroom milieu by objective observers, rating of the classrooms and the teacher by the principal and other supervisory personnel, are all evaluative techniques that may be used.

Mental health education poses the same methodological problems for evaluation as do the clinical and consultation programs. Most evaluation of mental health education has attempted to measure conscious, more or less rational attitudes, by some interview or paper and pencil survey technique. The relationship between verbalized attitudes and behaviors, both self-directed and other-directed, is not impressively high. In other words, a careful distinction must be made between what people *say* about what they think, feel, and do, and what, in fact, they *actually* think, feel, and do.

5. *Studies of special problem areas as related to the community, utilizing survey and epidemiological methods,* may offer considerable assistance to the community mental health center in developing an increasingly more effective and sophisticated program. Any of a number of problem areas— such as major mental illness, alcoholism, delinquency, dependency and neglect, unemployability, mental retardation— may be chosen by the mental health center as a focus of special interest and inquiry. In the initial description of the problem, an attempt should be made to answer such questions as: How many of these people are there? Where are they located? What are their demographic characteristics? What do we know about how they become that way? What are community attitudes about persons with such problems? What are social devices for assisting them in coping with their problems?

6. *Collaborative research* with other mental health agencies, or with a wide variety of educational agencies, may develop in a few mental health centers which are located near major training and research institutions. The community mental health center can participate in research in such areas as child development, the effect of day care programs for neglected children, psychological aspects of speech therapy, and so forth.

7. *Operational research* may be extremely useful as a management tool. By the use of such operational research methods, the director of an agency is essentially providing the agency with an "observing ego function." He might ask such questions as: What differences are there in the style of practice of various staff members of the center? Does their use of diagnostic categories differ? Are there differences in the rates of unilateral termination? Are there differences in the duration of therapy? Are there differences in "customer satisfaction" following termination? Why is it that staff member C seems to have so many "emergency appoint-

ments?" Why does staff member A seem to offer prolonged treatment only to young women?

The answers to such questions, tentative though they may be, are useful to the director of an agency in supervision, in developing individualized programs of staff development and inservice training, and in improving the operational efficiency of the agency.

Now, the mental health center cannot do all types of research at any one time. But unless there is active inquiry going on within the agency about some phase or another of mental health theory, practice, or experience, intellectual curiosity will wither, the staff members' sense of vitality and purpose may wane, and the center may find itself repeatedly losing personnel to more "exciting" job opportunities.

The help of a consultant in planning research, and in understanding and interpreting the data obtained, may often be necessary.

The direct and indirect gains from a research program, no matter how limited and how imperfect, are great for the community mental health center.

SUGGESTED READINGS

Adelson, D. (1964), Research in community psychiatry. In: *Handbook of Community Psychiatry and Community Mental Health,* ed. L. Bellak. New York: Grune & Stratton.

Churchman, C. W., Ackoff, R. L., & Arnoff, E. L. (1957), *Introduction to Operations Research.* New York: Wiley.

Community Mental Health and Social Psychiatry: A Reference Guide (1962). Cambridge: Harvard University Press.

Hertzog, E. (1959), *Some Guides for Evaluative Research.* Washington, D. C.: Dep't of Health, Education & Welfare.

Mercer, J. R., Dingman, H. F., & Tarjon, G. (1964), Involvement, feedback, and mutuality: Principles for conducting mental health research in the community. *Amer. J. Psychiat.,* 121:228-237.

Plunkett, R. & Gordon, J. (1960), *Epidemiology and Mental Illness.* New York: Basic Books.

XXVIII

Training for Community Mental
Health Practitioners

It would be unfortunate if this chapter, or others, tended
to overemphasize the uniqueness of community mental health
practice. Each of the professional persons, be he psychiatrist, clinical psychologist, or psychiatric social worker, must
be basically a person with identity and commensurate training and experience in his own basic discipline, who chooses
to work within the context of a community mental health
endeavor. By virtue of offering a chapter on this subject,
however, the author clearly implies that there should be
changes and improvements in training for mental health
practitioners in the community.

There is considerable disagreement concerning what constitutes necessary and proper preparation for community
mental health practice. However, there is reasonable agreement that the majority of the training programs, in all three
of the disciplines, are not entirely adequate in terms of preparing young professional people to practice community
psychiatry. To quote one recent study:

> The psychiatric resident upon completion of his training is likely
> to be proficient in personality theory and in the diagnosis and treat-
> ment (either organic or psychodynamic) of acute psychoses, psycho-
> neuroses, and psychosomatic disorders. He is less likely to be as
> competent in those aspects of psychiatry which make him able to
> function comfortably and effectively in public psychiatric services—
> precisely those in which there are the most serious shortages of psy-
> chiatrists [American Psychiatric Association, 1963].

412

Perhaps as a result of these implied criticisms of training programs, a number of individuals charged with the responsibility for psychiatric residency training have reacted with some uneasiness:

> In spite of a great deal of publicity in which social and community psychiatry has been presented as the newest and most progressive development in psychiatry, there remains considerable uneasiness in the profession, and a general unclarity with regard to the basic concepts in this area of psychiatry. This is perhaps most true among those responsible for the development of residency programs, as well as those teaching in such programs, who have become increasingly aware of the conceptual difficulty and problems when trying to convey these to their students [Pumpian-Mindlin, 1964].

Not only is there some disagreement in psychiatry concerning the amount and type of specific training in community psychiatric practice—the same dialogue is current in clinical psychology and psychiatric social work—but there is a basic disagreement as to whether such training should even be included as part of the basic psychiatric residency.

Doctor Pumpian-Mindlin (1964) states: "Social psychiatric concepts should be included in the curriculum to stimulate and arouse the curiosity of the residents, but the specific techniques and skills of social psychiatry should be taught on a post-residency level, after the firm establishment of a core identity as a clinical psychiatrist."

In contrast, the Conference on Graduate Psychiatric Education (1963) of the American Psychiatric Association implies that post-residency training may be "too little, too late":

> The present focus in the training years tends to make the young psychiatrist go into private practice, where, in addition to financial and other advantages, he feels most competent. Conversely, the focus of his training tends to keep him from being interested in public mental hospital work or community services where he will encounter chronic psychoses, and have to deal with chronically ill and relatively indigent patients with a wide variety of social problems [p. 113].

The answers to what constitutes good or complete psychiatric training, even irrespective of the question of training in community psychiatry, would undoubtedly be many and varied. However, probably as compact a statement, having as general acceptance as is possible by the current leaders in psychiatric education, might be the following comments from the American Psychiatric Association Conference on Graduate Psychiatric Education (1963):

TRAINING TO FULFILL SOCIETY'S DEMANDS

In so doing, we must ask, what does the psychiatrist need to make him a 'complete' psychiatrist, who may be expected to fulfill society's demands, not only today but in the foreseeable future? The answer, summarizing much of what has been discussed in the previous sections, was formulated as follows:

1. He needs, first and foremost, to be a physician, with the knowledge, ethics, values, and codes expected of a member of the medical profession.

2. He needs to expand his knowledge of biological, behavioral, and social sciences in the specific areas of mental health.

This, ideally, would include:

Biology of behavior, including chemistry, neuroanatomy, genetics, neurophysiology, endocrinology.

Psychology, including theories of behavior, testing, personality growth and development.

Behavioral sciences, including relevant areas of sociology, anthropology, social psychology, and penology.

Psychopathology, including child and adult personality disorders, and psychosomatic disorders.

Therapy—organic, and group and individual psychotherapy for children and adults.

Neurology, including basic neurological sciences and recognition and management of clinical neurological syndromes in psychiatric practice.

Mental retardation—diagnosis, treatment, prevention.

Public health—principles of prevention, health education, and epidemiology, and knowledge of public health organizations.

Administration.

Social Welfare.

Rehabilitation.

Positive mental health principles and practices.

3. He needs to learn techniques and to develop skills in diagnosis,

treatment, rehabilitation, prevention, agency consultation, research, administration, and education relative to mental health. These are the practical applications through specific techniques and procedures of the basic knowledge and principles enumerated above. Hopefully, these applications are gained through experience in as many areas as possible.

4. Finally, he needs to develop a mature attitude and values that will enable him to assign priorities and properly balanced emphases to the various functions of a psychiatrist.

The training program, it was proposed, should be so organized that each resident is given at least an exposure to pertinent areas in the biological, behavioral, and social sciences. To assure that such exposure is integrated into the general program, responsibility for carrying out the procedure needs to be vested in the director of education, with the full support of the faculty. The program as envisaged should result in a reorientation of training attitudes and directions, from a restricted concern with individual psychopathology and therapy to a broader involvement with the psychosocial problems of the entire community.

In respect to specialization, the basic program should give the resident enough familiarity with all the subspecialties to enable him to make an intelligent choice of whatever area is most suitable and congenial for him, rather than committing him to one area, as is often now the case, because this is the only one with which he is familiar. There appeared to be general agreement that specialization should be discouraged at least in the first two years. The implication was that the resident might in his third year begin to pursue interests which would lead him to a longer period of subspecialty training, as, for example, in child psychiatry or psychoanalysis. This approach, it was held, is preferable to an arbitrary lengthening of the basic training period as a means of introducing subspecialization.

Changes in Training Attitudes and Emphases

The proposals for expanding and broadening the residency program were questioned by some participants, chiefly on the grounds of practicality. In attempting to meet society's demands, it was said, we must not lose sight of what can actually be done, what the resident can be expected to learn. Some participants felt that it is unrealistic to attempt to provide formal training in so many areas and to assume that such training will automatically produce psychiatrists interested in meeting public needs and competent to do so. The tendency to expand training with relevant material from other areas seems to be the same as that now developing in internal medicine. The question was raised: Is this a desirable trend? The Renaissance notion of the all-embracing role of the psychiatrist was dubbed impractical, and there was some feeling that it would be impossible to implement such a broad factual program in the residency period.

Admittedly, the psychiatrist must be concerned not only with psychotherapy but also with the psychosocial problems of the general population. There are, however, dangers in attempting too diffuse an orientation in basic training. Instead, it was said, the three-year program should be generic and its aim should be to produce a generalist. The character of the educational experience, rather than the actual content of the program, will give the generalist the perspective that will enable him to relate to special problems and to function in the areas of unmet needs.

The Conference agreed that changes in the training program are needed, that the present educational base is narrow and should be widened, and that the primary aim is to develop a socially responsible psychiatrist. The immediate step is to reorient the basic residency program so that public and social psychiatry as well as psychopathology and therapy are emphasized. This will involve changes in attitudes and emphases by the training directors and some enrichment of content; such changes can be made by most training centers within their present resources and without major dislocation.

Such changes will not, it was recognized, in themselves satisfy all the unmet public needs. They may go far, however, in countering the present drawbacks of public services with an inner drive for service to society. The public agencies can do much in overcoming low salary schedules, administrative difficulties, intellectual isolation, and other factors which contribute to the low status of positions in public psychiatric service.

It may be postulated that training programs have no obligation to provide personnel for the state hospitals and other public facilities, or even to encourage residents to undertake such work. They are, however, obligated to avoid prejudicing the resident against public service or any other particular type of service. By implication, it may be said that they have an obligation to make the resident aware of all possible areas of employment, and to spark his imagination by giving him a clear picture of the professional gratifications obtainable in public service.

While there are few training centers that have wholeheartedly accepted the responsibility of preparing residents for community psychiatric practice in the basic three-year curriculum, the department of psychiatry at Albert Einstein Medical College has attempted to do so. It is the belief of the chairman of the department, Milton Rosenbaum, that there are four characteristics of community psychiatry which should be included in basic training: [1]

1. Information about group interaction and group dynamics, and experience in working in a variety of roles with small groups.
2. A knowledge about the characteristics and dynamics of social conflict, both by formal study and by experience in the small society of a therapeutic community.
3. Knowledge about the proper use of community resources.
4. Emphasis on the preventive, supportive, and rehabilitative focus (as opposed to diagnosis and treatment).

The Albert Einstein group believes that these aspects of community psychiatry must be considered in addition to the emphases of the usual psychiatric training, and that they must be coordinated with insights about the intrapsychic resources and conflicts of the individual patient. In order to prepare their residents for community psychiatric practice, they have four basic programs, combining didactic presentation and clinical experience.

1. The dynamics of groups.
2. Family diagnosis and treatment.
3. Consultation theory and technique.
4. Epidemiology of mental illness and community organization.

Not only does this particular training center believe that these elements of preparation for community psychiatry can be included in the basic residency program, but it holds that the bulk of the preparation of a psychiatrist can be completed in the first two years, allowing the third year for specialization and the development of special interests.

In marked contrast to this are such postresidency fellowships in community psychiatry as those existing at Columbia University (Bernard, 1960). While there is considerable

[1] Rosenbaum, Milton, and Zwerling, Isreal: *Training for Community Psychiatry in the Psychoanalytically-Oriented Department of Psychiatry.* Presented at a University of Wisconsin postgraduate program in medical education, "Community Psychiatry: What It Is and What It Isn't." Approximate quotation.

flexibility and individualization, the various training programs offered constitute one or two years beyond the basic three-year residency, in order to prepare psychiatric physicians for administrative and leadership roles in community mental health practice.

Portia Belle Hume, M. D., as director of the Center for Training in Community Psychiatry in Berkeley, California, has developed what is essentially a post-residency, part-time training experience for community mental health practitioners. The courses are open not only to psychiatrists, but also to psychologists, psychiatric social workers, and psychiatric nurses. Students in basic training programs are also accepted for some of the courses, which cover such areas as mental health consultation and education for non-psychiatric agencies and professions, research in community psychiatry, the epidemiology of mental disorders, community resources in the treatment of psychiatric patients, administration of community mental health programs, and community psychiatry and the law. In addition, reading seminars and field experiences are included.

Now, while the exact dimensions of the problem, decisions as to proper action, and experimental programs to improve the preparation of mental health professionals for community practice may vary widely, there does seem to be a consensus that improvement in the training of mental health professionals in all disciplines is necessary. Psychiatrists and clinical psychologists are most characteristically isolated from many of the realities of community life, and often have limited experience during their training programs in working in community agencies. Social work students, in contrast, usually have not only formal instruction in social organization and community dynamics, but also field experiences in agencies that are more rooted in the community than are the characteristic university medical center or university department of psychology.

In the preparation of community mental health practitioners, as well as those practicing in other settings, we cannot underestimate the importance of available, consistent, and sound identity models. The training of clinicians can only be done properly in clinical settings, and only by practitioners who have at least basic competence, and preferably outstanding ability, in the area in which training is being conducted. To the extent that the major training institutions are controlled and staffed by individuals whose experience has been almost entirely within settings not responsive to community desires and community pressures and attitudes, and serving patients that have been selected on a number of social and demographic criteria, the preparation of community mental health practitioners will be an imperfect, and far from satisfactory, process.

There is an inevitable cultural lag in all training enterprises. As conditions of practice change, persons in training institutions, out of necessity, are somewhat out of step with the shifting demands in the field. For example, psychologists tend to be trained for hours on end in psychological testing, while the majority of their future work will no longer be in psychological testing. Much of the upgrading of skills of practitioners to meet changing social demands must, in all likelihood, be handled initially through such extramural training programs as the Center for Training in Community Psychiatry. As time goes on, it is to be hoped that the more able and adventuresome practitioners in community psychiatry will assume positions of leadership in training institutions, so that experience may be fed back into the stream of research and teaching, and so that each generation of practitioners may stand on the shoulders of the generation that has gone before.

Such is the nature of progress.

SUGGESTED READINGS

Bonn, E. M. & Schiff, S. B. (1963), Clinical supervision of psychiatric residents. *Bull. Menninger Clinic,* 27:15-23.

Goldston, S. (1964), Training in community psychiatry: A survey report of the medical school departments of psychiatry. *Amer. J. Psychiat.,* 120:789-792.

Hammersley, D. W. (1963), *Training the Psychiatrist to Meet Changing Needs.* Washington, D.C.: American Psychiatric Association.

Rosenbaum, M. & Zwerling, I. (1964), Impact of social psychiatry: Effect on a psychoanalytically oriented department of psychiatry. *Arch. Gen. Psychiat.,* 11:31-39.

Sharaf, M. R. & Levinson, D. J. (1964), The quest for omnipotence in professional training: The case of the psychiatric resident. *Psychiat.,* 27:135-149.

Shively, M. L. & Phillips, W. A. (1963), Family oriented training for psychiatry. *Arch. Gen. Psychiat.,* 9:419-426.

XXIX

Perspectives

The first sentence on the first page of a recent book on community psychiatry states, "Community psychiatry might well be considered a third major revolution in the history of psychiatry" (Bellak, 1964).

The late President of the United States, John F. Kennedy, on February 5, 1963, informed the Congress of the United States:

> I propose a national mental health program to assist in the inauguration of a wholly new emphasis and approach to care for the mentally ill. This approach relies primarily upon the new knowledge and the new drugs acquired and developed in recent years which make it possible for most of the mentally ill to be successfully and quickly treated in their communities and returned to a useful place in society.
>
> These breakthroughs have rendered obsolete the traditional methods of treatment which imposed upon the mentally ill a social quarantine, a prolonged or permanent confinement in huge, unhappy mental hospitals where they are out of sight and forgotten. We need a new type of health facility, one which will return mental health care to the mainstream of American medicine, and at the same time upgrade mental health services.

In commenting upon the President's message, the author of another recent book on community and preventive psychiatry stated:

> The promise contained in the President's message and in the legislation to secure its implementation is that for the first time an organized program is being prepared that will seek to reduce the problem radically at the community level and that this nationwide program will be directed, controlled, and partly funded by the federal government and implemented by state and local governments and

421

private organizations. This should provide a framework within which
psychiatrists and their colleagues will have the possibility of meaningfully introducing a community and preventive focus into their
work. They will in fact be called on to do so by the leaders of our
nation [Caplan, 1964b].

In the same vein, another psychiatrist has proclaimed,
"Community psychiatry is designed to guarantee and safeguard, to a degree previously undreamed of, a basic human
right—the privilege of mental health" (Bellak, 1964).

In this climate of exalted hope, excitement, and hunger
for innovation, community psychiatry has stepped to the
center of our professional stage. The spotlight is on it, the
audience is knowledgeable and critical, and the curtain has
gone up. As the preceding quotes demonstrate, the score
and lyrics have already been written, rehearsal time has been
brief, and the star player is relatively inexperienced.

Will the play be a success?

What Is Community Psychiatry?

Ironically, there is doubt as to whether all the major
proponents and practitioners of community psychiatry agree
upon a definition. One that has been proposed is: "Community psychiatry can best be defined as a resolve to view
the individual's psychiatry problems within the frame of reference of the community, and *vice versa*" (Bellak, 1964).

Melvin Sabshin, Professor of Psychiatry at the University
of Illinois College of Medicine, suggested the following definition at a recent seminar on community psychiatry at the
University of Wisconsin:

> Community psychiatry is subsumed under the generic heading of
> social psychiatry. Social psychiatry may be defined as an emergent
> theoretical and research field in which social and psychiatric variables
> are used to study, and eventually to remedy situations related to
> mental illness. Community psychiatry, as a species of social psychiatry,
> is concerned more with application, but should not be strictly
> pragmatic or service-oriented if high quality personnel are to be
> attracted and retained. Community psychiatry involves the utilization

of techniques, methods, and theories of social psychiatry and the other behavioral sciences in meeting the needs of a defined population over a significant time span, and in turn feeding knowledge back and affecting the development of social psychiatric theory.[1]

Gerald Caplan (1964b) has written:

> . . . the term 'preventive psychiatry' refers to the body of professional knowledge, both theoretical and practical, which may be utilized to plan and carry out programs for reducing (1) the incidence of mental disorders of all types in a community ('primary prevention'), (2) the duration of a significant number of those disorders which do occur ('secondary prevention') and (3) the impairment which may result from those disorders ('tertiary prevention').

Preventive psychiatry, social psychiatry, community psychiatry, community mental health—are they only different words describing the same field of theory and practice, or do they refer to different aspects of theory and practice?

There does seem to be general agreement that we are in a transitional stage in the development of psychiatric science and art, and reasonable agreement exists concerning the antecedent phases and events that led up to it. Most authors indicate that the end of the 18th century marked the beginning of developments to improve the lot of the mentally ill. The work of Pinel, Joly, and Tuke is representative of this phase.

Most authors cite Freud as signaling the beginning of a second phase in the development of psychiatry, one which emphasized the elaboration of psychogenetic theories and practices.

And most authors agree that something is happening again to redirect energies and reshape American psychiatry today. The heritage of humane concern for the welfare of the patient, and the psychoanalytic emphasis upon intrapsychic life, genetic past, and psychodynamic causation both contribute heavily to the current scene. The influence of behavioral scientists—other than psychiatrists, clinical psy-

---

[1] *Note:* This is an approximate quotation of Dr. Sabshin's remarks.

chologists, and psychiatric social workers—such as Hollingshead and Redlich, and Stanton and Schwartz, is also of major importance. Similarly, attempts to extend public health theory and practice to include mental and emotional illness are relevant. The work of Lemkau and Passamanick is typical.

As John F. Kennedy's message indicated, the advances in psychopharmacology deserve equal credit for some of the developments in psychiatry today. It is paradoxical that this branch of our science, which has turned away from interpersonal and intrapersonal explanations of disorder to look for physical causes and cures, should be primarily responsible for triggering a reorganization of psychiatric practice—a reorganization which includes an increased emphasis on interpersonal and social factors in the cause and treatment of emotional illness.

Increased public awareness, through the activities of the National Association for Mental Health and such individual psychiatric leaders as Karl and Will Menninger, has also given impetus to the current realignment in psychiatric practice. Our experiences in World War II served to alert not only the public, but also key opinion-setters and decision-makers about the prevalence and seriousness of mental disorder in the United States. It also introduced segments of the psychiatric community to concepts of immediate, brief, battlefield psychiatry.

OTHER FACTORS

There may, however, be other factors at work which have not been mentioned so often, and perhaps should be touched upon here.

For example, the accelerating increase in absolute numbers of mental health practitioners cannot help but affect the focus and style of psychiatric practice. While the number of persons recognizing the need for and desiring individual psychiatric treatment has undoubtedly grown as rapidly or more rapidly than the number of practitioners able to supply this treatment, the number of individuals able to afford such treatment, and residing in major urban centers of population, has perhaps not increased as rapidly as the number of psychiatrists in private practice in such areas.

The ongoing dialogue in our culture concerning methods of financing *all* medical care and the resultant strong feelings and partisan alignments have not gone unnoticed by psychiatry. The public sense of need, the American Medical Association's sense of panic, and the politician's attitude of cautious readiness have all stimulated our professions to seek a way out of the seeming conflict between an entrepreneurial fee-for-service system, and the desire of our society to insure good medical care for disadvantaged citizens.

Nor should it be overlooked that psychiatry, more than any other branch of medicine in this country, encompasses large numbers of citizens from cultures that do not share the dominant American ethic. Immigrants from Europe, South America, and indeed from all over the world, have taken their places among the ranks of American psychiatrists. Many native born American psychiatrists do not stem from "typical" or "mainstream" subcultures. In other words, our profession is not typical of a cross-section of the American social, political, and cultural fabric.

REVOLUTION?

Metaphors have great impact upon us all. Draped in puissant and rich associations and affective connotations, metaphors speak directly to the preconscious and unconscious elements of personality and to some extent influence perceptive, affective, and action readiness.

Why is the metaphor of the "third psychiatric revolution" such a popular one? Why do we choose a metaphor con-

noting conflict and violence to describe present developments in our profession?

A revolution is defined as a "sudden, radical, or complete
change. A fundamental change in political organization, especially the overthrow or renunciation of one government or
ruler and the substitution of another."

Why do we choose a metaphor that emphasizes sudden-
ness, radicalness, complete change, overthrow, renunciation,
dethronement?

In addition to, or sometimes associated with, this appeal
to revolutionary wishes, there is resort to the metaphor of
historical realignment, "The wave of the future." The clear
implication is that we are in the midst of a crucial phase in
the history of human events, carry a heavy burden of responsibility because of this, and are privileged to witness and
participate in society-shaking realignments and innovations.

Why do we emphasize newness and stylishness in relationship to community psychiatry?

Why do we advance community psychiatry in terms of
competition and replacement, rather than supplementation
and expansion of existing services?

Why do community mental health programs tend to take
on an evangelical, moralistic, crusade-like quality?

Why do we resort to new stylish packaging and hard-sell
promotion?

Why does community psychiatry so often shout "I accuse"
at state hospitals, private practitioners, medical schools, and
other training institutions? Why is there so much self-ag-
grandizement, and so much criticism of others?

Answers to these questions might lead us to understand
why proposals for community psychiatric innovations have
so often been met with fearfulness, resistance, and passive
obstructionism from vested power interests in psychiatry.

WHY A STRIDENT QUALITY?

Perhaps all of these exhortations and battle cries are necessary to rally the faithful in order to overrun entrenched power blocks. Perhaps there is, indeed, a conspiracy between state hospital superintendents and university professors of psychiatry to subvert and destroy the community mental health movement. This would be a simple explanation, for which appropriate solutions might be found. However, I think our basic assumption should be that whatever resistance or destructiveness is met by community psychiatry and community psychiatrists, must be looked at from two vantage points:

First, what has the individual or the movement done to arouse and make necessary such obstructionism? And second, are there indeed valid issues rooted in scientific, social, and philosophical disagreements that call for discussion and compromise rather than combat?

Perhaps the strident quality of some of our proclamations about community psychiatry may be because all of us recognize, although we seldom clearly state, that we have neither sufficient manpower nor sufficient scientific knowledge to deliver on the promise that we can "guarantee and safeguard the basic human right—the privilege of mental health." Perhaps we should recognize the partial phoniness in our claims, and see clearly how large the gap really is between future expectations and present ability.

Perhaps also, the strident quality may be due to the secret reservations or doubts we have about community psychiatry. All of us may not be entirely comfortable about becoming agents of society, in the general and specific sense, rather than agents of the individual patient, as community psychiatry may require. Those of us who have been raised in the dominant American ethic, while hopefully aware of our societal and cultural weaknesses and shortcomings, may not have quite the eagerness to destroy existing institutions, or to replace the customary, comfortable, and reasonably effective modes of social organization with models which purport to guarantee greater harmony among men and more efficient conservation of human resources.

Although we may not talk extensively about it, perhaps we recognize that one of the basic problems is that we really have not developed a satisfactory mechanism for financing good psychiatric care. Even though President Kennedy said, "The services provided by these centers should be financed in the same way as other medical and hospital costs," it must be admitted that for the time being and probably in the foreseeable future, this is an unrealistic hope. Until and unless the cost per treatment of an individual patient is substantially reduced, our present economic and social system for financing medical care will *not* be adequate to meet the need for comprehensive psychiatric services for all citizens.

Or, is the strident quality due only to the fact that we recognize, secretly, that what is being billed as a revolution and a radical innovation, is nothing of the sort?

REALLY RADICAL?

If we for a moment abandon our ethnocentric position as psychiatric theoreticians and practitioners, and look at the proposals for community mental health services within a broader social context, I think we will have sufficient grounds for stating that this is neither a revolution, nor an innovation, but rather a definitely conservative, and in some ways even reactionary, movement.

For example, the comprehensive community mental health center was described by President Kennedy in terms that made it sound very much like the community general hospital, certainly not a radical innovation in our society. He said:

Private physicians, including general practitioners, psychiatrists,

and other medical specialists, would all be able to participate directly
and cooperatively in the work of the center. For the first time, a large
proportion of our medical practitioners would have the opportunity
to treat their patients in a mental health facility served by an auxiliary
professional staff that is directly and quickly available for outpatient
and inpatient care.

In terms of economics, Kennedy envisioned extending the
accepted mode of financing medical care to include mental
health services.

> Consequently, individual fees for services, individual and group
> insurance, other third party payments, voluntary and private contri-
> butions, and state and local aid can now better bear the continuing
> burden of these costs of the individual patient after these services
> are established. Long-range federal subsidies for operating costs are
> neither necessary nor desirable. The success of this pattern of local
> and private financing will depend in large part upon the develop-
> ment of appropriate arrangements for health insurance, particularly
> in the private sector of our economy. Recent studies have indicated
> that mental health care—particularly the cost of diagnosis and
> short-term therapy which would be major components of service in
> the new centers—is insurable and of moderate cost.

The federal mechanism for assistance in construction of
community mental health centers has been utilized in the
Hill-Burton program for almost two decades. Certainly most
of the proposals for community diagnosis and treatment are
in line with current medical thinking, and the basic conceptual models for prevention of mental illness are hardly
new to public health professionals.

Despite contradictions within the President's message,
within legislative enactments, and within pronouncements
and publications of the U.S. Public Health Service and constituent agencies, there does not seem to be any firm conviction that existing services can or should be completely
destroyed or entirely realigned. While in talking about community mental health center financing, President Kennedy
did refer to "the redirection of state resources from state
mental institutions," his message also recommended improvement in the quality of care within the state institutions.

This intent to improve the state hospitals has been implemented by Hospital Improvement Program and Inservice Training grants. There is no evidence of real intent to abandon state hospitals or to follow through, with consistent action, on the derogatory verbal attacks that have often been made upon the hospitals.

All of the developments envisioned in the National Community Mental Health Program, as well as the National Program for Mental Retardation, would seem to be—after they had been worked through and modified by our system of checks and balances—entirely consistent with the social fabric of an open and pluralistic society. In psychiatry for too long we have been tied to simple and unitary solutions and have been out of step with the temper of our time and our society. The major proposals concerning changes in psychiatric services in this country would lead, if successful, to psychiatric services becoming more and more like medical services and other health, education, social, and welfare activities. For example, the field of law enforcement has town marshals, sheriffs, city police, federal marshals, the Federal Bureau of Investigation, private protective firms (such as Brinks, which specializes in the transportation of money), national detective agencies (such as Pinkerton's), many local detective and special police agencies, and large numbers of watchmen and special custodians who serve essentially police functions in relation to specific private property. In addition, each state has a highway patrol and a state bureau of investigation or state police service. Military services have their own special police forces, some school systems have special police, transportation agencies have guards and police, etc. Anxiety about competition between agencies and eventual displacement of one group by the other is not, to my knowledge, as rampant in the law enforcement field as it is in psychiatry.

Similarly, we have private, public, and parochial schools

at the elementary and secondary level; colleges that are
operated under private, church, municipal, and state auspices; and special trade and vocational schools operated by
private and governmental groups. While at one point in the
history of education, conflict between these groups was
undoubtedly as sharp as it currently is in psychiatry, they
seem to have arrived at a successful *modus vivendi* within
our pluralistic society.

Within the medical subculture, a similar heterogeneity of
agencies is evident. For example, the private practitioner
sees private patients in his office. Some of them pay him
directly, a few with insurance benefits, some pay through
workmen's compensation, and some by state and local welfare arrangements, which are largely financed by federal
funds. If hospitalization is necessary, the physician places his
patient in a hospital that is usually operated by a self-perpetuating board. This facility was probably constructed by
a combination of local tax, federal, and private funds. The
physician bills his patient directly, while the hospital bills
him for room and ancillary care such as physical therapy,
occupational therapy, medical social work, X-ray, laboratory,
drugs and so forth.

Should more specialized diagnostic procedures be necessary, the physician might transfer the patient to a large
medical center in an urban area where additional diagnostic
and therapeutic modalities, as well as the services of specialized medical consultants, would be available. Or, he might
elect to have his patient transferred directly to a university-
related medical center, where even more complex and specialized services would be available. At the medical center,
an elaborate financial system would combine the utilization
of state tax, and in some instances local tax funds, federal
funds, insurance payments, donations, and patient fees to
support the operation of the facility and the reimbursement
of the medical staff. In all of these transactions, the inter-

dependent nature of the relationship would be clearly evident to all participants. While there might be rivalry and issues of prestige and authority, there would be no anxiety that, for example, the university medical center might "take over" and operate a general hospital in a small community, or that the reverse would occur.

So much for inspection of certain aspects of recent community mental health proposals, which are essentially conservative in nature.

Out of Step?

While the salmon successfully swims upstream, its heroic accomplishment is terminated inevitably by death. We should at least ask whether we are, in part, swimming against the tide of human events and social evolution.

Proposals for community mental health services unquestionably emphasize decentralization. The unfortunate application of the factory model to mental hospitals, and spurious justifications on the basis of economy by virtue of congregating "facilities" in one place, have led to the agglutination of unmanageably large groups of patients. There is no reason for this since there is little specialized equipment or procedures in psychiatric practice today. From this vantage point, decentralization could be seen as desirable and long overdue. However, most of the trends in modern society seem to run the other direction, towards increasing centralization of population, resources, and power. In countering this trend, is community psychiatry only subjecting itself to built-in disappointment and frustration?

The community mental health establishment, in theory at least, is conceived of as being democratically based. Recent guidelines for the administration of federal construction grants emphasize that services must be tailored to local needs and desires and that citizens must have a voice in policy-making and decisions. In an age when the majority of governmental processes are carried on by the consent, rather than the participation of the governed, is such a heavy reliance upon the citizen governing board—the usual mechanism for ensuring citizen participation—entirely realistic? In an age of bureaucracy, is the "servant of the people" model of sufficient viability and prestige to be attractive to mental health professionals?

Everyone wants to be a chief. No one wants to be an Indian. While we continue to culturally condition people in this way—which has proven to be functional during the steady history of expansion in our American society—there is some doubt as to whether the chief positions will continue to increase very rapidly in the years ahead. Along with the centralization and bureaucratization of power and authority, it is quite likely that there will be a decrease in the number of top-level positions where decision and power making are concentrated. In medicine, and consequently in psychiatry, physicians are trained and conditioned for leadership. In the context of the treatment of the individual patient within the medical institution and in relationship to other members of the medical team, this is a congruent model. When translated into agency practice, it has some limitations, since not every psychiatrist, psychologist or social worker can be director of an agency. A general cultural emphasis on social recognition and reward as a sign of personal worth only increases the urgency of strivings for leadership and power.

HARMONY?

If we are to achieve any harmony from our dissension, and distill any unity of purpose from our disagreements, we must give serious and continuing attention to defining our superordinate goals. What is the purpose of all this activity? Is it to make human beings conform more closely to acceptable norms for their particular subculture? If we expect psychiatric agencies and psychiatric practitioners to conform closely to the wishes of the citizens in their areas—as those employed in mental health centers directed by local citizen governing boards must—it is only reasonable to expect that this pressure and demand for conformity will be reflected in their interactions with patients. Are we primarily to serve as social control, humanizing, and civilizing agents for society? Are we to become more closely allied to judges, police, and teachers; or to physicians and private attorneys?

We must, as often as possible, step outside our technological and scientific ethnocentrism. Rather than asking so often whether a particular development is a psychiatric revolution or not, we should question its meaning in relationship to our society. Increasingly, we will have to pay attention to the fact that psychiatry is the tail and is wagged by the dog, society; not, as we tend to think in our more grandiose moments, the other way around. Psychiatry will always reflect current trends, conflicts, and ambiguities in our general society. Awareness, objectivity, and attempts at rational problem-solving, rather than messianic aspirations, should be our contribution to general social dilemmas.

We must always look carefully at a sense of urgency. The need to hurry, to move too rapidly, may raise tremendous clouds of dust that obscure problems or imperfections in our plans and designs. Our society has been somehow limping along for many years, without the special contributions that psychiatry now seems too ready to make to "life, liberty, and the pursuit of happiness." We should participate in needed, necessary, and possible social change with—as the U.S. Supreme Court phrased it—"all deliberate speed."

Motivations that lead men and women into psychiatry, psychology, and psychiatric social work are as diverse and complex as the individuals themselves. However, it is clear that many of us have a need to be somehow special or different. We also have a need for other people—not ourselves— to have problems, with which they want our help. We have been extraordinarily successful in discovering personal pathology. Having nearly reached the limits of that endeavor, so that everyone is sick, we may now be starting down another path by trying to discern how sick our society is (not a really new endeavor to psychoanalytic theoreticians) and to point out these imperfections as forcefully and loudly as possible. Let us hope that the forbearance and empathy which we extend to our individual patients will not be lacking in our communications with society as a whole.

IDENTIFICATION WITH THE AGGRESSOR

Perhaps now, to further confuse the whole issue, we should take the entire discussion out of the frame of reference of American culture and social process and view it in an even larger context.

The United States and the Soviet Union have been locked for some decades in an ideological and power struggle, with confrontations around a variety of issues. These confrontations, in real and tangible ways, reflect ongoing conflicts in the value systems of two major segments of human society. The basic question may be: Is man an autonomous, inner-directed, responsible, moral, God-like entity who moulds and shapes society to achieve the most good for the most people? Or is he a member of the herd, directed and controlled by mass opinion, bereft of inner-directedness and moral purpose, a mammal who is inordinately talkative and manipulative? This basic conflict between the inner-and outer-directed view of human nature has been reflected in our society. Our ability in America to ascribe to, and partly practice, elements of *both* views of man and his world has puzzled observers over the years. The need to be consistent has not greatly inhibited our national character.

However, is it possible that, as we find ourselves in continuing confrontation with a communist nation, we are tempted to unconsciously identify with the aggressor? Are we tempted to adopt, and make as part of our society, elements of the communistic man-and-world view—at least as we perceive them at a distance and with cultural bias and distortion? Are we overly eager to abandon the inner-directed view of man and embrace personal and social relativism? It is characteristic of opponents, when their powers are nearly equal, to secretly perceive the power of the other as being greater or somehow superior. Undoubtedly, citizens of the Soviet Union will increasingly identify with American values, at least as they perceive them, and will secretly tend to feel and fear that American ways are better. I am sure that it is not necessary to remind this audience that the Soviet Union has had, for quite a few years now, psychiatric facilities which sound very much like our comprehensive community mental health centers. Nor need I remind you that they, for many more years than we, have emphasized the social-rootedness of man and the social-relatedness of all human behavior. For years they have eschewed, and frequently attacked, the model of individual psychotherapy. Some proponents of community psychiatry in this country would seem to be doing the same thing: saying that the private practice of psychiatry and psychotherapy is probably ineffective, at any rate is greatly overpriced, and probably is basically immoral.

We have all seen individual patients who have been too willing to throw away accustomed and habitual ways of thinking, feeling, and acting. Overwhelmed by excessive input of new and troubling information, or finding themselves in an environment so strange as to be incomprehensible, or becoming frightened of their essential weakness and helplessness as individual human beings, or being subjected to fear of abandonment and group exclusion, individuals upon occasion enter into periods of rapid personality change and realignment. At times we refer to these periods as crises in ego identity; while at other times, and with equal validity, we refer to them as acute psychotic states. At such times, the patient tends to be highly suggestible, to be willing to adopt, often in an imitative manner, new modes of acting, thinking, and feeling; and to repudiate preexisting ties and affectional bonds. Hyperactivity and noisiness not infrequently accompany such crisis periods.

Just as the individual can become disorganized and fragmented as a result of too rapid change, so can a group or subculture. Exhortation and criticism, coupled with insecurity and self-doubt, and compounded by bitter struggles between authority and leadership figures, have perhaps precipitated psychiatry—or those of us at least who are concerned about community psychiatry—into a momentary identity crisis. As with the psychotic patient, perhaps we have been too eager to say that we have been born again, that we are a new individual, or that some mystical experience has reshaped our personality and our life. Perhaps, when we take stock, we are not so different after all.

Perhaps we will find that we are still imperfect and puny individuals, attempting for highly personal reasons to assist other puny and imperfect individuals become less puny and less imperfect, and to accept that part of their fate which cannot be remedied. Perhaps we will discover that in our brave new community mental health centers, we will be doing essentially the same sorts of things that we have been doing all along. Perhaps we will find that we do not really know enough to usher in paradise on earth, no matter how badly we want to.

THE FUTURE?

Heterogeneity is essential to progress. Unitary solutions and evangelical movements are inimical to genuine progress in psychiatry, as in other aspects of human endeavor. Just as we must accept that the individual patient lives the best life of which he is capable, we must assume that the state hospital professionals have individually and collectively done their best, as responsible and compassionate scientists and human beings, for the mentally ill. Our task is to be one of assistance, not criticism, defamation, or destruction.

Likewise, the private psychiatric practitioner and the private psychiatric hospital have afforded good psychiatric care to many patients, and really excellent and superlative treatment to not a few. In our society, the man who is more fortunate and/or more able, has a right to purchase for himself and his family psychiatric services that are superior to those available to all citizens. Consistently we have striven in our society, to the extent practicable, to level upwards. In public psychiatry, I would urge that we attempt to approximate the high level of practice that is obtained in the private and university-related segments of our profession, rather than criticizing, struggling with, or attempting to displace or degrade the private practice of psychiatry.

We live in a wondrously rich and complex society. Because it is open and pluralistic, and because we are, as Americans, committed to the pursuit of social justice, change and progress are inevitable. Most of us will be minor craftsmen in building a better society.

Hopefully, our devotion and respect for the basic element of society—the individual man—will grow and become wiser over the years. The individual human being is his own purpose for existing. As our Constitution and our political heritage have consistently stated, the purpose of government is to serve the individual and to advance his self-interests, so long as these do not infringe upon the rights of others. In this enterprise, and to this end, psychiatry—and its subspecialty of community and preventive psychiatry—can well dedicate itself.

CURRENT ISSUES

There are three general areas that are of overriding importance at the present state of development in community psychiatry:

1. The definition of community and social psychiatry, and historical antecedents of the community psychiatric "movement," discussed partially in preceding chapters.

2. The institutional lodgment, in a sociological sense, of the *comprehensive community mental health center,* as it is coming to be described and as the concept is beginning to solidify. Where does it fit? Is it a medical institution, a social institution, etc.? Comprehensive mental health planning in Kansas has evolved concepts related to institutional lodgment which will be discussed.

3. Models for financial support for comprehensive community mental health services. This is a particularly important area as it relates to the role of the private nonprofit organization, and its participation in providing comprehensive services.

DEFINITIONS AND ANTECEDENTS

Definition has concerned us in preceding pages; should we talk about community psychiatry as if we *really* knew exactly what we were talking about? The definitions of community psychiatry and social psychiatry indicate considerable discrepancy among authorities. Community psychiatry is coming to be more and more like morality and sin: everybody has his own definition.

The need for a basic research discipline to back community psychiatric practice is particularly relevant, however, to our current interests and issues. The child guidance and family service movements began with enthusiasm in this country quite a few years ago with a good deal of talk about prevention. "Mental health consultation" is not really a new discipline. It is new for *psychiatrists* to be concerned about it, but family service agencies have been writing about it for many years. The family service and child guidance movements, however, essentially lost their vision and bogged down. As they ceased to attract the best professional people, their programs became rigid and stereotyped. Both of these movements have ground to a halt in many areas of the country quite a few years ago. Why did this happen? Partly because they did not simultaneously develop adequate research mechanisms, or methods to evolve a body of theory and knowledge about what they were doing. They became bogged down on pragmatic application, on a day-by-day basis, of "standard procedures," trying to meet extremely heavy service demands. They built in no mechanism for evaluating or systematically expanding their knowledge about practice modalities as they went along.

In trying to understand these definitions and ideas, we should ask: Where does community psychiatry "come from" and what is it really? Is it an entity? Or is it just the most popular jingle we have at the present time for the advertisement of psychiatry? We should be suspicious of stylish innovations of all kinds. Having been subjected to the bombardment of television jingles and catch phrases, it is understandable why we tend to be annoyed and skeptical of promotional devices which attempt to sell us a variety of products, only a small minority of which significantly better the human condition. One question must concern us repeatedly: Is community psychiatry really a product? Is it something new or is it only a new way of packaging old products and a new way of promotion?

I believe that it is something *partly* new, in the sense of a new gestalt that has evolved out of a number of antecedents. I do not believe it is new in the sense of being a revelation, or something that has suddenly sprung upon the scene, or *that it brings within itself any unique concepts.* Community psychiatry combines a number of antecedent conceptual models, research traditions, and schools of appli-

FIGURE 1

The Origins of Community Psychiatry

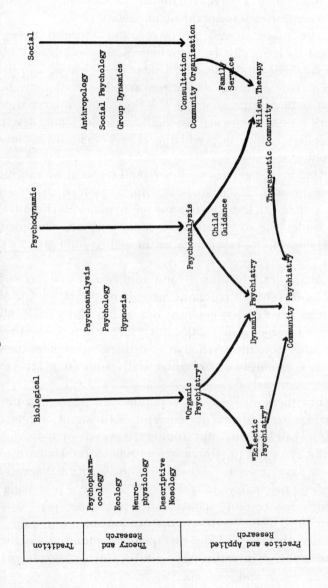

cation which I have attempted to schematize as follows, demonstrating some of the major trends.

The major trends in theory and research have been divided, traditionally, into biological, psychodynamic, and social theory and research. Under biological we can include such basic research disciplines as neurophysiology, biological ecology (the study of the organism's interrelationship with its environment), psychopharmacology and descriptive nosology (which in psychiatry follows essentially a biological typology).

Under psychodynamic theory and research we can include such areas as psychoanalysis, clinical psychology, and some of the research involving use of hypnotic techniques.

Under the social areas we could include, among others, sociology, social psychology, anthropology, and group dynamics.

At the level of practice and applied research (as opposed to basic research), organic psychiatry is one of the major disciplines that has emerged out of the biological tradition. Psychoanalysis is one major discipline of practice and applied research from the psychodynamic discipline. Under the social area, community organization and consultation are perhaps major derivatives.

But then, all these get combined and reshuffled into the various areas of practice currently existing. Completely organic psychiatrists and completely psychoanalytic psychiatrists, pure and untainted, are getting extremely hard to find these days. Eclectic psychiatry is one discipline that combines organic psychiatry and psychoanalysis into a practicing field which has certain characteristics. Dynamic psychiatry has combined these same traditions, but in a different ratio. Milieu therapy and the therapeutic community, as theories and styles of practice, are mixtures of psychoanalysis and social theory and research.

I believe the only thing that really distinguishes community psychiatry as a discipline, if we are quite frank about it, is that *it combines elements of all three of the major styles of practice.* We really cannot lay claim to having found anything wonderful and new, but only that we are attempting, in a vigorous and consistent way, to avoid a doctrinaire commitment to any particular field, to any particular theory of personality development or malfunctioning, to any specific type of therapy, and are trying to combine all relevant insights into some kind of functional compromise while proposing to deploy personnel in ways that are operational at the community level.

As we attempt to do this, key concepts about community psychiatry are beginning to emerge. Six of them—and there are many others that we probably could add—are as follows:

1. *Behavior is socially rooted.* People are affected not only by what they carry inside them, but by what is going on around them. This is not a terribly new idea. In fact, it is a partial return to an old idea of human behavior, which psychoanalysis for a while set aside by emphasizing the intrapsychic determinants of behavior. People have always known that we are affected by what goes on around us, and the only thing new is the attempt to use this in a practical way to develop a style of therapy.

2. The second major development or concept of community psychiatry is the *determination to emphasize the preventive aspects of psychiatric practice.* Again, this is nothing new. The child guidance and family service movements have both emphasized this for a long time, as have many other individuals and groups concerned about bettering the human condition. At the present time, the only thing different about the preventive emphasis is that the people who are practicing community psychiatry *think* they know more about how to go about it, and are attempting to deploy personnel to demonstrate that mental illness can be prevented.

3. The third major concept is *an emphasis on the social-rootedness of agency functioning*. The community mental health agency is embedded in a matrix of other social institutions. Just as the individual does not exist in isolation from the people around him, neither does the mental health agency exist in isolation from the surrounding agencies. This attempt to involve the mental health center with other community agencies has been justified on a number of grounds, but I think a major reason is that this kind of social rootedness is essential if the individual patient is to achieve continuity of care, comprehensiveness of care, and availability of care. If this is to be guaranteed to the individual, or all individuals in the community, the mental health agency must be related to other social and caregiving agencies and individuals in the community.

4. In community psychiatric practice there is a *flexible use of therapeutic modalities and an attempt to stringently avoid any kind of doctrinaire commitment to either a single theory of personality development or malfunctioning, or an exclusivistic theory of practice and therapy*.

5. Related to all of the preceding is a conviction that *professional resources will have to be redeployed if the goals of achieving preventive, therapeutic, and rehabilitative services for the community as a whole are to be even approximated*. Some aspects of redeployment involve the following:

a. *All professions must undergo a role expansion*. This is becoming increasingly important in a variety of mental health agencies. In some places it is called role *blurring*, which is an unfortunate term. In the process, each profession begins to assume additional skills, and responsibilities commensurate with the skills, so that the needs of the patient and of the community can be met more effectively. This whole area of role expansion may get caught up in anti-authoritarian wishes that all of us have from time to time, and lead to a conviction that it somehow will destroy medical prerogatives or social work prerogatives or psychological prerogatives. Role expansion does not mean, however, that all people or all professions are equal. There are many good reasons for expanding the roles of all professional people. However, I doubt very seriously if this role expansion will remove all distinctions in terms of hierarchy, skill, ability, or responsibility among different professional disciplines.

b. Another redeployment involves *the use of professional personnel to provide consultation to other community caregivers.* The professional person must leave his office—which he has been loathe to do for a long time. It also involves a new kind of commitment to the community and to other agencies. None of the disciplines is really prepared for this activity by basic professional training. A major need now is for training experiences both within the professional curricula, as well as in postgraduate or continuing education, for purposes of teaching consultation. Consultation is not simply talking to people; nor is it simply being friendly and patting people on the back while reassuring them that they are doing a good job (because they may not be doing a good job). Mental health consultation is a way of using oneself professionally, that involves just as much theory and just as much discipline as does psychotherapy, and deserves comparable training and experience.

c. An additional type of redeployment for professional resources is just beginning—and really may or may not develop very far. This involves the conviction that *perhaps there is a role for a professional mental health educator at the community level.* Perhaps we should reexamine the whole question of the potential role of a mental health educator within the context of the primary educational institutions of the community, in such areas as human growth and development, family-life education, sex education, human relations, group dynamics, etc. Again, this is an emphasis that was mentioned very strongly by the early child guidance people, but never was followed up in any organized way. The major disillusionment was that you cannot *demonstrate* that mental health education prevents mental illness. You cannot *demonstrate,* either, that liberal arts education at the college level modifies attitudes about oneself or about other individuals, or about the world; and yet we continue to have liberal arts education because we *believe* it is a liberalizing and humanizing experience. There is value in providing basic information and learning experiences for children, in the schools, about human beings, and human behavior. If you look at the curricula, and the materials available for most schools, a child can learn almost anything he wants to know about *things,* about physical science—but there is very little taught about *people.* And what little is taught emphasizes instrumental process rather than meaning. Civics books, for example, will offer extensive descriptions on how institutions are set up but tell us very little about what these institutions are to accomplish, why they exist, or how good a job they do.

d. The fourth major kind of redeployment of professional personnel involves *a determination to be cooperatively involved in social planning.* The mental health professional has a role, has something to offer in cooperation with other significant individuals in the community, to the whole area of social planning for the betterment of the human condition.

e. The community mental health movement, in many areas of the country, and certainly in Kansas, has *emphasized a decentralization of services.* This includes determination to avoid the accumulation of large clumps of patients, around which we deploy large clumps of professional people with the idea that if we get enough of them together, something happens. I think that we will eventually abandon this approach entirely. Therapy is not a "critical mass" phenomenon. Usually, by amassing large numbers of patients and staff, all that is accomplished is that they *leave each other alone*—

patients and staff go their separate ways. By decentralizing services, by maintaining small units, by keeping collections of staff and patients small, we hope to provide better care, to make it more available, more comprehensive, and very importantly, more continuous. Many professional people are simply not trained, however, to work with this degree of independence and freedom at the present time. Decentralized services involve realignment of selection procedures for all the professional disciplines, and certainly shifts in the kinds of education and training offered.

6. The sixth major concept of community psychiatry, which we emphasize more in Kansas than in some states—but which is emerging and has even been reflected in the federal regulations for construction funds—is that *citizens must participate in policy setting for the provision of community psychiatric services.* The consumer of the service, not just the purveyor, must be represented in arriving at policies and procedures to meet the needs of the community. The responsible citizen has to be involved in a meaningful way—not simply in being a front man for the operation through a position on an honorary board. He must be involved in a meaningful way in setting up priorities and developing services.

INSTITUTIONAL LODGMENT

In discussing institutional lodgment, we often begin with the assumption that mental health services are medical services, and that the model of mental health services should follow one of the many medical models. It has begun to dawn on me, as I have listened to people talk—"Well, no it's not this kind. It's not a medical service. Yet in one sense it's a public health service. No, it's not a public health service, it's a social agency. It's this, that and the other thing"—that this is really a serious problem requiring study and conceptualization.

We have been struggling with this problem in Kansas for 18 years now, but not conceptualizing it in these terms. For the first 15 years we said that the community mental health center is a public health agency, and it must rest in the public health department: this is the kind of agency it is, it fits the public health model. In 1961 the wisdom of the legislature was to say, "No, this is a new kind of institution and will be set up entirely independently and have an independent governing board which will answer directly to the elective representatives of the people. This does not fit the public health model, or any other existing model. It is a new agency."

This was a remarkable bit of wisdom for the legislature. In the last four years the number of centers, counties, professional man-hours a week, and the number of patients have all increased more than in the entire preceding 15 years. This rapid growth occurred once community mental health services were taken out from under public health.

I do not think this really says anything definite, to be honest, about the institutional nature of the community mental health program. In part, it gives us a picture of the political realities and the status of local public health services in Kansas, which have been going downhill for 15 years. This does not really answer the question of institutional lodgment, but it has helped focus our attention on it.

The following list of characteristics of social institutions, although by no means exhaustive, should help us to understand how the community mental health center fits into the institutional framework:

1. An institution has a *goal,* which is usually based on some kind of *concept*—either implicit or explicit—*of the needs of society*. This goal, once it is established, undergoes some process of social legitimation; society says, "Yes, there is a need for this sort of thing."

2. All social institutions operate on the basis of some

underlying, usually implicit rather than explicit, *concept of the nature of man*.

3. All social institutions incorporate a set of *value and moral judgments* in their operational philosophy.

4. Social institutions are *regulated,* by either formal or informal social control mechanisms such as licensing, funding, public opinion, etc.

5. Every social agency has an *ethos and a lore* which are built up as the agency functions over the years; an ingroup attitude and self-identity emerge and persist.

6. The agency has a set of *standard operations* that are more or less routinized and more or less consensually validated procedures for accomplishing alleged goals. These procedures may or may not be effective, and may or may not be logically related to the alleged goals of the agency.

7. The institution has mechanisms to insure *exclusiveness,* or to limit membership.

We spend a lot of energy trying to decide where the community mental health center should be lodged. A schematic diagram (Figure 2) of some of these possibilities is as follows:

Under the social control agencies such things as law enforcement, the courts and correctional institutions would be included. Community mental health centers have correctional elements increasingly, as they become more and more involved with other community agencies. This alarms and troubles many professional people, who have been reared on a model which stresses a cooperative engagement in the psychotherapeutic relationship by a willing and motivated patient, who consults the professional person on his own steam anad pays for his treatment. Involvement with community agencies such as courts and law enforcement agencies results in the professional person's seeing many people who are not coming to him because of their own wishes,

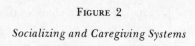

FIGURE 2

Socializing and Caregiving Systems

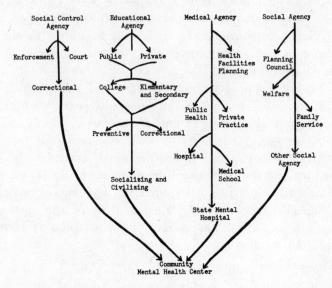

and who are not motivated in the sense that they go through the prescribed ritual for submitting to the examination and treatment process. Community mental health centers increasingly have some of the characteristics of social control agencies.

The second general rubric is educational agencies. These can be public or private at all levels of development. Educational agencies have primarily, I suppose, a socializing and civilizing role in our society. The public educational agencies particularly are in the business, at least partly, of implementing consensually held value judgments and promoting a consensually held view of the nature of man and his relationship to his environment. In part, the mental health agency does the same thing. The mental health practitioner promotes and communicates a particular view of man and his relationship with other men and with his inanimate environment, using different techniques than do educational practitioners, but still holding essentially similar goals. There is also a wide variety of private educational institutions for the children of well-to-do parents, which are essentially correctional institutions. There are some similarities between educational agencies and community mental health centers, but they are certainly not identical.

The third possibility is that the community mental health center is a medical agency, an idea which psychiatrists have tended to promote. There is also a tendency to advance, I believe unthinkingly, the concept that a psychiatrist is "just another doctor." This is the biggest myth of the 20th century. The psychiatrist is *not* just another kind of doctor. Perhaps we labor too much trying to bolster the psychiatrist's medical identity.

The number of alternative models *within* the general medical agency model is considerable. The private practice model is different from the community hospital model, and these are both distinctively different from the public health and medical school models. Moreover, all of these models differ considerably from the state mental hospital. The community mental health center differs from all of them, in significant ways.

We sometimes try to "fit" community health centers into the social agency model. Here we have such agencies as health and welfare planning councils, welfare agencies, family service agencies, and a variety of other social agencies, voluntary as well as public. In part, the community mental health center may be seen as fitting in here.

Yet I think it does not fit, really, any of these models or *any* of these kinds of institutional lodgments.

The reason we struggle so hard in our attempts to decide where to place community mental health agencies is only partly related to the question of what makes sense. It usually is related more to the question of *who is going to be director*. We tend to think that the social workers have an edge on directing social agencies, psychiatrists for medical agencies, and psychologists for educational agencies. We struggle as if the question were what kind of agency it really is; when the basic question really is, *who is going to run it*. Much of our thinking is a bit irrelevant and inexact. Some of the mental health centers in Kansas that operate on the most rigid, traditional medical model are run by clinical psychologists; and some of the mental health centers, in Kansas and elsewhere, that are run on the most radical, untraditional, unmedical models are directed by psychiatrists. We have gotten caught in rigid, cliché-bound thinking about the functions of physicians, social workers, and psychologists. It seems to me that any agency may serve as the base for the development of a community mental health center, and any discipline may direct or administer the center. This depends on a lot of things, including the characteristics of the individual member of the particular discipline.

The community mental health center—in terms of its basic goals, its concept of the nature of man, its value systems, methods of social regulation, the ethos of the agency itself, procedures, and technics of exclusiveness—really forms a unique gestalt. It does not fit into any of the existing agency models and is really a social innovation. Increasingly, it will emerge as a new kind of agency with a new combination of goals. None of these goals is new for society, but society is constantly deciding upon new ways to go about meeting them, and I think that the community mental health center is the latest conglomeration that we came up with.

Some of the current planning activities in Kansas, relating to the whole issue of the future of the community mental health center in Kansas, are relevant here.

In Kansas, planning committees have submitted over 300 specific, constructive, and distinct recommendations. Some of these planning committee recommendations were used to develop a set of proposals for immediate modifications in the Kansas mental health program, leading to a general upgrading of services. These recommendations are only a part of the abstract entity that is referred to as "The Kansas Mental Health Plan." There are several other documents that may be considered part of the plan: *Conservation of Human Resources,* which describes the general philosophy of community mental health services; *Standards for Community Mental Health Centers in Kansas,* which outlines specific details of organization, staffing and program, and "The Kansas Plan," published some years ago in *Mental Hospitals* and forming the basis for the present system of institutional services.

In addition, a plan for the administration of federal funds for the construction of comprehensive community mental health centers and community facilities for the retarded has also been prepared, and will constitute an additional element in the "Kansas Mental Health Plan."

In essence, the recommendations outline a system of echelons of service, allowing for an orderly evacuation of most severe psychiatric casualties from the community into specialized treatment resources, and providing for patterns of interdependency and mutual support between various mental health agencies.

The plan calls for 25 community mental health centers, existing in each of the 25 mental health districts in Kansas. Functions of these community mental health centers would consist of outpatient evaluation and treatment of children and adults, consultation services to other community care-givers, mental health education, and emergency psychiatric care. These community mental health clinics may be either under medical or nonmedical auspices. The one-half mill tax levy and existing administrative structure is sufficient to implement this level of the program, with necessary revisions in the present community mental health legislation to insure more uniform standards of quality.

Of the 25 *community* mental health centers, it is proposed that 11 add additional staff and services to become *comprehensive area mental health centers*. These 11 centers would provide, in addition to the functions of the smaller community mental health centers, short-term inpatient treatment for children and adults; partial hospitalization services, such as day hospitals; specialized services for such groups as alcoholics, the mentally retarded, patients returning from the state hospitals, and special diagnostic services for the juvenile and district courts; professional education, and research. As a minimum, the direct treatment activities of the comprehensive area mental health center would be under medical supervision. In addition, the comprehensive area mental health center would provide consultation and inservice training to the one or two associated community mental health centers in the mental health districts of the larger mental health area. Each of the 11 comprehensive area mental health centers would be related to the 11 state residential treatment units which now exist at our state hospitals, each of which serves a defined geographic area.

Each of the state residential treatment units would provide moderate and long-term inpatient treatment; rehabilitation services; extramural consultation services to nursing homes (which care for 1,400 former state hospital patients); special services to such groups as alcoholics and the mentally retarded; research; and professional education. In addition, the state residential treatment units would provide consultation and inservice training to the comprehensive area mental health center related to that unit. To establish and support such interrelationships, a clear definition of the role of the state hospital, guidelines for hospital-community cooperation, and redistricting to bring hospital section areas in line with mental health center areas would be necessary.

In essence, these proposals allow for improvement in our existing services. They are essentially conservative, and contemplate the indefinite continuation of a system of three types of psychiatric services; private, community supported, and state supported.

MODELS FOR FINANCIAL SUPPORT

However, in looking at the next 20 years, serious thought should be given to moving in new directions to return mental health services into the mainstream of American medicine, and to make them more congruent with other institutions in our democratic, pluralistic society.

Initially, we must ask how the present system of services came to be established, and what were the underlying assumptions of our present organization. It would seem that the assumptions were as follows:

1. *The mentally ill are dangerous and incurable, and must be segregated.* This is no longer believed by professional persons or knowledgeable lay people.

2. *Communities cannot and/or will not provide care for the mentally ill.* This mistaken idea was widely promulgated by Dorothea Dix over 100 years ago, and led to the assumption of responsibility for the mentally ill by state governments. If it had not been for the veto of the President, Miss Dix would have in fact succeeded in having the responsibility for the mentally ill assumed by the federal government, feeling that the states were not willing to care for them either.

3. *Mental illness is chronic and requires prolonged hospitalization.* Recent experience indicates that most mental and emotional illness has a good prognosis, and that the need for hospitalization is present for only a very short time in the total treatment process of even the most seriously ill.

4. *Mental illness is uninsurable.* A careful actuarial study

and demonstration project in New York City by Group Health Insurance, Inc., illustrated that this is untrue.

5. *Care can be provided more cheaply by the state than by private or nonprofit institutions.* Careful inspection will indicate that care can be provided more cheaply only if it is inferior. There is no magic by which equivalent staff and service can be bought by the state for less money, and there is perhaps some evidence to the contrary.

This has resulted in a denial of a civil liberty to the mentally ill; one which is held in considerable esteem by society, and which the mentally healthy citizen enjoys: *the right of choosing his own physician to diagnose and treat his illness.*

Actually, welfare services went through a similar phase of denying the choice of physician to the welfare recipient, and an elaborate system of welfare doctors and welfare hospitals was established in most of the states. Without exception, the experience was that such a separate system, set aside from the mainstream of private medical practice, resulted in an eventual and inevitable deterioration of standards of patient care. Rapid progress has been made in recent years in returning the medical care of the welfare patient to the private sphere of medical practice, with increasingly satisfactory mechanisms being established to provide for third party payment to practitioners who are licensed by the state and who provide services and facilities that have met certain minimal standards set forth by the state agency.

The issue at stake is primarily one of civil liberty under our system of social organization.

If we accept that state government will retain primary responsibility for care and treatment of the "indigent insane," we must examine alternative methods for discharging this responsibility:

1. The state may build and operate facilities.
2. It may contract with local units of government and/or

nonprofit groups to supply needed services (such as Short-Doyle legislation) .

3. It may institute a system of third party payment.

We should ask ourselves whether it is not now time to consider the possibility of returning the care of at least some of the mentally ill to the private sector of our economy. That is, rather than the State Mental Health Authority's assuming responsibility for constructing, staffing, and operating all mental health facilities, a system might be substituted whereby the State Mental Health Authority administers funds to allow individual citizens unable to support adequate psychiatric treatment, to obtain such care. The extent of state financial support would be only to supplement individual resources, and would be based upon need. With this support, the individual citizen, or in many cases his family (often with the help and advice of the private physician or other community caretakers), could decide where to receive the needed treatment. This would remove psychiatric care from its position as an isolated and largely socialized segment of American medicine, and would in the process accomplish three things:

1. It would enhance the dignity of the mentally ill by restoring to them a right enjoyed by other citizens in our democratic society.

2. It would end the inevitably unsuccessful attempt of state systems to compete for staff on the free market, with all the pressures of our open, entrepreneurial and pluralistic society mitigating against success.

3. By encouraging the establishment of small, private non-profit mental health facilities of all types, the availability, comprehensiveness, and quality of mental health services would be greatly enhanced over the years ahead.

The following schema, "Redeployment of Mental Health Services in Kansas," provides recommendations for three phases in the suggested 20-year program. After an initial

Table 1

REDEPLOYMENT OF MENTAL HEALTH SERVICES IN KANSAS

PHASE	PROGRAM GOALS	PROGRAM ELEMENTS	ONSET	COM-PLETION	COMMENTS
PHASE I	Decentralization of institutional services	1. Appointment of mental health program directors for urban areas.	FY 1965	FY 1970	Reduction of inpatient resident populations at Larned State Hospital, Osawatomie State Hospital and Topeka State Hospital with partial deployment of funds and resources, and establishment of alcoholism treatment unit.
	Strengthening and expanding community services	2. Grants-in-aid to community mental health centers for: a. Construction b. Expanded services in area centers (11)			
	Developing basis for comprehensive services	3. Establishment of adult day hospitals in urban centers.			
		4. Establish small retardation units at Larned State Hospital, Osawatomie State Hospital and the State Sanatorium for Tuberculosis at Norton.			

			FY 1970	FY 1978	
PHASE II	Amalgamation of institutional and community programs	1. Construction of comprehensive centers in urban areas. 2. Contractual arrangements with mental health foundations in urban areas for full range of services. 3. Establish alcoholism units at Larned State Hospital, Topeka State Hospital and Osawatomie State Hospital.	FY 1970	FY 1978	Additional reduction of inpatient populations at Larned State Hospital, Osawatomie State Hospital and Topeka State Hospital with redeployment of funds and resources.
PHASE III	Restoration of choice of therapist	1. Enact legislation for state third-party payment: "Psychiatric Medicare" 2. Encourage development of area mental health centers into quasi-public, quasi-private institutions similar to community general hospitals.	FY 1978	FY 1986	Additional reduction of inpatient population at Larned State Hospital, Osawatomie State Hospital and Topeka State Hospital with redeployment of funds and resources.

phase of improving present services and planning for future developments, a process of deliberate amalgamation of institutional and community programs (which would blur distinctions between state and community support through a series of contractual and shared staffing arrangements) would ensue. Following this period of transition, legislation could be enacted to provide mechanisms for third party payment. With this stimulation, a wide variety of private groups would establish needed services, and the direct care of the mentally and emotionally ill would gradually move from state and local control, into the private sphere of our economy. The role of the State Mental Health Authority in establishing standards and inspecting cooperating agencies to protect the public health and safety, and to insure the proper expenditure of state funds granted to individual citizens, would be a continuing necessity in such a program. To some extent, the present state facilities partly vacated by such a progressive shift in auspices of care, could be utilized in providing services to groups now without care in Kansas, such as the alcoholic patient; in improving services offered to some groups where needs considerably outstrip resources, such as the seriously retarded; and in continuing to provide treatment and rehabilitation services to citizens whose behavior is troubling to the extent that treatment and rehabilitation is ordered for them by society, rather than being sought by the patient because of his own discomfort and wishes.

In Kansas, for the foreseeable future, there would seem to be a place for all three types of service: for the fully state operated, for the locally based and state subsidized, and for state third-party payment. Private institutions could play a major, even dominant role if a public policy decision is made to enter into this system of third-party payment. The private agency is *already* playing an increasingly major role with the growth of contractual relationships between state government and local units of government, and/or between local units of government and nonprofit corporations in its efforts to provide both preventive and therapeutic services. The question of whether to institute third-party payment is a knotty one. The "chicken and egg problem" is ever-present; few private, comprehensive agencies will be developed until there is some system for adequate financing of services. On the contrary, there is no reason for having a system for third-party payment, because there are not enough private agencies to provide the service.

Somewhere the cycle has to be broken, and somewhere a public policy decision has to be made if we are going to shift away from large state-operated institutions, to smaller community and nonprofit entities, so that service may be equally available to all citizens.

SUGGESTED READINGS

Grinker, R. R. (1964), Psychiatry rides madly in all directions. *Arch. Gen. Psychiat.*, 10:228-237.

Appendix

Case Studies of Community Mental Health Centers

The following case studies are essentially based on fact. They are disguised so that they cannot be identified specifically. Since they are intended primarily as a stimulus for discussion groups, the bare outline of observed events is recorded, and an attempt is made to avoid any sense of closure or finality in reporting these episodes.

A seminar discussion could consider these individual cases from a number of vantage points. For example, what are speculations about the dynamic interplay of forces bringing about the reported sequence of events? What might be involved that is not described in the narrative? What are the core problems or issues, or latent themes? What needs to be done? How would one go about it? What emotional reactions might one have if found in a similar situation? Are there implications for research in any of the described episodes? What generalizations can be drawn?

CASE STUDY No. I

In 1948 a small budgetary item was placed in the budget of the health department of a Kansas university community. It was to provide for the employment of part-time mental health personnel, in order to develop what was then called a child guidance clinic. In reading newspaper accounts, as well as official publications and correspondence, it became clear that this social innovation was presented to the community with the following provisions:

1. It would provide diagnostic and evaluative services only.
2. No fees whatsoever would be charged for services, regardless of ability to pay.
3. Only children would be served.

The five-man Board of Health, legally responsible for determining policies for the clinic, utilized the services of a large advisory committee composed of citizens who had been influential in developing the clinic initially. Over the years, this advisory committee usurped authority and assumed direct, extralegal administrative control over the clinic.

A succession of part-time psychiatrists and psychologists, and of full-time psychiatric social workers, passed through the clinic. They were disparate personalities, but all had basically sound training and experience which qualified them for the work.

In 1957, the advisory committee was stripped of its authority, primarily at the instigation of the part-time psychiatrist employed by the clinic. The advisory group had become a static and ingrown body, which offered constant criticism and little constructive assistance to the clinic, and generally opposed any modifications, including improvements. Their dismissal by the legally constituted Board of Health was not received with particular pleasure by members of the advisory committee.

The first full-time psychiatrist was employed by the mental health center in July of 1960. This action resulted only after the resignation of a different part-time psychiatrist, who in effect presented the Board with the choice: "You have had 12 years to develop a full-time service. This is long enough to see if a mental health center is useful to our community, and it is time for you to make a decision as to whether to have a really good center, or to have none at all." A year previously, a sliding fee scale had been instituted for the first time over considerable objection from individual members of the old advisory committee. However, the county medical society had supported such a change, and most citizens viewed it as a reasonable development. Consequently, for the first time, financial resources became available to employ a full-time psychiatrist, in addition to a full-time social worker. Psychological services continued on a part-time basis for another year, and then a full-time psychologist was added to the staff.

In the fall of 1963, increasingly large groups of citizens began to attend all of the meetings of the city-county Board of Health. Leaders in the group were members of the old advisory committee, and several influential leaders in the county Association for Mental Health. The school psychologist also actively criticized the center, as did one physician. Complaints were as follows: 1) The fees charged by the center are too high. 2) The community cannot really afford a full-time mental health center. 3) Services should be limited to children and adults referred to a nearby state hospital outpatient department. 4) Services should only be diagnostic and evaluative, rather than therapeutic.

While newspaper coverage was fair, and generally favorable to the center, a columnist in the county weekly paper continued to attack the center, as he had done for at least ten years, as a socialistic enterprise which was not needed. While one-third of the referrals to the mental health center continued to come from individual physicians, the medical society took no official action to support the center. In fact, the only organized support of the center came from several local ministers who attended meetings regularly and indicated their support of the center, as well as of the director and staff.

Pressure continued to mount, and the director and other staff members became increasingly apprehensive. The chairman of the city-county Board of Health, also a county commissioner, announced that he intended to refer one letter of complaint to the professional grievance committee of the medical society. The director of the center was also chairman of that committee, but resigned his position so that the medical society might appoint an impartial chairman. However, the case was never actually presented, and the psychiatrist never discovered who his accuser was nor did he ever become aware of what the charge against him was. Instead, he grew weary of the constant struggling, despaired because of the lack of support of the governing board and the medical society, and resigned to accept a similar position in a federal outpatient facility.

CASE STUDY No. II

Kansas law requires that a mental health center, prior to establishment, must have approval by the State Board of Social Welfare. While its application for approval was pending, a community mental health center publicly announced its intention to employ a psychologist having only a Master's degree and less than six-months' experience in a state psychiatric hospital. Approval was subsequently denied on the basis that minimal standards recommended by the State Board of Social Welfare called for a psychologist with a Ph.D. Degree in clinical psychology, if he were the only, or senior psychologist in a community mental health center. This position had been supported by a formal endorsement by the Kansas State Psychological Association several years previously.

As a result of the denial of approval, several incidents occurred:

1. The board of the mental health center forwarded a letter of resignation from the psychologist, and indicated that it would comply with personnel standards.

2. Local psychologists, with Ph.D. degrees in clinical psy-

chology, objected to the position of the Board of Social Welfare, and themselves stated that the Ph.D. degree was *not* necessary for such a position. This was in direct opposition to the policy of the State Psychological Association, but they were adamant.

3. Rumors sprang up that approval was being denied because of a long-standing grudge between the psychologist in question and a member of the state-level staff.

As a result of the resignation of the controversial psychologist, the Board of Social Welfare extended approval for the establishment of the new clinic. Once the approval was official, the governing board of the mental health center immediately reemployed the untrained psychologist, which was possible since there were no statutory provisions for continuing licensure of the center. The governing board informed the state agency that it had reached a decision as to what was best and that it desired no further consultative services.

CASE STUDY NO. III

A fully-trained and experienced psychiatric social worker, who had served as the administrative director of a mental health center for several years, was being considered for a similar position in a newly established center. The governing board of the mental health center had about decided to employ him, when loud and persistent objections were raised by a minister in the community because the social worker had recently been divorced. The minister claimed that a divorced man had no business attempting to help other people with their problems and should not be allowed to work in the community. Reminders that the Governor of our most populous state and our former Ambassador to the United Nations had experienced similar difficulties, left the minister and his handful of supporters unmoved.

The governing board had no applicants with equivalent

qualifications available. It had to decide how to handle the general uproar and whether to employ the individual in question or not. In this dilemma, it turned to the State Mental Health Authority with the question, "What should we do?"

CASE STUDY No. IV

At the request of the governing board of the mental health center, the State Mental Health Authority conducted a program evaluation. It became apparent that all three staff members were well qualified by training and experience in their respective disciplines of psychiatry, psychology, and psychiatric social work. It was also discovered that each of these individuals essentially was functioning as an independent practitioner within the center and seemed to share no responsibility for cases. The psychiatrist was referred to as the "medical director" but he had no authority over the assignment of cases, the selection of personnel, the supervision of ongoing treatment, nor for a periodic review of the caseload of the staff.

In reviewing the records, it was further discovered that a large percentage of the cases at the clinic terminated unilaterally, without the knowledge or consent of the clinician.

When these findings were discussed with the staff, the psychiatric social worker responded with bland denial, the clinical psychologist with angry disagreement, and the psychiatrist was not even present for the meeting.

The evaluation team had to decide what should be included in the formal report to the governing board of the mental health center. What would be helpful and constructive in this situation? How much should the idealized model of team practice be stressed? Has it really been demonstrated that a team can more effectively meet the needs of patients than can an independent practitioner?

CASE STUDY NO. V

The State Mental Health Authority discovered, indirectly, that one of the mental health centers had employed a clinical psychologist who had recently been discharged from employment at one of the state hospitals because his credentials were found to be fraudulent. The community mental health center had, after some weeks, independently discovered, purely by chance, that his credentials were false and had discharged the individual. The mental health center had not notified the State Mental Health Authority, nor alerted other mental health centers in the state or region.

What is the responsibility of the State Mental Health Authority? What should it communicate to the mental health center? What is the responsibility of the State Psychological Association?

CASE STUDY NO. VI

A long-established mental health center was approached by an adjoining county concerning a merger, so that sufficient population and funds would be available to support a full psychiatric team. After the merger was worked out, the new county insisted that an office of the clinic be in its community, as well as in the original location. This was acceded to, and a psychiatric social worker became a full-time employee in each office, with temporary psychiatric and psychological assistance at both locations pending recruitment of full-time staff.

Each of the offices began dealing with the State Mental Health Authority independently. Even on such routine matters as the monthly report of terminated outpatients and the workload summary required for forwarding to the National Institute of Mental Health, separate reports were sent from the two offices of the clinic. It was also requested that communications from the state office be sent to both branches.

Increasing division within the governing board was noticed. Members of the governing board from the second community tended to deal directly and independently with the social worker in their county and regarded this as "their" mental health center. None of these issues was discussed openly in governing board meetings. The chairman of the governing board tended to deny their importance and to assure the state staff that everything was under control.

How should this situation be managed? What should the State Mental Health Authority do in relationship to the governing board and in relation to individual staff members? Should the separate statistical summaries be accepted and compiled in our office? Should we indeed communicate with both offices?

CASE STUDY No. VII

A Kansas county of 27,000 population, developed plans in conjunction with a state institution, to establish a jointly financed and staffed community mental health facility. These plans were developed without involvement of either the State Mental Hospital Authority or the State Community Mental Health Authority, and were first presented as definite and fixed local arrangements. Attempts to discourage the institution of such a service were met with angry rebuttals to the effect that local initiative was being stifled, and that "the state" was behaving in a dictatorial fashion. It was pointed out to local citizens that the role of the state institution did not include the direct provision of services to the community; that the state institution did not have a surplus of available personnel, but rather, had a long waiting list for admission; and that there were mental health centers in three adjoining counties, with whom the small county could merge in order to support adequate service. It was further pointed out that the state policy had been to encourage the establishment of multiple-county districts, since this seemed to be the only way whereby as sparsely populated a state as Kansas could build up a local population and taxation base, adequate to completely staff a comprehensive community mental health facility.

Local citizens were irate, intercounty rivalries and grudges grew sharp, and the staff of the community mental health agency found itself interposed between combatant counties, factions within the county itself, and between established state policy and local wishes.

In reviewing the situation, a previously unnoticed finding came to light: no county in the state which housed a state institution had, up to that point, levied a tax for community mental health services. While superintendents and staffs of the state institutions had, at the overt level, seemingly supported community mental health services, there was evidence at the covert level that they participated in local processes to subtly discourage and disrupt the development of community services near their institution.

What should the role of the state community mental health authority be in such a complex situation?

CASE STUDY NO. VIII

Over a period of several years, a local mental health association in western Kansas had, through the efforts of a small group of dedicated citizens, conducted a reasonably effective program of country-wide education concerning mental health needs and the development of improved local resources. However, the local Association for Mental Health was never able to arouse sufficient support at the opinion-setting or local governmental level in order to have a local tax levy which could support the development of a community mental health program.

Gradually, leadership of the group faltered and enthusiasm waned, so that the Association became dormant. After a period of a year or so, a new group of citizens developed an active interest in mental health, formed a new Association for Mental Health, and very quickly were able to arouse considerable support from influential segments of the community.

However, in the process, they completely excluded members of the old group. What should the role of the State Mental Health Authority be in such a situation? Out of loyalty and appreciation for services rendered in the past, should the state community mental health authority urge the inclusion of members of the old group in the community effort? Should it recognize the new group as a valid spokesman for community mental health interests?

Case Study No. IX

After several years of relatively placid organizational life, a new member enters an Association for Mental Health in a county of approximately 17,000 in central Kansas. Under the prodding and active leadership of this new member, the Association becomes actively involved in promoting the development of a community mental health center for its county, in requesting a tax levy from its county commissioners, and in approaching interested citizens and commissioners in adjoining counties to enter into a multiple county arrangement.

However, "old timers" and vested power interests in the community begin to express to the staff of state community mental health services, considerable uneasiness about the activities of this newcomer. It turns out that he has only lived in the community a few years, is seen as being pushy and brash, a big city boy, and somehow scornful or inconsiderate of the rural population.

Yet, his commitment, level of intelligence and education, vigor, and imaginativeness far exceed leadership potential displayed by any prior member of the Association for Mental Health in that area of the state. What should the role

of the state community mental health authority be in such
a situation?

CASE STUDY NO. X

A wealthy Kansas county, containing a number of suburban communities of a metropolitan complex, with the county
seat in a small Kansas town and with approximately three-
fourths of the county devoted to farming and farm-related
activities, levied a tax for community mental health services.
A governing board was appointed by the county commissioners with representation from the suburban area and from
the smaller communities. However, the chairman of the governing board represented the upper-middle-class level of
suburban society, and in over a year of planning and recruitment for staff suburban area representatives, tended to
assume leadership and authority positions.

Less than a month after the first two staff members were
employed, articles in county newspapers began to reflect criticism of the tax levy and of the community mental health
center development. County commissioners received verbal
and written objections, and eventually a public hearing was
set. A crowd of almost 100 representatives attended the
hearing, with the majority of them being representatives
whose attendance had been solicited by the county association for mental health, such as school psychologists, welfare
workers, state mental health representatives, etc. The county
Association for Mental Health had typically represented the
suburban upper-middle-class interests, and had never been
able to achieve real involvement and support from the small
town and rural population of the county.

At the public hearing, a handful of citizens at large, such
as farmers, small businessmen, and elected county officials,
represented the objection to the mental health center by such
statements as the following:

"Nobody has indicated that there is really any need for this."

"All they are doing is bringing in a power elite and paying them salaries higher than anyone else in the county makes."

"The salaries are too high."

"We haven't anything to say about how this is all going to be done, and it is being shoved down our throat."

Newspaper accounts of the meeting emphasized the objections of county citizens, and dismissed testimony by a wide variety of mental health and mental health-related professional persons from the state and local level, by saying, "Supporters of the mental health centers stood up one-by-one like a well-drilled team, and gave their rehearsed testimonials of support for the mental health center."

In an attempt to understand this violent community conflict, staff of Community Mental Health Services came to see that there was long-standing division between the northeastern portion of the county, which was suburban and upper-middle class, and the remainder of the county which was still a Kansas agricultural area. Property in the northeast part of the county was markedly underevaluated, so that county citizens could rightfully feel that county services were not adequately supported by the well-to-do residents in those houses. While the rural interests dominated county government, the urban interests had successfully supported, and succeeded in controlling the development of the community mental health program. The mental health center, then, was seen as potentially disruptive in a very delicate balance of power within this particular county, and became the target and "blank screen" upon which long-standing rivalries were projected.

With this understanding, the staff of community mental health centers made plans for remedying the situation. What would you suggest?

References

Allinsmith, W. & Goethals, G. W. (1962), *The Role of Schools in Mental Health*. New York: Basic Books.

American Psychiatric Association (1963), *Training the Psychiatrist to Meet Changing Needs;* Report of the Conference on Graduate Psychiatric Education, Washington, D.C.

American Public Health Association (1937), Evaluation Schedule for Use in the Study and Appraisal of Community Health Programs. New York. (reprinted)

— (official statement adopted Nov. 1, 1950), The local health department—services and responsibilities. *Amer. J. Pub. Hlth.*, 41:304, 1951.

— Area Committee on Mental Health (1962), *Mental Disorders: A Guide to Control Methods*.

Arieti, S. et al. (1959), *American Handbook of Psychiatry*. New York: Basic Books, p. 1958.

Bahn, A. K., Chandler, C. A., & Eisenberg, L. (1962), Diagnostic characteristics related to services in psychiatric clinics for children. *The Milbank Memorial Fund Quart.*, 40:289-318.

— et al. (1963), Gains in outpatient psychiatric clinic services, 1961. *Ment. Hyg.*, 47:177-188.

Bennet, A. E. et al. (1956), *The Practice of Psychiatry in General Hospitals*. Los Angeles: University of California Press.

Bernard, V. W. (1960), A training program in community psychiatry. *Ment. Hosp.*, 11:7-10.

Caplan, G. (1959), An approach to the education of community mental health specialists. *Ment. Hyg.*, 43:268-280.

— (1964a), *Principles of General Psychiatry*. New York: Basic Books.

— (1964b), *Principles of Preventive Psychiatry*. New York: Basic Books.

Freeman, H. E. & Simmons, O. G. (1961), Treatment experiences of mental patients ¹and their families. *Amer. J. Pub. Hlth.*, Vol. 51.

Freud, S. (1909), Analysis of a phobia in a five-year-old boy. *Collected Papers*, 3:149-288. London: Hogarth Press, 1948.

Gardner, E. A. et al. (1963), All psychiatric experience in a community. *Arch. Gen. Psychiat.*, 9:369-378.

Glasscote, R. & Canno, C. (1963), *The Plans for Planning—A Comparative Analysis of the State Mental Health Planning Proposals*. Washington, D.C.: The Joint Information Service.

Haylett, C. & Rapoport, L. (1964), Mental health consultation. In: *Handbook of Community Psychiatry and Community Mental Health*, ed. L. Bellak. New York: Grune & Stratton.

474

Hollingshead, A. B. & Redlich, F. C. (1958), *Social Class and Mental Illness: A Community Study*. New York: Wiley.

Houda, A. A. & Wiene, D. N. (1961), Service attitudes of board and staff members of community mental health clinics. *Ment. Hyg.*, 45:40-45.

Jahoda, M. (1958), *Current Concepts of Positive Mental Health*. New York: Basic Books.

Jellinek, E. M. & Keller, M. (1952), Alcoholism in the United States of America. *Quart. J. Studies of Alcohol*, 13:49.

Joint Commission on Mental Illness and Health (1961), *Action for Mental Health*. New York: Basic Books, pp. 63-64.

Lawrence (1962), Division of Institutional Management and Governmental Research Center, The University of Kansas. *Seminar for Directors of Mental Health Centers: A Report*. Special Report No. 114.

MacLeod, J. A. & Middelman, F. (1962), Wednesday afternoon clinic: A supportive care program. *Arch. Gen. Psychiat.*, 6:56-65.

Mahoney, S. C., *Mental Health Consultation*. Unpublished manuscript.

McCarthy, R. G., ed. (1964), *Alcohol Education for Classroom and Community: A Source for Educators*. New York: McGraw Hill.

Muth, L. T. (1961), *Aftercare Services for the Mentally Ill, A World Picture*. Philadelphia, Pa.: Smith, Kline and French Laboratories.

National Institute of Mental Health (1961), Data on Patients of Outpatient Psychiatric Clinics in the United States. Bethesda, Maryland.

National Science Foundation (1961), *Review of Data on Research and Development*, No. 31. Washington, D.C.

Ojemann, R. H. (1961), Investigations on the effects of teaching an understanding and appreciation of behavior dynamics. In: *Prevention of Mental Disorders in Children*, ed. G. Caplan. New York: Basic Books.

Ozarin, L. (1962), *Aftercare—Program Developments*. Report of the State Conference on Aftercare of the Psychiatric Patient in Kansas. Division of Institutional Management, Topeka, Kan.

Pumpian-Mindlin, E. (May 1964), *Resident Education in Community and Social Psychiatry*. Presented at the American Psychiatric Association's Annual Meeting. Los Angeles, Calif.

Report of the Surgeon General's Ad Hoc Committee on Mental Health Activities (1962), *Mental Health Activities and the Development of Comprehensive Health Programs in the Community*. Washington, D.C.: U.S. Dept. of Health, Education & Welfare.

Robinson, R. et al. (1960), *Community Resources in Mental Health*. New York: Basic Books.

Rooney, H. L. & Miller, A. D. (1955), A mental health clinic intake policy project. *Ment. Hyg.*, 39:391-405.

Sigler, J. E. (1963), *A Two Year Follow-up Study of Aftercare in Kansas.* Kansas City: Community Studies, Inc.

Srole, L. et al. (1962), *Mental Health in the Metropolis: The Midtown Manhattan Study,* Vol. 1. New York: McGraw-Hill Co.

U. S. Department of Health, Education and Welfare (1957), *Characteristics in Professional Staff of Outpatient Psychiatric Clinics.* Washington, D.C.: U.S. Public Health Service.

— Children's Bureau (1960), Report to the Congress on Juvenile Delinquency.

— (1962a), *Data on Patients of Outpatient Psychiatric Clinics in United States.* Washington, D.C.

— (1962b), *Data on Staff and Manhours Outpatient Psychiatric Clinics.* Washington, D.C.

— (1963), *Mental Retardation: A National Plan for a National Problem.* Washington, D.C.

Waggoner, R. (1962), Psychiatric units in general hospitals. *J. Hillside Hosp.,* 11:159-170.

Whittington, H. G. (1964), *Psychiatry on the College Campus.* New York: International Universities Press.

Winslow, C. E. A. (1920), The untoiled field of public health. *Mod. Med.,* 2:183.